DISCARDED

Daughters of the Game

THE FIRST ERA OF MINNESOTA
GIRLS HIGH SCHOOL BASKETBALL
1891-1942

Women's history matters!

Dorothy McIntyre

Daughters
of the

St. Paul 1902

LeSueur 1921

Montgomery 1930

Game

THE FIRST ERA OF MINNESOTA GIRLS HIGH SCHOOL BASKETBALL 1891-1942

MARIAN BEMIS JOHNSON
DOROTHY E. MCINTYRE

Jeannette Page Wright, Crookston 1912

The First Era of Minnesota Girls High School Basketball - 1891-1942

© 2005 by McJohn Publishing, LLC

All rights reserved. No part of this book may be used or reproduced in any form without written permission. This includes any electronic or mechanical means, including, but not limited to, photocopying or any information storage and retrieval system.

Published 2005

Printed by Sentinel Printing Company, Inc.

Writers and Editors: Marian Bemis Johnson and Dorothy E. McIntyre

∞ The paper used in this publication meets the minimum requirements of the American National Standard for Information Sciences –Permanence of Paper for Printed Library Materials, ANSI Z39.48-1992.

For information contact: www.daughtersofthegame.com or McJohn Publishing, LLC, P.O. Box 390043, MN 55439-0043.

Printed in the United States of America

ISBN 0-9766214-0-1

Jacket photos:

Front – center – Aileen Just Luther, Rapidan, 1928; clockwise from center right – Montgomery 1930; Grand Meadow 1930; Buffalo 1927; White Bear Lake 1920; Brainerd 1902.

Back – clockwise from upper left corner – **Passing the Torch** – Hutchinson, 1921; Lindsay Whalen, Hutchinson High School, 2000, University of Minnesota, 2004; **Strong Minnesota Women** – Belle Plaine 1926; Marie Weibeler Keeler, Belle Plaine, 2000, Marie holding ball in both photos; **Legacy** – Milan 1927; Ruth Olson Kleven with two great-granddaughters, 2004; Ruth Olson Kleven.

Dedication

To my mother, Elenora Schlaet Bemis, who gave me self-esteem and the confidence to try anything, inspired me to succeed; and through the college education she had been denied, enabled me to live her dreams.

Marian Bemis Johnson

To the women of the game whose stories were waiting to be told; and, to our future generations whose opportunity to play must be preserved.

Dorothy E. McIntyre

"Would each generation of women leaders have had to endure such a solitary struggle if they had known about those who came before them? One of women's greatest struggles has been that their history has not been preserved, and so each generation has had to rediscover over and over again the ideas and individuals that gave it strength."

Ann D. Braude, Ph.D

Contents of the Game

Warm-ups

Foreword	ix
Preface	xi
Acknowledgments	xiii
Introduction	xv
Chronology	xvii

First Quarter

A New Game Comes to Minnesota	1
A Game of Their Own	3
From Costumes to Uniforms	16
Free Throws	28

Second Quarter

Where They Played the Game	29
Getting to the Game was Half the Fun	35
Minnesota Hospitality and the Game	46
Benefits of the Game: Fun, Fitness and Friends	48
Tournaments, Trophies and School Awards	51
Free Throws	58

Halftime

Shooting Stars of the First Era	59

Third Quarter

Darwin, Women and the Game	65
End of the First Era	70
A Team for Every Girl and Every Girl on a Team	81
Finding Opportunities Beyond School Teams	84
Legacy of the Game	87
The Reunion of First Era Pioneers	93
Free Throws	100

Fourth Quarter

Introduction to the Teams	101
Team Profiles	103
Free Throws	311

Overtime — 313

Epilogue — 317

Rosters

Composite List of Coaches	319
Composite List of Players	325
Composite List of Teams	351

Credits — 357

Notes — 367

Index — 371

Family Memories — 386

Another Eagle Victory for Janet, Kim and their New York Mills team!!

Foreword

Now that I have been out of high school for 25 years, I have a better perspective of how my athletic experiences have shaped me as a person. Like the women you will learn about in this book, I have been blessed with many wonderful memories, friendships, life lessons and heart-pounding moments through basketball. It will always be a part of me – and for that I am grateful.

People talk about being in the right place at the right time. Growing up in the small community of New York Mills in the late 1970s, I was fortunate to be in high school during the post-Title IX era. Our athletic director, Carl Sundeen, had three daughters and believed that girls deserved athletic opportunities. During those years between 1971 and 1981, our basketball teams were coached by Kathy Lervold Goodrich and Peggy Zimmerman Stibbe, both former college players. With committed athletes, excellent coaches and a supportive community, our girls basketball team won three consecutive state championships in 1977, 1978 and 1979. It was said that we were finally "on the map of Minnesota."

I applaud the dedication of Marian Johnson to uncover the first era of girls basketball in Minnesota. She and her co-author, Dorothy McIntyre, combined their commitment and passion to preserving the history in this book. It is an important contribution to the history of women in sport before it is left untold and unknown. The book will serve to honor and safeguard the stories of girls like me whose athletic participation in the early 1900s was central to their lives. It will also serve to bring an awareness of the injustices experienced by the girls caught in the unfortunate gap between these sports eras.

Today, girls' sports are a part of society's fabric and are here to stay. It is difficult to fathom how generations of women were denied that opportunity for so many years. If my high school years had occurred during the gap like my own mother and sisters, my life's path would look very different.

Knowing this story will give us all an opportunity to applaud the great efforts of those who competed in the early days, to celebrate the achievements since Title IX, and to work to ensure the opportunities for future generations.

This book solidifies my personal mission to ensure that my young daughter, Sophia, will have an open door to pursue sports. I can only hope she will choose to do so and will also enjoy the memories, friendships, life lessons and heart-pounding moments that will last forever.

Janet Karvonen Montgomery
New York Mills, 1976-1980

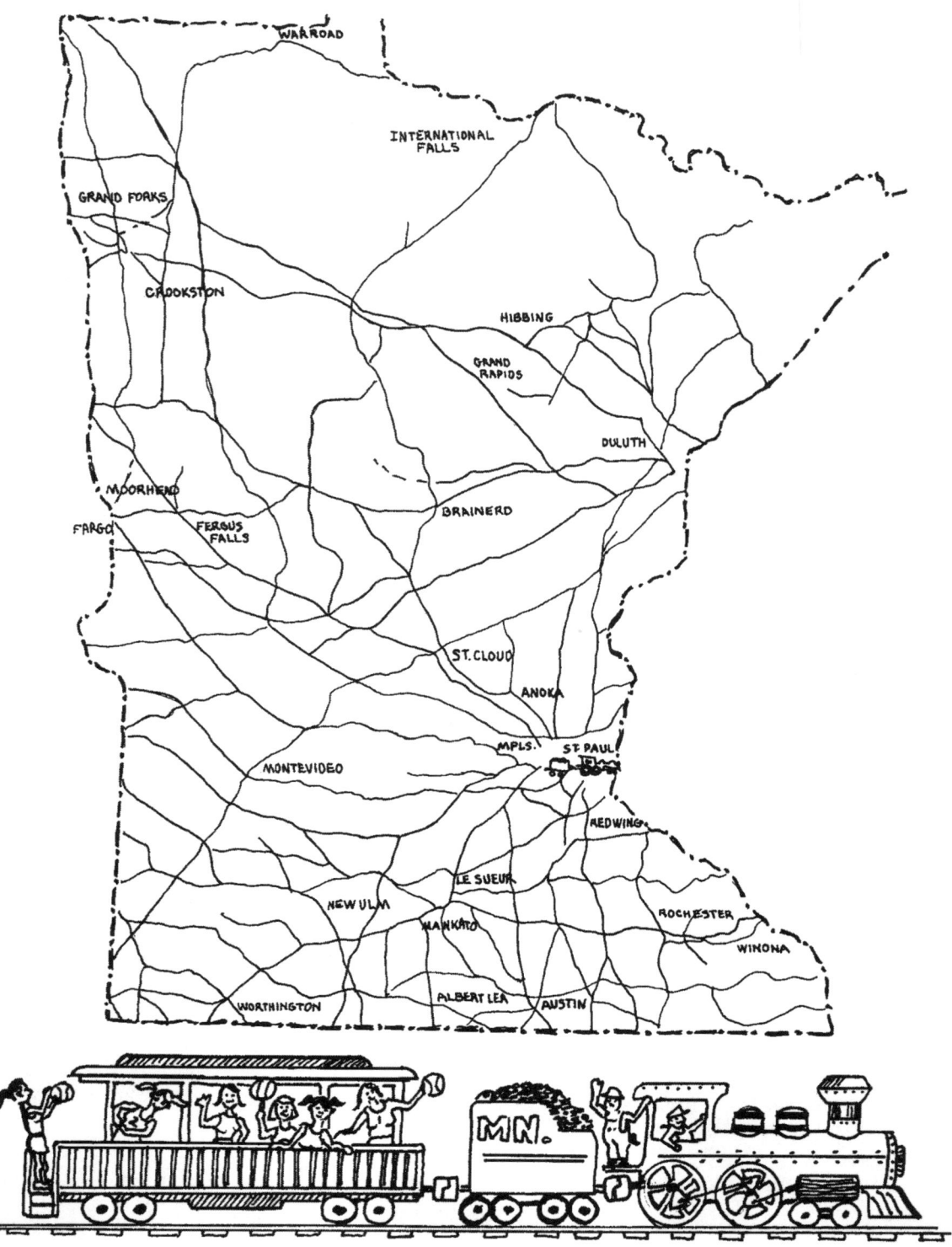

Railroads of the 1920s and the girls basketball teams who rode the rails

Preface

It was the look in their eyes when they told their stories! Each woman remembered games, opponents and scores as if it had happened just yesterday. It was, in fact, eighty or more years ago!!

The recollections of women who played high school girls basketball during the era from the late 1890s to the early 1940s turned into a fascinating story. They are stories nearly lost except for the curiosity of Marian Bemis Johnson of White Bear Lake. Marian was one of the generations of women who did not have the opportunity to play high school sports during the decades from the 1940s to the early 1970s. And she wondered why she wasn't allowed to play.

Women in the early 1900s and their daughters, found girls basketball teams in their schools. Why did these high school girls have interscholastic teams, only to lose that opportunity to play as early as the late 1920s and early 1930s? Why did some teams continue as late as 1942? And why didn't parents, players, or school administrators object to the announcements by their school boards that the girls' teams would be discontinued? What could cause such a drastic change in attitude toward girls and women in sport?

Marian began by searching through the boxes stored in the Minnesota Historical Society to find the answer. She discovered amazing original correspondence that provided a trail of correspondence by state and national figures, each pointing toward the close-down of girls basketball in Minnesota and in other states across the country.

With that information, Marian began searching for women who had played on the early teams. She began where she lived in White Bear Lake. One woman's story led to another, and that woman's story led to another. One school's season would provide names of other schools that they had played. The network began to grow. Marian's map soon had pins marking communities throughout the state.

Marian's car began to tally the miles as she found women in their 80's, 90's, and two women who were 100 years of age, all ready to tell their stories. Marian's tape recorder continued to spin, recording the vivid memories of the women. Soon, questionnaires were sent to women who shared their memories. When their handwriting was challenging, family members wrote down their stories and sent them to Marian. Preserving their memories was important to them all.

Like a treasure hunter, Marian began to unearth trophies won by girls' teams at various tournaments. Miraculously, some women had kept their uniforms, carefully folded and stored in boxes, and in one case, in a "hope chest." Letter sweaters were worn once again with pride. Scrapbooks filled with photographs and newspaper articles were lovingly opened and shared.

Marian contacted the Minnesota State High School League and offered to share her information. Dorothy E. McIntyre offered to help gather more information. Little did they anticipate the statewide program of high school girls basketball that would unfold before their eyes! Little could they anticipate the delight of locating and meeting so many real, very lively women who could tell them first-person stories of their playing days during this first era of girls basketball.

It was time to "put out the call" for information. The first opportunity came when Janet Karvonen Montgomery, the premier player of the New York Mills team of the mid-1970s, interviewed Marian during a televised game at the MSHSL State Girls Basketball Tournament. The screen showed the League's telephone number and asked the audience to call if they had information about this era of girls basketball.

The next day the telephone rang "off the hook." The callers were women who played on the teams during those years and wanted to tell their stories! If their call wasn't returned the next day, they called again!!

Many of the women said that they watched every year, wishing they could have been playing as high school athletes for a state championship on the floor of the Met Center or Williams Arena.

Information began to arrive. It came from the women and from families of women who had played and left mementos in their family archives. It came from schools that had opened their yearbooks and dug deep into trophy cases. It came from local historical societies that had archived photos and newspaper articles of local teams. A picture began to take shape that was much larger than anticipated. It pointed to a conclusion that nearly every community had sponsored a girls basketball team at some time during these early decades. Over 350 teams were identified and more are waiting to be discovered.

Marian Johnson and Janet Karvonen Montgomery "put out the call" for information

Many women commented that their families had never shown much interest in their basketball career. Others said they just never mentioned it to anyone. Some families regretted never knowing that their mother or grandmother had played basketball, on occasion discovering this information after her death.

The authors wrote articles and participated in radio and television interviews, asking for more information. Marie Keeler of Belle Plaine, Luella Anderson of Arlington, Irma Foley of Montgomery, Mabel Erickson of Mabel, and Jean Frarey Walters were featured as speakers at the 1999 MSHSL Women in Sports Leadership Conference. They "wowed" the audience with their tales and humorous stories of their high school days. They became sixteen year-old athletes again.

Now we are ready to tell their stories!

Luella tells stories of her playing days.

The reader is encouraged to review family records, to ask their women about their sports history, and to dig through those school yearbooks and historical files. Preserve and share the information with your local historical societies and schools.

There is more information yet to be discovered. But for now, here are their stories and what has been shared.....so far!

Acknowledgements

We wish to express our deep appreciation to the women who provided the first-person stories from their playing days on a high school girls basketball team in Minnesota. Each woman uncovered another piece of the history of girls basketball teams that had flourished during the first era of girls sports.

We appreciate the efforts of the family members who contributed so much information to this history by digging into family archives and sharing the photos and special memorabilia. It was touching to feel how important it is to you to have your family member's history preserved with her peers.

Marian's appreciation runs deep for the time and effort spent by Gail Bishop, her good friend and retired office assistant, for transcribing oh-so-many recorded interviews with women all over the state.

Thanks to each of our many friends who devoted so much time helping us to sort through the files and volumes of information that Marian had so carefully gathered. We could tell by your reactions to the stories that preserving this history was a worthy project.

For months Karen Kuhn, Crystal and Jane Christensen, Eagan, scanned photos, dug through files to track down the endless details, and then proofed and re-proofed files. Special thanks to our Manuscript Editor, Claudia Dodson, Charlottesville, Virginia, whose knowledge about grammar and punctuation is unparalleled and who could find the elusive commas and colons wherever they would attempt to hide. She could find almost anything and anyone on the world-wide web. Sylvia Logerquist, Edina, was our Food Editor, with the important assignment of keeping each editing crew happy and energy levels high. Dale Sattler, Edina, was our Technology Consultant, keeping computers and their technology running and viruses at bay.

Leslie Johnson, from Oahu, Hawaii applied her creative talents and developed a jacket that illustrates the essence of the book and its contents. Wendy Cutting, Apple Valley, Minnesota, and Rebecca Kurk, Eden Prairie, Minnesota, were key members of our team as they undertook the layout for all of the interior pages of the book. Thanks to Leslie, Wendy and Rebecca for sharing your artistry with us.

Bev Byington from far-away Alaska brought the Little Girl Bouncing Ball Team to the Book, so they could bounce through the free throw contest with you. Thanks, Bev, for those friendly faces!

We appreciate the map from Doug Kruse, Hugo, that illustrates the network of railroads that carried so many teams to their games. The photos of the Model T cars were generously shared by Elizabeth and John MacLeod.

Our grateful thanks to Brian Wise and his staff at Sentinel Printing, St. Cloud, MN. We were confident that you would invest your best efforts into the production of our book.

We gained new appreciation for the historical societies where local history has been so carefully preserved; and for the Minnesota newspapers' staffs who told the stories of teams during the first era, and now continue to inform our communities about past and present high school activities.

We offer this book to each of the school districts across the state, and especially those who assisted with the gathering of information for their teams of the first era. You and your community's commitment to all of your students will ensure that the second era of girls' sports can look forward to an enduring and healthy future.

Introduction

When you picked up this book, you may have wondered, "Why is this book about girls basketball only from 1891-1942? Girls are playing basketball now. Couldn't they always play on teams in Minnesota?"

Let's look at your first question, "Why focus on the years from 1891-1942?"

The game was created by James Naismith in 1891. A year later, Naismith's friend, Max J. Exner, brought the game to Carleton College, Northfield, Minnesota. As the game spread, girls loved this new game of "basket ball." Like wildfire, girls' teams sprouted in virtually every community in the state of Minnesota.

In the mid-1920s, state and national groups came to believe that intense competition was filled with the potential for negative effects on young women. These groups took a strong position against interscholastic and intercollegiate competition as well as competition conducted by community and sports organizations, including the Olympics.

Information was sent to schools and organizations throughout the country that girls' and women's competitive teams should be replaced with a recreational program open to all girls and women. In high schools, this organization was commonly known as the Girls' Athletic Association. In colleges, it was called the Women's Athletic Association.

Minnesota schools began to comply with the recommendations. Teams were being dropped by the larger schools in the 1920s with the smaller schools holding onto their teams into the late 1930s and early 1940s. The girls swimming teams on the Iron Range were also dropped after their state meet in 1942.

The purpose of this book is to share with you the rich history of the first era of girls basketball through the first-person stories of the women who played. And they have stories to tell!!

Why is it important to preserve the history of the first 50 years of girls sports in Minnesota and to know what caused its demise for several decades?

This answer is clear and simple:

> "Those who do not learn from history are doomed to repeat it."
>
> George Santayana

Sherburn trophy 1925

Chronology

*Official rule changes for girls and women's basketball

1848	A convention to discuss the social, civil, and religious condition and rights of women was held at Seneca Falls, New York
1849	Amelia Bloomer began publication of *The Lily*, a monthly paper that became an active voice for women's rights, including changes in the restrictive clothing worn by women. It recommended shorter skirts and the knee-length undergarments that came to be known as Bloomers
1858	Minnesota becomes 32nd state in the Union
1860s	Minnesota opened three teacher training schools – called normal schools – in Winona, Mankato, and St. Cloud
1869	The University of Minnesota becomes the first state university in the country to open its classes to both men and women
	Sara Burger Stearns started Minnesota's first suffrage group in Rochester
1886	The first true safety bicycle, the Rover, with rear chain drive and direct steering established the design of the bicycle very much as it is today. The 1895 Ladies' Schwinn New World bicycle came at the height of the bicycle boom
1887	Married women achieved the same legal existence as single women; they were no longer the property of their husbands
1891	James Naismith, as a teacher at the International YMCA Training School in Springfield, Massachusetts, invented a new indoor game that he called "Basket Ball." (The game was spelled with two words until the 1920s)
1892	Max J. Exner, a friend and roommate of James Naismith, was in Naismith's class and played in the first game. Exner moved to Northfield, MN to serve as director of physical training at Carleton College. He brought with him the rules for the new game of basket ball. He taught the women of Carleton the new game in the lower level gymnasium of Gridley Hall
	Senda Berenson introduced her adapted game of basket ball to Smith College students.
1899	The Women's Basketball Rules Committee held its first meeting at Springfield College, Springfield, Massachusetts
1900-1945	The Golden Age of railroads
1901	Senda Berenson served as editor of the first "official" publication of Basket Ball for Women (three-court game) by the Spalding Athletic Library. She served as editor for 17 years
1914	World War I began
1916	The Minnesota State High School League was organized as the state's high school activity association
	*No coaching was permitted during game (except halftime)
1917	The United States entered World War I
	The National Council of the American Physical Education Association appointed a nine-woman Committee on Women's Athletics; basketball was a subcommittee
1918	*A basket with an open bottom, instead of closed basket with pull chain, became official in the game of Basket Ball
1918-19	The influenza pandemic was the most devastating epidemic in recorded world history, killing between 20 and 40 million people around the globe. 675,000 Americans died in the worst epidemic the United States has ever known.

1919	Treaty of Versailles ended World War I
1920	Women received the right to vote with the adoption of the Nineteenth Amendment to the U.S. Constitution
1921	Women win the right to serve on juries
	*Two-hand overhead shots were reduced from two points to one point
1922	The Amateur Athletic Union (AAU) incorporated women's basketball into its program offerings
	Women won the right to serve in the Minnesota Senate and House of Representatives
1923-24	The National Amateur Athletic Federation – Women's Division was organized. The first meeting was held in Washington D.C. in 1923; the organizational meeting was held in 1924
	E.W. Everts was appointed the first Supervisor of Physical Education in the Minnesota State Department of Education.
1924	The NAAF-WD began disseminating information and recommendations throughout the country that competitive teams for girls and women should be replaced with "competition of the right kind," i.e., competition for enjoyment and without the stress of winning and losing
	The Minnesota State High School League sponsored its first state tournament for girls in the sport of swimming and diving
1925	Thirty-seven states hold state girls basketball tournaments. Minnesota did not sponsor a girls state tournament in basketball until 1976.
	Shot put style, two-handed underhand, and back-basket goals were reduced from two points to one point.
1926	The Amateur Athletic Union (AAU) held its first national basketball championship for women in Pasadena, CA
1928	NAAF-Women's Division protested women's entries in Olympic track and field events (and all events in 1932 and 1936)
1929	The Wall Street stock market crashed
1930s	The Great Depression plagued the United States
1932	The NAAF-WD recommended that no women's events be conducted in the Olympics held in California; Babe Didrickson won two gold medals in track and field
	*All basketball goals to count two points
1936	The All-American Red Heads women's basketball team organized, used men's rules, and competed against men's teams
1936	Olympics were held in Berlin and held the first men's basketball competition; Naismith observed games and handed out gold medals to the winning U.S. men's basketball team
1938	*Official rules changed from a three-court game to a two-court game with six players
1939	Harold Jack, the second Supervisor of Physical Education, reported to schools that "Interscholastic competition for girls of high school age was reported in 92 schools in 1938-1939 and in 38 schools in 1939-1940. This represents a decided change for the better"
1941	The United States entered World War II after the bombing of Pearl Harbor
1942	The first era of girls basketball ended
	The first era of girls swimming and diving ended with the 1942 MSHSL State Girls Swimming and Diving Meet
1945	World War II ended
1960	Wilma Rudolph won three gold medals in the Olympics for track and field (100m dash, 200m dash and 400m relay), raising questions as to why other U.S. women were not competing
1960s	Advocates for change in Minnesota became active in promoting and developing opportunities for girls and women in sports

1961	*The two-court, roving-player game rules were adopted
	*Three-bounce dribble adopted
1963	The First National Sport Institute was held to provide teachers with skills to teach gymnastics and track and field. Four additional institutes would be held to emphasize other sports and to discuss adding competition into these activities
1966	*A new rule allowing an unlimited dribble was introduced
1969	The Minnesota State High School League voted to add girls' sports to its competitive sports activities
1971	National Federation of State High School Associations published a girls basketball rules book
	*Five player-full court game adopted by DGWS and AAU
1972	The first MSHSL State Girls Track and Field Meet was held at St. Cloud Apollo High School
1972	Title IX of the Education Amendments of 1972 passed
1975	Some Minnesota schools were conducting their girls basketball seasons in the fall, and some preferred the winter season. To accommodate these two seasons, the MSHSL conducted both fall and winter basketball tournaments
	Title IX Guidelines published. Interpretations were issued to schools from the U.S. Department of Health, Education & Welfare (HEW) regarding the intent of Title IX. Schools were required to be in compliance by 1978
1976	At the end of the winter season, the first MSHSL State Girls Basketball Tournament was held at the Met Center, Bloomington. All games were played with the five-player, full-court game
	Women's basketball was added as a competitive sport for women at the Summer Olympics in Montreal, Canada
1984	The U.S. Women's Basketball team won its first gold medal in the Los Angeles Summer Olympics
	*Smaller ball for women's basketball introduced
1987	*Three-point field goals adopted
1988	Gold medal won by U. S. women's basketball in the Seoul Olympics
2004	Pam Borton, coach, leads the University of Minnesota women's basketball team to its first NCAA Final Four appearance
2004	In 2003-2004, the League reported 418 girls basketball teams and 13,017 participants

In 2003-2004, the MSHSL reported that a total of 105,152 high school girls participated in sports. League-sponsored sports for girls included: adapted bowling, adapted floor hockey, adapted soccer, adapted softball, alpine skiing, badminton, basketball, cross country, golf, gymnastics, ice hockey, lacrosse, Nordic ski racing, soccer, softball, swimming and diving, synchronized swimming, tennis, track and field, and volleyball

First Quarter

A New Game Comes to Minnesota

In 1891 Max J. Exner was a student at the Young Men's Christian Association International Training School in Springfield, Massachusetts. Fortunately for Minnesota, James Naismith and Max J. Exner were friends, leading to Exner's participation in the first game of basket ball.

In 1892 Max J. Exner's two-year pre-medical physical education course was completed and he headed to Carleton College in Northfield, Minnesota to enroll as a student. Exner was also hired as the college's first instructor of "physical culture." Exner was dedicated to his studies and to developing a variety of activities for his classes, including fencing and gymnastics for both men and women.

What was most important to Minnesota was what Max J. Exner brought in his suitcase to Carleton: the rules of this new game of "Basket Ball!!"

Soon reports were coming out of the lower level gymnasium in the women's residence, Gridley Hall, that Exner was teaching this new game of basket ball to the women of Carleton College.[1]

Max J. Exner

The Carleton College archives included a summary of the Gymnasium Work for the year 1892-1893. In the spring issue of the college yearbook, *ALGOL*, was a description of Exner's work during the winter term.

"A little later Basket Ball was introduced and you should have seen the fun. See the ladies on the floor, attired in loose dresses permitting free action of the body and tennis slippers upon their feet. They are divided into two sides, standing at opposite sides of the gymnasium; their eyes sparkling with excitement, ready to dash at the ball when put into play. The ball is thrown into the field of play and the fun begins. Now they are all in a bunch endeavoring to get the ball, now they scatter and again they rush together, every eye following the ball which is never for an instant in one place, and every energy bent upon obtaining a clear throw for the basket. Watch an individual player. Now she dashes to obtain the ball, now darts to obstruct an opponent and again to protect the goal; running, dodging, squirming;

Gridley Hall, 1890

1903 Carleton Women's Team

throwing the ball, again catching it, and all the time exercising her vocal organs to the best of her ability. When in course of the game a well-directed throw sends the ball into the goal a cheer arises which shows the complete relaxation of the mind to the enjoyment. Are girls fit for the drawing room only? Can they participate in active games as boys can.? Were you permitted to witness one of these games you would surely conclude that they can."[2]

In 2004, Max V. Exner of Ames, Iowa, told how his father brought women into athletics, demonstrating that women could play sports formerly deemed the domain of men. Max J. Exner did this in classes, demonstrations and on tours. He later traveled to China where he taught Western sports through the Y.M.C.A.

Max V. Exner described his father as "the perfectionist's perfectionist." He was committed in theory and in his personal life to the physical education belief in the harmony of body, mind and spirit. [3]

The Birth of Basketball in Minnesota

As a result of one individual, Max J. Exner, and his teachings at Carleton College of physical culture and the new game of "basket ball," the first era of girls' and women's basketball in Minnesota was born!

And it soon became a game of their own.

A Game of Their Own

In 1891 James Naismith was a young physical education instructor at the International Young Men's Christian Association (YMCA) Training School in Springfield, Massachusetts. (The Training School's name was later changed to Springfield College.)

"Carleton was founded in 1866 as a coeducational college right from the start, with its first graduating class composed of one man and one woman. Throughout its history, the college has a tradition of championing the right of the female student to have full access to the best educational experiences possible. It does our hearts good to know that the seeds sowed by Max J. Exner, one of Carleton's early physical education professors, originated a movement which has grown into the level of passion with which girls and women approach active sport today."
Pat Lamb and Ele Hansen, Professors Emeriti of Physical Education, Carleton College

Naismith was given an assignment by school director Dr. Luther Gulick to develop a new indoor game for the male students that would provide a good workout and a change from the traditional gymnastics exercises. During his childhood in Canada, Naismith had played a game called Duck-on-a-Rock. He incorporated some of its concepts into 13 rules of a game that he named Basket Ball, a two-word name that would last into the 1920s. [1]

Naismith posted the typed rules on the bulletin board so that his young men could learn the 13 rules for the new game. The ball was an Association foot ball (soccer ball).

1. The ball may be thrown in any direction with one or both hands.
2. The ball may be batted in any direction with one or both hands (never with the fist).
3. A player cannot run with the ball. The player must throw it from the spot on which he catches it, with allowance to be made for a player who catches the ball when running at a good speed.
4. The ball must be held in or between the hands; the arms or body must not be used for holding it.
5. No shouldering, holding, pushing, tripping, or striking the person of an opponent shall be allowed; the first infringement of this rule by any person shall count as a foul, the second shall disqualify him until the next goal is made, or, if there was evident intent to injure the person for the whole of the game, no substitute allowed.
6. A foul is striking at the ball with the fist, and any violations of rules 3, 4, and such violations as described in rule 5.
7. If either side makes three consecutive fouls, it shall count as a goal for the opponents. ("Consecutive" means that the opponent does not make a foul in the meantime.)

8. A goal shall be made when the ball is thrown or batted from the grounds into the basket and stays there, providing those defending the goal do not touch or disturb the goal. If the ball rests on the edge and the opponent moves the basket, it shall count as a goal.

9. When the ball goes out of bounds, it shall be thrown into the field and played by the person first touching it. In case of a dispute, the umpire shall throw it straight into the field. The thrower-in is allowed five seconds. If he holds the ball longer, it shall go to the opponent. If any side persists in delaying the game, the umpire shall call a foul on them.

10. The umpire shall be judge of the men and shall note the fouls, and notify the referee when three consecutive fouls have been made. He shall have power to disqualify men according to rule 5.

11. The referee shall be judge of the ball and shall decide when the ball is in play, in bounds, to which side it belongs, and shall keep the time. He shall decide when a goal has been made, and keep account of the goals, with any other duties that are usually performed by a referee.

12. The time shall be two 15-minute halves, with five-minute rest between.

13. The side making the most goals in that time shall be declared the winner. In case of a draw, the game may, by agreement of the captains, be continued until another goal is made.[2]

The custodian could not locate the rectangular boxes requested by Naismith, but did find two peach baskets. One peach basket was attached at each end of the overhead running track which circled the upper part of the gymnasium.

On December 21, 1891, the first game was played by students from Naismith's class at the YMCA. The 18-member class was divided into two teams of nine players each. The game was an instant success with the players. The players took the game to their home states on their holiday break and taught it to others.[3]

Women Find a New Game

In 1891 women enjoyed a number of sports such as riding horses, archery, croquet, bicycling, fencing, roller and ice skating, golf and tennis. Team sports were considered "unwomanly," involving playing against others where there could be physical contact and roughness.

According to James Naismith, only weeks after the game was created, a group of women from a nearby elementary school came by to watch the men playing this new game. They asked to play and Naismith made the arrangements and organized the first basketball game for women. The women played in their teaching and street attire, high-buttoned shoes with heels, corsets and dresses with the long sleeves. It didn't deter them from enjoying this new game. Soon other women organized additional teams with Naismith officiating some of the games. Naismith's future wife, Maude Sherman, was one of the first female players.[4]

James Naismith with peach baskets and ball

Senda Berenson arrived in 1892 at Smith College in Massachusetts to become its first director of physical culture. She was a popular instructor in her gymnastics clothing – long, dark woolen bloomers, long-sleeved blouse, dark stockings and flat-heeled soft shoes. Within weeks after her arrival, Senda heard about the new game of "basket ball." She contacted Naismith for information. She said, "We no sooner tried it (in class) than we liked it." [5]

Senda wrote about the timing of basketball's arrival.
> "Basketball came on at the right moment in the history of the development of games for women. One of the strong arguments in the economic world against giving women as high salaries as men for similar work is that women are more prone to illness than men. They need, therefore, all the more to develop health and endurance if they desire to become candidates for equal wages…And how valuable a training it is which enables a woman to meet an unexpected situation, perhaps of danger, with alacrity and success." [6]

Senda was concerned about a game designed for men that might be "too strenuous and too physically demanding for women." She determined that Naismith's rules should be adapted for a game that would be vigorous and yet "womanly" for her students as well as acceptable to her college and the parents of her students. Moreover, Senda was committed to developing a game that would provide women "with the physical and moral qualities demanded for the New Woman."

Her rules created a three-court game with nine players that would encourage teamwork, avoid physical contact and separate it from the men's game. Players were required to stay inside their own section, thus restricting the women from running and over-exerting themselves. Players could bounce up to three times and hold the ball no more than three seconds. On March 21, 1893, a team of freshman played the sophomore team. The gymnasium was filled with spectators and banners supporting their favorite class. No men were allowed to watch the game. [7]

Basketball was introduced in 1893 at Sophie Newcomb College in New Orleans by Clara Gregory Baer. Clara also felt the need to make changes to suit young women's needs, and she was the first to publish her rules under the name of "Basquette". To prevent any potential for overexertion, she divided the court into as many as 9 and 12 divisions. Baer also invented "Newcomb" an elementary school game that introduced basketball skills. [8]

Women's basketball was born! It spread through YMCAs and YWCAs, community organizations and high schools. The YMCAs and the YWCAs could provide coaching, officials and facilities to play the game. Another level of female players was served through the colleges and universities where teams grew quickly and spread across the country.

Keeping the Game Safe and Fun
As women's basketball spread throughout the educational and community structures, many variations of rules were written and published. Concern over the status of the game led to a conference of physical training leaders held at Springfield College in 1899. A committee was appointed to design a uniform set of rules. After two weeks, the committee produced the first official women's basket ball rules. The conference decided to publish the rules and did so in 1901.

The first rule book in 1901 was edited by Senda Berenson and published by Spalding's Athletic Library, an accepted source of rules for men's sports. From 1905-1917 Senda served as chairperson of the Women's Basketball Committee (WBC) of the American Physical Education Association (APEA). She was the first woman to hold such a powerful position in a national sports organization.

"The present age has witnessed a great awakening regarding physical development. The need of exercise for the human body has been recognized and has resulted in the introduction of all kinds of sports. That exercise is just as necessary to the proper development of girls as it is for boys ought to be apparent, but the fact is that much opposition had to be overcome in establishing courses in physical training in girls' schools. The traditions of ages had to be set aside, especially with respect to out-door sports. None of the newer games seemed suitable for both sexes, until basket ball appeared some fifteen years ago.

It was received with great enthusiasm and grew steadily in popularity, as it furnishes vigorous exercise, and along with the self-control and self-reliance it develops, is that training in co-operation which is so essential for social discipline today. This latter quality, that of subordination of self for the good of the whole, is especially desirable for girls, as their education in the past has been lacking in it. There has not been need of co-operation on the part of women before.

Today it is vital.

At first the same rules were used for both sexes, but soon it became apparent that it was too strenuous a game for girls, whose power of endurance is less than that of boys. Then, too, bodily exhaustion is far more dangerous to girls because of their more delicate nervous organism. It was found necessary almost at first to modify the rules so they might be played with safety. But as time went on this change did not prove sufficient, for the game seemed to be deteriorating and public opinion likely to withdraw its approval of it. This was due to various causes. The game was played with men's rules, the girls were coached by men, they were treated as men, and public contests took on the character of mere exploitation of a winning team, as men's athletics often do. The girls themselves affected mannish airs and in some cases the game seemed to be degenerating into rowdyism.

It was clear something must be done, or this delightful, interesting, beneficial game would fall into disrepute. So at a National Congress in 1908 of those interested in that important phase of modern education, recreation, the question of girls' athletics was especially considered. The trend of opinion was almost entirely in the direction of differentiating their sports from boys'. And it was unanimously decided to further the establishment of girls' rules for girls, under the direct supervision of women coaches. The primary consideration being that of health this was felt to be the only solution of the question. These conditions prevail throughout the East and the Pacific Coast, but not entirely through the Middle West as yet. However, it is hoped that before long there will be unanimity everywhere, for aside from its being for the best good of our girls, contests cannot be fair where different standards are followed." 1910 Crookston yearbook.

The rules created by the Women's Basketball Committee were only one set of rules used across the country. Many teams continued to play with Naismith's game with rule modifications that they created to suit their situations. In addition to the rules developed by the Women's Basketball Committee (WBC), the Young Men's Christian Association (YMCA), the Amateur Athletic Union (AAU), and other organizations also published rule books. It soon became a power struggle over who would control the rules and the game. [9]

Minnesota and Its Girls Basketball
During this first era, the state activity association did not adopt girls basketball as one of its sponsored programs and did not establish statewide rules. It left the schools to mutually agree on the rules for the girls' games in their area. As early as 1924-1925, the Minnesota State High School League provided its member schools with the following rule and interpretation.

> The 1924-25 *Minnesota State High School League Official Handbook*; Rule 8, p. 28, "Question: May girls inter-school basketball games be played according to boys' rules? Interpretation: No. This is strictly prohibited by the Constitution of the Minnesota State High School Athletics Association. Members of the Association have no more right to violate this rule by mutual agreement than they have to violate any other provision of the constitution." [10]
>
> **1917, The Duluth Central yearbook, the *Zenith***
> "Although for the last few years it has been the custom for the girls to play boys' rules it was decided to follow the example of the leading 'normals' (teacher preparation schools) and colleges and to play girls' rules. There was difficulty finding games."

Several women recalled being told by their coaches that it was necessary to switch to "state rules" in order to play interscholastic games.

> **1923, The Cloquet yearbook, the *White Pine***
> "The season began with use of *boys' rules*. A change took place in the playing after the Alumni game. Coach Drew was told that a High School Girls' Team belonging to the State Athletic Association must play girls' rules. This was a shock to all concerned *as girls' rules were practically unknown*. Mr. Drew was willing to coach the team in girls' rules so practice began. The change seemed as though it would be for the worst but some of the fastest games ever played on the gym floor were played with girls' rules."

Early in the 1900s, high school girls' teams in various parts of the state did play a full-court game.

> **1907, Grand Rapids yearbook, the *Pine Needle***
> "The basketball season came to a close with a grand 'double bill' so to speak. The Eveleth High School *quintet* and a team from the Young Men's Club of Eveleth came over and contested with the girls' and boys' high school teams. The twenty-seventh of March was the day elected by the Eveleth team 'to bite the dust' and they were not disappointed in their purposes. The girls' game came first; 15-minute halves were played. Both teams played a hard game and were so evenly matched that spectators were kept in an enthusiastic mood during the entire game. It ended up with the score 10 to 9 in favor of Grand Rapids, and again the loyal rooters of the home team were delighted. The lineup was as follows:
>
> | | | |
> |---|---|---|
> | Edna Bonarhar | C | Alice Tyndal |
> | Molly Donavan | RG | Mary Hepfeld |
> | Rose Wiegle | LG | Gunia Hettly |
> | Georgia Powell | LF | Hazel Tyndal |
> | Cora Williams | RF | Carrie Beckfeld |
>
> Substitutes- Irene Davy, Margaret McAlpine
> Eveleth girls 9, Grand Rapids girls 10

Players spoke of changing rules and the challenge of playing different rules. When traveling

Grand Rapids 1907

for a weekend of games, teams would play two or more sets of rules. There were occasions when the game was split and different rules used for each half of the game. The host team determined the rules according to the number of players and the size of room where the game was played.

1914-1915 Willmar High School yearbook
"On January 16, both girls and boys went to Howard Lake for a double-header. Here we met a new and puzzling situation; the Howard Lake girls had previously played boys' rules only, while we had played according to girls' rules. For a time the outlook was dark, but finally a special edition of rules was put into use and the game was played according to girls' rules in the first half, and according to boys' rules in the second. The final score was: Howard Lake 13, Willmar 26."

There were several types of girls' rules being played, thus the definition of "state rules" varied from place to place.

1920 Two Harbors yearbook, the *Agate*
"Practice was found all the more difficult because in previous years we had all been used to playing boys' rules, and because we wished to take part in interscholastic contests we found it necessary to change to girls' rules. Imagine our disappointment when we learned that instead of playing and traveling all over the floor we had to stay in our own little division or court as it is called. Of course, we all rebelled at first, but our desire to play outside teams won out and so we buckled down to learn girls' rules; that is, we tried to.

The first game with Proctor started at last, and although the 'outside' umpire called only 18 fouls on us for over-guarding, it ended in our favor. Later, we were rather indirectly informed that we played boys' rules instead of girls'. Of course, this was a thorn in our side so we began immediately to reform."

Leona Siewert Gray, Byron and Dodge Center - 1922-1924
"We played boys' rules, three-court, and two-court. We played them all. The rules to be played were determined by the host team.

The three-court game wasn't as fast because you had to stop when you came to the line. You couldn't go over that line, either into the center or out of the center. I liked half-court better than three-court. We were called running centers in half court, one on each side of the half. The games weren't very rough unless if we were very far ahead it might get that way. We couldn't touch a person. If we did we were fouled. We had to be careful. We couldn't take the ball away; we couldn't get too close. My favorite was boys' rules.

The positions we played were marked on front of the uniforms. We were playing Elgin, and that was boys' rules, and we had lost one of the five off the team with fouls. There were only four of us and we were one point behind. My sister was a pretty good-sized girl, and she had pretty good-sized hands. There were two guarding her and she came out with the ball in one hand, and threw it up and it went in and we won the game.

One Friday we went by train to Eyota and played girls' rules. We stayed over night and went by train to Elgin and played boys' rules."

How the Game Kept Changing

Teams sometimes played games that were a hybrid of local and national rules. It was common practice that if two teams used different rules they played half a game of each set of rules. Choices were two-court, three-court, full court, or a game with a roving center.

Clara Mae Donlin, Excelsior - 1917-1921

"We had three courts when we first started. When we had three courts I was a forward. When we had two courts I was a center and I could run all over the place. I liked that because I could run around. We had it one year that we could go all over, regardless. They changed the rules every once in a while."

Charlotte Johnson, Hutchinson - 1921-1922

"When we went to Litchfield to play, then I just played for a half of the game because they had only five players. They didn't have a running center. We played half that way, and half our way."

Three-Court Game

To play the three-court game, two lines were drawn across the width of the court dividing it into three sections. No player could step on or cross these lines. For a short time 12-inch lines were recommended and players could step on the line. Courts marked for both girls' and boys' teams had line widths required by the boys' rules. If games were played in temporary facilities, court lines were not permanent and chalk was used.

Ruth DeLaHunt Rawn, Willmar -1913-1914

"I had to stop and pull up my pants all the time, and I got fouled for that. I guess I took too much time. We also got fouled for stepping over the line as the floor was divided into three parts. There was a place where the forwards and guards could stay and didn't dare go any farther. You didn't run all around the floor. We were running and we'd get that far, to that big white line, and we had to stop. If you got your feet over the line, the whistle blew and you fouled.

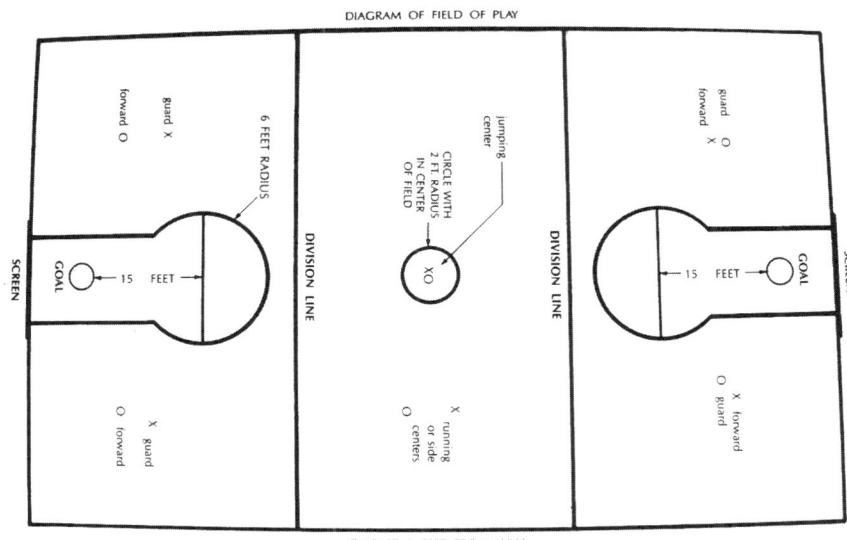

1899 official basketball court for girls and women

There were six players on a team, two forwards, two guards and two centers in that middle area. There were subs of course. Centers did not go out of the middle area. They stayed right there. I don't think anybody ran all around the field there. The forwards were the only ones who could score. Guards gave the ball to the forwards and that was it.

After someone made a basket we went back to the center and the two centers would tip off, and try to make another basket. After a foul I think they had free throws.

I can remember the feeling of being there and I was always running and chasing after my forward and guarding her. That was my job. I couldn't make baskets or anything like that. You had rules about how close you could get to her, but I had to try to keep her from throwing that ball. You had to be as fast as she was. I was about average height. The taller the girl the better the chance she had to be a good forward or guard. If I stepped over the line or if I got too close to her, it was a foul. They were very strict about that. They called most of the fouls on the guards.

If you did things you weren't allowed to do, you got fouled immediately. Three fouls and you were out. Maybe they let you in the next period. We were out and sat on the sidelines. If there were no bleachers in the gym, we sat down on the floor."

Marie Weibeler Keeler, Belle Plaine - 1922-1926
"We played the three-court game. Two guards, two forwards, and two centers. One was the jumping center, and the other was the side center. I was a side center. The game started with a jump ball in the center. It was the running center's job to get that jump ball and get it to her forwards who couldn't go across the line. The floor was divided into three areas. It was the forward's job to get a basket. If the guard from that side happened to intercept the ball she would try to get it to her center (and) to the forwards on the other end. Sometimes the opposite team could get the ball and we'd get it back again where we felt it belonged. That was about the major way of doing things. Once in a while you would get a girl who would try to throw it from the guards to the forwards. It was legal but in those days it was quite a shot for a girl. She has to be able to throw that far and we in the center would jump and try to bat it down and get it back to our own forwards. No dribble was allowed. One bounce— that was it, and you couldn't take any steps. When a basket was made the ball was returned to the center for another jump ball."

Ella Mae Bauer Pease, Delano - 1921-1925
"I can remember about the difference in the rules. The boys used to kid us about our game so we challenged them to play with us using girls' rules. We beat the pants off of them! They couldn't play like we did. After that they didn't tease us so much. The court was split in half and there were two forwards, two guards, and a center; five players on each team. I was jumping center."

"Bunny" Bernice Halverson, Delavan - 1926-1930
"Basketball was very different in my day. First of all the gym was divided into three parts and we were not allowed out of our part. We had a jumping center, a running center (me), and each end had two forwards and two guards. We were only allowed one dribble after we received the ball. We had plays. It helped a lot to have a tall center so I could get the tip-off and get the ball to our forwards. As I've always been short, I had to work hard to get and keep the ball."

The Two-Court Game
For the half-court game, the floor was divided by a center line across the width of the court dividing the area into two equal sections. The small center circle remained, and later a larger circle of greater diameter was put around the center circle. During 1914-1917, the two-court game was recommended for use only when the area was small. One center from each team could then play the entire court, using either five or six players. Sometimes these roving/running centers were allowed to shoot and other times they could not. The roving player game was recommended, approved, then eliminated

and then reinstated as the committee cautiously moved toward full-court basketball. It wasn't until 1938 that the committee finally made official the two-court game that was already in common use.

Eleanor DeLaHunt Strand, Willmar - 1917-1921
"We had a court divided in the middle at Willmar High school. You couldn't put your foot or toes over the middle line or it would be a foul. They tossed the ball up between every score and we had to try to bat it in their direction. I was a guard. We were on half of the court. No one could go all over the court. The running center was a forward. There were six on the team. I was the jumping center. I couldn't wait to play basketball at St. Cloud when I got there. The basketball was different from high school. In fact the floor was divided into three courts. They moved me to a running center. Then you had to stay on your side of the line. I could get a basket once in a while because the running center was a forward. These two in the middle had to pass the ball. I think there were just six on the team."

In some areas, the team captain or one forward could be a "rover" and play the length of the floor.

Margarethe Romo Thoreson, Red Wing Seminary - 1920-1921
"We played two-court games. I played center and was captain of our team. As captain, I was the only one that could go all over the floor. None of the other players could cross the center line. Only the two forwards and the center could score. There were five playing on a team at one time-a center, two guards, and two forwards. I can't remember that we dribbled much –we passed the ball quickly around. It was fun, but we never had much time to practice so scores were low as only forwards and the captain could score.

Jane Varner Breimhorst Jordan - 1928-1932
"The court was divided by a center line. We played three guards on one side and three forwards on the other. Only one of the forwards, the center, could cross back and forth. The other forwards and guards had to stay on their side of the line. The game was started with a jump ball, and after each basket the ball was returned to the center for a jump ball.

New Prague was always our rival. They were good players, but they played rough. Montgomery girls were always nice."

Scores began to get higher in the two-court game.

Inez Uglum Schissel Adams - 1927-1932
"Scores for the girls' game averaged from 35-40 points. We played by girls' rules with three offensive players on one end and three defensive players on the other end of the court. The three offensive players were the only ones that could shoot and score baskets. The defensive players could only defend against the opposing players but could never score. Players were allowed only one dribble so passing was a key part of the game. Play began with a center jump. And there was also a center jump after each basket. There was a jump ball whenever the ball was tied up. There were no jump shots and no three-second lanes. Two free throws were awarded if a player was fouled in the act of shooting, but other fouls earned just one free throw."

The Full-Court Game
Players were allowed to run the length of court and were not restricted to one section. Players often referred to these rules as the "boys' game." An outside boundary line was supposed to be three feet from the wall but this was not always possible.

Oline Christianson Anderson, Greenbush - 1920-1924
"After traveling by train to most of our games the girls played first and the boys second. We played real boys' rules and there were officials"

Kathryn Meade Shinn, Browns Valley - 1926-1929
"We played full court most of the time. We could run the full length of the court and we were allowed to dribble. First we started out with half court, but we had some tall gals, on there you can see (referring to a picture) and they couldn't stop fast enough. We played full court about half the time. It all depended on who you were playing. We went to different schools and some were in South Dakota."

Size of Teams

The number of team members varied with the rules. Originally groups were divided into teams of equal numbers and played the full-court game. The number of players was found to be too large so the number on the floor was reduced to 10 on the floor at one time. The Women's Basketball Committee recommended the following number of players per team:

1898 - 5	1906 to 1922 - 5-9
1901 - 5-10	1937 - minimum of 6
1903 - 6-9	1938 - 6

The number of players in some of the early high school photos showed five players. They may have been playing the Women's Basketball Committee rules for a two-court game with a roving center. Players' positions were described as that of running, racing or jumping center, with some women claiming they could shoot baskets, and others saying they could not. The use of the word "Quint" to describe a team after 1914 may have described a full-court or a roving center type game with five players.

The following newspaper referenced five players.
"Cathedral Girls' Quint to Play - Team meets Sauk Rapids Girls Fri. Night on Rapids School Floor. The St. Cloud Cathedral girls' quint will play its third game of the season against Sauk Rapids Friday night on the Sauk Rapids floor. The game should be an even contest as the local quint won from Holdingford and the Sauk Rapids girls won one game and tied one with Holdingford. The Cathedrals dropped a game to Melrose." The *St. Cloud Times*, January 6, 1927

Court Markings

Basketball was played in any available space in both school and community facilities. Opera houses, dance halls and armories were often the site of games. Games were also played outdoors on grass or hard surfaces including packed dirt which could get muddy with rain and snow.

Court markings were of more concern than the actual dimensions of the floor. Chalk was used to mark the three-court dimensions or lines could be scratched in the dirt. Recommended floor dimensions were frequently changed by rules committees and there were few standard basket ball courts available until the late 1920s.

A circle with a small diameter was in the center of the floor. This was used for jump balls. The first rules books show a six-foot free-throw lane coming out from the basket, with a free-throw line across the center of a six-foot radius circle, much like today. It was indicated that an outside line should be three feet from the wall with the court divided cross ways into three sections. As the game changed so did the court markings.

Baskets and Backboard

The peach baskets that James Naismith attached to the running track were 10 feet from the floor, a height still maintained in current rules.

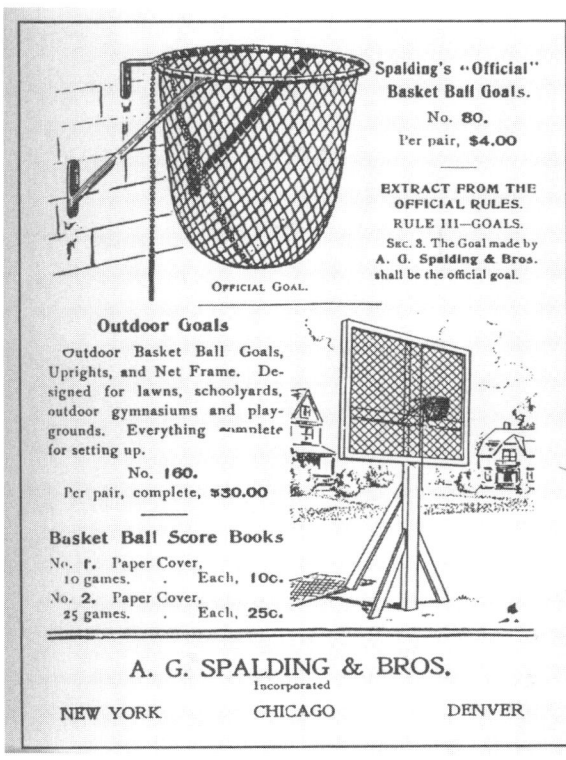

Baskets and outdoor goals, Spalding Athletic Library 1901

The peach baskets were soon replaced by baskets made of wire mesh, hammock cording, or sometimes just a rim. The Narragansett Machine Company started making baskets in 1893 with a pull cord to release the ball after a goal. This speeded up the game. Open-bottomed baskets were introduced in 1912 for use in YMCA rules and soon were in common use. The official rules change by the Women's Basketball Committee was made in 1917-18.

There were no backboards in the original game. A basket was fastened on the balcony or wall. Photographs of outdoor courts show a basket on a pole with no backboard. A net or screen was soon put behind the basket to prevent interference from spectators on balconies. The YMCA rules recommended backboards in 1895. Its dimensions followed the present backboard design.

Women's team circa 1900 before backboards were adopted

Boundary Lines

The first rules did not include rules for balls leaving the court. The game continued even when the ball went bouncing down steps or out in the hallway. Players scrambled to be the first player to retrieve the ball and throw it back onto the court. The game was filled with pushing and shoving as players tried to get to an out-of-bounds ball.

The *St. Cloud Times*, January 9, 1925, "In the girls' game, the Rapids cagers overcame a 7 to 14 lead for Big Lake at the end of the first half, and in the second half piled up four points while holding the Lakers scoreless. Sauk Rapids won by a count of 8 to 7."

Chicken wire was placed around some courts to keep the ball in play. Basketball players became known as "cagers." The term was frequently used in newspaper reports describing players.

Playing conditions varied greatly. Sometimes spectators' feet extended into the court which added to the hazards of the facilities. The boundary line was sometimes the wall itself or so close to the wall that there was no room to stand out of bounds. Later, a rule was added that the player could place one foot against the wall. One rule even made it legal to play the ball from a bounce off the wall. The WBC 1906 rules stipulated that an outside boundary line could be eliminated if the coaches both agreed. Local rules prevailed if there were obstacles on the court or if the ball touched a low ceiling, climbing rope or ceiling fixture.

Dribbling the Ball

Bouncing the ball or dribbling was illegal at first, but was quickly added to the game. The first girls' rules in 1889 allowed only three knee-high bounces. Then around 1910, no bounce was allowed. A single bounce became legal again between 1914 and 1915. No bounce, two bounces, three bounces and the continuous dribble were all legal at some time. The Women's Basketball Committee was maintaining a limit of three bounces as late as 1961. They were concerned that the continuous dribble was too much like the boys' game. A player could also juggle the ball. This meant to throw it into the air, run and catch it yourself. Bounce passing to another player became legal about 1918.

Guarding

Guarding could only be on a vertical or horizontal plane. A guard had to stand with her feet planted and not lean over a player or put her hand over the ball. To wave her hands or move her arms up and down was a foul. A blocking foul was called if a player put her hands out to a player without the ball. Two players guarding a player with the ball was considered a foul called "boxing up." The rules changed in 1932 so guards could guard on any plane.

Shooting Techniques and Scoring

Shooting techniques have greatly changed. Underhanded shots were once recommended to prevent "compression injuries" to the chest muscles of female players.

Montevideo 1913

Restrictions on guards and different point values for baskets led to some unusual ways of shooting. A field goal always has counted two points with three exceptions: only one point was earned by a shot taken with one hand (the shot put), a two-handed overhead, and the back-to-the-basket shots. These were impossible to guard against and did not count two points until guarding was changed to any plane in 1932.

Jump Balls and Tie Balls

The rules regarding the center toss and jump balls required the jumping center to stand with feet together within her half of a small circle, facing her team's basket. A whistle was blown at the height of the toss between the players and after the whistle the centers could jump. At first the ball could be batted or caught by the center, but the 1914 rules changed. The ball could no longer be caught. The jumping center had to hold her hand at waist height behind her back until after the ball had been tapped. In 1927 someone realized that the free hand was important to jumping height and balance. The rule was changed and the free hand no longer had to be placed behind the back.

Jump balls were used to start games, get the ball into play at quarters, after every goal, and for tie balls. Tie balls were settled with a jump ball where the incident occurred. A questionable out-of-bounds call was settled with a jump a few feet inside the boundary line where the ball went out of bounds. Jump balls were gradually removed to speed up the game.

Penalties, Fouls, and Violations
In 1916-17 the Women's Basketball Committee began to differentiate between types of rule infractions. Until then all infringements carried the penalty of a free throw. This was very time-consuming so the committee reorganized this part of the game. Five line violations still could disqualify a player, but a penalty called the 'unguarded throw' was instituted. This was an unguarded throw to a player on the floor. No basket could be attempted.

A double violation was settled by a jump ball. In 1918-19 more changes were made and fouls became defined as 'personal' and 'technical.'

Traveling, double bounces, holding the ball more than three seconds, stepping on a line, handing the ball or striking the ball with a fist became violations and resulted in a throw-in rather than a free throw.

General fouls pertained to the ball and game regulations. Specific fouls were person-to-person fouls. The descriptions used to define specific fouls indicate the game was not gentle. Terms included shouldering, hacking, tripping, striking, kicking, hair pulling, tackling, and unnecessary roughness.

It was not until 1949 that the ball became dead at the whistle before a free throw. Until that time if a free throw was missed, players grouped under the basket fighting for the ball, causing rough play and personal fouls. It was taken out of bounds by the team not shooting the free throw.

Coaching Restrictions and Player Conversations
Captains were allowed to speak quietly to their teammates in 1915. A year later in 1916, all the players could speak quietly to one another. In 1951-52 players were allowed to confer with their coaches during time out and at intermissions. The Women's Basketball Committee did not allow coaching from the sidelines during time outs and intermissions until the 1950s.

Minnesota players from the late 1920s indicate that this rule was considered a local one determined by the coaches.

"In our second year of high school basketball, an official made a call that Marie McIntyre did not like and she slammed the ball to the floor and it bounced up and hit the low ceiling of the gym and back down and part way up again- she didn't like the next call very much either."
1924-26, Agnes King McIntyre, International Falls

Length of a Game
Originally the game was played in 20-minute halves. In 1903 halves were shortened to 15 minutes with a 10-minute halftime rest.

The game remained this way until 1918-19 when the 15-minute halves were divided into two eight-minute quarters for secondary schools, with a two-minute rest between quarters. No coaching was allowed. Halftime remained at 10 minutes. This recommendation became an official rule in 1924. By 1971 the game had evolved back to two 20-minute halves with a 15-minute halftime.[11]

Summary
The variety of rules and games appear not to have deterred the enjoyment of the game for Minnesota girls. In true Minnesota tradition, these young women were flexible and could adapt to the type of game selected for any game. They only wanted to play the game. Decades have passed and the standardized rules now allow players to fully utilize their abilities and enjoy their favorite sport of basketball.

From Costumes to Uniforms

Looking through family photos and school yearbooks, we can observe changes in clothing fashions for women that cause us to wonder, "Why would they wear such uncomfortable and restrictive clothing?" Quite simply, the social mores of the times were strong and nonconformity carried public and social penalties as well as negative reactions for the woman in her own home. Perhaps we should not judge our predecessors too harshly. Today's fashions will also receive the critique of future generations, and they may appropriately ask, *"Why would they wear that?"*

In Days Past

The clothing fashions of the twentieth century made it difficult for women to live a healthy life, and they did restrict women's participation in sports to recreational, more passive activities.

Corsets for the Princess and the Dowager

Women in the wealthier class were expected to dress in a manner which reflected their status in society. They were buried under layers of fabrics that made it very difficult to move or even breathe. Getting dressed in the morning was a challenge. A fashionable woman had to put on the following garments: a chemisette, pantalets, long stockings, a garter belt, her corset upon which was hung about three layers of petticoats, and finally a bustle. A layered, ruffled and fancy floor-length dress with long sleeves followed as the top layer. This was all quite heavy. Small feet were in fashion so she would have squeezed into the smallest pair of shoes possible—high top with high heels. Finally, gloves would be added, and she could now go out into the public.

Movies and books illustrate the efforts of women and their helpers to lace corsets as tight as possible to achieve the small waist that was considered essential. The shoe styles were difficult for walking, as many remain today. Little wonder that a woman might welcome the helping hand of a nearby "gentleman." The appearance of delicacy and fragility were acceptable if not encouraged for a proper "lady" of the times.

"Women's bodies were pressed into a grotesque S-bend, breasts pushed outward into a sweeping curve, while an exaggerated, projecting bottom curved in the opposite direction as a counterweight beneath the tightly corseted waist and flat abdomen." [2]

The "Lady," so dressed, reflected the status of her family, and their place in the upper or upper middle class. It also implied that this woman would require help with her house, another reflection of wealth and status. [1]

It becomes obvious why women would experience difficulty in breathing because of the extremely tight corsets. Some women experienced light-headedness and could faint.

"An unprecedented passion for decoration characterized this time. Corded embroidery, appliqué, lace inserts, glass beads, sequins, frills, and pleats covered women like a glossy, flickering web.[3]

These conditions were referred to as the *vapors*. A piece of furniture in homes of that era was actually called "a fainting couch." It was a long couch where a woman could recover her breath. It is little wonder that the physicians and others believed that women should not exert themselves because their lungs were too weak.

Fashions from France and England traveled across the ocean to the new country and spread throughout all levels of society. Women who were not in the upper class in terms of wealth would dress with similar fashions, adapted for their needs. Long dresses, hats and gloves were considered essential for special occasions. Fashion styles were modified as needed to accommodate their participation in the hard work required on family farms and businesses.

Going for a walk in 1902

Leisure Time Activities
During the late 1800s fashion began to yield to women's interests in new leisure-time activities. Social station, wealth, and especially leisure time were key elements in allowing women to participate. The upper class had access to facilities provided by private clubs. Croquet, archery, golf and lawn tennis were available, though difficult while wearing the restraining corsets and layers of skirts and high heels.

Women's primary role was considered to be child-bearing and rearing, so the health of women was important to their families and the medical community. Walking was a recommended activity though the clothing and shoes were limiting. Speed walking and running marathons were not within this sphere.

Women went to the beach wearing a heavy, sometimes woolen, bathing costume, long stockings, bathing shoes and a ruffled cap. So attired, women could play on the beach and wade in the water, but even strong swimmers were limited until clothing styles changed to a lighter one-piece bathing suit. It would be years in the future before women wore what would be called "swimming suits."

The medical profession of those times tended to accept, and even promote, the premise of women being the 'weaker sex.' The research that would dispel this myth would not be available for another hundred years.

The Birth of the Bloomer Costume
In the 1850s, the word "bloomer," came into the language when Amelia Jenks Bloomer of New York promoted an outfit that consisted of a tunic and full pantelettes. Bloomer promoted the attire in her newspaper, *The Lily*. It was worn by Elizabeth Cady Stanton, among others, and became known as "The Bloomer Costume," even though Amelia Bloomer had no part in its creation.

These educated and courageous women worked for and demanded women's rights. They wrote and spoke about social issues such as temperance and slavery. They worked for suffrage, i.e., obtaining the vote for women. They believed that women should be able to own property.

As women worked to correct social injustice against women, they included working for changing apparel that was unhealthy and restricted activity. They wore bloomers, experiencing social ridicule and public abuse. In later decades, women would experience similar reactions when they began wearing slacks and pant-suits.[4]

Clearly, social pressure to dress in certain styles can be one way to restrict and control women and their lives.

Women and Their Bicycles
Primitive versions of the bicycle began in the 1400s, but the first designs that included pedals began in the mid-1800s. In 1860s and 1870s, a velocipede with steel wheels and the high-wheelers became favorites for men willing to risk the falls, called "taking a header."[5]

In the 1880s, limited by the clothing fashions of the time, women first rode adult tricycles where their skirts could be safely tucked away from the wheels. There were social rules that didn't allow women to ride alone without a chaperone.

There were women, however, who chose to ride a tricycle without a chaperone. In 1888, the Philadelphia Tricyclist's Club had 118 members, 18 of whom were women. That year the club's "Captain's Cup" that was annually presented to the member who covered the most miles during the year, was won by a woman 'for her mileage record of 3,304 miles.'[6]

In 1885, the Rover safety bicycle opened the door for women. It was the first true safety bicycle, with two wheels of the same size, a rear chain drive and direct steering that established a bicycle much like the design of today.[7]

The 1890s were called the "Golden Age of the Bicycle." One-third of the world's bicycle production was of women's models.

The invention of the bicycle also had a great influence on women's fashions. In 1896, *Godey's Lady's Book*, the most popular women's magazine from 1830-1877, recommended the following costume for women on their adult-size three-wheeled tricycles. "A straight, side-pleated skirt of wool serge, worn over one underskirt and full trousers lined with flannel and made of material to match the dress. A warm jersey and jacket trimmed with fur, with a 'tricyclist's' cap to match, completed the outfit."[8]

Before long, women began to shorten their skirts, sometimes weighing down the skirt with lead weights into the hem. Women could now ride without their getting their clothing caught in the wheels or gears.

Women began riding bicycles in large numbers. This created a negative response from those who believed that it was breaking the rigidly defined gender roles, and it was! Women were leaving their homes without chaperones and going into the world without supervision. The Victorian era was ending, but not without conflict and stress for both men and women.[9]

To women, the bicycle meant one thing: *freedom*!

Bloomers would become the riding costume for the woman, her two-wheeled bicycle, and for her growing participation in active sports.

Bloomers and This New Game of Basket Ball
Into this social environment filled with social expectations for women in dress and behavior, came this new game of "Basket Ball." Women not only began playing it, but they began to play it in public

"Let me tell you what I think about the bicycling. I think it has done more to emancipate women than anything else in the world. I stand and rejoice every time I see a woman ride by on a wheel. It gives a woman a sense of freedom and self-reliance. It makes her feel as if she were independent. The moment she takes her seat she knows she can't get into harm unless she gets off her bicycle, and off she goes, the picture of free, untrammeled womanhood."
Susan B. Anthony, interviewed by Nellie Bly, *New York World*, February 2, 1896[10]

wearing bloomers. It was inevitable that there would be serious conflict and arguments over the game and its perceived negative influence on women.

A segment of the population continued to look upon bloomers as inappropriate wear and girls' and women's ankles and knees as something to be hidden. The term "bloomers" acquired a negative name because they defied social customs and allegedly encouraged negative behavior while girls and women played this new game.

Consider the impact when these two forces merged: *basketball*, a real team sport that included physical contact during the game, and *bloomers*, a style of clothing that challenged the accepted dress for women out in the public eye.

Minnesota, Basketball and Bloomers

When the young women of Minnesota began playing basketball in 1892, they were also wearing the bloomer attire. The loose, shorter dress was supplemented by bloomers under the skirt of the dress. Even so, the costume was an improvement over the longer dresses and corsets of their mother's generation and provided greater freedom of movement for the players.

Sweaters were worn on early teams. The 1901 Crosby-Deerwood team wore light colored sweaters. Some wore a "C" for Crosby and others have a "D" for Deerwood.

Another early team photo is of St. Paul Central in 1902. The team wore wearing dark sweaters with "C" on the front, paired with long bloomers.

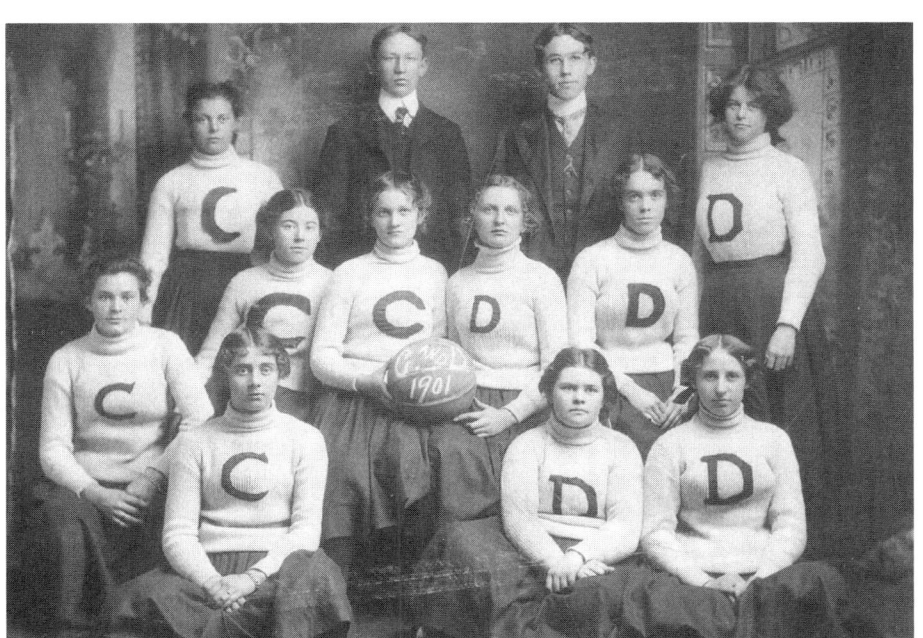

Crosby-Deerwood 1901

The next team is the 1903 Cloquet team wore a middy style top with the letters CHS across the collar. Did you see the middy with the "S" reversed?

All of the teams wore long stockings and long sleeves to cover arms and legs. If an ankle or knee could be seen during play, it would have to be properly covered.

St. Paul Central 1902

The early uniforms were frequently made by the players or their mothers. The amount of material used in the bloomers accounted for a variety of styles among players on the team. The 1902 Brainerd team shows several types of homemade uniforms among the team members.

The ancestor of the pony tails of today's athletes was the "Gibson look" that appeared in *Life* magazine in 1890. It was said, "The physical attributes of the Gibson Girl were a tall and commanding appearance, 'thick dark hair swept upward in the prevailing pompadour style.' She had a thinner rather than a more voluptuous figure but roundness of bosom and hips. Her casual attire and frequent appearance in a sport setting, according to Charlotte Perkins Gilman, bespoke a woman 'braver, stronger, more healthful and skillful and able and free, more human in all ways.'"[11]

Wearing Bloomers from the Players' Perspective
Bloomers and middy blouses were being worn by college women and they soon became the costumes for the early girls basketball teams.

While bloomers were an improvement over corsets and long dresses, they were often made of wool or materials that were hot and scratchy for basketball players. The construction of the bloomers often led to amusing moments for players.

Ruth DeLaHunt Rawn, Willmar - 1913-14
"Uniforms? We wore middies and bloomers that were like baggy pants. After awhile the elastic in the legs got worn out and mine would keep falling down and I had to stop and pull up my pants all the time, and I got fouled for that. I guess I took too much time."

Cloquet 1903

Brainerd 1902

20   Daughters of the Game

Zumbrota 1904

Clara Mae Donlin, Excelsior - 1917-21

"Our uniform was a beautiful black wool. The pants were so big that it was like a skirt. On top we wore a middy blouse that went with it. It was a real nice uniform. The wool was warm. We had a lot of underwear on.

The school furnished the uniform. If my mother had to buy it, I wouldn't have had one. I'd have had to play in my birthday suit. They didn't have money; my father earned a dollar a day. They didn't have any money to throw away on stuff like that."

As years passed, the fabric gradually became lighter and the bloomers became shorter. Players began to roll down their long stockings and pull the bloomers above their knees.

Grand Rapids 1907

Vera Learned Templin, Buffalo - 1922-1926

"Bill Hoffer was our coach, and he had us out on the field doing our warm-up exercises—we were in our basketball suits at that time—bloomers, middies, anklets, and tennis shoes. A woman from across the street

Goodhue 1910

In 1919, an Iowa parent admonished her daughter, Maud Pfeffer, to ensure that she would dress properly and conform to the acceptable code of their community of Hampton.
"You can climb on the barn,
You can shinny down the roof,
You can climb the windmill,
But you can't play basketball in those bloomers!"

was watching us, just staring at us. I said to Eileen, 'Why is she staring at us like that?' We later found out she went to the school board and she reported to the school board that those girls were out there 'half-naked,' jumping up and down in front of that man, and she thought it should be stopped. Of course the school board called us in and they told us about her visit. They said, 'We can't have a complaint like that going around town, so we have to do something about it.' What they did was we had to wear long stockings after that."

A Minnesota parent shared her concerns.

Marie Weibeler Keeler of Belle Plaine - 1922-26
On one fateful night, Marie's mother learned that she was playing basketball against her mother's wishes. For two years, Marie had been telling her mother that she had orchestra practice or trips, and would hide her flute in the bushes. One night, Marie's father invited her mother to see the girls basketball game and to ride in their new car.

During the game, Marie saw her mother in the stands and knew she was "in for it" when she got home. When they got home her mother asked Marie if she realized that she was embarrassing her family and making a spectacle of herself. Marie said it was the first time that she, as a young girl, went against her mother's wishes.

Marie said it was very difficult to do, but she said to her mother, "I'm sorry that you feel that I am making a spectacle of myself playing basketball and that it brings disgrace to our family….*but I am going to play basketball*!" Her mother's response was, "well, all right, but I am not coming to your games."

In 1999 when Marie and other women of the era were honored at the MSHSL State Girls Basketball Tournament, Marie lifted her plaque and her eyes upward, and quietly said, "Mother, I hope you are watching."

Gradually bloomers became shorter, less full, and hot woolen bloomers gave way to lighter material. Some middy tops were borrowed from young sailors returning from World War I.

Kay Nolan Wetter, Brainerd - 1924-28
Brainerd Dispatch, Wed. Jan. 13, 1993. "Uniforms were designed to cover skin and make a fashion statement. The girls wore either store-bought sailor blouses made of heavy material with sailor collars, and neck ties, or borrowed the sailor blouses of returning sailors. The black satin bloomers had elastic cuffs at the knees to pull securely over the tops of long black stockings. The stockings were held up by garters, and were stuffed securely into the tops of flat soled, high, laced up leather or canvas tennis shoes.

We played in the bloomer days. They were loose and big, but they were hot. Although my dad didn't mind me playing basketball too much, he didn't like me wearing those bloomers. We'd pull them up above our knees and he thought that was just terrible.

Locker rooms were not available, so we wore our uniforms under our school clothes until the afternoon game. Then we sweaty girls had to go home to clean up."

Leona Briard Hanson, Gaylord - 1920-24
"We made ourselves black bloomers. I had a middy from my sister's brother-in-law who just came home from the Navy. I had his necktie too. That's what I wore. My sister Belle had a white blouse."

Uniforms Become Colorful
Colorful bloomer and middy uniforms made by the players may surprise those who assume that they were all black and white. With no color film available, the colors are lost. What appear to be black bloomers and black or white tops were frequently a variety of bright colors. Players made bright middy tops of red, orange, green, blue or gold all trimmed with contrasting school colors. There were brightly colored scarves, colorful striped stockings, and some even wore "beanies" between games.

Two Harbors Yearbook, *The Agate* - 1920
"Our first game came after the Christmas holidays, in our own gymnasium; but, nevertheless, we were all rather nervous because so far the visiting team, Proctor, had not been defeated. Of course, it being our first game, we wished to make a good impression, so we purchased suits, or rather had them made, by ourselves, which consisted of red middies, black bloomers and the rest of the paraphernalia that goes with a suit. With this attractive attire and a 'bold front' which we managed to put on, we looked fit for either defeat or victory."

Rochester 1921

Edith Anderson Bergan, Cloquet - 1920-25
"Our school colors were purple and white. The first two years we wore a red sailor middy blouse and big black bloomers and socks that came over our knees. We each had our own stockings so they all did not match. Sometime during our senior year (1925) we got new uniforms. They were purple with white trim. The top had a v-neck and capped sleeves. We had a "C" on the front of the shirt. The bottoms of our uniforms were purple shorts. It was a big change from our other uniforms. We had purple and white stockings. The uniforms were furnished by the high school."

Vera Learned Templin, Buffalo - 1922-26
"At first we had middies with the square collar down the back. We wore big bloomers made of wool serge. Boy, were they hot!. That is what we had when I first started. Then Mrs. Doctor Catlin (they were such supporters of athletics), she made purple corduroy knickers for all of us and a white, kind of heavy, rayon blouse with a purple corduroy collar. We thought they were pretty foxy."

Cloquet 1925

Marie Weibeler Keeler, Belle Plaine - 1922-26
"The girls wore black bloomers with elastic at the waist and below the knees. Our shirts were a pinkish orange and were worn with black ties that were always in the way. The girls made their own uniforms. Paid for 'out of their own pocket.' I had a good father and in my freshman year when they asked for people to come out for basketball, my friends were all going so I felt, why not, so I went too. When we needed money to make our uniforms I went to my dad and told him that in sewing we were making this outfit and I would need some material and I needed some money. He didn't ask questions, he just gave me the money for the material and I went to the store and bought it. I brought the material to school and the teacher helped us make our uniforms. I had no problems with that part."

Blanche Line Kingsley, Cromwell - 1926-31

"I was chosen as captain of the team for my junior and senior years. Our uniforms were updated from black bloomers and a white middy top with black tie, to new red and white outfits. The bottoms of the legs were tight and the body of the pants draped over them. The shirt was fashioned with a V-neck and I believed them to be quite attractive. The uniforms were all red, trimmed in white."

Cromwell 1927 champs

"Bunny" Halverson Wheeler, Delavan - 1926-30

"We wore huge wool serge pleated bloomers for pants—non-washable—can you imagine? Tops were cotton, green middy shirts with a white letter D on the front, and green and white striped socks. Our tennis shoes were black and white and they cost maybe $2.98."

Thea Sletkolen Stay, Montevideo - 1931-35

"Our uniforms were maroon and gold wool uniforms furnished by the school. They were pullover jerseys and bloomer-type pants. The pants were baggy, like knickers. They were hot and scratchy. I'm a very allergic person to wool. I hated those uniforms."

Delavan 1927

Best-Dressed Teams

The uniforms made a fashion statement for players and their team. Some tournaments even chose a "best-dressed team."

Dorothy Svenson Viker, Hayfield - 1921-25

"Our girls' team was outfitted by the school, as was the boys' team. In 1924 we had reason to be very proud of our uniforms. They were gold cotton sateen middy blouses and bloomers, socks and beanies. The beanies were not to be worn while playing, all with purple trim. The middy blouse had a purple trimmed sailor-style collar. The wool socks were striped in the same colors to the knee. Although the bloomers were supposed to go below the knee, the girls usually pulled them up higher.

At the Ellendale tournament in 1925 we missed the championship, but we went away happy to have been named 'the best appearing team, both on and off the court.'"

From Bloomers to Shorts: Change is in the Air

Players began to adapt uniforms and how they were worn. Materials become lighter and less fabric was used. The biggest change in uniforms came when bloomers were exchanged for shorts. The change was not always acceptable to parents and community, but the young women were pleased. The movement of the players must have become easier, improving the overall quality of the game. Legs and arms were finally free to run, pass and shoot. The players were excited, and sometimes a bit nervous, to be the first team to wear their new uniforms of shorts and short sleeved tops.

Hayfield 1925

Gertrude Zeibarth Bloom, Coach, Park Rapids - 1928
"I remember when I was playing on my high school team at a neighboring town, and we were a daring, devilish group. We rolled our stockings down below our knees and wore red kneepads. The superintendent of schools of said opponents wouldn't let the game go on until we rolled our stockings back up where they belonged. That tells you what they thought of our scanty attire. My early teaching was all done in bloomers."

Aileen Just Luther, Rapidan - 1922-30
"Our uniforms in 1923 consisted of a white middy with black collar and long black bow, black bloomers, and blue and white stockings worn over the knees. The bloomers were made of black sateen using about five yards of material pleated and very full so they hung below our knees. Since almost all other girls' teams in the area had women coaches at that time, Miss Pear Ware coached the 1926-27 season. Miss Ware, being a bit more fashion-minded, dared to change the traditional black bloomer white middy uniform to a medium blue with white trim in keeping with our school colors. We retained the bloomer-type bottoms but with a yard or two less material in them. So in 1928-29, we again changed coaches. We were happy that Gladys Wandersee Mohr became our coach. The first thing she changed was our uniforms. She really went modern with all white suits with blue trim. We had small unpleated bloomers worn above the knees and were even permitted to roll our stockings below the knees or to the ankles."

Kathryn Meade Shinn, Browns Valley - 1926-29
"The popularity of the boys' and girls' teams was about equal. Of course as soon as we got the shorts everybody in town had to come to see that, because that was disgraceful. First we played in bloomers. When the team started to wear shorts, the whole community was interested. Some were shocked and they thought it was scandalous. There was trouble at home with some of the men who would get the gossip downtown about the girls' teams, you know, with their shorts. My dad didn't think they were disgraceful, but my mother kind of held her breath a little bit because shorts were not popular in those days."

Ruth McCarron Dahlke, Sherburn - 1924-27
"In 1926 the school bought the short outfits for us. We were the first team in Martin County to wear shorts."

Rose Robinson Wichser, West Concord - 1925-29
"Uniforms were supplied by the school. In 1925 when I started playing, we wore short uniforms. Two senior members and one junior talked the superintendent into the short uniforms and we were the only ones in Dodge County to have them.

Browns Valley 1929

The pants came three-fourths of the way to our knees (a lot of bare skin) and we all felt very naked the first time—we pulled our socks up to below the knee to cover our legs. Word spread through town and the attendance at the next game was large. All the curious men came to see those short uniforms!"

Ruth Olson Kleven, Milan - 1925-1929
"To start we had our own white blouse and black bloomers. In 1927 the school bought us uniforms. They were red v-neck shirts of lighter weight material than the shorts. Red shorts with white socks. Colored trim and high-top tennis shoes. We also wore cloth headbands with 'M' on the front. Uniforms had a white 'M.' We were the first team to have real uniforms.

The shorts were red, and we were so self-conscious—they were a little wider at the bottom. We had to make little red bloomers to wear underneath them. We talked mother into going one time, but she didn't think too much of the bare knees."

Mabel Thompson Erickson, Mabel - 1927-31
"Once when we were playing in Spring Grove, I got my foot caught in the pocket of the jumping center. We had to laugh and our coach was madder than a hornet. She said, 'get up, get up, get up.' We got up right away, but of course it was funny because it opened up the placket. That was when we wore bloomers. Then we switched to shorts and sleeveless tops in 1929. Our mothers made the entire outfit. We were the first team to have shorts in Fillmore County. Our school colors were purple and white.

Ruth Olson Kleven, new uniform, 1927

Jane Varner Breimhorst, Jordan - 1928-32
Jane was proud of "being the first girls basketball team at Jordan High School to wear shorts. Before that they wore bloomers—we were considered pretty risqué with our shorts and t-shirts."

Evelyn Olson Kukkola, Underwood - 1934-37

"The school gave us uniforms. My first two years they were like a jumpsuit, but by my junior year we got regular uniforms in red and white. They were sleeveless, like a tank top with a big letter and satin short shorts."

Warm-ups

The only photo of a team with warm-ups came from Glyndon in 1934.

The photos of the first uniforms in 1903 to the last in 1939 reflect the dramatic changes in attitude and social expectations both for basketball and for women in general.[12]

Jordan 1932

Underwood 1937

Glyndon 1934 in warm-ups

First Quarter 27

Warm-ups and First Quarter Free Throws

"Hello!! My name is Ima!! I am a member of the LGBB team! Can you guess the name of our team? We are the "Little Girl Bouncing Ball Team.

What's the name of your team? _____
Let's play a game while you are reading our story, shall we?! Great!!

Here are the rules for the first quarter. Read the sections in the Warm-ups and First Quarter. Then shoot your 'free throws' by answering the questions below. You will score 1 point for each correct answer. After you shoot your free throws for each quarter, total the score for your team after the Fourth Quarter. The team with the higher score WINS!!!

Here's a practice question, "If my first name is Ima and my middle initial is 'B,' what is my last name? Answer: My last name is Ball!! Ima B. Ball. Did you get it?! I knew you would!! Here we go!"

Warm-ups and First Quarter Questions

1. What was the Rover that freed women from chaperones and the restrictions of dress?
2. Name the apparel for women that would help them participate more freely in sports.
3. Name the woman who promoted this apparel through her newspaper, *The Lily*.
4. What does the word "suffrage" mean?
5. What was the name of the person who invented basketball?
6. What was the name of the school where basketball was invented?
7. In what year was basketball invented?
8. What did players use for baskets in the first games played?
9. What was the year that basketball was brought to Minnesota?
10. Who brought basketball to Minnesota and taught the women to play this new game?
11. What is the name of the college and where is it located?
12. Name the Smith College woman who adapted Naismith's rules for a women's game.
13. Why have basketball players been called "cagers?"
14. Name the condition created by extremely tight corsets that caused women to faint.
15. Name the piece of furniture women used when they became 'light-headed.'
16. Name the most influential women's fashion magazine from 1830-1877.
17. What U.S. constitutional amendment gave women the right to vote?
18. In what years did the influenza epidemic result in the deaths of 20-40 million people?
19. Did the Great Depression plague the U. S. economy in the 1920s, 1930s or 1940's?
20. What year did the Minnesota State High School League adopt sports for girls?
21. What was the first year for the MSHSL State Girls Basketball Tournament?
22. In what year was women's basketball added as an Olympic sport?
23. How many Minnesota girls' varsity teams played in 2004?

Score   Home_____   Visitor_____
Answers:

1. A bicycle
2. Bloomers
3. Amelia Bloomer
4. The right to vote
5. Dr. James Naismith
6. YMCA International Training School, Springfield, Mass
7. 1891
8. Two peach baskets
9. 1892
10. Max J. Exner
11. Carleton College, Northfield
12. Senda Berenson
13. They built a cage of wire around the perimeter of the court to prevent the ball from rolling away
14. Vapors
15. Fainting couch
16. *Godey's Lady's Book*
17. 19th amendment
18. 1918-1919
19. 1930s
20. 1969
21. 1976
22. 1976
23. 418

Second Quarter

Where They Played the Game

Today's athletes walk into gymnasiums that are complete with floors, baskets, spectator seating, showers and are appropriately heated and cooled. Locker rooms have taken the place of coal bins, school rooms, or space in nearby community buildings. Playing floors are clean and well marked.

Before the invention of basketball, gymnasiums were used for group exercises and often contained gymnastic equipment. These gymnasiums were in colleges and universities, YMCAs, private clubs and occasionally in the attics or basements of public schools.

The first gymnasiums and playing fields for women were built at private women's colleges in the eastern states. When women began going to college in the mid 1800s, physical exercise was part of the curriculum. It was intended to strengthen women for the intellectual stress of using their brains. Women were found to be surprisingly strong and their brains withstood the rigors of study.

As the game grew in popularity, games were held in a variety of facilities. The dimensions of the court, ceiling height, basket height and playing surface varied from site to site. Dancing was a popular activity. When games were played in the Opera House and other community facilities after one of these social gatherings, the floor was frequently slippery with the corn meal spread for dancing.

They Played the Game in Any Available Space

Many communities did not have gymnasiums so games were played in local community buildings, dance halls, opera houses, tin shops, or basements of buildings.

Souvenir edition of 100 years at Alexandria's High School
"The girls' gym was in the attic of the school, until the superintendent caught the girls hanging from their knees on the bars. He shouted, 'Girls, I'm shocked,' and promptly closed the gym."

The Alexandria High School newspaper, the *Alexandrian*, 1904
"Basket ball was not played this year because the girls could not find a ball and the city council prohibited the boys playing in the city hall, which was the only place large enough that could be used."

Grand Rapids yearbook, the *Pine Needle*, 1908-09
"The second game was at Floodwood. At this game we failed to pile up quite such a score as we had done on Hibbing, owing to the slippery floor and the high baskets. But, because of a number of enthusiastic rooters, who certainly helped 'some,' and also, because of 'rubbing a little rosin,' which helped some more, and of course, because of good, scientific playing, the final score was 15-1, in favor of the black and the orange. There was 'dancing in the hall' after the game (should anyone desire further information on this point, just ask our captain,) and we tore ourselves away barely in time to catch the midnight train. It was a tired but happy crowd which Miss Burlingame marshalled back to town to the tune of "Lo, the Conquering Heroines Come."

Clara Mae Donlin, Excelsior - 1917-21
"We played in Excelsior at the grade school that is over there. That was built when I was in the sixth or seventh grade. That was the first school in the area that had a gym and shower. It is three stories high. I look at it and I think I use to run up and down those steps, and then I'd have to go down because I ran up, and have to do it over again. When we traveled to other towns they usually had gymnasiums, but they didn't have lockers or rooms to dress in or things like that. Excelsior had a low court and then the seats were on the side and went up gradually. It was a real swanky place and we felt pretty good with the school we had with all this modern equipment."

Warroad travels to Roseau, 1919
"The games were played in the Opera House which can hardly be called a "gym" being both low and poorly heated and no provision to accommodate the audience. The girls' game was called first and resulted in another victory for our team."

Clara Corcoran Lawrenz, Gaylord - 1919-22
"Gaylord had a high ceiling that's why we liked Gaylord's court. Gibbon used a dance hall."

Virginia Irwin Kruger, Belle Plaine - 1920-24
"We played outside, in the town hall, the Knights of Columbus (KC) Hall, and Wyblier's Hall."

Margaret Huffman Thompson, Gaylord - 1920-24
"For our games, the old city hall was just full. They stood up in back where they put the movie theater things. It was all full on the stage. We charged and made money because we had to pay all our own expenses. We even brought money to pay the light bill at the city hall, and brought wood to build the fire. There was a stove in the corner, and we had to sweep. The boys always wanted to come in and watch us play. They would try to play before we did. They would sneak in, carry wood and do all kinds of things for us."

Leona Briard Hanson, Gaylord - 1920-24
"We went to Fairfax, Hutchinson, Excelsior and Gibbon. We went on the train to Excelsior."

Marie Weibeler Keeler, Belle Plaine - 1922-26
"None of the schools had gyms. We played in town dance halls mostly. At St. Peter we played in the gym at Gustavus. That was keen. The halls were different sizes — some were heated by

a large stove in the corner, and had low ceilings. One time at Carver we were late getting there and the coach told us we would all have to change clothes together in the coal room. He would be there, and we were to hurry and get our clothes out so he could turn off the lights. We would have to dress in the dark, as the boys were also changing. When he turned the lights back on, one girl had a boy's uniform on and the boy had the girl's on. Of course the kids exploded in laughter, but the coach was as angry as I ever saw anyone be.

We had some boys that were on the team that were probably 6 feet tall and they could touch the ceilings in Carver. It was difficult to make baskets, and it was difficult to throw the ball."

Leona Seiwert Gray, Byron 1922-24; Dodge Center - 1924-26
"Our gym was about the worst. The rest had a place to sit and we just had benches around the side, and the two stairs that came down from the hallways were packed with people to watch the game. The basket was on the wall. It had a backboard on the wall, and the basket was right on that. When I moved to Dodge Center they didn't have a gym at the school. We had to change our clothes at the school, and run two blocks, up the stairs to the hall that was above the hardware store. When we got through we had to go back to school to change our clothes again. In the winter time that wasn't very nice."

Vera Learned Templin, Buffalo - 1922-26
"We played in a gym. The gym was small but had a high ceiling. At one end of it was a stage because the auditorium was used for the plays and programs, and things we had in school. Then there was a balcony. Under the balcony they wrapped up these maple seats that were on stringers, which they pulled down during the game for spectators. The spectators feet would be sticking out, and they had to pull their feet back in to be sure that wouldn't trip anybody. Not all the other communities had gyms. in Howard Lake they had a great big room up over another building, which was probably more like a dance hall. They marked it off for basketball, and we played up there. Maple Lake and Annandale had gyms. In Rockford we played in a great big room in a hotel, which was a dance hall."

Aileen Just Luther, Rapidan - 1923-29
"At Waldorf, there was an area screened off for the heating unit. If the ball would happen to bounce just right it would land down in the boiler room. Then a time out was necessary to retrieve the ball. Pemberton had support beans on the edge of the playing floor. We were warned not to bump into them."

Ann Martinson Neuman, Grove City - 1924-26
"We usually played in the old town hall. In Eden Valley we played upstairs over a grocery store."

Ruth McCarron Dahlke, Sherburn - 1924-27
"We always played in a gym except at Ceylon where we played on a dance floor. During time-outs, we stepped out the front door and stepped into resin. We walked on our heels back to the floor. We were down more than we were up. All of us had skinned knees and elbows."

Inez Uglum Schissel, Adams - 1927-32
"The girls' team practiced a few nights each week in the small school gym which had no room for spectators. The new gym wasn't built until the late 1930s. The boys practiced downtown above the Krebsbach store or across Main Street in Mike Schneider's large building. The games were played in the downtown buildings which had more room and were always played on Friday nights."

Ruth Bratrud Jacobson, Grand Meadow - 1929-30
"Our school had a gymnasium, but it was kind of small and we didn't even practice there. We'd walk up to the Opera House (the Woodman's Hall), that was a big floor, and that's where we played. We'd dress at school and run up to the opera house even when it was winter. Some of the girls were from the country, you know, and they would even walk home. They wanted to practice and they did what they had to do to practice. Sometimes they'd stay in town with friends. I lived real close to the school."

Grand Meadow Opera House

Thea Sletkolan Stay, Montevideo - 1931-35
"We usually didn't play this team, but they wanted to play with us so we decided that we would go to Clara City and play. It was a small space, I would say about the size of my little house here. We got over there to play and we were used to playing on a big armory floor and playing half court only, but had a big space. We just about killed ourselves because we kept running into the wall. We never expected it. There were people standing around the edge and at the ends. They had backboards, but it was funny. That was the smallest place we ever played."

Audrey Moe Froiland, Dawson - 1930-34
"Our team played in the National Guard Armory as did most of the other schools with National Guard quarters. The smaller schools had tiny floors in their gyms, bordered on one end by the stage for plays and walls close around the other edges with hardly any room for spectators."

Unexpected Encounters with Stoves, Posts and Radiators
When games were played in facilities that hosted community dances and other events, a supporting post or more might be located inside the playing court.

Belinda Corcoran Eckert, Gaylord - 1919-1922
"There were radiators in each corner of the city hall and along the walls. They didn't have any mesh or covering over them. Sometimes there was a stove on each side. We stayed away from them. The ball would then be taken out of bounds."

Irma Nelson Post, Deer Creek - 1924-29
"When we first started in 1924, some towns (New York Mills or Frazee) had a post just off the center of the hall where we played. None of us ran into it, but the girls that played and practiced there really took advantage of that mean old post. We played on lots of dance floors and halls. Wadena and Bertha, I think, were the first schools to have gyms."

Blanche Line Kingsley, Cromwell - 1925-31
"When I began playing in the eighth grade, we played in the basement of the school. The south end of the school basement served as the gym. It was quite small which made it difficult to play in the larger gyms during competition. They acquired access to the Farmer's Hall which was a little larger, and this meant driving three miles south from the school for our practice and games. After the IOOF Hall (Independent Order of Odd Fellows) in Cromwell was completed in 1929, we played there. It was much easier having a place near the school for practice. Both halls were equipped with a barrel stove for heating the building, and

were located in one corner of the hall. A rope fence was placed around them for protection. The IOOF Hall contained a stage, which extended across the front end of the building. A balcony above the other end of the hall, added seating space for the various activities of the school. There were no shower facilities so we changed in the bathrooms, which didn't seem to hurt the fun and competition."

Alice Aaenson Lervold, Nielsville - 1927-31
"We played mostly teams from North Dakota. We played often in a gym heated by a pot bellied stove so a couple of men stood by it so players wouldn't run into it."

Jane Varner Breimhorst, Jordan - 1928-32
"Jordon's gymnasium was one of the nicest. We played basketball at one school where we had to play around a stove in the center of a hall. At Montgomery we played in a hall, too, because they had no gym."

Norma Booth Krats, Big Falls - 1939-43
"We played in a hall above a store and tavern. The hall had a low ceiling so we had to adjust our shots. The hall was heated with two big barrel stoves that were covered with chicken wire. More than one fell against them, but I don't remember any burns though! We had to run downstairs to an outdoor toilet. If we needed water we had to get it in the tavern which was below the hall. We played against the boys when we couldn't travel anymore because we didn't have enough for a girls' team. Then we played boys' rules."

Finding a Place to Change into Their Team Uniforms was a Challenge
Girls would have to search for places to change into their uniforms and almost any space would have to do.

Sarah Meffert, Arlington - 1919-1920
"All the games were played in old Esser's Hall, which was where Brau's car lot is currently located. There was no place for us to change in the hall, so we would go upstairs in my father's furniture store to change into our uniforms. This was about a block away from old Esser's Hall."

Marie Weibeler Keeler, Belle Plaine - 1922-26
"Our dressing rooms were the coal bin."

Lucille Beckman, Jordan - 1924-28
"Lots of schools did not have a gym. We played in city halls. In Henderson we dressed in the basement. I am sure it was a coal bin. Then we had to walk outside around the building to get to the stairs to play on the top floor. I enjoyed every bit of it."

Aileen Just Luther, Rapidan, 1923-30
"When the Rapidan school was built, it seems that they did not anticipate a girls basketball team, so they did not provide for a girls' locker room and shower. The girls were permitted to use the boys' room and shower when not in use by the boys' team. One evening we were all waiting our turn for a shower after a game. Hilda Schwanberger saw a bar of soap on the upper ledge of the shower she could not reach. She climbed on the lavatory to get the soap but fell to the floor with the bowl, plumbing and all. By the time we could all get dressed so the custodian, Mr. Dougherty, could get in, the room was full of steam and water. The Athletic Department got the bill for the repairs and it was the last time the girls were permitted to use the room. However, this prompted the school district to construct a locker room for the girls in the basement on the west side. By this time the interest and enthusiasm for girls basketball had grown to new heights in Rapidan."

Edith Dalen Bjornlie, Milan - 1925-27

"We had our little suitcases with us, with our clothes in them and when we got there, wherever we were going to play, either it was any empty office that we used or a girls' rest room. No special place, but they found a place for us to change our clothes. I remember it was in Currell that they had a heating pipe that came right close to the

Rapidan school 1922

basket, so we had to shoot up and around like that to get the ball into the basket. You know it wasn't much of a gym and I'm sure all the baskets weren't that high or exactly the same. The baskets were on a backboard."

Ruth Olson Kleven, Milan - 1925-29

"One time we got to a town and we were going to play, and there wasn't any place for us to dress and we just kind of scrounged around town to see if there was some place. There was a filling station that had a big office and there was room behind there and we got in there to get into our uniforms. The gym was in a separate building behind the school house. We had only one janitor and he wasn't able to keep up with everything. The floor was pretty dirty and all of the girls on the team decided they should wash the floor. We were on our knees washing the gym floor before our game.

> "The floor was pretty dirty and all of the girls on the team decided they should wash the floor. We were on our knees washing the gym floor before the game."
> Ruth Olson Kleven, Milan

My sister played in a tin shop. The girls had to help with that. The tin shop was a repair shop. Edith's brother played in the tin shop and after the game was over with they would run in their suits to the barber shop and shower. Wonder that they didn't catch a dickens of a cold all the time, but that's what they did. We girls never had a chance to shower."

Rose Robinson Wichser, West Concord - 1925-29

"There was no gym. We played at the movie theater. There were two stoves in the northeast and southwest corners. The only seating was around the edges and in the movie projector area. Only a few people attended. The baskets were in front of the door and in front of the movie screen. We dressed for home games at home or in the hotel across the street in the ladies' bathroom. If it was not real cold we dressed at home- no slacks then. We froze in Dodge Center. We played in a hall above the hardware store and there was no heat."

West Concord City Hall

Teams changed into uniforms in West Concord Hotel

> **Eileen Maxner Grove, Cromwell - 1930-33**
> "We played in a big dance hall with a high ceiling that was rented by the school. There was a big clothes closet, and that's where we changed into our uniforms. There was a kitchen in the basement and when company teams came to play us, somebody would use that for a changing room. No water, no showers or anything like that."

> **Evelyn Olson Kukkola, Underwood - 1934-37**
> "We played in the Woodman's Hall in Underwood. It had two stories. We practiced and played in this big hall. We had to dress upstairs in the kitchen hoping no one would come upstairs. This hall was used for dances every Saturday night".

Overview
The players of the early 1900s played in facilities where the conditions for playing a game were challenging, at best. No matter! These young women would play in any facility, just so they could play the game.

Getting to Games Was Half the Fun

Girls who played on a basketball team had a built-in challenge — how to get to a game and back home again. Walking several miles to school or for practice and games was frequently the only option young women had; leaving parents waiting long hours for their return with no way to get in touch with them. Girls who lived on farms a distance from school would occasionally stay in town with relatives, or even board in a rooming house during the week, going home only on weekends.

On occasion, a favorite horse would be ridden to town by a young woman so she could get to her practice and games.

> **Marie Hippert Larson, Our Lady of Good Council, Wilmont - 1920-21**
> "We lived three and a half miles from town so when we were to practice, either I walked the railroad tracks, which cut down a mile, or rode the horse."

The following stories about traveling during the early 1900s are a reminder of the risks involved when young women and their parents or drivers traveled on muddy roads, in snowstorms and with little or no communication available for emergencies. As a result, plans tended to go on as scheduled with teams traveling in conditions that could and did create accidents and other dilemmas.

Horse-Drawn Vehicles
In the early 1900s, horses were a primary mode of transportation. They could pull buggies, sleighs, bobsleds and even school buses. Elementary students were very familiar with the horse-drawn school bus, as were the basketball teams. A canvas-covered bus was preferred during the cold weather.

Cromwell horse-drawn school buses

One horse is in the photo of the Cromwell buses. Can you see it?

Hurry up! The bus is here!

Parents used their horse and buggy or sleigh to get to games to watch their daughters play.

When snow filled the roads, teams frequently traveled by horse and sleigh, bobsled or bob sleighs. Sometimes they simply took to the fields and traveled cross country to the next town.

In the early 1900's, a primary mode of transportation during fair weather was the horse and buggy. A cutter, sleigh or bobsled would be used during the winter. Parents and community supporters frequently would provide transportation for the teams, sometimes forming caravans of horses, sleighs and bobsleds. It added to the fun to travel together as well as providing safety in the cold weather.

Visualize a string of horses and sleighs and bobsleds, filled with lots of clean straw, adults and kids, all bundled against the cold as they

Heading for town with horse and buggy

plowed cross country through the snow to the next town for a game.

Roads were frequently poorly maintained and after rains, could be filled with deep and muddy ruts.

Oline Christianson Erickson, Greenbush - 1920-24
"We lived eight miles from Greenbush so we had to find a place to stay in town during the week when school was on. Most of the games were held on Friday nights.

Horse and buggy on Main Street in Grand Meadow

Edith Anderson Bergan, Cloquet - 1920-25

The 1923 Cloquet yearbook, the *White Pine*, reported, "On a cold, bitter night the basketball teams went to Lincoln in a sleigh. It turned out to be a cold ride, but the girls' score warmed us. The score was 32-12 in favor of Cloquet. On another night, Cloquet's girls' and boys' teams went to Carleton in a sleigh. Several other sleighs followed with rooters. The boys and girls traveled by train. Sometimes they had to stay overnight. Sometimes the teams traveled by cars. The girls played first and then the boys played next. The boys and girls traveled together if they were playing the same teams."

The *Ellendale Eagle*, January 23, 1924.

The headline read, "Ellendale High Wins and Loses, - 1924" The article read, "Tuesday evening of this week the New Richland High School girls and boys basketball teams journeyed over here in bob sleighs for a doubleheader with the Ellendale High School boys' and girls' teams".

Alice Dahlman Carter, Cromwell, 1924-28

"Our school bus was a box-type thing with canvas curtains. It had wheels in the spring and fall, and runners for wintertime. Many times the snowdrifts were so big that we tipped over. The boys' team always liked that as they had to help set it back up. The bus was pulled by a team of horses."

Clara Digre Johnson, Hendricks - 1928

The *Hendricks Pioneer* newspaper, January 6, 1998, stated "Hans Hanson and Slim Buseth of Hendricks often took the team by bobsled to the various towns. Clara said the sleds were quite long, and that once when they were transporting the boys' team to one of their games, the girls sneaked in the sled also."

Riding the Rails

Girls and boys basketball teams rode the rails for games "down the line." Sometimes it required changing trains to another railroad line. Trains were especially helpful when roads were closed with snow.

Proctor rails, 1893-1933

Spectators were sometimes left waiting for the teams to arrive. When the trains were running late, the spectators simply waited at the gymnasium and the games began when the teams finally got into town.

On many of their trips by train, teams would frequently stay overnight and then catch an early morning train home. It was also common to stay overnight in host players' homes. Occasionally teams also stayed in hotels or in schools and other community buildings when returning the same day was not an option.

The first railway was built in the United States in 1830 and by 1869 the first transcontinental railway was finished in Promontory, Utah. From this point on there was a rush to build rail lines to connect cities all over the country. By 1915 there was a network of railroads all over the country.

As an agricultural state located in the north central part of the country, Minnesota had many miles of track. By 1890 there were 10 railroad companies operating in Minnesota. Three of the transcontinental lines crossed the state. Short lines were built out from the main lines to small towns to aid the farmers in getting their produce to the main line. By 1900-1910 there were 15 railroad companies, and several served the northern part of the state. Between 1900 and 1910 railroad mileage continued to expand from 6,794.68 to 8,483.56 miles. The number of passengers during the same span of time increased from 5,122,004 to 14,266,516 persons.

Every town on a line had a depot, and many new communities were established along the rails. Railroads served to carry ore to Duluth and Two Harbors and lumber south to Minneapolis and St. Paul. Spur lines ran passenger cars which made it possible to travel almost anywhere in Minnesota by train.

Towns developed along waterways and along railway lines. Minnesota was scattered with small agricultural towns linked together by rail.

The greatest number of tracks existed between 1920 and 1930. Rail traffic came before good roads. Roads, which were little more than dirt tracks, led out from the rail lines so that farmers could get their crops and produce to depots and off to market. There were no snowplows or graders to smooth out the rutted muddy roads, and farmers made extra money with their teams of work horses pulling out of the mud holes the first horseless carriages to venture from the city.[1]

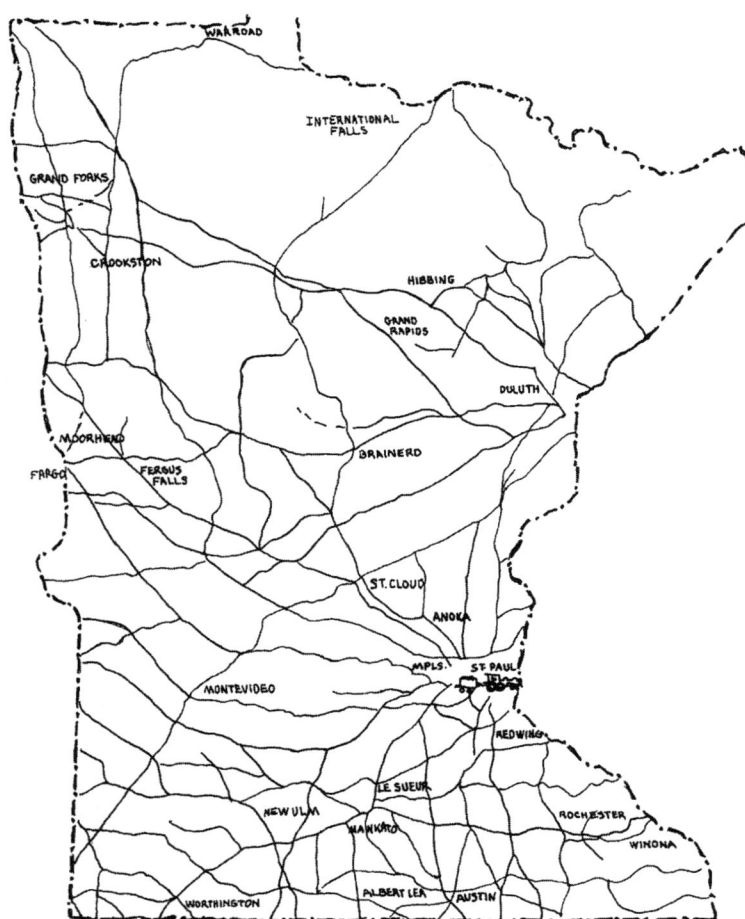

Railroad lines 1920s

This history comes alive through the stories told by the women who rode the rails with their basketball teams.

In cities such as Minneapolis, St. Paul, and Duluth, the players told of riding the electric streetcars in the metropolitan and suburban areas. Sometimes schools were able to charter private streetcars for the basketball teams and they had the streetcar to themselves.

In Minnesota, the Great Depression and the automobile eliminated the streetcar by 1932.[2]

Eleanor DeLaHunt Strand, Willmar - 1917-21
"Once or twice there were enough cars to go like to Maynard, but mostly

we traveled on the train, the Great Northern. It left Willmar early, and we got to the town on that line. The Flyer they called it, the one that went through to the coast was supposed to pick us up later on. There was one earlier than the Flyer that they had scheduled us on. I remember that night when we played at Dassel and we all wanted to stay for the party after the game, but no, we had to get down to the depot and get ready to take the train back to Willmar. So we all got down to the depot and our superintendent was there. That was his job to see that we got on the train. I can still remember what he looked like when the train went by, swoosh! We went back to the party and we had to stay there until the later train that came from the coast took us back to Willmar. That was really great!"

One of Minnesota's most influential railroads was James J. Hill's Great Northern Railway which eventually stretched from St. Paul to the Pacific Northwest.³

Clara Mae Donlin, Excelsior - 1917-21

Clara recalled that they went to Waconia, Hopkins, South St. Paul, North St. Paul and possibly Stillwater. The team traveled to South St. Paul by streetcar. It took a couple hours to get there. If it was chartered for the team, Clara said, "We were the only ones on it." In winter weather, the team traveled by sleigh or bobsled with the boys' team.

Clara reminisced, "One time we were going up to Waconia, and they got a livery stable that had a small truck for moving furniture and put eight bales of hay in there. It was cold winter time and we all piled in there and went to Waconia and played basketball. They didn't have a school with a gym or anything. We stayed overnight because we got out there in the 'boondocks,' and couldn't get any place. It was so cold and I didn't get home until five in the morning. My mother said, 'It's the last time you do that!!' The boys' and girls' teams traveled together,' Clara said. "We also traveled in the winter in a hay wagon with runners on it. We went to Hopkins that way. To keep warm we sat together boy-girl in the hay. We had lots of fun on those hay rides."

Twin City Rapid Transit Company streetcar, 1902, St. Paul

Charlotte Johnson Johnson, Hutchinson - 1919-1922

"When the roads were full of snow, we went by bobsled. Both the girls and boys would ride in the sled to the other towns, like Glencoe."

Dorothy Svenson Viker, Hayfield - 1921-25

"We played neighboring towns and traveled in cars and, if necessary, by train with an overnight stay. We, in Hayfield, often times hosted visiting teams overnight. What fun!"

1910 Minnesota bobsled used for transporting school children and teams

Leona Siewert Gray, Byron, 1922-24; Dodge Center - 1924-26

"We went to Mantorville, three miles west of Kasson. We went cross country with team and sleigh. Mantorville is seven or eight miles cross country. We had foot warmers, and blankets and we sat in the hay. We had no buses to take us. When you could go by car the parents had to take turns taking you. I remember one time my brother was to take us and he, of course, had to milk cows. We were a little late getting started and we were to go to Hayfield. He said, "We are going cross country. I think it's shorter." We slid off the road, so we girls had to get out and push the car back up onto the road. We got there not long before the game was to start. We were so cold the coaches sent somebody out to get us hot egg sandwiches. So we ate a hot egg sandwich before we played.

When I was a sophomore we played 16 games and won them all. One Friday night we went by team and sleigh to Mantorville. Saturday we went by train to Owatonna and transferred north to Medford and played that night. We had housed them when they came to Byron, but they wanted to charge us, so we had the janitor flag down a late train and we went to Owatonna, stayed in a hotel, and went home by train on Sunday morning. When we traveled, we had lunches after the games and stayed in the homes of the host team players. Sometimes followers of the team came with us on the trains."

Grand Meadow train depot

Marie Weibeler Keeler, Belle Plaine - 1922-26

"Parents drove cars, sometimes teachers drove. We went by train if weather was bad. The cars were Model-Ts with eisinglass curtains we could roll down in case it rained or the weather was cold. Once I remember going by bobsled.

We stayed overnight once at St. Peter, once at Montgomery, and also at New Prague. We had gone to these places by train. We left Belle Plaine at 6:00 p.m. St. Peter was on the same railroad line and we were there by 6:30 p.m. We stayed at the hotel and we were to be on the train at 6:00 a.m. One of the boys slipped into the coach's room and turned off the alarm clock so we missed the train. There was no other train out of St. Peter until about 5:30 p.m., so we roamed St. Peter. The coach was mortified and the assistant principal promised us all kinds of discipline, and dismissal from school for the 'guilty party.' As I recall we all, girls and boys, had to write 100 times on the blackboard we would never do that again. We all had to write, as no one 'squealed' on the one who was guilty.

Another time we stayed overnight at Montgomery. Montgomery was on the Minneapolis and St. Louis train route (the M & St. L), so we who were on the Northwestern train route had to change trains at Merriam Junction. We were on the Chicago Northwestern Line and in order to get on the Minneapolis and St. Louis line we had to change trains at this Merriam Junction which is about where they have the Renaissance Festival on Highway 169 today. We arrived in time for the game, and at night the opponent we played against had us for her guest. We liked that, as the mothers were very good cooks. We had a light lunch before bed, and breakfast before we left. The food was scrumptious. We always wished for a storm so we would have to stay overnight in Montgomery or New Prague.

"Marie recalled that on a very cold windy night, the driver of the bobsled sometimes joined the passengers in the sled, leaving the horses to find the way home."

We went by bobsled about seven miles to a game at Jordan. It was cold, but we had a lot of fun. We had a real deep pile of hay, and we were told to get our feet in that hay, and we all brought blankets of course. We had a lot of fun. We managed to sit girl-boy, girl-boy, even though we weren't going with that particular person. Marie noted that on a very cold windy night, the driver of the bobsled sometimes joined the passengers in the sled, leaving the horses to find the way home.

Jane Varner Breimhorst, Jordan - 1928-32
"When we played at Carver, we often took the "dinky"(a small train) after school. Its schedule was such that it could then pick us up and deliver us home by about 11:00 p.m. that night. Otherwise we traveled by cars driven by parents or community volunteers."

Motorized Vehicles: Cars and Buses
The first cars were run by steam, electricity, and finally by gasoline engines. They were slow, and small, carrying one or two people.

Cars began to be mass-produced in 1901 and the Detroit automobile industry was underway. Within the decade, Henry Ford invented an improved assembly line at Highland Park, Michigan. Ford's famous Model-T was assembled in 93 minutes. By 1927, 15,000,000 Model T's had been manufactured.[4]

Rapidan train depot 2005

The bicycle blazed a trail for the advent of the automobile. The construction of the bicycle, the invention of pneumatic tires and the push for better roads all helped the automobile become the preferred mode of travel. Bicycles were left behind in favor of the "Tin Lizzy."[5]

When the favorite and faithful horse was frightened by the approach of these noisy vehicles, conflict was inevitable. A common name for the early cars was "Tin Lizzies." Lizzy was a popular name for a horse.

The open cars and poor roads combined to create a challenge for the passengers. Both men and women wore coats and goggles as protection against the elements from both the weather and the car.

Some of the names of cars of that era may not be familiar today, such as Franklins, Hutmobiles, and Case cars.

The outcry to help get goods to market by building better roads was stymied by the entrance of the United States into World War I. During the 1920s and 1930s, roads were built to accommodate the growing numbers of vehicles. During the Great Depression, the federal government helped states provide jobs for building roads. World War II spurred the building of roads but after the war ended, the congestion continued until the 1950s when the interstate system was created.[6]

Margaret Thompson, Gaylord – 1919-24
"When we went to St. Peter, we got stuck in a snow bank between Gaylord and St. Peter. It was terrible weather. We stayed overnight there because I went home with the teacher. We traveled in cars. Some people in the town had big cars — Everett Reimer — he always had a big car and we always hired him."

Winifred Swanson Stromberg, Milaca –1920-21, *Mille Lacs County Times*
"Road games to Princeton were a bit easier than those to Hinckley, but not by much. In 1920 the girls rode in cars on bad, muddy roads. Stromberg remembered one return trip from Princeton when she had to ride back with the coaches because she had been running late. The car carrying the team broke down south of an area called Wendell Brook. The girls were forced to spend the night in an old school house and in the morning a nearby farmer transported the girls into town. Stromberg did not get stranded that night, but did not get home until after midnight. She was dropped off at the school and then had to walk a couple miles home on an ankle she had sprained during the game.

The following year the girls rode to Princeton in pickup trucks that had been converted into buses. The back ends were covered with a tarp and benches were installed which sat six people. The basketball team crammed eight girls in the so-called buses in order to transport the team to Princeton."

Vera Learned Templin, Buffalo - 1922-26
"At first the parents or friends of the school would take us privately in cars; old Franklins, Hutmobiles, and that type. Then Mr. Leaderbach started a bus route in town and the first bus had a cab with the driver and associate with him. Then along both sides of this long bus were wooden seats, the boys sat on one side and the girls sat on the other, and the coaches and cheerleaders were in the back. The cheerleaders were very good. It was mid winter and we were in this bus going to Howard Lake. The blizzard was so bad that the driver just couldn't see the road, so the boys of the team would take turns and walk in front of the bus to lead it. They didn't have anything for their heads, but in those days the girls always had those long wool scarves. We'd give them our scarves, and they'd put those over their heads. A couple boys would take turns to lead the bus. We didn't get to Howard Lake until after 9:00 p.m., but all the people were waiting, and we played the games. The girls played first and won; winning the Wright County Championship. Then the boys played winning their game also. The bus was reloaded and we came back the same way with the boys taking turns leading the bus. We got back in the wee hours of the morning.

I still remember the trips. Before we had the bus, we would get on a train in the afternoon and play at Maple Lake, or Annandale. We would play the game and stay overnight with the players or in a hotel. There wasn't always a train to bring us home, so we'd come home the next day."

Ruth McCarron Dahlke, Sherburn - 1924-27

"We usually traveled by car. Business men usually volunteered their cars and drivers. On Friday afternoon at school the players went to the bulletin board in the gym to see what car they would ride in. One time the car I was riding in went into the ditch on the way to Winnebago. The windshield was broken, and we were late arriving to the game. It was 10 below zero and we had to return home without a windshield.

In 1927 we went to Winnebago on a Friday afternoon on the Milwaukee Railroad. Both teams stayed in the hotel. The chaperones were the two coaches. We returned the next morning to Sherburn. Our expenses were paid by the school. After we came home from a game away, both teams went to a local restaurant and were allowed 15 cents for lunch."

Anna Martinson Neuman, Grove City - 1924-26

"Dads of players would drive, usually cars. To play Kerkovan we took the train. We left at 4:00 p.m. and came home the next day. At Kerkovan we stayed at the school. Opponents served lunch and visited. Drivers were volunteers, but the school paid when we went by train."

> "One time the car I was riding in went into the ditch on the way to Winnebago. The windshield was broken, and we were late arriving to the game. It was 10 below zero and we had to return home without a windshield."
> Ruth McCarron Dahlke, Sherburn, 1924-27

Irma Nelson Post, Deer Creek – 1924-29

"We rode to the games by car or truck. Parents drove and filled their cars with players and subs. Sometimes the cheering section was scarce and other times there would be a lot. The local trucking men (the Rodekuhr Brothers) often cleaned out the truck bed, put in straw, and if it was cold put a tarp over the truck. Those trips were usually a riot. Usually both the boys and girls teams rode in the truck. I wondered sometimes if the R. Brothers would stop and put us out, but those brothers were a couple of O.K. men.

Our trip to Battle Lake after the big snowstorm was exciting as even the trains didn't go. Many volunteered to drive, and all agreed to take the same route. Roads were not plowed like these days. Una Rector and I were to ride with Rev. Keefer. He took a different road than the rest and I wish I could remember how many times we were stuck. He shoveled, we shoveled, he drove and we pushed. Well when we came to Battle Lake our girls' game was in the fourth quarter. Una played, but I didn't because I was so cold my hands were numb. The minister felt bad, but it was just a game and we had a good time pushing the preacher's coupe out of one drift after another. I remember Una and I were both sore and stiff the next day. The others all got there on time. You can't guess how much we were kidded because the minister was young, single, and handsome to boot."

Model T Roadster

Dorothy Schultz Schuster, Freeborn - 1924-27
Dorothy recalled a makeup game against St. Clair that was played on a Saturday afternoon, and riding the train from Freeborn to the game. At that time the school district did not have motorized buses. The buses were horse-drawn and consequently too slow for distant games. Either families with cars took the girls or a gentleman with a truck took them. They would ride in the back of the truck, and there was no top on the box either.

Rose Robinson Wichser, West Concord - 1925-29
"We traveled to the games by cattle truck; boys on one side and girls on the other. Sometimes we traveled by train leaving West Concord on the 5 o'clock train and returning on the 10:30 p.m. train. Other trips we went by driving a very fast team and sleigh. One time we nearly tipped over in the sleigh.

Three subs traveled with our team, except by train, when only two were allowed because of the cost of tickets. Games were usually played at 7:00 p.m. Friday. One time we got stranded in Hayfield and got up at 4:00 a.m. and flagged down a train to get back Saturday morning."

Blanche Line Kingsley, Cromwell - 1925-31
Our neighbor drove the bus for the first two years I played and my dad the last two. The boys and girls rode to the games in the same bus. The boys' game was played first, and after a short interval, the girls competed in theirs. Each team watched while the other played and thus was able to cheer for the other team. We were taught good sportsmanship and never harassed the teams we were playing. Although playing to win, we were good losers, and always shook hands with the other team.

At times, a little diversion from the usual occurred on our trips. One night while returning from a Floodwood game, the school bus stalled on the railroad crossing and needed some repair work before we could go on. We waited in the bus until the work was completed. I didn't arrive home until 4:00 a.m. Bill was the driver, and he brought me home.

> "We waited there until they had the bus on the road again. I arrived home at 5:00 a.m. and my brother, Jack, was just starting the fire."
> Blanche Line Kingsley, Cromwell, 1925-31

Cromwell first motorized school bus

One night following a Barnum game, the bus slid into the ditch. My father was driving and the roads were glare ice. I never understood why we had the game that night when the roads were so bad. A farmhouse was located up the hill from the accident. We waited there until they had the bus on the road again. I arrived home at 5:00 a.m. and my brother, Jack, was just starting the fire.

One night on our way to play at Denfield High School in Duluth, our bus broke down. The players all jumped out and boarded a streetcar. I just followed the other players; never realizing you needed a dime to pay the fare. My dad was the driver and he stayed with the bus. He always paid for expenses that occurred for me when he drove. When the conductor came to collect the fare, I didn't have any money to pay it. Luckily, one of the girls had an extra dime, and she took care of it for me - very embarrassing!"

Bunny Halverson Wheeler, Delavan - 1926-30
"Boys and girls played the same night with the girls playing first. Girls and boys rode together in the same bus. Sometimes we rode by train in the winter. I had many sleepovers after the games as I lived five miles from town and didn't drive."

Kathryn Meade Shinn, Browns Valley - 1926-29
"We stayed overnight one time because we were going to be part of a tournament and the town was 60 miles from home. When you were going with a Model T car it was a little distance. Mostly Model T's took us where we wanted to go. We very seldom ever had to miss a game. We traveled with the boys' teams, and the boys played first. Either we had to wait, or they would have to wait which they would rather not do. It just depended on who the coach was for the men's team."

Ford Model T 1922

Edith Dalen Bjornlie, Milan - 1925-29
"We traveled in cars when we went to games. People offered to drive a car full of students. Somebody had a Case car that had many seats-it was the only Case Car I ever heard of.

One time there were two cars with kids in them and we were going up to play a game in Bellingham. The car that I was in was the last one. It was snowing to beat the dickens, and of course, at that time there weren't any ditches to amount to anything. It was snowing and we followed right behind the car in front of us and he was in the ditch! We went in right after him. We sat, laughed, and got out and pushed the cars up on the road. It wasn't much of a ditch, but it was off the road."

Evelyn Sponberg Young, New Richland - 1925-27
When weather permitted Evelyn and her brother, Herb, would travel five miles each way from the farm to New Richland with a horse and buggy, a cutter or wagon.

When the winter weather arrived, they would stay for days at a time with family friends in town; Herb with one family and Evelyn with another. Herb's brothers would do his farm work during the basketball season.

Hilda Zander Anderson, Brownton - 1926-28
"Our school was relatively new. At that time we had a new superintendent, Mr. Handke, who introduced basketball in 1921. My sister played on the first team. When we traveled he drove us in his car."

Ruth Bratrud Jacobson, Grand Meadow - 1929-30
"Even though we won all our games, we were not allowed to ride on the bus with the boys. We usually were going to the same places, but the girls had to find their own transportation — usually their parents' cars."

Early cars on Main Street of Grand Meadow

Staying in Town
Ella Mae Bauer Pease, Delano - 1923-25
"My family lived on a farm and my parents never came to the games. I stayed in town overnight. For a while there were a couple other girls who lived in Maple Plain, but they went to Delano High school. They had housekeeping rooms where they could cook their meals and sleep. I used to stay there. Of course if they went home I had a key to their place."

Ruth Bratrud Jacobson, Grand Meadow

Overview
Basketball teams from the 1890s through the 1940s faced a variety of obstacles, just to get to the game, and home again. These stories remind us of the strong commitment and desire of these young woman and their families.

The challenge of roads filled with muddy ruts or snow, cranky automobiles, and late trains did not deter them. It was viewed as just another of life's challenges. If one wanted to play basketball, then "getting to the game was half the fun."

Minnesota Hospitality and the Game

In communities and cities of every size, the activities of their children brought people together. Parents could gather at the game to cheer for their children and get caught up on the "news around town." As electricity came to a community, it encouraged people to gather in those facilities like the community's Opera House or school gymnasium.

By 1882, Westinghouse was furnishing electric current to residences and businesses as well as powering streetcars in Minneapolis and St. Paul. Some independent power companies were furnishing power to the small cities and towns throughout Minnesota. In 1914, electrical current was made available to farms outside Red Wing, Fargo and Granite Falls. It was not until 1935 that a federally-funded program called the Rural Electrical Association (REA) was started under President Franklin Roosevelt, leading to more farms having access to electricity.[1]

True Minnesota hospitality emerged when a community hosted basketball games. Combining social events with the game would add to the fun for everyone and provide a way to show their visitors a good time.

In Minnesota, as elsewhere, food was required for any and all gatherings, from weddings to funerals, neighborhood parties and community celebrations. Athletic events were no exception. Entertaining the visiting girls' and boys' teams was an important part of hosting games and often the whole community would be involved. Visiting teams were often treated to banquets, tours of their town, and dances after the games.

Grand Rapids *Pine Needle* - 1908-09

"The date set for the great double game — boys' and girls' – was to take place at Cass Lake. But it arrived, as all things will, and a jolly crowd numbering about 20 in all started out under the able chaperonage of Misses Burlingame and Backes. We found a friend on our way — the jolly conductor — who attended our game and proved himself possessed of almost as much voice as heart, both strangely enough on the right side. We were shown about the village during the afternoon, and were entertained at different homes for supper. The business events of the evening were the games, most undeniably. The girls played first, with Mr. Stanton as referee. The game was close at first; those baskets were not so easily made as they looked to be. But at the close of the first half the score stood 10 to 2 in our favor. In the second half our opponents scored twice to our twice, leaving us eight points to the good.

The boys' game followed ours immediately, and resulted in another decisive victory for the Rapids. The Lakers are good losers, and showed themselves to be 'true blue' in their entertainment of us. After removing all traces of our strenuous exercise, we were invited to trip the 'light fantastic' to strains of sweet music. Not until the hour when ghosts begin to walk, did we return to the high school, where a sumptuous banquet was prepared for us. There we ascertained that Cass Lake had domestic as well as athletic girls. After all had done justice to the banquet, Superintendent Larson addressed us saying some very pleasant things for the Rapids, among others, that he believed 'the Lord was on our side.' He asked our referee and our captain to explain our victories otherwise, if they could."

"Not until the hour when ghosts begin to walk, did we return to the high school, where a sumptuous banquet was prepared for us."
Grand Rapids 1909

Parties after the games sometimes lasted into the night, with teams still facing the trip back home.

Grand Rapids *Pine Needle* - 1910

"The first game was played on the 18th day of December at Hibbing. Hibbing won, and Hibbing rejoiced; but we took our defeat in silence, for we knew our day was coming. After the game the Hibbing girls took us to the grand opening dance at the new Armory, where we danced until the wee tiny hours of the morning. Happy, and yet unhappy, we boarded the Merry Widow for home, where we were warmly welcomed, though we had failed to completely sustain the reputation of the school along athletic lines."

When teams traveled a distance in the winter, a social event with food was sometimes served before the games were started.

Zumbrota News - 1912

"Zumbrota played St. Charles in the City Hall that served as a playing court. The girls defeated their opponents 10-5. Boys' and girls' teams from both communities attended a banquet before the games."

Warroad Travels to Roseau, *Warroad News* - February 13, 1919
"The trip to Roseau was splendid from start to finish. Being the train arrives during the noon hour practically the whole student body was at the station to meet the visitors. The afternoon was spent in visiting school and in practicing. For supper, the visiting teams were given a banquet at the schoolhouse which put everyone on good speaking terms as two opponents of each team were seated at each table. Needless to say the repast was much enjoyed by all."

When teams did not stay overnight the host teams usually provided a light lunch or refreshments after the games. Playing social games was a way for visiting teams to enjoy the company of their hosts.

Margaret Hauck Morrill, Madison - 1916-18
"We had fun parties with hot cocoa after the games. They played games at the parties. We did a lot of cooking for the parties. Everyone who came to the game came to the party."

Greenway of Coleraine, the *Blast* -1923
"The victories of our undefeated team were celebrated by a party which was held in the school gymnasium. Games were played and a delicious lunch was served."

Irma Nelson Post, Deer Creek - 1924-28
"Some places we played, like Sebeka, Bertha, and Parkers Prairie, served hot chocolate and cookies after the game and when they came to Deer Creek we returned the treat. We got acquainted with the other team that way."

The experience of staying in the homes of the host team for the night fostered many long lasting friendships among the players and provided many young women with contacts beyond her family circle.

Evelyn Olson Kukkola, Underwood - 1934-37
"Each girl took one of us home for the night. I ended up at one of those beautiful big farm homes. I came from a very poor family and really didn't know how to act, plus being shy. I had my own room and breakfast was outstanding. *I'll never forget that place.*"

Overview
Reading and listening to the stories from the women of the first era confirms that high school sports of any era can teach lessons that last a lifetime.

Benefits of the Game: Fitness, Friends and Fun

In the early 1900s, girls wanted to play basketball for the same reasons as they play today: it was fun! It made them feel good! They enjoyed being with their friends!

There were individuals during this era who spoke of the benefits that could result from playing on a team:
- Playing sports would develop fitness including endurance and strength;
- Sports were fun to play and were a positive balance to the hard work expected of young women;
- A team sport would develop the skills of cooperation and teamwork;
- Playing a game would help players to make quick judgments and maintain self-control as they won or lost games. This could aid young women in their future careers; and,
- Sports could provide social contacts with others and broaden their experiences.

So, let's learn how the young women of Minnesota saw the benefits that resulted from playing basketball.

Ruth DeLaHunt Rawn, Willmar - 1913-14, at 100 years of age.
"I felt running was good for me when I was young so I ran everywhere — all the time. I started running because after waiting for the bathroom with eight siblings, I was always late and had to run to school in order not to be late."

Dorothy Iversen Viker, Hayfield – 1921-25
"Our girls' team was as popular as the boys' and was outfitted by the school as was the boys' team. We were enthusiastically backed by the town's people, and the business men showed their approval with boxes of candy when we played well. I don't think anyone questioned our ability to physically play the game."

Vera Learned Templin, Buffalo - 1922-26
"When I did a few things I was taught to do, I began to gain that confidence that I could do it. Self-confidence carried over into the rest of my schooling and into the rest of my classes. I felt if I could do that, I could get up and do anything in class too, and I did."

Frieda Zander Lord, Brownton - 1923-26
"It was great! I loved every minute of it. We had a great team and did most of the winning. It was fun to meet the girls from the other teams. It certainly did give us confidence and self-esteem, besides being good for us."

Lucille Beckman, Jordan - 1924-28
"I think it did build self-esteem in girls — at least it did for me. I was kind of a little rough-neck."

Vera Templin honored at Lynx game

Belle Plaine 1925, Marie Keeler and Mildred Engfer

Virginia Kruger and 1923 Belle Plaine teammates and coach having fun

Second Quarter

Kathryn Meade Shinn, Browns Valley - 1926-29
"I always felt that I benefited from playing basketball. It is very hard to be a standout in a small town like that unless your father was a banker, but everybody was proud of us when we came home. We exercised all the time anyway. We played cricket and all the outdoor games too. As a matter of fact, we practiced some. I was proud of the fact that I made the team. We got a lot of attention from younger students and teachers. We were "heroes".

Jordan Independent, **March 24, 1932**
"Fans were there with automobile horns and razzers, and Pete Schmidt of the Hub assumed the cheerleader's role with ultimate success. The stands were eager and anxious to lend vocal support to the teams."

Rosalind Knutson and teammate Dolores Kirkeby, Clarkfield, 1931

Willmar 1927, Lorraine Ackerman and Addie DeLaHunt

Kasota 1930, swinging fun

Team-building, Mabel, 1931

50   Daughters of the Game

Hancock teammates, Irene Angier Jensen and Marian Halvorson Solvie, 1999

Evelyn Olson Kukkola, Underwood - 1934-37
"Playing basketball gave me confidence and built up my self-esteem. One experience is a highlight. We were playing a game; the boys team that was to play our boys were there watching. I threw the ball from over on the side and, as luck would have it, it went in the basket. I heard one of the boy's say, "Gee! We could use her on our team." That probably made my day!"

Mildred Wick Gorden, Northome - 1934-37
"We developed very close relationships with team members; I'm still in touch with some of the girls. I learned to be in the public eye. It gives one lots of confidence and it never bothered me to be in front of people to speak or take part in any activity."

Tournaments, Trophies and School Awards

During the period from 1892-1942, the Minnesota girls basketball program grew into a statewide program with teams found in virtually every community. Minnesota schools did not take action to sponsor a state girls basketball tournament at any time during this 50-year period.

As more information was gathered, it became evident that teams all over Minnesota had participated in tournaments. Players described their experiences and were proud to report their achievements at tournaments. Mementos kept over the years included school letters, tournament programs, and individual player awards like rings and gold basketballs. Sadly, only a few of the trophies have been saved, though more may still be stored in a school and could be brought out, polished and enjoyed by the community.

The neighboring state of Iowa was active in girls basketball and became nationally known for its high-profile state tournaments. Iowa began conducting a state girls basketball tournament in 1920. In 1925 after creating a separate organization to conduct girls' sports, the state never looked back. More than one Minnesota player asked her parents to move to Iowa where she could play basketball.

Area Championships
Invitational tournaments were held with other schools in their geographical area. One school would challenge others to play and then lay claim to the championship of that area. On one occasion, they claimed the title of 'state champs.' Schools in several areas of the state conducted district and region tournaments and provided the champions with trophies and awards.

The 1908 Grand Rapids yearbook, the *Pine Needle* reported,
"Thus it is that the Grand Rapids High School, since it challenged every high school basketball team it knew, heard or read of in North Central Minnesota, lays claim to the championship of this section, tho' it played but three games. Moreover if any team in this region, that has or has not declined to meet the Grand Rapids High School on the basketball field, dares not to come forth and accept the challenge, Grand Rapids stands ready to vindicate her claim to the championship this year or next."

Second Quarter

The 1911 Alden girls basketball team photo reported that its team was the "1911 Southern Minnesota Champion Girls Basketball Team."

In 1919 Owatonna defeated Austin, Kasson, Albert Lea, New Ulm, Osage (Iowa), and the State Public School. They sent a letter to 25 area schools sponsoring girls' teams and challenged them to contend for a state championship.

The letter pointed out that "The girls will play any recognized high school on a regulation court under girls' rules of the game." New Ulm accepted the challenge and the game was a "winner-take-all game" in the Owatonna Armory. Owatonna won, 24-18. They proudly claimed the title "State Champs."

Grand Rapids 1908

Owatonna 1919

The *1921 Proctorian* wrote of its girls basketball team, "Proctor High has one possession indeed which other schools cannot boast of. What is it? The champion girls basketball team. Champions of the Head of the Lakes and St. Louis County."

In 1921, the northern Minnesota "Range Championship" was claimed by the Greenway of Coleraine after it defeated Proctor.

In 1922, Proctor claimed the Northwestern Championship after winning and losing games with Coleraine. Coleraine declined a third game play-off, so Proctor claimed the championship.

In 1923 the Greenway of Coleraine team defeated Cloquet for the "Northwest Championship," with a reported 700 spectators enthusiastically cheering for the teams. The school yearbook, The *Blast*, recorded that,

> "A promise was made that if we won the return game with Proctor we might play a game with the Cloquet six, who had won a victory over our late opponents and various schools. The second game with Proctor ended in our favor with a score of 22-20. The promise was carried out after many difficulties.

Owatonna 1919 game announcement

Greenway 1923

The largest crowd that had ever assembled in the Greenway gymnasium to witness a game was present at this Cloquet game. A band concert was held before the game started. No two teams could have been more evenly matched. Cloquet fought hard but Greenway fought harder. The ball went from one side of the floor to another and ended in Greenway's basket, giving us the game. Hurrah! We had won. The victorious season was over and we could claim the Northwest Championship."

Invitational Tournaments

In southeastern Minnesota, Ellendale hosted an invitational tournament in 1925. Ellendale won and was presented with a loving cup and individual medals. The loving cup is on display in the Ellendale Community Building.

Ellendale 1925 tournament medal

Ellendale District Trophy 1925

A photo of one surviving medal is shared by the family of rotogravure star Helen Johnson. The medal is inscribed around the top "Girls BB Tournament." Around the bottom, it reads, "Ellendale." Across the basketball in the center, "1925."

An invitational tournament was held in Sherburn in 1925. Sherburn was chosen as the site because it had a 48 X 64 gym with a five-foot out-of-bounds all around. The Businessmen's Association purchased the trophy for $26.00 and provided other prizes. Dr. Farrish volunteered his services in case there were injuries to any of the players. The rules were a kind of combination of both boys' and girls' rules, mostly boys', except the quarters were shortened to reduce the strain on the players. The tournament was held in March. It snowed and Elmore could not get there. Alpha substituted for them. Sherburn won three games on the way to the title, defeating Alpha 22 to 4, Jackson 18 to 6, and Ceylon 20 to 11 in the finals.

Sherburn program

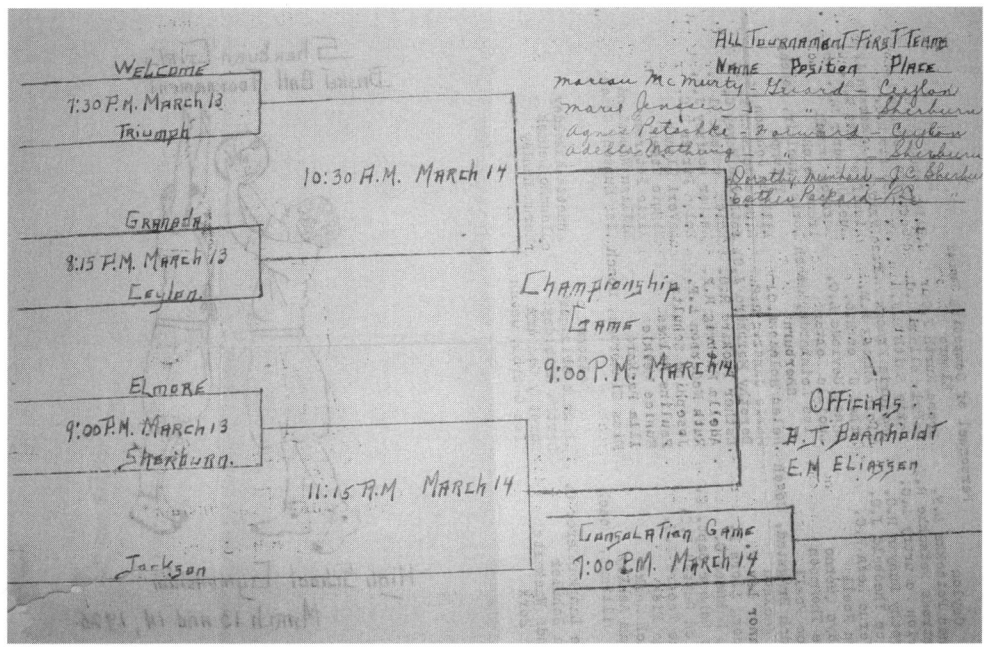

Sherburn 1925 tournament pairings

The champions were awarded a magnificent silver basketball atop a pedestal. The plaque on the front is inscribed "Invitational Tournament Champions, Sherburn, 1925." Individual players received a ring with the top of a basketball that read, "SHS."

Ruth Dahlke described the loss of her ring. She said, "I was a sophomore when our team won the tournament. At a high school assembly, the squad was awarded sterling silver rings. In the summer of 1925, I went swimming in Fox Lake and dived off a raft. When I came up for air, I realized my ring was gone. My friends and I dived for some time but couldn't locate the ring. When I realized it really was gone, I cried many times. The years went by and in 1995 my daughter, Carron Klukow, attended an estate auction. Later I called her to find out what she had bought. She had bid on two rings – one a 1925 class ring and a smaller one (she didn't know the story of the basketball ring). When she showed it to me I cried, realizing I now had an identical ring which had belonged to Adella Mathwig, our captain. Even though the sands and waves have washed over my ring for 80 years, I have one of its 'sisters' to remind me of those enjoyable basketball days." Ruth wears the ring at all times and has said that it will be buried with her.

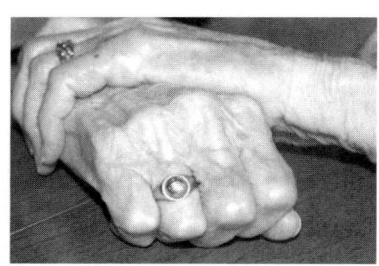

Ruth Dahlke wearing Sherburn tournament championship ring

Ruth Dahlke, Sherburn, 2005

In recent years, the team members gathered with their trophy.

Sherburn players reunited with trophy

Teams in Wright County played for the County Championships from the early

1920s into the early 1930s. The Buffalo team won in 1928 and 1931, and has a silver trophy in its school archives. Other teams active in the tournament were Annandale, Maple Lake, Howard Lake, Monticello, Rockford and Kimball.

Thea Sletkolen Stay (Montevideo, 1931-1935) said, "The schools had a playoff and the two best teams played for the championships. The coaches organized the games. We got a large trophy if we won. And we won several times!"

All-Tournament Teams were named in many of the tournaments and reported in local newspapers.

County Championships

The St. Louis County schools conducted county championships in basketball, and also in volleyball and track and field. Toivola won trophies in these activities.

Buffalo won its county championships in 1927.

Buffalo 1927

Grand Meadow Mower County Cup 1931

Grand Meadow won the Mower County Cup for three years, including 1931. The Cup was awarded based on the team's season record.

District and Region Tournaments

District tournaments, based on the administrative districts established by the League, were conducted in several areas of the state. Trophies were awarded to the championship team.

In 1925 Hancock won the District 25 Tournament.

In 1928 and 1929, Rapidan and scoring sensation Aileen "Point-A-Minute" Just won the Southern Minnesota Tournament. The championship team received a silver trophy and individual members received medals and school letters.

Rapidan trophy 1928

Rapidan trophy 1929

Montevideo was dominant in their area and won the district championship every year between 1926-1935 except 1930 and 1932.

Montgomery 1930

Irma Malone and Evelyn Vitha, Montgomery, with 1930 District trophy.

In 1927 Cromwell won the Carlton County Championship, the sub-district championship, District 5 championship which included over 20 schools, and the championship of 14 counties from Proctor to Brainerd and from Hibbing to Minneapolis.

The District Tournament was won once by Montgomery, twice by New Prague and twice by Jordan, 1929 and 1932.

In 1932 the championship Jordan team was given small gold basketballs. Since 1932 Jane Varner Breimhorst has worn her basketball on a chain around her neck.

Jane Varner Breimhorst's gold basketball

The Litchfield team won its district tournament in 1931. After it won 73 consecutive games, the school announced it as a national record.

Mankato Teachers College hosted the finals of the district tournament won by Rapidan in 1929.

"It was really great to win the District Championships and the trophy for your school. School spirit was so great back then. It was a big confidence builder. We thought we were so important."
Jane Varner Breimhorst, Jordan, 1928-1932

Jordan District Champions 1932

Luverne 1937

Mabel Thompson Erickson from Mabel with her school letters

The District 8 Tournament was won by Luverne in 1935 and 1937. Wheaton played in a region championship in 1937.

School Letters
Schools awarded school letters, and sometimes school sweaters. Many of the women interviewed had carefully saved their school letters, team photos and other memorabilia.

Edith Anderson Bergan, Cloquet, 1920-1925, said, "We received a stripe for each year we played. I got three stripes for the three years I played. We had purple and white school sweaters."

Marion Halvorson Solvie, Hancock, 1925-1928, said, "I worked one whole summer to earn money for a letter sweater and letter by milking cows and taking care of babies for a local family."

The 1933 Aitkin yearbook reported that the team members must play in one quarter for each major game played by the team, a minimum of six quarters, to earn a letter. The six-inch chenille letter "A" was maroon with a black border.

Rose Creek 1928 school letter

Overview
The importance of receiving recognition was important to the athletes of the first era, just as it is today. Young women who saw their name in a 1913 school yearbook, or their 1919 town newspaper had the same warm feeling as today's athlete who has had the experience of seeing herself on a family video recorder and on television. Those young women of the early 1900s who received school letters and sweaters wore them as proudly as their counterparts do today.

Second Quarter

Second Quarter Free Throws

"Hi there! You met my sister, Ima, when you competed in the First Quarter Free Throws.

My name is Hava!! So you already know my last name!! So, let's start the competition, and remember to 'have a ball!'

Are you ready? Remember your score at the end of the First Quarter Free Throws so you can add it to your score for the second quarter. Score 1 point for each correct answer.

Here we go!!"

Second Quarter Questions
1. What were two of the obstacles in facilities where girls played basketball?
2. Why were the playing floors frequently very slippery for basketball?
3. What was the name of the team that had to bring money to play the light bill and wood for the stove to heat the room?
4. What was the name of one of the schools that played its games in the Woodman's Hall?
5. What four-legged animal was used to pull buggies, sleighs and school buses to take teams to games?
6. What does playing schools "down the line" mean?
7. What was the name of James J. Hill's railroad?
8. What important invention brightened homes and eliminated the use of kerosene lamps, lanterns and candles?
9. Was it the 1930s or 1950s when farms begin to receive electricity through the Rural Electrical Association?
10. What kind of vehicle had eisenglass curtains?
11. What was the full name of the railroad called the M & St L?
12. What was the name of the team that received gold basketball charms when they won their district championship?
13. What was the name of the team that won 73 consecutive games and declared it a national record?

Score: Home_____ Visitor_____

Answers:

1. Hot stoves, posts in the court, slippery floors, radiators, spectators
2. Dances had been held and corn meal was spread on the floor for the dancers
3. Gaylord
4. Grand Meadow; Underwood
5. The horse
6. Towns that are connected by the railroad track.
7. Great Northern Railway
8. Electricity
9. 1930s
10. Model T cars
11. Minneapolis & St. Louis
12. Jordan
13. Litchfield

Halftime

Shooting Stars

During the first 40 years of high school girls basketball in Minnesota, there were individuals and teams who were highly accomplished and received recognition within and outside their communities. They were "shooting stars," brightening the skies over Minnesota.

Helen Johnson, Star of the Rotogravure
Ellendale High School
1923-1925

Helen Johnson Davidson played from 1923-25. The *Ellendale Eagle* newspaper, February 18, 1925, reported that Ellendale scored three and a half points a minute, winning 114 to 5 against Freeborn. "Good use was made of the time between halves in allowing the baskets to cool and in ordering another gross of pencils for Wesley Steele (scorekeeper), and a new arm and a few boxes of chalk for J.C. Jensen, the honorable keeper and chalker of the abacus." Helen Johnson scored 64 points.

On March 11, 1925, the *Ellendale Eagle* newspaper stated that the tournament was won by Ellendale. The team received a loving cup and the players received individual medals. The officials selected Helen Johnson and Violet Jensen for the All-Tournament Team. The article was titled: "Are We Proud? Well! Well!"

Helen Johnson, Ellendale 1925

On April 1, 1925, the Ellendale newspaper headlined, "High School Star in Rotogravure" and pointed out "The rotogravure section of the Sunday (*St. Paul*) *Pioneer Press* this week gave a little well-deserved credit to the Ellendale High School's star basketball player. A very good picture of Helen Johnson in uniform in characteristic pose getting ready for one of her dead-sure free throws appears in this pictorial section."

Ellendale 1925, Helen Johnson, holding trophy

LLENDALE

ELLENDALE, MINNESOTA, WEDNESDAY, APRIL 1, 1925

HIGH SCHOOL STAR IN ROTOGRAVURE

The rotogravure section of the Sunday Pioneer Press this week gave a little well deserved credit to the Ellendale high school's star basket ball player. A very good picture of Helen Johnson in uniform in characteristic pose getting ready for one of her dead-sure free throws appears in this pictorial section. The text explaining the engraving reads: "Miss Helen Johnson, Ellendale, star of the Ellendale high school girl's basket ball team, who scored 290 of her school's 504 points during the past season. She produced a bigger score than the total made by opposing teams, 230 points, and made 64 of these while. Ellendale was winning from Freeborn by a record breaking score of 114 to 5."

SLEEPING SICKNESS PROVES FATAL

Miss Emma Anderson Succumbs to Lethargic Encephalitis With Complications

Miss Emma Anderson was taken sick with measles on the 18th of

"Ellendale newspaper 1925"

Aileen "Point-A-Minute" Just
Rapidan High School
1923-1930

Aileen Just Luther played from 1923-1930 and became known as the "Sensational Aileen Just." In one game, she made 60 points; another time 50 points in four eight-minute quarters. In 366 minutes of play during one season, Aileen Just scored 410 points. Thereafter, she became known as "Point-a-Minute Just." In another season, Just scored 453 points in 416 minutes of play. The Rapidan team scored a season total of 614 points compared to a total of 224 points by the opposing teams.

A picture of Aileen Just was sent to all corners of the United States, appearing in papers in Chicago, Massachusetts and Denver, among others. The caption read, "Aileen Just, Outstanding Girl Basketball player of the State of Minnesota. A 16-year-old and a sophomore at Rapidan, Aileen has brought her team through to 40 victories in 43 games played in three years. Scoring 30 to 35 points in a game is a common occurrence for her."

Aileen Just, Rapidan, 1928

Rapidan 1928, Aileen, right end of back row

Rapidan poster

Thea Sletkolen
"A One-Girl Scoring Machine", *Montevideo American News*
Montevideo High School
1931-1935

Thea Sletkolen Stay played on the Montevideo Girls Basketball team from 1931-1935.

In her senior year, she scored 15 more points than all of Montevideo's opponents. It was said that Thea rarely missed an opportunity to score and opponents could not come up with a defense to stop her.

The Montevideo American News, February 24, 2000, called Thea, "A one-girl scoring machine."

Montevideo dominated the district from 1926-1935, winning every year except 1930 and 1932.

In 1985 Thea Sletkolen Stay was inducted into the Montevideo Hall of Fame. It was held during her 50th class reunion. Thea said, "They had a large parade in Monte. We rode in a red convertible! What a thrill!"

Montevideo, 1935, Thea, left end of back row

Thea Sletkolen, Montevideo

Thea Sletkolen Stay, 2003, Montevideo

Litchfield High School
Calls 72 Game Winning Streak a National Record
1926-1932

The Litchfield girls basketball team from 1927-1932 won a total of 73 games without defeat and claimed a national record.

The winning seasons began with the 1927 team. Front: Frances Risdon, Myrtle Grendahl, Marian March, captain; Elva Sederstrom, Ila Peterson. Back: Harriet Harmonn, Myrtle Anderson, Coach Horton, Agnes Grendahl, Hazel Bendickson, Beatrice Palm, Charmion Baker. Edith Anderson (not pictured).

The winning season extended into the 1931-1932 year. The 1932 team members were: Front: Peterson, Pauline Shoultz, Cassady, Capt. Peterson, Muriel Sederstrom, Peterson. Middle: Coach Becker, Mortenson, Phyllis McGraw, Nelson, Jeannette McGraw, Brown, Coach Horton. Back: Erickson, Deilke, Stoner, Nelson, Berens, Lahr, Longworth.

Litchfield 1927

It was a great honor to be on the Litchfield girls' team because of its incredible winning record."
Iris McGraw Campbell

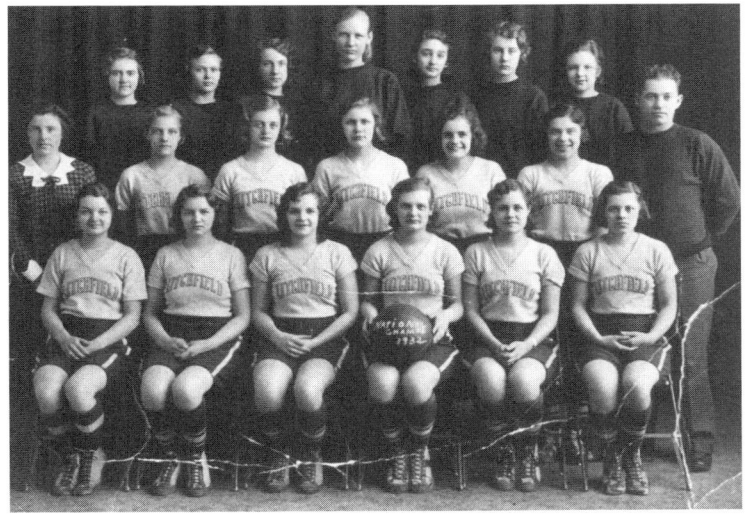

Litchfield 1932

Grand Meadow High School
Sets Record 94-Game Winning Streak
1929-1939

Grand Meadow 1930

The Grand Meadow girls basketball teams from 1929 – 1939 did what no team has done before or since: they won every game that they played during those 10 years. They never experienced the loss of a game. The team averaged over 38 points a game and held their opponents to an average of just over 12 points a game. The teams were coached by Lila Reiersgard for the first seven years, Marian Nestande for two years and Carol Rem for the final year.

The winning seasons began with the 1929-1930 team. Front: Phyllis Rother Torgrimson, Mildred Berg Gilbert, Helen Gunderson, Gladys Nelson Travis, Marie Tommerson Berg. Back: Supt. Hugh Jones, Ruth Bratrud Jacobson, Pearl Tommerson Jacobson, Madeline McDonough Perry, Mildred Wakefield Olson, Gladys Peterson, Fruth, Miss Reiersgard, Coach.

"Our games were played in the Opera House. Many times the place was packed for the girls' game but many people left before or during the boys' game."
Ruth Bratrud Jacobson, Grand Meadow 1929-30

Grand Meadow 1939

The winning season extended into 1938-1939. Front: Norraine Thorson Handke, Kathryn Skaran Losey, DeVera Bratrud Proeschel, Irene Mahoney Bye, Dorothy Allen Blanchard. Back: Daniella Blanchard Peterson, June Wright Kramer, Winifred Goodsell Peterson, Mae Harvey Gross, Alice Jenson Gevling, Coach Carolyn Rem.

Overview

These "shooting stars" truly did brighten our skies during their era. They began a legacy that will be passed on to the second era of basketball players in Minnesota.

Third Quarter

Darwin, Women and the Game

Over the centuries when young women wanted to play sports like their brothers, they often encountered negative reactions. Even now, many women only have to look into their own experiences to bring back memories that are painful and result in that familiar feeling in the pit of the stomach that comes from the anger and frustration of hitting yet another barrier.

Denial of equal rights based on gender has its roots in Western culture that goes back for centuries and even thousands of years. It reaches deep into the heart of sports.

Laws of Nature

Western culture has tended to define females as inferior and dependent, passive and submissive. Women have been portrayed as biologically and physically limited. These beliefs permeated every sphere of women's life and became accepted simply as the "laws of nature."

In the 1890s, the concepts promoted by Charles Darwin focused on the division of roles based on gender. According to Darwin and his biological determinism, women were lower than men on the evolutionary scale and were therefore inferior to men.[1]

> According to Darwin and his biological determinism, women were lower than men on the evolutionary scale and were therefore inferior to men.

When basketball arrived in 1891 and women began to play this new game, they ran headlong into these cultural beliefs, stereotypes and prejudices. Basketball challenged the view of what was termed "appropriate behavior" for women. It raised fears that a young woman would neglect or ruin her opportunity to marry, bear children and care for her husband and family. Sports just did not fit the mold reserved for young women.

When the young women challenged these restrictions, some were frequently confronted with negative reactions from their family and community. They were told they would lose their femininity and that exercise would result in unsightly muscles, i.e., a masculine appearance. Some young women were raised in a supportive family with parents who believed in the same opportunities and education for their daughters as for their sons. Even so, the world around them would still intrude on their dreams.

The Medical Community and Basketball
Doctors of the 1800s and early 1900s tended to support the theory of the weak female whose "constitution" should not be pushed beyond its limits. Women were expected to be weak and ill. When women began attending college in the mid-1850s, there was great concern that it might cause severe mental strain on the female brain. Nonetheless, many of the theories became accepted as fact and have persisted for decades.

When young women asked their parents if they could play high school basketball, the response may have been influenced by the prevailing attitude of their community and the attitude of their local physicians.

"Many a young life is battered and forever crippled in the breakers of puberty; if it crosses these unharmed and is not dashed to pieces on the rock of childbirth, it may still ground on the ever-recurring shallows of menstruation and lastly, upon the final bar of menopause where protection is found in the unruffled water of the harbor beyond the reach of sexual storms."
George J. Engelmann.[2]

Adolescence was a time of great concern. When a young woman's reproductive organs were being developed, it was believed that a sport such a basketball could impact her health on a long-term basis. An overriding argument was the threatening admonition that exercise could result in a female's inability to bear children. As basketball became a game of choice for girls and women, the arguments began to center around the potential for weakening a woman's already inadequate vital force, the very force needed for reproduction. Scientific knowledge of the female body and its structure was limited. There appeared to be little awareness that a female's internal organs were in a shock-resistant structure and more conducive to absorbing blows than the structure of their male counterparts.

One area of concern was the impact of exercise on a young woman's menstrual cycle. It was recommended that school rules prevent girls from participating during the first three days, or longer, of her menstrual cycle. It would become the team captain's responsibility to enforce them. [3]

The medical community believed that exercise could over-stimulate the female's endocrine system. The doctors warned that the cheering and the pressure to win at competitive events could cause females to fall victim to fainting or over-stimulation.

The key word of warning to females of all ages was that an activity could only be healthful if indulged in "moderation."

When females were viewed as weaker and in need of protection, it justified restriction of their activities and limiting them to their primary roles as caretakers of the home and family.

"Our coach during my last year was great. I was chosen captain, so he called me aside one time and told me to tell the girls that they couldn't play if it was 'that time of the month.' I almost died because we didn't talk about those times. We had just six girls playing that year, no substitutes, so if we told, there would be no games. So the girls decided not to tell. Now one of the girls usually had fainting spells at that time so we would just say she was tired and was pretending. Her sister also played on the team and it was up to her to have "smelling salts" along at that time. It happened twice during that year."
Marie Weibeler Keeler, Belle Plaine
1922-1926

Rules for the Game for Young Women

Sports do not exist in a vacuum separate from the culture and society in which it is conducted. Basketball is a prime example of women caught in the swirl of cultural expectations.

During the 1890s Senda Berenson and her colleagues were adapting Naismith's rules to fit the concept of women's biological makeup and the social mores of the times. The women justified dividing the game into multiple courts and restricting the players from running, based on their belief that special rules were required for their female students. Their beliefs reflected their acceptance of biologically-based differences.

The problem was that the young women enjoyed the game! They preferred basketball to the individual sports that were acceptable for women, playing in their corsets and long dresses. It was great fun playing as a team against another team. They enjoyed moving about on the court and scrambling after a loose ball. Their competitive instincts began to stretch what their "elders" considered appropriate behavior.

Basketball became a game that could be, and was, rough. There were allegations of hair pulling, slapping, scrambling on the floor after a loose ball and kicking. Before long, basketball had become a vigorous, challenging game, but it did not fit the accepted roles expected of young women.

The storm clouds began to gather. There was consternation expressed by educational and medical groups.

As the women leaders of physical education worked to gain public support for women to play basketball, they also supported the theory of "moderation." Young women were urged to rest between the mental and physical exertion. The rules for females even built in a rest period between scoring a goal and a center jump ball for the players to regain their strength.

From the View of Minnesota Parents and Players

Rural communities tended to understand that the females in their families were strong and capable of contributing to their family and community as well as participating in sports. After all, their daughters were expected to work in the fields and the home, and help with the livestock. If they wanted to get to practice and games, sometimes it meant that the young women would walk several miles to get to practice or games and then walk home again.

The women who played on girls' high school teams during the first era never mentioned basketball as being too strenuous, or that they were concerned about being "unladylike" playing basketball. They believed that it developed physical fitness and provided exercise that was fun. They learned to be confident in their skills from being in front of an audience cheering them on.

But Minnesota parents also struggled with the desire of their daughters to participate in sports.

They knew that their physicians and other educators believed that young women could 'over-do' while playing basketball. There were young women whose parents were concerned about what she would wear, out in public and in front of their community. Wearing the comparatively less-restricting bloomers brought reactions from mothers whose own dresses were longer skirts and 'no skin' showing up to their necks. They were concerned about "what the neighbors would think." When bloomers gave way to shorts, the reactions were equally as concerned.

Aileen Just Luther, Rapidan, 1922-30
"Throughout these eight years these fine coaches not only taught us how to play the game of basketball, but other values as good sportsmanship, fair play, discipline, poise, balance, coordination, and leadership."

Windom 1917

"Myrt came out to play with the pretty big ball this year; despite the remonstrance of papa and mamma that little daughter would ruin her health playing that awful game. Nevertheless she still appears to be surviving the terrible ravages of basketball, and as far as we can see, Myrt's frail constitution has been little injured."
The 1917 Windom *Cricket* yearbook

Leona Siewert Gray, Byron 1922-24, Dodge Center, 1924-26
"I believe I got a lot from playing basketball. Being together with others and learning how to get along. I had some very good friends in basketball and we remained friends for a long time. There are only two of us left now, all the rest are gone. I think that basket ball helped me be strong. I never got above 5' 3", and I never weighed more than 138 lbs. After I got married I could swing a can of milk into the tank or I could swing a hay bale."

Agnes King McIntyre, International Falls, 1924-26
"Playing sports gave us self-confidence and self-esteem. I became active in anything that improved my active life and good health. I am 92 years old now."

Irma Nelson Post, Deer Creek, -1924-29
"We played to win, but I do not remember any of us ever shedding tears because we lost. We all had fun. Basketball kept some of us girls from quitting school. I'm sure, as I was one that worked at the drug store and the café. We had to keep our grades to passing. We won our fair share of games and lost them too. We were proud of our efforts, especially if on any of these trips when the girls won and the boys lost."

Leona Siewert Gray

Ruth Olson Kleven, Milan-1925-29

"The fellowship was the most important part of it—the being together. I think you learned if you lost a game that you couldn't pout about it or anything like that you just had to be stronger for the next game. It was scary playing in front of an audience. I know I was very timid when I started because I had gone to a country school all the time, but as the years went on I got a lot braver."

Jane Varner Breimhorst, Jordan, - 1928-1932

"It was really great to win the District Championships and the trophy for your school. School spirit was so great back then. It was a big confidence builder. We thought we were so important."

Kasota 1930, swinging fun

Mary Champlin Tonkin, Lake Crystal, 1930-32

"Great exciting memories! Being one of the younger sophomores, everything and everyone was larger than life to me! I ran and played my heart out. I weighed 110 and was not one of the stars — Yet!"

Ruth Norelius DeLapp, Luverne, - 1937-39

"It was a thrill to be listed as high scorer in the newspaper. The experience of playing gave me confidence and I felt good about myself."

Overview

One wishes that these attitudes had dissipated and disappeared over the years, but they stayed intact through women's suffrage, the Great Depression and two world wars.

Similar objections were raised when the first discussions in the 1960s proposed to create inter-scholastic teams for girls. What about the female body? Is it structured for sports or will it shake something out of place? Will she develop unsightly muscles? Will it affect a young woman's femininity if she is an athlete?

It would require years of hard work by enlightened educators and medical professionals to break down the myths and stereotypes that have plagued women far too long.

In today's society the public, parents, the medical community and the schools are moving from apprehension to tolerance to acceptance.

Young women play today for the same reasons their great-grandmothers and grandmothers played in the early 1900s. They will not accept unjust and unnecessary limitations which would restrict their opportunity to participate in sports.

They only ask for a fair chance to play.

The End of the First Era

This little story describes how the high school girls basketball program became caught in a tug-of-war between conflicting philosophies and organizations.

The Story of Little Girl Bouncing Balls

Once upon a time in Minnesota, there were lots of little girl basketballs that loved to bounce, and bounce, and bounce. Because they loved to bounce, they looked for a place where they could bounce together. They bounced into a gymnasium and found a basketball court. They bounced all over the court and had so much fun.

Then someone came in and said, "Let's play a game! I'll teach you the rules." So some of the little bouncing balls played in the game and some sat and watched, sitting on the sidelines and on the ball racks. Once in a while, the balls on the sidelines went into the game and bounced too. The little bouncing balls began playing other teams down the railroad track. It was such fun to play!

Then a new someone came in and said, "I'd like to pick some of you to play on a team for me! And you can play other teams of bouncing balls. You could wear pretty uniforms and people would cheer for you. We might travel to other cities and maybe go to the Olympics. Wouldn't that be fun?!"

The little balls said, "Yes, that would be fun!" But that 'someone' only picked a few of the little balls, those who were really good bouncers. Even so, it seemed o.k. because the other little girl bouncing balls still got to bounce all over the court and see who would bounce the highest.

Then one day, the school principal and superintendent came into the gymnasium and said, "We have studied what might happen to little girl bouncing balls if they bounce too much or too high. Those who know tell us that too much bouncing might hurt your little insides and you wouldn't be able to have babies later on." The school principal said, "Our school has hired a teacher trained in physical education and she can teach you how to bounce in lots of fun games. She knows what is best for you so listen to her. If she tells you to bounce only to knee height (the principal's knee), you must do what she says so you will be healthy all your life. But from now on, there will be no more bouncing with

other little girl bouncing ball teams."

The little girl bouncing balls were very sad. Bouncing to knee height just wasn't as much fun as bouncing as high as you could. They missed bouncing in competition against little girl bouncing ball teams from other schools. And they didn't want to cheer for the boys' bouncing ball games. (You see, the principal and superintendent said it was o.k. for the little boy bouncing balls to bounce as high as they could).

So, while the little girl bouncing balls enjoyed bouncing in their Little Girl Bouncing Ball Athletic Association (LGBBAA), they still wondered how high they might have been able to bounce, if only they could try.

For many, many, many years little girl bouncing balls bounced no higher than knee high in lots of fun activities. But some went to other gymnasiums where they were allowed to bounce higher! Some became national champions, some dyed their hair red and bounced for the Red Head Bouncing Ball Team, and others bounced in other sports. But most little girl bouncing balls just bounced a little and wondered why bouncing was bad when it felt so good.

Many, many, many years later, after the little girl balls had grown and many were raising their own little girl bouncing balls, someone came in the high school gymnasium where their daughters and granddaughters were bouncing at knee height and said, "Let's see how high you can bounce!"

At first, they sat quietly and wondered if this was o.k. And gradually one after the other, they began to bounce higher than knee height and even higher! And their mothers and grandmothers bounced with happiness, and cheered from the sidelines. They were so happy for their little girl bouncing balls!!

However, the mother and grandmother bouncing balls did wonder how high they might have been able to bounce, if only they could have.

Now that little girl balls are bouncing as high as they want, the story continues.

And *they all bounced with happiness ever after!*[1]

Why Wasn't I Allowed to Play?
The most commonly-asked question from women who went to high school in the 1940s, 1950s, and 1960s is, "Why wasn't I allowed to play?"

As you recall the experiences of the "Little Girl Bouncing Balls," apply them to the conditions that combined to bring about the closure of the first era of girls sports in Minnesota.

The National Story
In the early 1900s as girls basketball in Minnesota was rolling happily along, storm clouds began gathering at the national level.

The primary battle was between the women physical educators and the leaders of the Amateur

Athletic Union (AAU) and similar sports organizations. The women physical educators were concerned that women's sports would soon take on the perceived elitism and exploitation that they believed had infiltrated all levels of male sports at the national and international competition.

The first publication addressing these issues was the "Official Handbook of the National Committee on Women's Athletics," published in 1923. The editor, Elizabeth Burchenal, pointed out the concerns of the Committee on Women's Athletics (CWA) as follows:

> "Insistent and increasing demands coming in from all parts of the country for assistance in solving problems in connection with the athletic activities for girls and women demonstrated the need for a set of standards which should be based on the limitations, abilities, and needs of the sex rather than the continuation of applying a set of rules and standards designed primarily for men." [2]

The National Amateur Athletic Federation
During the early 1920s, there were concerns expressed over the health and fitness of all young men and women throughout the country. Statistics had shown that a high percentage of young men had been unfit for service in World War I.

These concerns coupled with the perception that competitive sports for girls and women had developed unacceptable practices and abuses. It led to the formation of an organization called the National Amateur Athletic Federation (NAAF). It was intended to serve as a national forum for discussing the status of the programs for men and women.

The membership of the organization included individuals and organizations from throughout the country. Colonel Breckenridge was the president of the NAAF. Elwood Brown was named a vice-president to head the NAAF-Men's Division. Lou Henry Hoover (Mrs. Herbert Hoover, Future First Lady) was named a vice president to head the NAAF-Women's Division.

The NAAF- Women's Division would have a significant and long-lasting impact on the world of female sports.

The NAAF–Men's Division collapsed when its leader, Elwood Brown, died in 1924. The boys and men went on playing.

The National Amateur Athletic Federation – Women's Division
Lou Hoover promptly organized a two-day conference in Washington, D.C. in April of 1923. The conference was planned to precede the national conference of the American Physical Education Association. It resulted in a large and representative attendance of leaders from across the country.

The conference was a working event with the discussion centering on the status of girls' and women's athletics. The conferees adopted a set of resolutions that reflected the fundamental policies on which girls' and women's athletics should be based. Dr. J. Anna Norris of the University of Minnesota prepared the proposals for the conferees and they were enthusiastically passed.

The NAAF – Women's Division was formally organized a year later in 1924.[3]

Lou Henry Hoover was its first chair and was generous with her time and personal finances to support the goals of the NAAF-Women's Division and other programs that would aid girls and women.[4]

The Purpose and Goals of the NAAF-Women's Division

The purpose of the NAAF-Women's Division was to study the athletic programs for girls and women and become a standard-setting organization.

The membership of the NAAF-Women's Division was composed of lay individuals and organizations as well as educators and their institutions. The Women's Division included a strong force of women physical educators from large universities around the country. They were also leaders in the Committee for Women's Athletics (CWA). After 1932, the CWA became the National Section on Women's Athletics (NSWA) of the American Physical Education Association (APEA).

The CWA was primarily a rules-making body for educational institutions.

The NAAF-Women's Division would take a strong stand opposing the national and international competition sponsored by the Amateur Athletic Union (AAU), industrial leagues and community-based organizations, as well as competition sponsored by educational institutions.

The philosophy of the NAAF-Women's Division was that girls and women should experience a variety of athletic activities under the leadership of qualified coaches and physical educators. Competition should be "of the right kind," which referred to games without the pressure of winning and the trappings of competition that could lead to exploitation of the participants. They argued that competition of the "wrong kind," i.e., the varsity and elite competition, limited opportunities for the majority of girls and women.

Mabel Lee of the University of Nebraska wrote, "But the men promoters of girls' sports were not giving up without a fight. They accused us women of trying to ban all competitive sports for girls. Nothing was further from the truth. We were fighting to correct abuses and to abolish only the wrong kind of sports." [5]

The platform of the NAAF-Women's Division consisted of the following 12 goals.

The Women's Division, National Amateur Athletic Federation of America aims to:
1. Promote such programs of athletic activities for all girls and women as shall meet their needs, and as shall stimulate interest in activities that are suited to all ages and capacities.
2. Promote competition that stresses enjoyment of sport and the development of good sportsmanship and character rather than those types that emphasize the making and breaking of records and the winning of championships for the enjoyment of spectators or for the athletic reputation or commercial advantage of institutions and organizations.
3. Promote interest in awards for athletic accomplishment that have little or no intrinsic value.
4. Promote educational publicity that places the emphasis upon sport and its values rather than upon the competitors.
5. Promote the use of suitable costumes for athletic activities.
6. Promote the provision of sanitary and adequate environment and facilities for athletic activities.
7. Promote the apportionment of adequate time allotment for a physical education program such as shall meet the needs of the various age groups for growth, development and the maintenance of physical fitness.
8. Promote the training and employment of women administrators, leaders and officials who are qualified to assume full responsibility for the physical education and recreation of girls and women.
9. Protect the health of girls and women through the promotion of medical examinations and medical 'follow-up' as a basis for participation in athletic competition, and of a system of supervision that shall assure a reasonable and sane attitude toward participation in activities at times of temporary physical unfitness.

10. Protect athletic activities for girls and women from the dangers attendant upon competition that involves travel, and from their commercialization by interest in gate receipts.
11. Promote the general adoption of approved rules for the conduct of athletics and games for girls and women.
12. Promote the study of the existing rules of all sports to the end that they may be changed to meet the specific needs of girls and women."[6]

In 1924 the NAAF-Women's Division adopted the slogan, "A Team for Every Girl and Every Girl on a Team." It would become the standard for physical educators into the 1960s.[7]

Support Comes From the Medical and Educational Circles

Members of the medical community also supported the standards and recommendations of the NAAF-Women's Division. They would express their concerns about the negative impact that strenuous sports and the pressure of winning would have on young female bodies, their endocrine systems and the impact on their ability to bear children.

At the high school level, the NAAF-Women's Division strongly recommended the replacement of interscholastic teams with intramurals conducted through a Girls Athletic Association (GAA), led by a qualified woman physical education teacher.

The position of the NAAF-WD was joined by the National Association of Secondary School Principals (NASSP) who expressed concern about the explosive growth of girls' athletics and the perceived abuses that were involved in competition. In 1925 the NASSP passed a resolution recommending that high schools eliminate varsity girls' teams and their state tournaments. The organization's decision would reach high school principals across the country.[8]

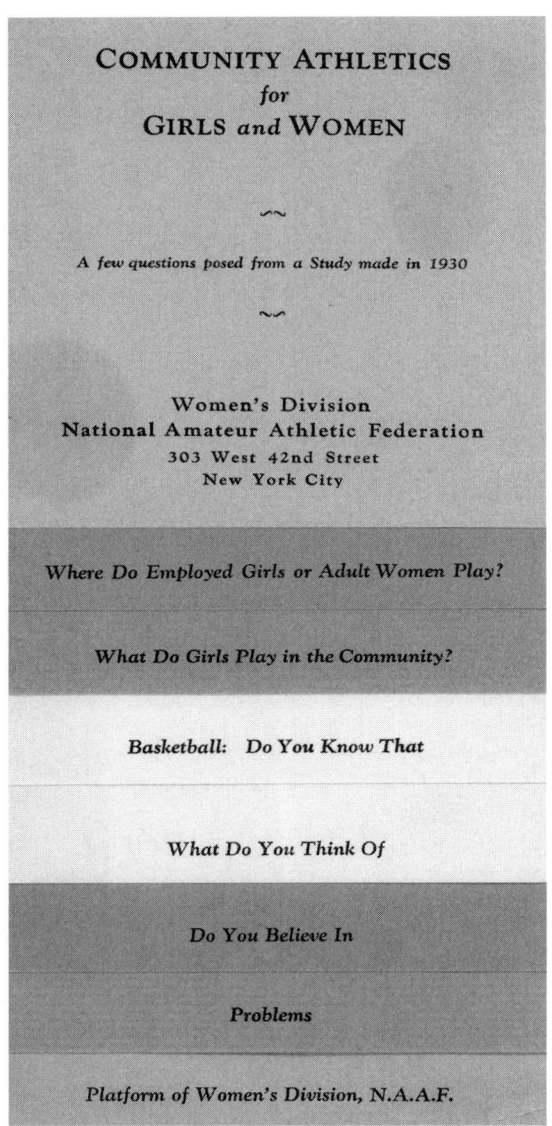

NAAF-WD Platform

Thirty-seven states conducted girls state high school basketball tournaments in 1925

"The committee, therefore, recommends that the NASSP throw the weight of its influence against interscholastic athletics among girls and that wherever possible state athletic associations be induced to legislate against them."
Report on the Committee on Athletics, NASSP, Ninth Yearbook, 1925[9]

74 Daughters of the Game

"Interscholastic competition for girls is to be discouraged in schools with an enrollment permitting of an intramural program, and all teaching, coaching and officiating must be in the hands of competent women teachers. Girls' rules must be followed for all games and activities for which such rules have been adopted."
The Sixth Yearbook of the Department of Superintendence, 1928 [10]

"External stimuli such as cheering audiences, bands, lights, etc., cause a great response in girls and are apt to upset the endocrine balance. Under emotional stress a girl may easily overdo. There is widespread agreement that girls should not be exposed to extremes of fatigue or strain either emotional or physical."
Agnes Wayman, 1933, President of the American Physical Education Association [11]

Taking Aim at the Collegiate and Olympic Levels

The scope of the recommendations of the NAAF-Women's Division extended to all levels of competition. It recommended the elimination of girls' high school and women's collegiate teams. The NAAF-WD took aim at the AAU's involvement with international competition and formally protested the participation of women in the 1928, 1932 and 1936 Olympic Games. [12]

Ethel Perrin, chair person of the Executive Committee of the NAAF-Women's Division, voiced her opposition to the 1928 Olympic participation of women.

"Girls are not suited for the same athletic programs as boys. The difference between them cannot be ignored…Under prolonged and intense physical strain a girl goes to pieces nervously…The fact that a girl's nervous resistance cannot hold out under intensive physical strain is nature's warning. A little more strain and she will be in danger both physically and nervously." [13]

The Minnesota Story

The NAAF-Women's Division sent its platform and recommendations to all organizations responsible for or conducting competition for girls and women.

The impact of the NAAF-Women's Division, and the organizations supporting its platform, was first felt in the mid-1920s as the larger schools began to replace their girls basketball teams with a Girls Athletic Association (GAA). The smaller schools continued with their girls basketball teams into the 1930s until they, too, made the decision to discontinue their teams.

The Letter That Tells the Tale

In the administrative structure of the Minnesota State Department of Education, one section was headed by a Supervisor of Health and Physical Education.

The first State Supervisor of Health and Physical Education from 1923 – 1931 was E.W. Everts. Everts' successor, Harold Jack, began as Supervisor in 1936.

This letter is one of the most significant as it reflects the impact of the platform of the NAAF-WD as it reached into the schools across Minnesota.

Read the language carefully and note the rationale for its recommendations.

> State of Minnesota
> Department of Education
> October 26, 1938
>
> To the Superintendent of Schools and
> Girls' Physical Education Instructor:
>
> Enclosed are two copies of the report on the Girls' Athletic Association as prepared by a committee of the Minnesota Health and Physical Education of the State Department of Education. It is suggested that the Superintendent retain one copy for his use and that the other copy be turned over to the Girls' Physical Education Department.
>
> In the same manner that the interscholastic and intramural athletics provide physical activity of an extracurricular nature for boys, and skilled athletes of the school, so the Girls' Athletic Association program provides for the girls of the school. If your school does not foster such a program, it is strongly urged and recommended that such a program be adopted.
>
> In those few remaining schools still sponsoring a program of girls' interscholastic athletics, it is recommended that the interscholastic program be dropped and that the Girls' Athletic Association program be installed in its place. The G.A.A. program will adequately meet the needs of the girls from a physical and recreational standpoint. Furthermore, it is in harmony with modern educational aims and objectives and contains none of the objectionable features of the girls' interscholastic program which women's organizations in physical education and athletics abhor.
>
> Questions relating to the installation and conduct of the G.A.A. program in your school will be promptly answered by the Division of Health and Physical Education.
>
> Very truly yours,
>
> Harold K. Jack
> Supervisor of Health and
> Physical Education

"The GAA program will adequately meet the needs of the girls from a physical and recreational standpoint." Letter to schools from Harold Jack, Supervisor of Health and Physical Education, 1938

The recommendations included in the letter clearly state that "the interscholastic program be dropped and that the Girls Athletic Association be installed in its place."

The letter specifically states that the boys' interscholastic athletic program and the Girls Athletic Association are considered comparable.

A year later in September of 1939, another letter from Harold Jack praised the schools' actions in dropping their girls' competitive teams.

"Interscholastic competition for girls of high school age was reported in 92 schools during 1938-1939 and in 38 schools during 1939-1940. This represents a decided change for the better."
Harold Jack, Supervisor, in letter to Minnesota schools.[14]

"Interscholastic competition for girls of high school age was reported in 92 schools during 1938-39 and in 38 schools during 1939-40. This represents a decided change for the better."

The State Department of Education continued to monitor the school programs. Surveys in 1940 and 1942 showed that these letters were not popular and brought response from many communities. However, the eventual loss of competition caused more and more districts to comply with the recommendations.

The policies of the NAAF – Women's Division continued until 1940 when it closed its books and merged with the American Association for Health, Physical Education and Recreation (AAHPER).

The first era of girls basketball was over.

A Neighboring State Takes a Different Stand.
The first state girls basketball tournament in Iowa was sponsored in 1920 by Drake University. From 1923 to 1925, the Iowa High School Athletic Association sponsored both girls' and boys' activities. In 1925 a meeting was held in Des Moines to discuss the recommendations that the girls basketball program should be dropped by schools and the state tournament discontinued.

One advocate for dropping the girls' program said, "I coached girls basketball once, and my conscience has bothered me ever since for the harm I might have done the girls."

A second speaker, John W. Agans, then superintendent at Mystic, Iowa had a different position.

"Gentlemen, if you attempt to do away with girls basketball in Iowa, you'll be standing in the center of the track when the train runs over you!" With that, the small schools of Iowa established a new organization to sponsor the state girls basketball tournament. Since 1925, the Iowa Girls High School Athletic Union, has conducted the state girls basketball tournament and the expanded sports program and tournaments for girls in Iowa.[15]

The Influence and Philosophy of Women in Physical Education
Women physical education teachers were trained at colleges and universities whose instructors in the women's physical education departments advocated the change from competitive programs to a physical education program available to all girls in the school.

> "Gentlemen, if you attempt to do away with girls basketball in Iowa, you'll be standing in the center of the track when the train runs over you!"
> John W. Agans, Supt., Mystic, Iowa

Gertrude Zeibarth Bloom was a physical education teacher who received her training at the LaCrosse Teachers College in Wisconsin, the University of Minnesota, and in California where she earned her doctorate. In a letter written in 1978, she recalled the training received by physical education teachers during that era. Gertrude coached girls basketball at Park Rapids from 1926-1928, and was a member of the State Referee Association. She came to White Bear Lake in 1928 and coached girls basketball one year before switching to a Girls Athletic Association.

> "The first year I was at White Bear, my assistant coach, Lorraine Redding Monson, and I had fair success at interscholastic basketball, but then decided to go GAA where more students could participate and more interest could be generated in a greater variety of activities, including track. Too much emphasis was placed on basketball and it was too time-consuming for the benefit of a few.
>
> My training at LaCrosse, WI Teachers College was very much against interscholastic sports. It was hammered into us that the female body construction was not geared to that strenuous activity. Female shoulders, arms, legs, muscles, heart, and especially the pelvic bones are completely different from the male."[16]

This philosophy would be taught well into the 1960s before the second era of girls' sports would emerge.

Girls Swimming and Diving Also Impacted by Recommendations

A second girls' high school sport shared the same fate as the girls basketball program. The recommendations from the Supervisor of Health and Physical Education, Minnesota State Department of Education, extended to the girls swimming and diving teams on Minnesota's Iron Range, located in the northeastern corner of the state.

The Minnesota State High School League sponsored a MSHSL State Girls Swimming and Diving Meet from 1924-1942.

Taxes from the iron mines resulted in beautiful schools with pools that were a centerpiece of their school district. Several area schools hosted the state swimming meet. Teams included Virginia, Eveleth, Aurora, Biwabik, Ely, Mountain Iron, Chisholm, Hibbing and Nashwauk. The meet usually included about 130 swimmers and divers.

For several years, the letters from the State Department of Education had recommended that the schools drop the girls swimming teams. In the fall of 1939, the superintendents again reviewed the recommendations from Harold Jack and voted that all of the schools would discontinue the girls' teams. There was negative response from the communities and news media to the decision. Local newspapers stated the concerns expressed by school board members about the loss of opportunity for Range swimmers to qualify for the Olympics. Anne Govednik of Chisholm had participated in the 1932 and 1936 Olympics and other prospects were preparing for Olympic tryouts.

Anne Govednik of Chisholm qualified for the Olympics in 1932 and 1936, performing well in her events. Anne remained a local hero throughout her life, with the Chisholm Junior High natatorium re-dedicated as the "Anne Govednik Pool."

The superintendents reconsidered their decision and voted to allow each school to decide for its own community. The schools chose to continue the girls swimming program for another two years through the 1942 State Meet.

At the 1999 MSHSL Women in Sports Leadership Conference, Jean Frarey Walters of Rochester shared recollections of her high school swimming years at Virginia High School. In 1942 Jean won the last championship in the girls' free style competition and her medley relay team established a record in that meet. When the recommendations came from the State Department to drop the girls' teams, her father was a member of the school board. He and others opposed the recommendations for dropping girls swimming and diving, but as other schools dropped their teams, the Virginia High School girls swimming team found itself without competition.

The *Official Handbooks* of the Minnesota State High School League annually reported the State Meet results and champions. After 1942 the handbooks made no mention of the girls swimming and diving programs.[17]

The Perspective of Minnesota Athletes

Girls playing on interscholastic basketball and swimming teams in Minnesota were devastated and frustrated by any attempted explanations of the reasons for the cancellation of their programs. Some tried to challenge the decision but eventually failed in their efforts to get the school superintendent or school boards to change their minds. It can be assumed that there were voices of support including high school principals and superintendents who coached varsity girls basketball teams.

Reactions to the loss of their girls' teams remained vivid memories throughout the lives of the women who lost the opportunity to play.

Ruth McCarron Dahlke, Sherburn, 1924-1927
As a senior, Ruth wrote a section on girls' athletics for the 1927 yearbook, "As we go to press, the editor and associate editors have heard the sad news that there will be no interscholastic basketball for girls next year. The girls of S.H.S. have our sincerest sympathy and we hope you don't get so stiff in the joints that it will hinder you from participating in interclass games."

Ruth said, "At the time girls basketball was discontinued for the 1927-1928 year, we were led to believe that it was detrimental to our health. The real reason was that the schools were not producing good boys' teams. By getting rid of the girls they could then have a 'B' squad for the boys, and eventually the 'A' team would be better. We are 22 miles from the Iowa border where all these years they have had girls basketball. I played basketball all four years in high school, two years at Mankato State, and coached it two years at East Chain. In my adult years I have played softball and golf. I am 88 years old so I am sure basketball never hurt us physically."

> "Our parents respected the school authorities who were among the most educated people in our community. So, if that is what they said should happen, our parents accepted it."
> Ruth Norelius DeLapp, Luverne, 1936-1938

1927 Tracy yearbook, the *Teton*
"At the beginning of the year the news was spread that the girls would be out-of-luck as far as basketball was concerned. They would have class teams, but would not play out-of-town games. The girls were disappointed that they couldn't play the different towns, but they decided interclass games 'would be better than nothing.'" Seth Schmidt, *Tracy Headlight-Herald*- Wed. July 1, 1998

Grand Meadow – 1929-1939
"Kathryn Losey was a student working in the school office the day news of the ban arrived, and when asked what the superintendent did with the letter she replied, 'The superintendent threw the letter in the trash.' 'We were shocked, angry, sick,' echoed the women of the 1930's basketball teams. There was a consolation prize for the girls; they could be cheerleaders for the boys. Some of them did so the following year, but their heart wasn't in it." Sue Doocy, the *Meadow Area News*, 1992.

Gladys Dahl Clark, Cromwell - 1930-1933
"We were told in the fall of 1932 that there would be no more basketball games for the girls. Excuses were plenty. Girls did not have the stamina, it wasn't good for our health, it was not ladylike, and more. Some thought that it was because they wanted a 'B' team for the boys. Mae White's mother thought playing would give her varicose veins. In November of 1932 a group of the remainder of the 1931-32 basketball team plus some of the girls that played in 1930-31 decided that we were going to play basketball. The boys were practicing basketball in the Odd Fellows Hall here in Cromwell. My dad was janitor and he let us in. As soon as the boys were through practicing we marched into the hall and demanded that we should be able to practice and have a team for the year of 1932-1933. Which we did! But that was the last girls basketball for many years, almost half a century. What a shame!

Alta Creger Heikkenen, Brainerd - 1932
"A group of us was determined and we went with Margaret Jackson, our gym teacher, to confront the school board, but the school board was a bunch of "old fogies" that had decided basketball was too rugged for girls. They said women's sports, especially when spectators came to watch, was just a display of our bodies and wasn't 'ladylike.' We kept trying to tell them that times were changing." From an interview by staff writer Michelle Willette, *Brainerd Daily Dispatch*, Jan. 1993

Mary Champlin Tonkin, Lake Crystal - 1931-1933
"They closed women's basketball the year I was a junior, to our disgust of course. The reason we were given was 'It was too hard!' We thought it was a disgusting reason."

The Growth of Physical Education

Physical Education and interscholastic athletics share a common timeline in Minnesota.

Medical examinations conducted during the First World War (1914-1919) found one-third of the young men in the country unfit for military service. There was national concern that something must be done to change this situation.

In 1923 the State of Minnesota passed legislation that required all schools to offer health and physical education for all girls and boys as part of the curriculum. This legislation brought about a statewide building program to provide gymnasiums that would enable school districts to comply with the law. Federal monies also became available to help to build facilities. Both physical education and interscholastic athletics benefited as schools finally gained facilities such as gymnasiums, changing rooms, and showers.

Additional legislation affecting physical education was passed in 1938-1939. The State Department of Education began to require that all teachers must be properly certified to teach full-time physical education. During the same school year, of the 1,226 teachers teaching physical education in the 465 school districts, only 402 teachers were fully qualified with a major in physical education.

It is significant that this legislation coincided with the recommendations to replace girls' interscholastic teams with intramurals and GAA.

The Last Schools to Have Competitive Teams

All the schools in Minnesota did not switch to the GAA format at the same time. The pattern shows that the first schools to eliminate interscholastic competition were the larger schools where physical education was part of the curriculum. The physical education teachers in the larger school districts would have been trained by collegiate and university physical educators who were supportive of replacing competitive teams with physical education curriculum for all girls and women. The smaller rural schools in Minnesota frequently did not have a trained physical education teacher during these years. Their teams were supported by their community and the girls' parents and they continued their competitive basketball teams into the 1930s and early 1940s.

"The one purpose of sports for girls and women is the good of those who play."
The National Section for Girls' and Women's Sports, AAHPER, 1937, 1948, 1953

The last teams known to play interscholastic games were in northern Minnesota. One of the teams was Big Falls. Norma Booth Krats and Beryl Regal Miller played from 1939-1942. Big Falls played

Northome, Kelliher, Littlefork, and Fort Francis, Canada. Norma indicated in her information that when her team could no longer travel during her senior year, they played the boys' team.

Overview

It would be easy to throw stones and cast blame on those who were part of the movement to eliminate the girls basketball and swimming programs, leaving so many young women without interscholastic teams for so many years.

The schools did develop a comprehensive physical education curriculum and hundreds of Girls Athletic Associations. These programs did provide enjoyable opportunities for thousands of young women. In spite of very limited time on any activity, the girls enjoyed learning about a variety of team and individual sports. They were provided with the opportunity to develop their leadership skills. They were taught by qualified women physical educators, and they participated in a wide sampling of indoor and outdoor activities through their GAAS. It was a program that could also have been a model for a Boys Athletic Association for the young men who wanted to experience a variety of sports at a recreational level.

However, for those girls and boys who prefer to compete at the highest levels, it is the interscholastic program that provides that opportunity. In hindsight, valid questions remain. Why did it have to be an "all-or-nothing" decision affecting only girls? Why couldn't schools keep the competitive teams and add physical education for all students, girls and boys? After all, we can observe the boys had competitive teams before, during and after the decisions to eliminate girls' competitive sports.

For all who believe in equal opportunity, this remains a sad ending to an era that had brought so much fun, enhanced physical health and enjoyment to so many young women in Minnesota.

Duluth Central GAA 1936

A Team for Every Girl and Every Girl on a Team

When the last schools dropped their girls basketball teams, it left behind countless young women who were confused, upset with the adults around them, and downright angry. Unfortunately, it was only the beginning!

For the next two to three decades, high school girls would find little or no interscholastic sports in their Minnesota high schools.

The Girls Athletic Association

Into this void, Minnesota schools expanded their physical education programs and employed qualified individuals to teach young women the skills of many sports and recreational activities.

For those girls who wanted opportunities beyond the classroom, there was the Girls Athletic Association, commonly called the GAA.

In a well-organized GAA, all girls in the school could participate. The activities were as varied as the creativity of their physical education teacher allowed. She could include indoor sports of every variety and depending upon the season might include outdoor winter activities like skiing and skating, as well as canoeing, camping, hiking, etc. The GAA was a healthy outlet for many young women during those decades.

The 1925 Marshall yearbook reported,

> "Seven Girls' Clubs were organized at the Marshall High School during the second semester of the school year of 1924 and 1925. The purpose of these organizations is to promote physical development through exercise and personal hygiene talks, also to promote a better spirit of fellowship and service among the girls of the high school: to aim at higher ethical and moral standards and by these means to prepare the girls for the responsibilities which they will have to assume after they are graduated from high school. Among the sports that have been indulged in are hiking, basket ball, golfing, skating and folk dancing."

In the 1926 Rochester yearbook, an article headed, "Girls Athletics," describes the type of activities provided in lieu of competitive sports.

> "Miss Townsend, director of Girls' Athletics, has proved to be a very capable and enthusiastic promoter of girls' athletics. She was graduated from the State Teachers College of Cedar Falls, Iowa. Under her instruction, many girls have passed various athletic tests. Her plan, to further the ideals of good sportsmanship, has proved very successful during her first year in R.H.S. "Class attention! Ready for roll call!" It's a gym class and we are going to have a triple test. Much emphasis has been placed in posture work this year, with a triple test each semester. A Posture Contest added much enthusiasm to the work. The most perfect posture in each grade was chosen and finally the most perfect posture in Junior High and Senior High. Aside from the regular calisthenics, folk dances and games, the high school girls have had two tournaments to play off. The basketball tournament was won by the two upper grades: The freshman in Junior High, and the seniors in Senior High. The volleyball tournament followed later with stiff battles for all grades. A Gym Demonstration in March, giving the public an idea of what we do in gym was the formal ending of the gym work this year. In swimming, many of the girls passed their swimmers' test, and fourteen of them went on to take extra work in the special Life Saving Class to become either a junior or senior lifesaver. The work in swimming ended in an Inter-class Swimming Meet. Four senior girls, all-prominent in girls' athletics, won their R.H.S. monograms this year by earning the required number of points. The points were earned in swimming, hiking, skating, skiing, and tennis; and in being, in general, good all around athletes. These girls were: Grace Foster, Edna Maass, Helen Thomas, and Harriet Quale. This year, athletics for girls, more than ever before, have been recognized as having an important place in the school curriculum. Interest in this phase of school work is growing, among the girls who participate and among the student body in general, as illustrated by the enthusiastic turn-outs for the basketball and volleyball games."

"A Girls Athletic Association has been started, headed by Miss Everts. The purpose of it is to get every girl interested in some form of athletics. Laws and by-laws have been drawn up by a committee for that purpose. Every kind of athletics available in Proctor will be introduced."

1926 Proctor yearbook, the *Mallet*

The Stillwater *Kabekonian* in 1930 includes an article about the Girls' Athletic Association, GAA, with members earning points for participation in a variety of team and individual athletic activities. The organization held a Big Sister Party and participated in skating, skiing, and hiking. A banquet was held at the conclusion of the year with GAA awards given to those who had earned from 100 to 1,000 points. The article ends with, "The GAA has proved successful, and has taken the place of other girls' organizations."

That said, the GAA was not designed to meet the needs of the female athlete who wanted to compete at higher levels. She watched from the sidelines while her brothers played on teams, competed in tournaments, were awarded school letters, and were selected for special honors. She played in the gymnasium when it was not being used by the boys' teams, or found her activities cancelled when the boys and their coaches wanted the space.

And she knew that it was not fair or right. It did not make her feel valued as an athlete or as a female.

It simply did not make sense.

And it made her angry!!!

The decades of the 1940s and 1950s continued on, leaving more and more unhappy young women in their wake. Then, in the 1960s, new pioneers and advocates began to speak and take action. With each step forward, cracks began to weaken the barriers. As the momentum grew, voices of reason and conviction overrode the myths and stereotypes that had limited the female athlete. The barriers began to fall.

"Our female student-athletes are fortunate to experience so many positive opportunities through participating in athletics. It is important for them to know that these opportunities were not always available.

I was a student at Litchfield High School during the GAA era when we could only play one night a week in the gymnasium. During my collegiate years, barriers were coming down and I had the opportunity to play competitively. However, I still regret not having the opportunity to wear the Litchfield High School uniform and represent my school and community as a member of an athletic team.

Seeing the opportunities for female student-athletes develop and expand in the early 1970s is an important piece of history that I will never forget. Now as a school administrator, I work with my colleagues to ensure equity in the high school sports program so no other young woman will miss that opportunity. I am so very proud to have been a piece of the history that allows for the equitable programs that we see in our schools today."

Sharon Euerle, Director of Activities,
Mankato West High School

School administrators listened and responded. In 1969, for the first time in the state's history, girls' athletics would be sponsored by the Minnesota State High School League. The rest, as they say, is history! Today's high school girls have teams, uniforms, fans, and state tournaments in a variety of team and individual activities. The best part is, these young women cannot fathom that it ever was or could be any different.

And yet, each year at a MSHSL State Girls Tournament, there are women watching with tears of frustration, for what "might have been."

To each of you sitting on the sidelines or in the bleachers watching today's young women enjoy the thrill of competition, wishing that you could have played: we only wish that those years could be a "do-over." But our wish cannot change what is forever etched in history.

We can do one thing. We *can* commit to ensuring that no future generation will ever experience limited opportunities, nor will we allow our young women to feel that they are less valued or less qualified to participate in any part of their world.

It is a commitment that must be made and honored by each of us.

As time passes, and yet another century rolls into view, when someone asks if young Minnesota women and their peers across the country are enjoying fair and equal sports opportunities, our answer will be: "*You bet'cha!!*"

Finding Opportunities Beyond School Teams

By the 1920s employers organized teams of their young employees to fill their leisure time and to inspire loyalty to the company. It was also good advertising. Some of these teams were the catalyst for criticizing the competitive programs and recommending that they be dropped in favor of recreational activities. However, independent teams continued to provide opportunity for many young women.

Independent teams were formed in many communities. Sometimes they were simply organized by women who wanted to play, organizing their own schedules. Many teams were sponsored by a local company or by their local YWCA, church or community organization.

When the first era of girls' interscholastic teams ended in Minnesota, a void was created and only a few young women among those who wished to play could find the competitive outlet for their talents.

Independent teams
After they graduated from high school in 1928, Kay Nolan Wetter and Alta Creger Heikkenen of Brainerd spoke of playing on a community team called the Flying Queens.

In 1929 the Stillwater girls basketball team played a professional women's team from Minneapolis, sponsored by the First National Bank (FNB). The FNB team played teams across the area and claimed the championship of the Northwest. In 1930 the Rapidan girls' team was scheduled to play the FNB team, but the FNB team experienced an accident returning from a game in Canada and the game was cancelled.

Irma Post from Deer Creek spoke of playing the Frazee Cane Women's team in the early 1920s, indicating that independent teams were organized for the post high school players.

Professional teams were organized with women selected from various states and who played against men's teams playing "men's rules." Some of these professional women's games were held as fundraisers, designed to entertain crowds with their skills and incorporating fun activities during the game and at halftime.

The All-American Red Heads
The All-American Red Heads played from 1936-1986. The team was created in 1936 by C.M. "Ole" Olson of "Olson's Terrible Swedes." Doyle Olson, wife of the team coach, was a hairdresser. Two of the players had red hair, so the players as a prank and with the aid of henna, all became Red Heads for a game. They were a hit! The Red Heads were born!

Throughout the years, the team played skilled basketball against men's teams and entertained crowds across the country. The All-American Red Heads hold attendance records in arenas all over the sports world. They have been featured in publications such as *Life, Look, Colliers, Sporting News,* and *Sports Illustrated*. They appeared on "The Ed Sullivan Show," "I've Got a Secret," and Art Linkletter's "House Party."

Dolores Petersen, Park Rapids

In 1948 Orwell Moore was hired to coach, and in 1955 Coach Orwell Moore bought the All-American Red Heads from "Ole" Olson.

The team was an outlet for the following six Minnesota women to play basketball – Dolores "Dody" Petersen Clack, Lynnette Sjoquist, Lynnea Sjoquist, Sherri Mattson, Gretchen Pinz Hyink, and Jackie Wrage Zitlau.

In the 1940s Dolores "Dody" Petersen Clack of Erskine High School only wanted to play her favorite game of basketball. She would play against neighborhood boys and shoot endless baskets using a wire hoop attached to the barn wall.

There was no opportunity provided by her school so she organized a women's basketball team, playing by the boys' rules, dribbling the length of the floor. In her senior year, the All-American Red Heads team came to Erskine for a game. The coach saw Dolores playing in a preliminary game and asked if she'd be interested in joining the Red Heads. She was! It began a life of travel across the United States, playing every night and two games on Sunday.

At halftime Dolores was selected to do a behind-the-back and over-the-head shot, and a piggyback shot. Other players performed their specialties. One stood on her head and shot from her feet. Another player shot 20 of 20 free throws from her knees. Dolores played with the Red Heads from 1950-1953. Dolores declined an invitation to play with a team in the women's professional baseball league. The team was later portrayed in the movie, "A League of Their Own."

Orwell Moore, All-American Red Heads Coach and Owner

Coach Moore said that 6'7" Jackie Wrage from Aurora was an excellent player and played with the Red Heads for many years. She is currently living in California.

The Red Heads won a high percentage of their games in 1972. They won 558 games out of 642 games played, all against male teams. Red Head uniforms, artifacts and one of the limousines that took the team from town to town can be seen at the Women's Basketball Hall of Fame in Knoxville, Tennessee.

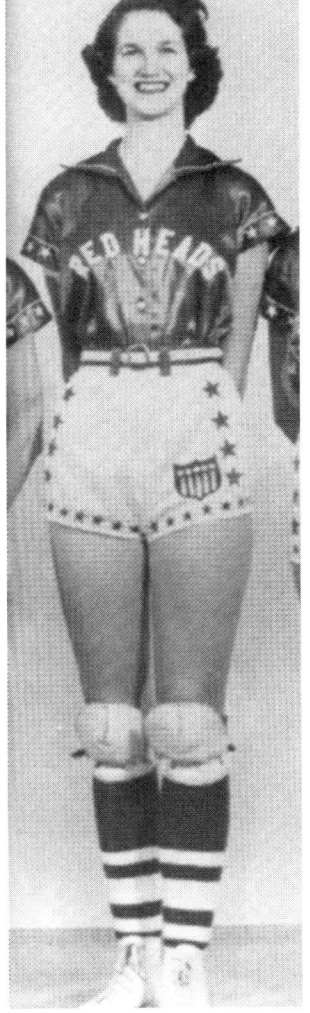

Jackie Wrage Zitlau, 1956, Aurora

Orwell Moore was very generous in providing information about his team, its history and photos of the Minnesota players.
See Notes, page 370 for link to additional information.

In 1973 the 6'2" Sjoquist twins, Lynnette and Lynnea, were the No.1 draft choices of the Red Heads. The twins had seen the Red Heads play in their home town of Cannon Falls and knew they wanted to join the team after graduation from Golden Valley Lutheran College where they played volleyball, softball and basketball. Lynnette played with the Red Heads until 1977 and Lynnea until 1978.

Lynnea served both as team captain and business manager during her last two years with the team. In 1978 Lynnette went on to play with the Minnesota Fillies, a franchise in the Women's Professional Basketball League.

Lynnette and Lynnea Sjoquist

Sherri Mattson participated in volleyball, basketball, and track & field at Braham High School (1969-1971) and from 1971-75 competed in volleyball, basketball, softball and field hockey at the University of Minnesota, Duluth. Sherri was drafted by the Red Heads in 1975 and played for two years. In 1997 she was inducted into the UMD Hall of Fame.

Gretchen Pinz Hyink grew up in Isle, Minnesota and attended the University of Minnesota, Duluth where she participated in volleyball, basketball, and softball.

During their senior year, Gretchen and Sherri saw an ad on the Physical Education bulletin board and were later hired by the Red Heads.

The 1976-1977 photo identifies Gretchen Pinz Hyink, second player from left, Sherri Mattson, fourth player from left, and Lynnette Sjoquist, seventh player from the left.[1] (see photo p. 87)

Sherri Mattson

GRETCHEN PINZ – "Doing a Nifty Balance"

Gretchen Pinz

86   Daughters of the Game

The Texas Cowgirls, Shooting Stars-Arkansas Lassies, and Arkansas Gems

Elvera "Peps" Neuman of Eden Valley was a 1962 graduate of Eden Valley High School and did not have the opportunity to participate in high school girls' athletics. As a student Neuman organized a Girls Athletic Association at Eden Valley. The GAA basketball team played against Paynesville and Grove City. She scored a career high 54 points in one game.

In 1962, "Peps" joined the Texas Cowgirls as a player/manager of the women's professional basketball team. From 1964-1973, she became co-owner and player for the Shooting Stars-Arkansas Lassies and was the sole owner, player and coach of the Arkansas Gems from 1973-1988.

Red Heads 1976-1977

Neuman's uniform has been enshrined at the Naismith Memorial Basketball Hall of Fame. She was inducted into the Minnesota Girls Basketball Coaches Association Hall of Fame in 1996.

Legacy of the Game

"Leg-a-cy: Something handed down from an ancestor or a predecessor from the past"

What a wonderful thing it is to have traditions and a legacy!

In the early 1970s as girls' sports began to grow, it was believed that the "new" teams were the first competitive teams and that it would require decades to develop traditions and a true legacy. But the women who had played during the first era knew better. They were the first high school girls' teams in Minnesota.

Elvera "Peps" Neuman

There is tradition! There is a legacy!

Now, with their history in hand, it can be said with confidence that the first era of girls basketball began the traditions and legacy for today's girls' sports teams.

The teams of the second era are now adding to their rich history of their foremothers.

The legacies that follow came to light during the gathering of information from families and schools. There are many yet to be discovered in your communities and in your family records.

From Champions to Champions

St. Paul Central

One of the early Minnesota teams was the 1902 St. Paul Central girls basketball team. The 1909 and 1915 St. Paul Central teams won the Twin Cities Championships during their era.

St. Paul Central 1902

St. Paul Central 1915

The legacy of the St. Paul Central teams was passed on to the 1976 St. Paul Central girls basketball team. The 1976 team participated in the first MSHSL State Girls Basketball Tournament and won the Class AA Championships.

A Family Legacy

As many of the young women of the first era began to raise families, they passed their love of basketball to their daughters, granddaughters and great-granddaughters. Families shared photos of their family legacy.

Dawson to Dawson

Ann Jerde played for Dawson in 1910 and her daughter, Audrey Moe Froiland, played for Dawson from 1931-1934. Audrey's daughters missed the opportunity to carry on the tradition because the school did not sponsor girls basketball during their high school years.

Audrey said, "Everything is more elaborate and organized now, but I think perhaps we had as much fun and enjoyment as they do now, almost 70 years later or, as my mother did 90 years ago."

St. Paul Central 1976 - Lisa, back row, 4th player from right

Dawson 1910

Cromwell to Cromwell to Cromwell

Blanche Line Kingsley was the first of the three-generation legacy of female athletes in her family. Blanche played at Cromwell from 1926-1931; her daughter June played at Cromwell and later coached her daughters, Tammy, April and Julie.

Three generations of Cromwell basketball - June, Blanche and Julie

Austin 1914

Austin basketball 1976 - Liz, front row, 3rd from left

Austin to Austin

In Austin, the school yearbook included photos of teams in 1914 and 1915. By the 1920s, a Girls Athletic Association had replaced the basketball teams.

When girls basketball began its second era in the 1960s and 1970s, the Austin girls basketball team participated in the first MSHSL State Girls Basketball Tournament held in 1976. Liz Erickson was a member of this pioneering team of the second era.

Megan, Liz and Annie, 2005

Liz passed her enjoyment of sports to her two daughters, Megan and Annie — both members of Austin girls basketball teams in 2005.

Madison 1919 - Margaret, 1st player on left

Madison to Anoka

Margaret Hauck Morrill played on the Madison team from 1916-19. She later went to the University of Minnesota and played on the women's field hockey team, earning a University letter. Her granddaughter, Margaret Chutich, played basketball and tennis at Anoka High School. Margaret won the second MSHSL State Tennis Championship in

1975. Margaret went on to play basketball at Stanford in 1976-77 and tennis at the University of Minnesota, 1978-80.

Milan to Willmar and Lac qui Parle

Ruth Olson Kleven, Milan, was a member of the first Milan girls basketball team. They were an early team in the area to change from bloomers to shorts. The photo of Ruth reflects her obvious pleasure in her new uniform.

Margaret Chutich at Stanford

Milan 1927 - Ruth, 3rd from left

Ruth was the first of four generations of basketball players in her family. Her playing days were followed by her son, Jim; his daughter, Missy; and now two great-granddaughters.

Ruth attended an exciting game in 2004 when two great-granddaughters were playing one another as members of the opposing teams. Lauren Struxness, left, played for Lac qui Parle Valley School and Ali Unger, right, played for Willmar. Ruth, of course, cheered for both teams.

Ruth Olson Kleven and two great-granddaughters, 2004

Ruth Olson Kleven, Milan, 1927, new uniform

New Richland to Edina

Evelyn Sponberg Young played for New Richland from 1925-1927. Her two granddaughters, Sara Sampsell-Jones, 1993, and Laura Sampsell Hoffman, Edina, 1995, inherited their love of the game and played for Edina, in the mid-1990s. Sara played at Dartmouth and has established a website dedicated to women's basketball.

Laura Sampsell Hoffman and Evelyn Young

Sara Sampsell Jones

90 Daughters of the Game

Jeannette Page Wright, Crookston, 1912

Crookston to St. Charles

Jeannette Page Wright, a member of the 1912 Crookston girls basketball team, set the standard for her granddaughter, Lori Ann Wright Severson. Lori played for the St. Charles girls basketball team in the early 1980s.

Franklin to Willmar, Mound and Jordan

In Franklin, basketball was a sisterly affair. Alice Schroeder McFarland played on teams with her two sisters, Esther and Bertha. After high school Alice and one of her sisters played on an independent team, the Wesley Church girls basketball team, in Minneapolis.

Lori Wright, St. Charles, 1982

Alice Schroeder McFarland, Franklin

Stephanie Hall Moran, Mound

Lynn Trochlil Crist, Willmar

Alice's granddaughters shared her love of the game. Three granddaughters played basketball: Michelle McFarland Bursch, Jordan; Lynn Trochlil Crist, played on a state tournament team at Willmar, and Stephanie Hall Moran at Mound.

Nielsville to New York Mills and Woodbury

Alice Aanonsen Lervold played on the Nielsville girls basketball team, beginning a three-generation family of basketball players. Alice's daughter, Kathy Lervold Goodrich, played basketball and became the coach at New York Mills.

Coach Goodrich's New York Mills team won its first MSHSL Girls State Basketball Tournament in 1977. Alice's granddaughter, Heather, played at Woodbury and her team was a participant in the 1997 and 1998 MSHSL State Girls Basketball Tournaments.

Michelle McFarland Bursch, Jordan

Heather Goodrich Schrider, Alice Lervold, Kathy Lervold Goodrich

Nielsville 1928 - Alice, 3rd from left

Jeffers and Westbrook to Elk River

Teri Takle has a special heritage — she had two grandmothers who were basketball players in the first era. Avis Hofslund Piper of Jeffers, 1929 and Clarine Knudson Takle of Westbrook, 1929.

With her grandmothers' legacy, Teri played basketball at Elk River from 1980-1983 and at Hamline University from 1983-1986.

Teri Takle, Elk River

Jeffers 1928 - Avis, middle row, 3rd from left

Pelican Rapids – A Uniform Lives On

Ethel Lyden Anderson played on the 1912 Pelican Rapids girls basketball team. After high school, Ethel kept her uniform and, after altering and decorating it, the uniform was also used as her swimming suit.

In 2005, Ethel's great-granddaughter, Heidi Robbins, wore the uniform that has been preserved over the decades by the family.

Pelican Rapids 1912 - Ethel, 3rd from left, front row

Heidi Robbins wearing her great-grandmother's 1912 uniform

Carrying the Tradition to the Professional Game
Hutchinson to University of Minnesota and Beyond
In 1921 the Hutchinson girls basketball team began a legacy being expanded by Lindsay Whalen. Lindsay was a member of the Hutchinson High School girls' team in 1996, graduating in 2000. Lindsay went on to play at the University of Minnesota, leading the Gopher Women's Basketball Team, under Coach Pam Borton, to its first Final Four in 2004.

Lindsay was drafted by a WNBA team and in 2005 was playing with the Connecticut Sun of the Women's National Basketball Association.

Hutchinson 1921

The 1999 Reunion of First Era Players

It was time to gather the women who had played during this first era of girls basketball, and what better place than the MSHSL Girls High School State Tournament!!

Invitations went out to the women, their families and schools: "you are invited to come to a special reception to be held in your honor on March 13, 1999 at the MSHSL State Girls Basketball Tournament. The reception will be held in the Williams Arena Club Room from 1:00 – 3:00 p.m. Family and friends are invited. At the halftime of the game, you will be introduced on the floor of the arena to the fans and television audience." *And they came*!!

Their smiles were closely matched by those of their family members and school representatives.

Welcome to the Basketball Pioneers - Janet, Dorothy and Marian

Lindsay Whalen, University of Minnesota

Twenty-nine women from across the state were reunited with former teammates and with players from other teams. There were reunions of players who had not seen one another since their high school years in the 1920s and 1930s. Some brought scrapbooks and more than one wore her school sweater with its basketball letter on it. Uniforms and trophies from the era were on display.

Memories were sharp and clear of their playing days. They recalled specific games played against another team. They remembered rough play in some games. They also shared their respect for neighboring teams and individual players. Stories were told of riding on trains, sleighs and cars to neighboring towns. They reminisced about playing in the community halls with the hot stoves in the corner and spectators lining the edge of the floor. They recalled attending dances and receptions after the games and staying in the opposing players' homes overnight.

Most touching and apparent was their lifelong love of basketball and its importance in their lives. Each woman received a complimentary basketball while family members looked on, with proud smiles on their faces. Happy tears flowed freely.

Sharing Memories at the Reception

Receiving plaques on the floor of Williams Arena - 1999

Jane Varner Breimhorst, Jordan, and Irma Malone Foley, Montgomery, enjoying their basketballs

At the halftime of the game, they walked onto the floor of Williams Arena and were individually introduced. Each woman received a plaque, commemorating the day and their attendance. One woman kissed the plaque when it was placed in her hands.

Marie Keeler, Belle Plaine, with her basketball

The following letter was received from Blanche Line Kingsley, Cromwell High School. It reflects the feelings expressed by many in attendance:

"I have to thank everyone who took part in planning and hosting the reception for us at the arena. I was concerned my doctor would say I shouldn't go, but he said, "Go for it!!" On my next visit I brought my plaque and official program for him to read. I think he was as excited as I was. He told me that he thought it was worth the risk for me to go. He even had to copy the write-up about it to show his wife and daughter. It was a great experience to have during my 85th year. I treasure the plaque and other memorabilia as do my other family members, and it will be passed on through the generations that follow me. My girls and I purchased enough official programs at the arena for each of the grandchildren, and they were all thrilled to get them. My children and grandchildren are all thrilled and happy for me.

"Mother, I hope you are looking down and enjoying this."
Marie Keeler, 1999

> I was fortunate in having played while my family and school supported the game. Our team was discontinued soon after my graduation from high school (1931). My family and I are all very grateful to all of you. Thank you!"

Marie Keeler wrote: "There aren't enough words in the English language to thank you for the wonderful time I had on March 13th. Everything was so perfect and wonderful. I enjoyed the game immensely. Sure wish we could have played in a place like that! Thank you so much!"

When Marie walked onto the floor of the arena to receive her plaque, she smiled, looked up and said, "Mother, I hope you are looking down and enjoying this."

Lillian Sovari said, "And I love my very own basketball!"

Saima Savela told us, "I have had great fun telling my friends how I was honored for something I did 60 years ago. Then I told them it was for playing girls' interscholastic basketball in high school. Many of them also had done likewise. Perhaps this research could be extended and expanded."

Mary Champlin Tonkin wrote,

> "While I was at the 100th anniversary of our high school, I saw three of the team members. They were all thrilled to hear the story of the event at Williams Arena. Also, when the video came, I invited Mrs. Ruth Rawn, the 100 year old, and her daughter to our house to see the video that you sent to each of us after the event. They do not have a VCR, so they came here. While she was sitting on the davenport, hearing about the event, I put the basketball in her hands. It was a very charming picture. She is such a beautiful woman and she smiled as she turned the ball over in her hands. I could almost see her dream of putting that ball up through the hoop as she held it. She enjoyed the reference to her in the video, as did her daughter. I want to thank you again for making it possible for me to be a part of the wonderful day at Williams Arena. Our daughter and granddaughter, Lisa, were as thrilled as I was. It was grand that they could also be a part of it all. I really think it is an important and intriguing idea that you have of preserving the history of women's basketball."

Ruth Rawn, Willmar and daughter Florence

Jane Varner Breimhorst wrote, "It was good to show the young girls there is 'life after basketball,' and girls who share this experience become life-long friends."

Ruth Norelius DeLapp wrote, "The pioneers of girls' basketball in Minnesota owe you a debt of gratitude *because you remembered them*."

Roster of Participants in Reunion

Players	Home Team	Years Played
Luella Bandelin Anderson	Arlington	1925-1928
Carolyn Bandelin Matz	Arlington	1925-1926

Carolyn and Luella are sisters. They held a reunion in Arlington in 1998 with their coach, Susanna Hensler. It was a special day for all. Their games were played in the town hall with chairs along the wall and the team's fathers guarding the hot stove in the corner.

Marie Weibeler Keeler	Belle Plaine	1924-1926

Marie began playing basketball against her mother's wishes. Her mother believed that Marie would make a spectacle of herself and bring disgrace to the family by playing in bloomers in front of a crowd. Her mother relented but never attended one of Marie's games. Because of Marie's persistence, her younger sister played with the support of both parents.

Gladys Dahl Clark	Cromwell	1930-1933
Blanche Line Kingsley	Cromwell	1928-1931
Eileen A. Maxner Grover	Cromwell	1929-1933

The three teammates recalled staging a sit-in when the school announced that the girls' team would be dropped. The team went down fighting the decision which eventually wiped out teams across the state by 1942.

Cromwell teammates and friends for life

Mae Beasman White, Gladys Dahl Clark, Blance Line Kingsley, Eileen Maxner Grover, Alice Ddahlman Carter

Bernice Halverson Wheeler	Delavan	1928-1930

Bernice played three-court basketball in pleated woolen serge bloomers that she remembers were very hot. She still loves the game of basketball.

Margaret Huffman Thompson	Gaylord	1923-1924

Margaret's team was called "The Bloomer Girls" because of the uniforms. Margaret said that she played basketball when she was 15 years of age and now she is 91 years of age. She didn't believe that basketball was detrimental to her health.

Ruth Bratrud Jacobson	Grand Meadow	1929-1930

Gaylord Hub reports on Recognition Ceremony

The GHS girls basketball team of 1924 was nicknamed "The Bloomer Girls." Their uniforms consisted of loose-fitting bloomers and middy blouses, according to team member Margaret (Huffman) Thompson, far right, back row. Others are: L-R, front: Ruth Borchert, Edna Lichtenegger, Leona Briard, Bertha Hyzer. Back row: Marie Spaude, Cora Warnke, Margaret Scheman, coach, Thusnelda Doering, Julie Huelskamp and Mrs. Thompson.

Ninety-one-year-old was a member of GHS girls basketball team in 1924 -

Margaret Thompson honored at girls basketball tournament

Margaret Thompson of Gaylord was among those recognized by the Minnesota State High School League at the girls basketball tournament held at Williams Arena in March.

In a ceremony at halftime of the AA championship, women who played interscholastic basketball in Minnesota from 1900-1942 were honored with a plaque.

Ninety-one-year-old Thompson was a member of the 1924 Gaylord High School team. A few of her teammates included Leona (Briard) Hansen and Ruth Borchert, both of Gaylord and Cora (Warnke) Lemberg, who now lives in Elysian.

According to Thompson, Gaylord High School's first girls basketball team was organized in 1907. The girls took a train to Arlington for their first game which they lost 9-6. That same year they defeated Henderson 20-0, the only shutout in Gaylord history.

There were six girls on a team, Thompson explained. Two forwards, two guards, a running center and jumping center. Forwards, the only players that could shoot, were not allowed to go past half court. They depended upon the guards to get the basketball.

Interscholastic basketball began in Gaylord in 1907 and ended in the late 1920's. It returned here in 1973.

Grand Meadow holds the state record of 94 consecutive wins between 1929-1939, never losing a single game playing against teams in southern Minnesota and Iowa. Ruth played on the first team to begin the winning record.

Oline Christianson Erickson   Greenbush   1923-1924

Oline traveled to the recognition ceremony from Badger, a trip of over 400 miles one way to Minneapolis. Oline's team played a 10-game schedule. It was one of the few teams to play full court with five players. Oline says she loved every minute of it.

Jane Varner Breimhorst   Jordan   1928-1932

Jane played on the district championship team in 1932 and on a chain, she wore the gold basketball that team members received at that tournament.

Mary Champlin Tonkin   Lake Crystal   1931-1932

Mary weighed 110 pounds in high school and, as she said, "ran her heart out" playing basketball. She was disgusted when basketball was dropped during her junior year because people said it was too strenuous for girls.

Ruth Norelius DeLapp   Luverne   1936-1938

As a fast and competitive player, Ruth scored 20 or more points a game and contributed to the championship teams at Luverne. Ruth says that playing basketball developed her confidence and self-esteem.

Mabel I. Erickson   Mabel   1928-1931

Mabel played five years of basketball and was the center of a fast-running team. Mabel still runs and works out regularly at her local fitness center.

Mary Dickmeyer Todnem   Mankato   1921-1923

Mary played high school and college basketball at Mankato. She began teaching and coaching at 17 years of age. Mary was a physical education teacher throughout her career and a leader in the 1960s to bring girls' sports back into school programs.

The Reunion was hosted by the Minnesota State High School League and the State Girls Basketball Coach Association. The association provided the memorabilia for each player.

Life-long friends Paula Bauck and Mary Todnem

Lorraine Stussy   Mantorville   1935-1936

Lorraine's team played a full schedule against area teams including archrival Kasson, and teams from Hayfield and Claremont.

Bernice Pexa	Montgomery	1926-1930
Irma Malone Foley	Montgomery	1929-1932
Eunice Washa	Montgomery	1929-1932

Bernice was a member of the 1930 district championship team as a high scoring forward. Irma played on the 1930 district championship team and was a fast player. She remembers a snowy day when the local train engineer offered to fire up the engine and take them to their game in a neighboring town. Eunice was the third member of the 1930 district championship team as the high scoring center. Eunice was also a softball player and golfer.

Alice Aanenson Lervold	Nielsville	1927-1928

Alice traveled to the reception from her home in Halstad on the North Dakota border, north of Moorhead. She played guard for Nielsville and Climax. They played full court, five-player rules. Basketball is a three-generation affair in her family. Fifty years after Alice played, she enjoyed seeing her daughter, Kathy Lervold-Goodrich coach New York Mills to a State Championship. Twenty years after this event, she watched her granddaughter, Heather Goodrich Schrider, play in the MSHSL State Girls Basketball tournament for Woodbury High School.

Adeline Kamish Musil	New Prague	1928-1930
Monica Janda Simon	New Prague	1926-1930
Ida Picha Welter	New Prague	1927-1931
Anne Sticha Juni	New Prague	1921-1925

These four women are four of the six players who played between 1927 and 1930 and all six still live in New Prague. Adeline's team uniform was black bloomers and a short-sleeved orange wool sweater. Ida remembers scoring the winning basket from the center line in a game with Belle Plaine. Anne's games were played in the local dance hall and they traveled by train to away games.

Paula Bruss Bauck	Roseau	1935-1937
Muriel Quanbeck Turritin	Roseau	1935-1937

Roseau's girls basketball team of the 1920's had been dropped by 1935, but Paula and Muriel played with the boys' teams. Paula was a pioneer in the renewal of girls' sports in the 1960's. As a coach in the 1970's, Paula's girls track and field teams were frequent region and state champions.

Saima Saari Savela	Toivola	1936-1939
Lillian Lahti Sorvari	Toivola	1933-1937

Lillian says basketball was great fun, but they didn't like rules for the two-court game. She says they wanted to play full court like the boys. Saima played running center. Her team won the county basketball championships in 1937 and also won trophies in volleyball, softball and track and field.

It was a day to honor and to remember. It was a day to link the past, present and future!

Third Quarter Free Throws

"Hi There!! Remember, there is only one quarter left after this one! Do you have your score for the first two quarters of free throws? Good!

Ready? Let's jump into the questions!"

Third Quarter Questions
1. What was the name of the man who said that women are lower on the evolutionary scale than men and are inferior to men?
2. What does LGBBAA stand for?
3. What was the name of the national organization with a Women's Division that recommended replacing girls basketball teams with Girls Athletic Associations?
4. Who was the NAAF-Women's Division's first chair person?
5. In what year did the NAAF-Women's Division hold its organizational meeting?
6. What was the name of the second Supervisor of Health and Physical Education who sent a letter to school superintendents reporting that they were making great progress in dropping girls basketball teams?
7. What did the superintendent of Grand Meadow do when he received one of the letters from the Supervisor of Health and Physical Education recommending that the school drop its girls basketball team?
8. What was the second interscholastic girls' sport that would lose its teams to the recommendations of the NAAF-WD?
9. Name the Chisholm swimmer who participated in the 1932 and 1936 Olympics.
10. What was the source of the taxes that would help the Iron Range schools to include swimming pools in their schools?
11. What do the letters GAA represent?
12. What was the name of the independent team that dyed their hair with henna?
13. What was the home town of Dolores Peterson Clack?
14. What was the name of the independent women's basketball team that Rapidan was scheduled to play?
15. What caused the above game to be cancelled?
16. What was the name of the independent women's basketball team in Brainerd?
17. Whose uniform is enshrined in the Naismith National Basketball Hall of Fame?
18. What was the name of the first women's professional basketball team in Minnesota?
19. Which one of the Sjoquist twins played for this team?

Score: Home_____ Visitor_____

Answers:

1. Darwin
2. Little Girl Bouncing Ball
3. National Amateur Athletic Federation
4. Lou Henry Hoover
5. 1924
6. Harold Jack
7. Tossed the letter in the wastepaper basket
8. Swimming and diving
9. Anne Govednik
10. Taxes from the iron mines
11. Girls Athletic Association
12. The All-American Redheads
13. Erskine
14. First National Bank (FNB)
15. A traffic accident returning from a game
16. Flying Queens
17. Elvera "Peps" Neuman
18. Minnesota Fillies
19. Lynette

Daughters of the Game

A Profile of Their Teams in Minnesota – 1891-1942

From 1891-1942, hundreds of high school girls basketball teams in Minnesota sprouted, flourished and disappeared.

Their history was nearly lost. It was buried in the personal scrapbooks of players, school yearbooks, the archives of local newspapers, and the memories of the women who played the game.

There was little opportunity for the women to tell their stories until now!!

As you read the stories from 148 of Minnesota girls basketball teams, try to picture the lives of these young women in the early 1900s. Their schools were usually in rural areas. The young women lived on farms, in small communities and larger towns and cities.

The common denominator was that girls loved this new game of basketball!

For many years, the horse and buggy, train or sleigh were the primary modes of transportation. Later, they would experience the invention of electricity, the telephone, and the early motorized cars and buses.

The social mores of society were changing. You'll see the change in the teams as clothing changed from heavy dresses and corsets to bloomers and lighter apparel. The struggle for suffrage would provide women with the vote and other legal rights. Their world would be impacted by World War I, the Great Depression, and the clouds gathering in the late 1930s for World War II.

The sports world was not always fair during that era. In some stories, the girls tell of making their uniforms while boys were provided school uniforms. They recall gathering parents to drive the girls' team to games while the boys rode in buses.

You'll also read of schools and parents who were equally proud of their teams and provided the same opportunities and support. Girls' and boys' games were played on the same night with teams traveling together by train, sleigh, bobsled, or early motorized vehicles. Parties were held after games and visiting teams were included. Banquets were held for both teams at the close of the season; team photos and season summaries were included in their school yearbooks. Local newspapers headlined the girls' games and provided game summaries and box scores.

In some areas, girls' teams participated in various forms of tournaments. The players received trophies, individual medals, and school letters. Some of their memorabilia survived the decades, carefully preserved in scrapbooks and in their family archives.

From the mid-1920s into the early 1940s, Minnesota schools began to respond to the recommendations of state and national organizations to drop their interscholastic programs and replace them with a recreational level program for all girls. Sad and poignant stories are told by the women when they came back to school in the fall, only to learn that the school would no longer sponsor a girls basketball team. One can feel the anger and frustration of young women who could not understand why adults would "do such a thing." The disappointment of their loss remained with them throughout their lives.

So, here are their stories as told by the women, the first daughters of the game!

The 148 team profiles include:

Adams, Agricultural Schools, Aitkin, Albert Lea, Alden, Alexandria, Arlington, Austin, Belle Plaine, Bigelow, Big Falls, Bigfork, Bingham Lake, Blooming Prairie, Braham, Brainerd, Bricelyn, Browns Valley, Brownton, Buffalo, Byron, Cambridge, Cass Lake, Clarkfield, Cloquet, Cromwell, Crookston, Crosby-Deerwood, Cyrus, Dawson, Deer Creek, Delano, Delavan, Derham Hall, Dodge Center, Duluth, Dundee, Eden Prairie, Elkton, Ellendale, Excelsior, Faribault, Franklin, Frazee, Freeborn, Gaylord, Glyndon, Goodhue, Grand Meadow, Grand Rapids, Granite Falls, Greenbush, Greenway, Grove City, Hancock, Hartland, Hayfield, Hendricks, Herman, Heron Lake, Hibbing, Hutchinson, International Falls, Jeffers, Jordan, Kasota, Lake Crystal, LeRoy, LeSueur, Litchfield, Luverne, Lyle, Mabel, Madison, Mankato, Mantorville, Marshall, Mazeppa, Milaca, Milan, Minneapolis, Montevideo, Montgomery, Monticello, Moose Lake, Morgan, Morris, Morton, Mountain Lake, New Prague, New Richland, New Ulm, Nielsville, North Branch, North St. Paul, Northfield, Northome, Olivia, Onamia, Owatonna, Paynesville, Pelican Rapids, Pine Island, Preston, Princeton, Proctor, Rapidan, Red Wing, Red Wing Seminary, Redwood Falls, Rochester, Roseau, Rose Creek, Royalton, Rush City, Sauk Rapids, St. Cloud Cathedral, St. James, St. Paul, St. Peter, Sherburn, Slayton, South St. Paul, Starbuck, Stillwater, Swanville, Thief River Falls, Toivola, Tracy, Two Harbors, Underwood, Verdi, Wadena, Wanamingo, Warroad, Waverly-St. Mary's of; Wayzata, Westbrook, West Concord, Wheaton, White Bear Lake, Willmar, Willow River, Wilmont-Our Lady of Good Counsel, Windom, Winona, Winthrop, Zumbrota.

Key: NA – name not available
photo identification: names of players are listed from left to right

For photo and graphic credits, see Credits, pp 357-366

Adams High School

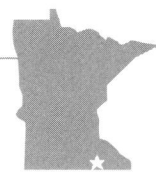

Southeastern Minnesota, south of Rochester; 20 miles southeast of Austin on #56
Years Represented: 1927-1932

Juletta Kasel, first generation American, was born in 1911 in Taopi, MN. She played basketball at Adams High School in 1927, 1928 and 1929, during grades 10, 11, and 12. The gymnasium had a small stage for the fans, sharing the gymnasium with the boys' team. The team practiced two days each week. Juletta and her sister, Catherine, had to walk three miles to their home in Taopi. On winter evenings this was a long, cold trek for the two girls.

Adams played neighboring teams from Le Roy, Elkton, Lyle, Grand Meadow and Rose Creek. The boys' and girls' teams usually traveled together to games by train or bus. Both teams were coached by the same coach. The girls wore long, dark, satin bloomers as a team uniform.

Inez Uglum, also a first generation American, was born in 1914 in Grand Meadow, MN. Her family moved to Adams where she played basketball in 1927 as a seventh grader until her graduation in 1932. She was tall and played a forward position the first years but moved to center for grades 11 and 12.

During those years, the team won some and lost some, always losing to Grand Meadow, who had an outstanding girls' team. The girls' team played 10 to 12 games a season.

Mr. Stockton was the coach of the girls' and boys' teams. The teams rode together on a bus to away games. The girls' game was first, followed by the boys' game. The team uniform had evolved to shorts and a v-neck top in the school colors of purple and gold, with white athletic shoes.

The photo of the 1932 Adams High School girls basketball team lists: Front: Norma Christianson, Myrtle Mattson, Louise Schneider, Florence Ulven. Middle: Priscilla Morgan, Myrtyle Quale, Margaret Schneider, Marian Thorson, Leone Halvorson, Inez Uglum. Back: Coach Ray Stockton, Alvira Anderson.

Adams 1932

The girls' game was played with three offensive players on one end and three defensive players on the other end of the court. The three offensive players were the only ones that could shoot and score baskets. The defensive players could only defend against the opposing players but could never score.

The team usually scored 35 to 40 points in a game. The rules allowed the ball to be bounced only once so passing was a key part of the game. Play began with a center jump, and there was also a center jump after each basket. There was a jump ball whenever the ball was tied up. There were no jump shots and no three-second lanes. Two free throws were awarded if a player was fouled in the act of shooting but other fouls earned just one free throw.

Basketball was the only sport available to girls in Adams.

The girls' team practiced in the small recessed school gymnasium in the center of the school. It had no room for spectators. The boys' team practiced downtown above the Krebsbach store or across

Main Street in Mike Schneider's large building. Both teams played their games in a large room above the town's furniture store with spectators sitting around the edge of the court. Both teams played on Friday night.

Inez's sister, Alice, played a few years before Inez, and the girls then wore large bloomers as their uniforms. Her younger sister, Lorraine, played a few years later. They were all good players.

After practice and games, they would get a ride home to their farm from their dad or a neighbor, but they often had to walk over three miles home.

Agricultural Schools

Morris, Crookston, Grand Rapids, Waseca, and the University of Minnesota
Years Represented: 1914-1920s

There were schools of agriculture in rural Minnesota sometimes referred to as "Ag schools." Their teams were called the "Aggies." Four schools were located in Grand Rapids, Morris, Waseca and Crookston. The schools in Morris and Crookston later became part of the University of Minnesota system.

The schools in rural Minnesota were open to high school level students and graduates from area high schools. School was in session on the campus only six months out of the year, from October to March, which allowed students to take part in the farming operations at home.

> Their teams were called the "Aggies."

The curriculum consisted mainly of agriculture, home economics, history, English, math, physics and chemistry, business and music. Students lived on campus in dormitories. The schools sponsored athletic teams for boys and girls.

The School of Agriculture at the University of Minnesota was established in 1888. It was a two-year program for young men at least 15 years of age. Young women were added later. The St. Paul schools reported games with the "Agriculture School."

In Morris, the school was called the West Central School of Agriculture and operated from 1909 to 1963. In Morris, an average of 400 students attended school and lived on campus. They sponsored West Central women's basketball. In later years, high school teams in the area list games with the "Aggies on their schedule."

The school yearbook, *The Moccas*in 1914, summarized that a girls' and boys' class tournament was held in the Armory that was beautifully decorated by the young women. One of their courses was home decorating.

The Moccasin described the inter-class tournament, with some 'tongue-in-cheek' language. "Excitement ran very tense when the girls, precisely at the stroke of eight, trotted forth very scantily clad in heavy bloomers, blouses, shoes and stockings. A gasp of astonishment went up from the bleachers at their audacity. Surprise and wonderment were printed on many faces as the boys were suddenly the recipients of the information that girls were bipeds."

Olive Peterson Kenely was in the Class of 1914. Mrs. Kenely's basketball team wore black caps with gold wings on them. Their colors were black and old gold. Team members of the West Central School of Agriculture are identified on a photo. Olive Farwell, left forward, is in the back row, first player on the left end. Other players listed as members were Bertha Kleven, captain, right forward; Olive Farwell, left forward; Cora Tessen, left guard; Ida Lewis, right guard; Alice Brandt, center; Agnes Reisrud, substitute.

West Central School of Agriculture 1914, Morris

Northwest School of Agriculture 1928, Crookston

Olive's daughter, Jean Peterson had saved her mother's information and asked her daughter Mary Ness to send for the book after seeing a request for information during the MSHSL State Girls Basketball Tournament. Olive lived to 101 years of age and was among one of the oldest graduate to return for reunions.

In Crookston, the Girls Basket Ball Team of 1928 included Clara Ness LaVoi, captain. Her son said that in 1999, his mother, age 91 years, could still dribble her basketball from the Northwest School of Agriculture. The photo includes a handwritten note, "Seventy years ago Grandmother's team could beat the Minnesota Gophers – Girls Basketball Team."

Aitkin High School

North central Minnesota; 20 miles north of Mille Lacs Lake on #169-
Years Represented: 1903-1936

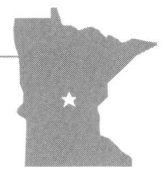

The first known Aitkin girls basketball team was in 1903.

GIRLS' BASKET BALL TEAM
"Our Girls"

Aitkin 1910

The photo identifies the players – Front: Naplin, Buringsrud, Breiland, C. Buck, Dobias. Back: Coach Gerber, Hamre, Blair, Viker, Badden, Clara Ness LaVoi.

In 1910, the team played two games. Both girls' games were against St. Cloud Normal with St. Cloud winning the first game 100 – 3 and the second game with St. Cloud winning 13-3. Verification of the first score appeared in a poem included in the high school yearbook.

Fourth Quarter 105

> **"St. Cloud vs. Aitkin**
>
> Put away the pretty bloomers
> That our basket ball girls wore.
> Hide the striped hose and sweaters;
> They're not needed any more.
> Pull the basket from the ceiling.
> Lay the Aitkin ball away;
> We've been handed a lemon.
> Who ever said we could play?
>
> Hazel Cluff was once our peaches,
> Lila G our sugar plum;
> Catherine Carlson and Miss Simpson
> Once our tutti-frutti gum.
> Bessie Seavey was our candy,
> Barbara, too, our sugar lump;
> They resemble two dill pickles
> Since that St. Cloud slump
>
> Miss McMullin, once the "frappe,"
> Dr. Dales our "woollen goods,"
> Now are down and out forever,
> Like babies in the woods.
> Hide the striped hose and sweaters,
> Let the pretty bloomers be;
> St. Cloud should be happy
> With one hundred to our three!"
> Author: W.B.G. (name unknown)

Aitkin 1928

The 1928 team photo listed members as Gladys Groves, Elsye Hyovalti, Susie Shisler, Ruth Kinney, Elmira Smith, Helen Holden, Harriet Wiita and Bernice Baker. Their game was a one-dribble, half-court game with uniforms that consisted of middy blouses and knee-length bloomers. Two photos from 1929 and 1930 showed the change from bloomers to shorts and v-neck tops.

Eva Turnock Alberg of Cromwell, MN, went to high school in Aitkin from 1932 to 1936. She recalls playing Crosby-Ironton, Brainerd and Deerwood, traveling by bus. Their gymnasium was on the top floor of the school.

In 1932-33 the athletic department set criteria for "winning a letter." Under the girls basketball section, it identified the rule and outlined the letter description. "A girl must play in one quarter for each major game played by the team. A minimum of six quarters must be played to be eligible for a letter.

Aitkin 1929

Aitkin 1930

Color: Chenille letter, maroon with black border, over a maroon background made of felt.

Style: Old English Script.

Six-inch script letter 'A' "

By 1936-37 a Girls Athletic Association (GAA) had replaced the basketball team. Points were earned for participation in athletics of all kinds. The purpose of the club was to further athletic interest for the girls in junior high and the sophomore class.

Albert Lea High School

South central Minnesota, 15 miles north of the Iowa border; on #35
Years represented: 1908-1921

Albert Lea 1908

Albert Lea 1909

The earliest photo in 1908 shows six girls in dark uniforms and a pennant with "ALHS – '08." A 1909 photo shows six girls in similar dark bloomer uniforms, standing with a young girl about three years of age.

The 1910 team photo provides the names of the following players. Front: first player unidentified, Ida Morrison. Middle: unidentified player, Laura Leusman, Helen Tingley. Back: Abbie Johnson, Myrtle Emmons.

A photo of the 1913 team shows six girls wearing dark bloomers with a white middy blouse and dark scarf. One is holding a ball dated "1912-13." The coach in the photo is identified as Miss Hanson. Players are: Helen Jensen, Sadie Devine, Laura Tveit, Agnes Stadhem, Marjorie Thompson, Beulah Westrum. The team played Wells, Owatonna and Waterville, winning three and losing two games.

Albert Lea 1910

Albert Lea 1913

Albert Lea 1914

The school yearbook, *Tiger*, reported on a 1913 game between Albert Lea and Wells." After the game the girls were entertained at one of our popular high school dances and the Wells team all reported a splendid time and the best of treatment."

The 1914 team consisted of Theodora Smeby, Alma Wall, Beulah Westrum, Marjorie Thomson, Esther Lundstrom, and Helen Jensen. Miss Hanson was the Coach.

The 1914 *Tiger* covered the girls basketball season with the following excerpt. "On December 12th, the girls played the Wells Girls team. The game was well played, considering that the girls had not been together in practice a half dozen times. The score was 15 to 16 in favor of Albert Lea. Beulah Westrum secured the entire score for Albert Lea by shooting eight field baskets."

The team lost the next game with Wells, 32 to 12 and won the next game against Austin, 13 to 11. The yearbook recorded that "The next game was at Owatonna, with the Pillsbury Girls. We won this by 23 to 4. Beulah Westrum was responsible for 21 points out of the total number. Esther Lundstrom did good work at forward."

The next game was with Lake Mills, won by a score of 27 to 2. The last game of the season was with the Pillsbury Girls, won by Albert Lea 19 to 17. Beulah Westrum was credited with scoring eight baskets.

The *Tiger* school yearbook also reported, "With a winning percentage of .733, the girls captured the championship of Southern Minnesota. Much credit is due Coach Hanson for the amount of work she has done in training the team. The girls worked unusually hard this year, and they deserved all that they won."

On January 12, 1917 the school newspaper, the *Ah-La-Ha-Sa,* summarized the first girls' game of the season,

"The game was slow at first until our girls became accustomed to the floor. Ruth Petran made the first basket, but it was void on account of a foul. From this time on to the end of the half the Blue Earth girls practically held the floor, in spite of Albert Lea's best efforts. The Albert Lea forwards did their utmost, but they just could not find the basket. In the second half Florence Gregg was put in for Ruth Petran, and May Jensen for Dorothy Augur, this leaving no substitutes on the bench. The guards did exceptionally well, holding their opponents down to two baskets. Just when the girls were doing their best and were beginning to lessen the distance between the scores Pearl Peterson sprained her ankle. As there were no substitutes on the bench the game had to be called."

The school newspaper featured the game with Owatonna on January 26, 1917: "Fooled by a slippery floor which had been waxed and danced on the night before, the Albert Lea girls, unaccustomed to such conditions, were defeated by the Owatonna girls by a score of 26 to 9. This is the second of the

Albert Lea 1920

local girls' games and they just cannot see how Owatonna defeated them, unless it was due to the condition of the floor."

Team members were Florence Gregg, Margaret Strand, Dorothy Augur, Georgia Petersen, Naomi Nelson, Pearl Petersen, Ruth Petran and May Jensen.

The 1920 team photo shows seven players and a coach. The school yearbook indicated that, "Albert Lea had a girls' team this year of championship caliber, a team of veterans that easily surpassed any girls' team Albert Lea has had for some time. The Influenza epidemic broke up the girls' schedule so they played only four games, but of these four they won three and lost the other after a hard fight." The team played the faculty women, winning by a score of 39 to 0; Northwood, winning, 24 to 9; Pillsbury Academy, losing 23 to 17; and Northwood, winning 18 to 14.

The *Minneapolis Tribune*, February 27, 1920, included an article with the headline, "The Other Side of the Story: Local Girl Who Witnessed Girls Basketball Game Gives Account in Own Words. Claims Game was Lost through Referee."

"In a rough game which included use of both words and fists, the Pillsbury Academy girls' team defeated Albert Lea at basketball here tonight, 12 to 17. One member of the visiting team was put out of the game on personal fouls, while several other players were close to the limit before time was called." The *Times Enterprise* newspaper expanded on the report "By Girl Eye Witness." It concluded, "As to the roughness, we have our share of the blame. It is our intentions to let it be understood that it was started by the Academy. Nevertheless, it is hoped that we will meet Pillsbury on our floor for a real game with what is a real referee."

The 1921 yearbook showed that the team was defeated in the three games played, but made a "good showing against some of the strongest teams in this region."

"After doing this project for my class, I now realize the great deal of work that is put into historical research."
Mary Thomes, student, University of St. Thomas, St. Paul.

Albert Lea 1921

Alden High School

South central Minnesota; 8 miles west of Albert Lea on #90
Years Represented: 1911

The 1911 Alden girls basketball team photo, provided by the Freeborn County Historical Museum, identifies the players as Hazel Lockwood, Isabel Mathison, Amelia Nielsen, Grace Robertson, Grace Sinderson (referee), Iris Howe, Ruth Anderson and Alphreta Cottrell.

The Freeborn County Historical Museum pointed out that the following statement was on the back of their file photograph. "1911 Southern Minnesota Champion Girls Basketball Team."

The uniforms were dark blue with white trim, and red silk ties.

Alden 1911

Alexandria High School

Western Minnesota on #94; 70 miles northwest of St. Cloud
Years Represented: 1904- 1935

Information on the Alexandria girls basketball team was located in the school yearbook, the *Alhias*, and at the Douglas County Historical Society.

Excerpts from the souvenir edition of *"100 Years at Alexandria's High School,"* included these statements.

1890 – 'No extracurricular activities – just education.

1894 – The girls' gym was in the attic of the school, until the superintendent caught the girls hanging from their knees on the bars. He shouted, 'Girls, I'm shocked,' and promptly closed the gym."

The 1904 Alexandria High School yearbook contains this statement: "Basketball was not played this year because the girls could not find a ball and the city council prohibited the boys playing in the city hall, which was the only place large enough that could be used."

From the Alexandria *Alexandrian*, February 1913: "On January 31, our girls and boys went down to Glenwood. Owing to the slippery condition of the floor, both teams were defeated. Glenwood will play a return game in a few weeks. Everybody turn out and help the teams redeem themselves."

The 1914 Alexandria High School yearbook, *Alhias*, summarized the girls basketball season, "This season the girls were unable to arrange a regular schedule, only three games being played. The last one was played at Battle Lake with a very close score, Alexandria winning by two points. The score was 8-10. The team members were Florence Noonan (center); Margaret Venoss and Luella Hougan (guards); Helen Wedum and Lorayne Larson (forwards); and Gladys Alton (substitute)."

"Owing to the slippery condition of the floor, both teams were defeated."
Alexandrian 1913

The 1915 *Alhias* recapped the season.

"The girls were only able to get one game with Villard whom they beat decisively. Villard had a win over Glenwood to their credit. Only one of last year's players, Luella Hougen, made this year's team. Esther Lundstrom was the only other veteran high school player. Both are seniors and will be missed greatly next season. Katie Augustine, a substitute forward, was a good all-around player and we wish we could keep her with us for another year. "Babe" Aberle, Marjorie Taylor, Annie Owen, and Adelia Hanson made up a scrappy, aggressive, and fast quartet. They will be hard to beat out for positions on next year's team. It is their great wish to make the coming first team a team of seniors. The team showed lack of practice together, but one could easily see that the material was there. We feel assured that with a long season they would have developed a fast and snappy team."

The souvenir edition of *100 Years at Alexandria's high school* indicated that, "In 1920, it was voted to install hot water tanks in the girls' showers."

The 1922 *Alhias* recorded: "This is the first year since 1916 that there has been any girls basketball at Alexandria." For the most part, classes played each other. However, a school team played St. Cloud, losing 12-9, and Osakis, winning 11-7.

Arlington High School

50 miles southwest of Minneapolis on Highway 5
Years Represented: 1907-1928

An article, "Hyst-orical Sports" by Mike Heibel, appeared in the *Arlington Enterprise* newspaper, circa 1991, and provided an excellent overview of the high school girls basketball teams in Arlington.

Heibel's articles reported, "Girls high school basketball in Arlington began in the first years of this century. The book, *Gaylord – Hub of Sibley County*, reported that one of the first girls basketball games in the county was in 1907 when Arlington defeated Gaylord 9-6."

In the decade of the 1920's, the Arlington girls' team would play its game before many of the boys' games. There were no post-season tournaments for girls' sports during that era.

Many of the girls basketball games were not covered in local papers. Sarah Meffert was a member of the 1920 Arlington team. Meffert said that all the home games were played in old Esser's Hall, which was where Brau's car lot is currently located.

"There was no place for us to change in the hall," said Meffert, "so we would go upstairs in my father's furniture store to change into our uniforms."

Meffert's furniture store was located where the present day Worm's grocery store is, only a block from old Esser's Hall.

Sarah said that the uniforms that they wore in the 1920's were "very roomy" black bloomers and full-vested white middies. She said that the bloomers were so baggy that if the opponents would stumble into them, they would have to worry that their bloomers would drop.

The article revealed, "Arlington's first organized girls basketball team consisted of forwards Eileen Altnow and Edna Geib; jumping center Eileen Ryan; running center Susanna Hensler; guards Ruth Sweeney and Sarah Meffert. Also playing for the 1919-20 team were Ruth Noack, Martha Stoefen, Clara Timm and Ruth Heidmann. Their coach was the high school principal, Gladys Miller." Susanna Hensler would become the coach in 1926-27.

Meffert said that the court was in three parts and that the players did not leave their respected areas. The basketball was thrown through the court with little or no dribbling.

The Arlington girls finished their first season with an unblemished 7-0 record. They defeated Winthrop twice (24-20 and 30-23), Norwood-Young America Central twice (14-4 and 16-3), Glencoe (29-26), Fairfax (18-13) and Hutchinson (19-10). Altnow was the leading scorer with 78 points.

In the 1920-21 season, the local girls had a 3-2 record with Altnow being the top scorer for the second straight season.

In the 1921-22 season, there were no articles available except for the season opener against Henderson. Arlington won this game 6-1. Members of this team were Martha Stoefen, Elinore Timm, Susanna Hensler, Edna Geib and Ruth Heidmann.

The local girls had a 4-2 record in the 1922-23 season. Their losses came against N-YA Central by the scores of 10-8 and 8-5.

The locals finished with even records in the next three seasons. They had a 4-4-2 record in 1923-24 and 3-3-1 in 1924-25. Two of three ties came against Gaylord. Helen Timm was the captain during these two seasons. Some of the other members during this period were Ruth Meyer, Ella Welch, Margaret Tierney, Lillian Theis, Cora Winters, Ellen Higgins, June Welch, Mabel Sweeney, Marie Ryan and Sylvia Geib.

In the 1925-26 season, Arlington finished with a 4-4 record. The team began this season losing its first three games. After this losing streak, the local hoopsters went on a rampage as they won their next four games by defeating Waconia twice (26-13 and 40-4), Henderson 28-8 and Gaylord 23-3. The girls ended the 1925-26 season with a 7-5 loss to their old nemesis, N-YA Central (Norwood -Young America).

Arlington 1926

1926 photo lists – Front: Luella Bandelin Anderson, Agatha Rieckert, Sophie Steffer, Helen Timm, Martha Bullert, Edna Timm, Irene Meyer Kienitz. Middle: Bernice Moorman, Trimbo, Clara Mueller, Muller, Norma Beseke; Carolyn Bandelin Matz; Carolyn Zimmerman, Helen Riechenbach, Leona Quast, two names missing. Back: Deloris Timm, two unidentified players, Bernice Eggen.

The 1927 photo lists – Front: Sophie Steffer, Agatha Reichert, Melva Geib, Lorraine Kienitz. Middle: Luella Bandelin, Irene Meyer, Bernice Peters. Back: Anna Sutton, Coach, Edna Timm.

The 1926-27 season was the most successful season for Arlington in the 1920's. Coached by Susanna Hensler, the locals cruised to a 10-0 record and defeated Waconia 24-7 for the unofficial district championship.

In the 1927-28 season, Arlington continued its winning ways by finishing with a 9-2-1 record. The girls had a 10-game unbeaten streak before they lost the final two games to Glencoe (16-9) and Belle Plaine (11-10). With the 10 straight victories from the season before, the Arlington girls had 20 straight games without a loss.

The 1929 team photo lists: Front: Anna Jasken, Bernice Peters, Violet Von Eschen, Lorraine Kienitz. Back: Mae Trimbo, Gertrude Higgins, Ruth Schauer, Ruth Sander, Grace Bunday, Coach. In its last competitive season in 1929, Arlington had a record of 1-4.

Arlington 1927

Arlington 1929

Arlington's girls basketball program had a record of 46-21-3 in the decade of the 1920's. Many of the games were not accounted for, so the record is unofficial.

The article concluded, "Some of the top players for Arlington in the 1920's were Velma Altnow, Edna Geib, Susanna Hensler, Helen Timm, Mable Sweeney, Edina Timm and of course, Sarah Meffert."

Special Stories

In the late 1990s, Luella Bandelin Anderson, her sister Carolyn Bandelin Matz and Coach Susanna Hensler made a surprise appearance in the television spotlight reminiscing about their high school basketball heydays.

It was no small feat to get them on the air!
The unsuspecting women were brought together by Luella's daughters, Juel Anderson and Karen Anderson, who drove their mother to Arlington to have Sunday dinner at Carolyn's home with Susanna, their former coach. But they didn't know what was ahead for them!

A buzz of activity preceded their arrival at the hall where the interview was secretly scheduled to take place. With the help of Dorothy E. McIntyre, Associate Director, Minnesota State High School League, KARE 11-TV producer Jane Helmke contacted the manager of Arlington's community hall where the women played basketball in the mid-1920's. He warned Jane that this town hall venue was being used for a wedding reception the night before and with a big football game on Sunday, the space wouldn't be cleaned up until Monday. Of course, "no" was not an option when there was an opportunity to interview these extraordinary women. So when Dorothy arrived mid-morning, Jane, now volunteer janitor, was sweeping debris from the main floor of the hall! Soon, Dorothy and Jane were both working to clear the area of leftover wedding cake, food and beverages. Family members stopped by and, learning of the surprise television interview, quickly began to help clear out chairs and remnants of their festivities.

At the appointed time, Luella, Carolyn, Susanna and the co-conspirators, Juel and Karen, arrived at the building where the women had competed in high school basketball decades before. The women's eyes sparkled as they looked around the hall. You could see the rush of memories from an era gone by suddenly revived in their faces and speechless first steps on their old gym floor. Two KARE-TV videographers, a reporter and producer caught every magical moment. As the former players and coach sat on chairs in the middle of the court, they described how the hall looked as it was during their playing days; how their parents and fans sat in chairs alongside the court with fathers in position to protect them from falling into the hot stove in one corner of the hall. Luella spoke about playing for fun but, she added with emphasis, "We played to win!" Susanna agreed.

When the segment was broadcast, the pride of these pioneers was shared with the television audience around Minnesota, western Wisconsin and into Canada, bringing even greater response from women who played decades ago.

Newspaper excerpts reprinted with permission by the *Arlington Enterprise*

Austin High School

Southeastern Minnesota, located 12 miles from Iowa border, 16 miles east of Albert Lea on Interstate 90
Years Represented: 1913-1915

The Austin High School yearbook, the *Austinian*, was first published in 1914. It included a photo of the Austin girls basketball team. The names of team members are not in order on the photo but included Frances Baird, Dorothy Barr, Corinne Jahren, Ida Hartje, Marcia Daigneau, Mable Barr, Gertrude Gleason, Captain; Marie Hartje, and Hazel Thomson. Coach: Miss Weedel.

Austin 1914

The team played nine games with Albert Lea, Lanesboro, Owatonna, Osage, Iowa and Pillsbury of Minneapolis, winning five and losing four.

The yearbook credited the coach by saying, "Miss Weedel, the able coach for the girls is deserving of praise from the High School. The success of the season is in no small part due to her patience and unselfishness in devoting her time to the girls' practice."

The *Austinian* included a photo of the 1915 team and provided information about the team and its season. In a list of milestones in the *Austinian*, it indicated that the girls basketball team played Carleton. Other games were with Albert Lea, Wells, Osage, Rochester, and Minneapolis with Austin winning a majority of the games.

The yearbooks from 1926 through 1942 include a section about the Austin Girls Athletic Association (GAA) and the teams in a variety of sports that competed by grade level teams.

Legacy

In 1976 Liz Erickson was a member of the Austin High School girls basketball team that participated in the first MSHSL State Girls Basketball Tournament. In 2005 Liz Erickson continues to enjoy the game with daughters, Megan and Annie, members of the 2005 Austin teams.

Austin 1915

Belle Plaine High School

Between Jordan and St. Peter, on Highway 169 to Mankato
Years Represented: 1920-1932

Virginia Irwin Kruger provided photos from her scrapbook of her teammates in 1923. The players are practicing outside with a large leather basketball. Individuals named in photographs, and their current residence, included Ruth King Brandel, Virginia Irwin Kruger of Minneapolis (1920-24), Mildred Hahn Mason of St. Louis Park; Harriet Hahn Schultz of Waconia; Viola Tolzman Bowser of Belle Plaine; Marietta Moore Sharkey of New Prague; and Marie Weibeler Keeler of St. Paul (1922-26).

The 1925 team photo included seven players and a female coach, holding the ball. Marie Weibeler Keeler is in the back row, fourth player from left.

Belle Plaine 1923 practicing outside

Belle Plaine 1925

Belle Plaine 1923

Fourth Quarter 115

The 1926 team photo includes seven players and one male coach. Marie Weibeler Keeler is holding the ball, center front row.

The 1927 team photo shows nine players and one male coach.

Belle Plaine 1926

Belle Plaine 1927

The 1930 team photo lists the following players – Front: Aurelia Sullivan, Helen Foedesi, Louise Widmer, Agnes Weibeler, Carol Olson, Ella Ische, Margaret Halloran, Florence Blume. Back: Dolores Engfer, Evangeline Nelson, Cordelia Maenke, Annabelle Klers, Marian Meierbachtol, Evelyn Steer, Betty Morearty, Rosemary Shaughnessy.

One official remembered from their games was Jack Grafs.

Games were played in dance halls or at the Knights of Columbus Hall. They would attach the baskets and backboards to the wall on either end of the room. The height of the baskets

Belle Plaine 1930

depended on how high the ceiling was. Marie recalled that at Carver, the ceiling was so low that the taller boys on the boys' team could touch the ceiling. Virginia said that their game officials came from Gustavus Adolphus College, St. Peter.

Schools played included Jordan, New Prague, LeSeuer, Henderson, St. Peter, Montgomery, Cleveland and Carver.

The court was divided into three courts with a team of two guards, two forwards, and two centers. The game began with a jump ball in the center. It was the running center's job to get that jump ball and get it to her forwards who couldn't go across the line. The forward's responsibility was to get a basket. If the guard from that side intercepted the ball, she could get it to her center to get to the forward on the other end. One dribble was permitted. After a basket, a jump ball was held in the center court.

The following letter was written by Marie Weibeler Keeler, May 1998.

"I attended Belle Plaine High School in the years 1922-26. During that time, I was one of those practicing basketball. We played the three-court game, two guards, two forwards and two centers, one the jumping center, the other the side center. I was a side center.

For the first two years, I was mostly a substitute. It was in September of 1925 that I was named co-captain of the team. We had officials at all games, home and away.

We played at Henderson, LeSueur, St. Peter, Jordan, New Prague, Montgomery and Carver.

Parents drove their cars and sometimes teachers drove. We went by train if weather was bad. Once I remember going by bobsled.

We stayed overnight once at St. Peter and once at Montgomery and New Prague. We had gone to both places by train. We left Belle Plaine at 6:00 p.m. St. Peter was on the same railroad line and we were there by 6:30 p.m. We stayed at the hotel where we were to be on the morning train at 6:00 a.m. One of the boys slipped into the coaches' room and turned off the alarm clock so we missed the train. There was no other train out of St. Peter until about 5:30 p.m. so we roamed St. Peter. The coach was mortified and the assistant principal promised us all kinds of discipline and dismissal from school for the 'guilty party.' As I recall, we all, girls and boys, had to write 100 times on the blackboard we would never do that again. We all had to write as no one squealed on the one who was guilty.

Another time we stayed overnight at Montgomery. Montgomery was on the Minneapolis-St. Louis train route. We were on the Northwestern train route and had to change trains at Miriam Junction. It is located southwest of Shakopee on #169, near the location of the summer Renaissance Festival. There was a big depot there. We arrived at night, so the opponent's team members each took one of us as her guest. We liked that as the mothers were very good cooks. We had a light lunch before bed and a breakfast before we left. The food was scrumptious. We always wished for a storm so we would have to stay overnight in Montgomery or New Prague.

One time we stayed overnight in New Prague. That also was on the M & St. L. This time we stayed in the hotel which is now the famous Schumacher Hotel. In our day there were no locks on the doors. Coaches, teachers and kids got no sleep that night. Someone was always coming into your room, mostly to aggravate the teachers.

None of the schools had gyms. We usually played in town dance halls. At St. Peter we played in the gym at Gustavus. That was keen. The halls were different sizes, some heated by a large stove in the corner, and low ceilings. One time at Carver, we were late getting there and the coach told us we would all have to change clothes together in the coal room. He would be there and we were to hurry and get our clothes out so he could turn off the lights and we would have to dress in the dark as the boys were also changing. When he turned the lights back on, one girl had a boy's uniform on and the boy had the girl's on. Of course, the kids exploded in laughter, but the coach was as angry as I ever saw anyone.

The girls wore black bloomers with elastic at the waist and below the knees. Our shirts were a pinkish orange and were worn with a black tie that was always in the way. The girls made their own uniforms and paid for the materials out of their own pockets.

We had a female coach in 1923-24 and in 1924-25, a male coach and female chaperone. In 1925-26 we had a male coach whose wife was chaperone. There were always a lot of other teachers along. The teams were well supported by faculty, hometown folks, parents and kids. The *Belle Plaine Herald* always gave us an honest opinion of all games.

The train trips were paid for by the school. If we were able to go by cars, the school did not reimburse anyone for driving. The boys and girls always traveled together. The girls played first. The boys cheered us on. When the boys played the girls cheered. There were no special cheerleaders.

One night the teams, coaches and chaperones traveled by bobsled to a game with Jordan. Marie recalled that "It was fun. We had real deep piles of hay and they told us to get our feet into the hay. We brought blankets, of course, and had a lot of fun. We managed to get girl-boy, girl-boy, even though we weren't going with that particular person. The coach was 'sweet' on one of the teachers, so they weren't paying much attention."

Marie continued,

"Our coach during my last year was great. I was chosen captain, so he called me aside one time and told me to tell the girls they could not play if it was 'that time of the month.' I almost died, because then we didn't talk about those times. We had just six girls playing that year, no substitutes, so if we told, there would be times there would be no games. So the girls decided they wouldn't tell. Now one of the girls usually had fainting spells at that time, so we girls decided if she fainted during a game, we would just say she was tired and was pretending. Her sister also played on the team and it was up to her to have 'smelling salts' along at that time. It happened twice during that year.

The official during our senior year was a friend of the coach, who was putting himself through college by officiating at all our home games. He was single, good looking and very nice to us girls, but if he had to call fouls he would and he would bawl us out later. It broke our hearts at first, but later we decided he wasn't against us and then we really played hard.

Our last game was with New Prague, a team we were never able to beat. This night, we decided this was our last chance, and we were going to do our very best. We all gave our watches to the coach's wife and she wound them around her two hands with the crystals on the inside of her hand. The game was close, up and down; we played our hardest but lost by a very small score. When we went to get our watches, the lady's hands were full of blood and every crystal on all the watches was broken. She had to go to the doctor to get all that fine glass out of her hands. We felt so sorry for her but she said it was worth it, as that was the best game we had ever played."

On March 17, 1932, the *Jordan Independent* reported that Jordan won the District Tournament in New Prague. Belle Plaine lost to Jordan in the first round game, 26-12 and defeated New Prague for the consolation honors, 14-13. They were presented with a basketball as their prize for the tournament. The team lineup included Koos, Enger, Effertz, Meier, Moelcher, Meierbachtol, Stier, Westhoff, Olson and Moenke.

Special Stories
In the 1990s Marie participated in several activities sponsored by the Minnesota State High School League. She spoke to the MSHSL Women in Sports Leadership Conference, was interviewed by several television stations and is an example of the benefits of girls' participation in sports. Marie has been a life-long sports fan.

Marie was fond of telling the story about the time when her mother learned that she was playing basketball. For two years, Marie had been telling her parents that she played the flute in the orchestra at the basketball games. Marie said she would wear her uniform under her dress and hide the flute in the bushes outside her house. Her parents didn't go to the games and her mother thought basketball was 'unladylike.' But one night during her junior year, Marie's father went to a game. She said she looked up into the stands and was shocked to see her father sitting there. As they walked home after the game, her father told Marie that she would have to tell her mother. Marie agreed but put it off until one fateful night when her father was driving their new car to see the game. Her mother decided to ride along in the new car. Marie didn't know if her father had warned her mother before the game, but she knew she was 'in for it' when she got home. Her mother asked Marie if she realized that she was embarrassing her family and making a spectacle of herself. Marie said it was the first time that she, as a young girl, went against her mother's wishes. But Marie said to her mother, "I'm sorry. But if that's how you feel, I'm going to embarrass the family and make a spectacle of myself because I am going to play basketball." Her mother's response was, "well, all right, but I am not coming to your games." Marie relates that when her younger sister, Agnes, wanted to play basketball, there was no opposition from her mother. Marie does regret that her mother never came to see her play.

In 2005, Marie Keeler is 96 years of age with a remarkable memory that has contributed greatly to the historical research on girls' basketball in Minnesota. She is the mother of 11 children, with 25 grandchildren and 35 great-grandchildren. Marie believes that her life should contradict the myth that participation in sports would be negative for the health of female athletes.

Marie was a member of a panel of sports pioneers at the 1998 MSHSL Women in Sports Leadership Conference. She was honored at a Lynx game in 2000 as a girls' basketball pioneer. She was featured in the October 2001 *Minneapolis-St. Paul Magazine*.

"Mother, I'm sorry that you believe that I am going to embarrass the family and make a spectacle of myself, but *I am going to play basketball.*" Marie Keeler

Bigelow High School

Southwestern Minnesota near the Iowa border; five miles south of Worthington on #60.
Years Represented: 1920's

Marilyn Hall provided the name of her oldest sister, Beulah O. Wick, who played on the Bigelow girls basketball team in the mid to late 1920's.

The family confirmed that Beulah was captain of the team and there was a championship involved. One of her sons has the trophy.

Big Falls High School

Northern Minnesota, 30 miles southwest of International Falls on #71.
Years Represented: 1939-1943

The hall was heated with two big barrel stoves covered with chicken wire. More than one player fell against them.

The Big Falls team played Northome, Kelliher, Littlefork, and Fort Francis.

Beryl Regal Miller played from 1936-39, traveling by bus to other schools. Games were played above a store. There was no gymnasium at school.

The uniforms were purple shorts and top. They traveled by school bus and had female coaches. They played in a hall with a low ceiling so they had to adjust their shots.

Norma Booth Krats recalls that when they couldn't play other schools, the girls played against the boys with boys' rules.

The hall was heated with two big barrel stoves covered with chicken wire. More than one player fell against them. She doesn't remember any serious burns. They had to run downstairs to an outdoor toilet. If they needed water, they had to get it in the tavern that was below the hall.

Norma played from 1939-43. The team was dropped by the school before her senior year. The reason given was that the game was too hard on girls.

Bigfork High School

Northeast Minnesota, 40 miles north of Grand Rapids on #38.
Years Represented: 1933

In the 1933 Grand Rapids High School yearbook, *Pine Needles*, page 47, there is a photo of the 1933 Bigfork girls basketball team.

The yearbook identifies the photo as "Girls' Basketball," and shows seven female basketball players in uniform. The yearbook's description says, "Basketeers Moors, H. Tagtgren, Evenson, Coolen, A. Skallman and V. Tagtgren. Pleasant, as you see, but very aggressive, these girls helped round out an unusually fine basketball season."

Bigfork 1933

Bingham Lake High School

South central Minnesota, located 5 miles northeast of Windom on #60
Years Represented: 1921-1929

The Windom school yearbook, the *Cricket,* reported that the Bingham Lake team played Windom from 1921-29.

The 1927 Bingham Lake girls basketball team photo lists – Front: Lily Redding Minion, Ruth Smith, Ivah Pietz Tjentland, Iva College, Bertha Smith Johnson, M. Phillips. Back: Miss Frasier, Mary Gravlev, Laverne Halvorson, Beatrice Smith, Gerdy Roll, Ethel Stephenson Messer, Professor Lauman.

Bingham Lake 1927

Blooming Prairie High School

Southeastern Minnesota, 14 miles southeast of Owatonna on #218
Years Represented: 1905-1934

A book, *Blooming Prairie Update*, was published in 1980, sponsored by the First National Bank of Blooming Prairie. The information was collected from area schools and individuals by Harold Severson, a long time employee of the *Rochester Post Bulletin*. Margaret Zwiener Hogan, a player in the 1930s, provided information about the Blooming Prairie girls basketball teams.

Blooming Prairie 1905

Members of the Blooming Prairie girls basketball team in 1905 were identified as - Lena Zweiner, Agnes Leahy, Anna Langan, Ina Solberg, Kate Keefe, Marie (N/A), Myrtle Fuller, Ethel Murphy, Kate Hanlon and Nan Keenan. Miss Lansing was their coach.

The photo of the 1925 team members included Emma Mortenson, Ruth Nelson, Alice Grass, Ione O'Malley, Margaret Schrier, Emily Engle, Marie Schrier, Ardella Ingvalson.

Margaret Zwiener Hogan played in the mid 1930s. In 1933-34, the lack of funds for uniforms resulted in the team playing in their gym outfits. The team photo listed members as - Elene Peterson, Signe Benson Pelinka, Ida Wylie, Irene Zwiener Wakefield, Juliann Johnson, Orene Hanson Lickteig, Helen Jolson Konz, Ruth Bales Thompson, Captain Margaret Zwiener Hogan, Lola Belle Bibus, June Granger, Coach.

Blooming Prairie 1925

Blooming Prairie 1934

The team played the two-court game. A neighboring school of Hayfield played the five-player game. According to Margaret, the Hayfield girls always won because they were permitted to practice against the boys' team and consequently soon developed considerable skills.

Margaret recalled that Ruth Woods, a coach and English teacher, was the one that persuaded the Blooming Prairie school board to give the girls basketball after Margaret and other girls had agitated for the program. She added, "However, after a few short years, no more girls basketball at Blooming Prairie. It seems the state said no more varsity for girls as it 'jarred their organs!' So the local school board obeyed. Hayfield and Grand Meadow continued."

Braham High School

50 miles north of metro area on #70
Years Represented: 1928-1929

The team played with two courts, guards and forwards could not cross the line into the other half of the court. The new school had a gymnasium.

Goraline Johnson Peterson played basketball from 1927-29. The uniforms, black bloomers and a middy top, were provided by the school. Goraline said her team had female coaches.

Braham 1927

The 1927 team photo lists – Front: Merle Mattson, Joyce Ostrom, Genevieve Johnson, Helen Sundberg, captain; Clarice Skjod, Claribelle Nebel. Back: C.C. Wiberg, Coach; Ordella Malm, Evelyn Johnson, Evelyn Olson, Gladys Mattson, Miss Mossberg, Assistant Coach.

The 1928 team photo lists – Back: Gertrude Horman, coach, Ordella Malm, Merle Mattson, Goralene Johnson, Alice Skjod, Evelyn Olson, Evelyn Johnson. Front: Genevieve Johnson, Lucille Skjod, Fern Medeen, Claribelle Nebel, Lorraine Findley. The girls' team played four games, winning one, tying one, and losing two.

Braham 1928

The 1929 photo lists the following players – Front: Ordella Malm, Margareta Erbstoesser, Claribelle Nebel, captain; Fern Medeen, Alice Skjod. Back: Margaret Olson, Dorene Mossberg, Gertrude Horman, coach; Lucille Skjod, Goralene Johnson. Their opponents were Cambridge and Pine City. The team won three games, tied one, lost three. They played Ogilvie, North Branch, Cambridge, and Milaca.

Goraline said, "I enjoyed all sports and there wasn't a lot to do in the 1920's so it was fun. It was something to go to and be with friends. I remember when one of our forwards was taking a free throw and the ball got entangled in her bloomers. Not funny then, but now we can laugh."

The benefits of playing on an interscholastic team, according to Goraline were, "I think it gave me self-esteem and confidence to perform in front of an audience.

Special Stories
The Braham yearbook stated in its 1927-28 edition that," The *boys* will find little difficulty in adapting themselves to the new rules in regard to dribbling. Previously, the rules in boys' basketball have not restricted dribbling, but under the new set of 1928 and '29, only one dribble can be taken."

Braham 1929

Brainerd High School

60 miles north of St. Cloud on #371
Years Represented: 1902-1928

The Brainerd girls' basketball team was started as early as 1902. The photo shows the team of nine with a small girl holding the basketball dated "1902." No names are available.

An interview with Kay Nolan Wetter provided information of the teams from 1924-28. Her team of nine girls wore "store-bought" black satin bloomers with elastic at the knees to cover the tops of long black stockings. The stockings were held up by garters. If they pulled the bloomers above their knees, they risked the displeasure of their parents and the school. The sailor blouses were made of heavy materials with uncomfortable flaps and ties. Their tennis shoes had flat soles and were laced up like hockey skates.

Kay recalled that she occasionally drove the car through mud and roads full of deep ruts.

Brainerd 1902

Nolan's father had reservations about the rough nature of their game and Kay remembered that he would say, "Basketball is too physical for the girls, they should be playing the piano."

There were no lockers so the girls wore the uniforms under school clothes all day. Showers/baths came only upon their return home after the game.

It was a two-court game, with three guards and three forwards that were limited to playing in their own half of the court. Players could dribble once and could not touch another player without risking a foul.

Members of the 1926 team were: Miriam Michael, Alta Storm, Iva Trask, Katherine Early, Grace Alzant, Katherine Nolan, Helen Beggs, Gladys Reuter. Coaches: Miss Cederstrand and Mr. Rosel. Teams played included: Crosby-Ironton, Staples, and Motley. Season totals: Brainerd: 150; opponents: 60.

The game attracted many enthusiastic fans who packed the stands to cheer their teams. Alta Creger Heikkenen was one of the little girls in the stands, watching with starry eyes, and waiting for the time when she could play. Kay Nolan Wetter was her basketball idol.

Excerpts from Newspaper
The following information is reprinted with permission from the *Brainerd Daily Dispatch*. The first article appeared on January 10, 1993, written by Mike Bialka.

The article titled, "Brainerd to salute female athletics," noted: "Female athletes throughout history have faced resistance and adversity in response to their desire to participate in athletics. According to Minnesota State High School League research, females in the early 1900s had fought for the right to play and had won. MSHSL research also indicates that right was lost in the late 1920s when President

Hoover's wife and the National Amateur Athletic Federation created a 'dark hole' which endured for nearly 50 years."

The article reported that a committee of 16 women planned a local celebration of National Girls and Women in Sports Day by celebrating the history of Brainerd area women's athletics. A program was conducted which included a basketball game in which each quarter was played using a progression of rules and uniforms of various eras.

The second article in the *Brainerd Daily Dispatch* appeared on January 13, 1993, written by Michelle Willette.

The article titled, "The school board wanted them to be ladies," stated:
"The Roaring '20s.
- A decade rich with history.
- Flappers with short hair and shorter skirts dancing the Charleston.
- Speakeasies that sold bootlegged liquor during Prohibiton.
- Jazz Music.
- The automobile.
- Silent movies.
- And Brainerd girls basketball.

From 1924-28, Kay Nolan Wetter and the Brainerd High School girls' basketball team made history, doing what no Brainerd woman athlete would do again until 1972.

Wetter and her teammates played girls basketball – competitively."

The article went on to say, "Girls basketball had been nothing more than a lesson in physical education until the day that nine short-haired girls donned bloomers and tennis shoes, road-tripping in a Model-T Ford to play their first game against Crosby. And although that first year handed the team two disappointing losses, the fighting spirit of Brainerd girls basketball had been born. But not without complications. Despite the seemingly progressive times, girls' sports made its debut to the shock of many less-open-minded folk. Girls were to act like ladies, not ruffians chasing basketballs with their bare knees teasing the minds of young men. How uncouth."

Alta Creger Heikkenen and Kay Nolan Wetter exchanged stories and memories of playing basketball. Nolan played on the team from 1924-28 and was Heikkenen's idol when she was growing up. After the 1928 season, the high school and its gymnasium burned down, leaving the boys to practice and play in empty stores and the basement of the YMCA, but no space for the girls' team. When the school was rebuilt several years later, Heikkenen recalls going with their physical education teacher, Margaret Jackson, to the school board to request reinstatement of the girls' team. They were informed that the team would not be reinstated and that girls would play only in intramural programs. The reason given was that girls playing basketball was an inappropriate display of their bodies and wasn't ladylike. Heikkenen described how heartbroken the girls were with the decision.

Nolan and Heikkenen continued to play basketball with an independent city team called the Flying Queens. The team was composed of players who were from an unbeaten season during their high school years.

During their adult years, they supported their sons' athletic opportunities and were supporters when the Brainerd girls basketball team was reinstated in the 1970s. They watched the Minnesota State High School League's (MSHSL) State Girls High School Basketball Tournament on television and could only wish that they had had the opportunity, noting that they had simply been born too soon.

Kay reflected that she thought it was great that today's generation of young women can play the game. She said, "We were just born too many years too early!"

In March of 1993, the women were invited to the MSHSL State Girls Basketball Tournament at the Met Center, Bloomington. It was a nostalgic moment when Kay Nolan Wetter was interviewed on television by Janet Karvonen Montgomery, one of the state's premier players from New York Mills.

Newspaper excerpts reprinted with permission from the *Brainerd Daily Dispatch*.

Bricelyn High School

30 miles west of Albert Lea on #253
Years Represented: 1928

Alice Armstrong Anderson played on the 1928 Bricelyn girls basketball team.

Bricelyn 1928

The 1928 photo shows a team of nine girls, most wearing letter sweaters. They are identified as - Lillie Thompson, Nedra Lund, Alice Armstrong Anderson, Alma Peterson, Bea Anderson, Birdie Abrehampson, Violet Thompson, Marion Peterson, Miss Gugesberg, Coach. Alice is in the front row, holding the ball.

Alice said that she and Violet Thompson were guards. Only forwards could shoot to score points. Alice fondly recalled that after the game, lunch was served.

In 2004, Alice was 94 years of age.

Browns Valley High School

On the South Dakota border, 40 miles south of Breckenridge on #28.
Years Represented: 1926-1930

Kathryn Meade Shinn played on the Browns Valley team from 1926-29. The game rules depended on the game played by the opponent's team. The first games were full court where players could run the full length of the court and were allowed dribbles. Later, games were played as a two-court game.

Kathryn Meade Shinn recalls that they played basketball outside until they had a coach, a female English teacher, who had previously played basketball. The coach "stirred things up" and insisted the girls have their games inside, play other schools and have practice time provided in the gymnasium. A member of the board liked basketball and approval was received. The team would practice at noon and then after school. Occasionally, they would trade times with the boys.

In the two-court games, Kathryn played guard and guarded the center. The team usually traveled in Model T's, with games sometimes as far as 50 to 60 miles away in South Dakota.

The boys usually played first and the girls' game was last. The girls' and boys' teams traveled together. Kathryn said, "The boys played first; either we had to wait or they would have to wait, which they would rather not do. It depended on who the coach was for the boys' team."

Kathryn recalled staying overnight once in Morris when a snowstorm closed roads. Kathryn said, "When you were going with a Model T car, it was a little distance."

The team uniforms began with bloomers and ended the last two years with a big change to shorts and a v-neck top, knee-high socks and athletic shoes. Some community members said it was "scandalous" and "were shocked," creating quite a stir in town. Kathryn said, "The girls' and boys' team were about equal in popularity. Of course, as soon as we got the shorts, everybody in town had to come to see that, because that was 'disgraceful.'" Kathryn recalls that her father didn't have any problem with the team wearing shorts. Her mother "held her breath a bit" but didn't object. The girls paid for their uniforms and kept them after the season was over.

> "Of course, as soon as we got the shorts, everybody in town had to come to see that, because that was 'disgraceful.'"
> Kathryn Meade Shinn

Kathryn said, "My dad and my mother and most all of the relatives even backed us up to the tip top of our heads. As long as it was some of their family playing, they stood behind us."

In the 1928 team photo, Kathryn Meade Shinn is identified as the player on the far right end. In 1929, Kathryn is the second from the left. In the 1930 photo, she is in the back row, on the left end.

Browns Valley 1928

Browns Valley 1929

Browns Valley 1930

The schools played were Wheaton, Beardsley, Ortonville, Graceville, Wilmont, South Dakota, Sissiton, South Dakota and Clinton. The season was four months long. A tournament was played at Morris and Ortonville.

Kathryn told that a local photographer took lots of pictures of the team. The team was supported by other students and the people in the community. The boys' team would help the girls with shooting and defensive skills.

Kathryn's favorite memories were that she made the team, the attention from younger students and teachers and that the team members were "heroes."

Special Stories

When a group of boys from an opponent's school came over looking for trouble, Kathryn recalls, "We knew that they had come to boo us and things like that, you know, so we saw what they drove up in, and we knew what they were fixing to do. They were getting ready to do something against our team. So a couple of us found out where they were parked and they had the old screw type gas tanks. So we just got a little bit of sugar and waited until we saw they were inside looking the teams over. Then we put about a cup of sugar in their gas tank."

Brownton High School

60 miles west of Minneapolis on #212.
Years Represented: 1907-1928

The first organized girls basketball team in Brownton High School was in 1906-07.

Brownton 1907

The 1906-1907 photo lists – Front: Mabel Brown, Esther Duehn, Lizzie Teich, Virginia Baker, Gertrude West, Myrtle Cook. Back: Ida Streich, Leonora Ewald, Marjorie Butler, Mabel Butler, Miss Waller, Coach, Anna Knoerr, Bessie Dieter, Ella Neitzle.

A 1922-23 photo lists the team as District Champions – Front: Emily Etter, Frieda Zander, Bessie May, Corrinne Zimmerman. Back: Katherine Sheldon, Ilo Zimmerman, Gertrude Horman, Miss Hallberg, Coach, Lucille Zimmerman, Goldie Streich, Florence Zimmerman. The team outscored opponents by 172 points to 48.

A 1923-24, photo lists – Front: Frieda Zander, Bessie May, Emily Etter, Corinne Zimmerman. Back: Goldie Striech, Lucille Zimmerman, Gertrude Horman, Ilo Zimmerman, Florence Zimmerman.

A 1924-25 photo lists – Front: Cora Nagel, Florence Zimmerman, Gertrude Horman, Frieda Zander, Mary Hagen. Back: Ethel Kohls, Corinne Zimmerman, Superintendent/Coach R.W. Handke; Emily Etter, Bessie May.

Brownton 1923

The 1925-26 team photo lists – Front: Cora Nagel, Bessie May, Frieda Zander, Ethel Kohls, Corinne Zimmerman, Florence Wall, Mary Hagen. Back: Supt. Handke, Coach, Florence Zimmerman, Hazel Wall, Miss Yennie.

Corinne Zimmerman Janke played in 1921-26. Corinne recalls that the game began with three courts and became a two-court game. They had two referees from Minneapolis.

Schools played were Buffalo Lake, Hector, Silver Lake, Gibbon, Stewart, Green Isle, Hutchinson. The team traveled by car and sometimes the team stayed overnight with the other team's families. They played from fall to spring.

The 1926-27 team photo lists – Front: Mildred Deuhn, Hilda Groth, Ruth Zimmerman, Eleanor Booth, Captain. Middle: Emma Zander, Helen Hochsprung, Hazel Wall. Back: Miss Waldo, Coach, Arline Zimmerman, Helen Arnold, Hilda Zander, R.W. Handke, coach.

Brownton 1924

Brownton 1925

Brownton 1926

Hilda Zander Anderson's sister, Frieda Zander Lord played on the first team. Hilda's father had a grocery-confectionery store and the girls worked in the store before school, noon, after school and weekends. Hilda could not play until her sister graduated and could work in the store.

Hilda describes the game in 1924-28 as a three-court game with players limited to their section. The school provided uniforms that were black knit shirts trimmed in orange and black knee-high shorts.

The girls' and boys' teams traveled together with the girls' game played first. Parties were held after the games and they got to meet many other players. She remembered the fun they had and that "winning wasn't a matter of life or death."

In the *Todd County Bulletin*, February 28, 1924, Supt. R.W. Handke praised the conduct and sportsmanship of players and fans. "The girls are above criticism. Not only have they developed a team that is the best in this section of the state who has acquitted themselves with glowing honor in all games, but they have acted like real ladies in all games.

Brownton 1927

Their scholastic work is far above the standard. The team is (composed of) the best students in the school and believe in good hard work whether playing basket ball or school work. They are girls who will acquit themselves with honor whatever their future vocations may be. Eight games won and one lost is their record."

Special Stories

Frieda Zander Lord recalls, "I loved every minute of it. We had a great team and did most of the winning. We were allowed to practice a lot and it really helped, especially shooting baskets. We had great coaches too. One man wanted to bet with our coach that I couldn't shoot 15 baskets and never miss. He wanted to bet 100 dollars and my coach said, 'I'd bet it in a minute but we're not allowed to bet.' She said that her father was on the school board and he never missed a game. The other fathers attended most of the games too.

Freida said," Basketball gave us confidence and self-esteem, besides being good for us. Keeping students busy with sports is the best ever."

The women believe that the girls' team was discontinued either in 1928 or shortly thereafter. They recalled, "They said basketball was too strenuous for girls."

Buffalo High School

35 miles northwest of Minneapolis on #55
Years Represented: 1911-1932

The first team was organized in 1911.

In a 1914-15 photo, one player is identified as Myra Little, second from the left. Teams traveled by train to Annandale and Maple Lake and stayed overnight either in the homes of players or a hotel, returning the next day. Later, a bus was used to transport the teams.

Buffalo 1915

Ann Studt, a graduate of Winona Normal School, coached the Buffalo girls' basketball team from 1919-21.

1923-24 photo - Armella Welkele, M. Elsenpeter, Mary Nagel Stark, Alma Pickruhn, Coach Hawker, Ethel Anderson Cummings, Eileen Catlin, Margaret Sexton, Vera Learned Ilstrup, Minnie Templin. The school yearbook indicated it was "one of the best ever representing Buffalo High School".

The *Wright County Journal-Press* provided an article on March 9, 2000, written by John George, with a headline, "What's it like to be a Basketball pioneer? Ask Buffalo resident Vera Ilstrup-Templin."

The article opened with the following: "Picture this. It's the early 1920s. The City of Buffalo has just purchased a new bus and loans it out to the school. A dedicated bunch

Buffalo 1924

of athletes, boys and girls alike, are on their way to Howard Lake, a mighty journey in those days, for a basketball game.

Without the benefit of Doppler radar, or even a radio, the team has no idea they are heading into one of the worst snowstorms of the year. Determined to get to their game, the boys take turns walking in front of the bus to guide it down the road. The team finally arrives at the Howard Lake gym and finds a full set of stands waiting for them at 9 p.m., several hours after the game was scheduled to begin.

The girls played first and won, earning the Wright County Championship; then the boys play their game. They won, then they reloaded the bus to arrive back in Buffalo in the wee hours of the morning.

'I loved it,' Buffalo native Vera Learned Ilstrup-Templin said. 'I loved everything associated with playing the game. Being with friends, the competition, going to games. I loved it all.'"

The article continued, "Vera is a fantastic woman who's 92 years young." In 2005, Vera remains a fantastic woman at 97 years young.

Vera played throughout her high school years on the Buffalo girls basketball team and one year at St. Cloud Teachers College.

The 1925-26 photo – Front: "Babe" Vivian Robarge, Doris Berg Mithun, Vera Learned Illstrup, Eileen Catlin, Orpha Hendershott Brown, Mildred Elsenpeter. Back: Dorothy Mattison, Jennie Ellen Sturges May, Mary Swanson Hastings, Marguerite Elsenpeter.

Buffalo 1926

The team played in a small gym with a high ceiling and a stage at the end. Vera Templin recalled two black eyes, one from running into an obstruction under an overhanging balcony and the other from tripping over the feet of spectators.

Howard Lake and Rockford had big rooms over another building, like a dance hall. Maple Lake and Annandale had gyms.

Their uniforms were middies, square collar down the back with big bloomers made of wool serge. Later on, the wife of the town doctor, "Mrs. Dr. Catlin," made purple corduroy knickers with a white heavy rayon blouse with a purple corduroy collar. Vera says, "We thought we were pretty foxy."

Vera described the game as two-court at the beginning, but after they practiced several times with the boys, they practiced with full court in 1925. They continued to play half court with others towns: Howard Lake, Maple Lake, Annandale, Monticello, Rockford and Kimball.

The team traveled in cars named Franklins and Hutmobiles. Then a bus route was started. The first bus for the team had a cab with the driver and an assistant with him. Along both sides of this long bus were wooden seats; the boys sat on one side and the girls on the other. Coaches and cheerleaders were in the back.

The team traveled in cars named Franklins and Hutmobiles.

A social time with lunch was held after the games to get to know the players from the other towns.

Dr. Catlin, the town doctor, Mrs. Dr. Catlin and others ensured that the girls' and boys' teams received news coverage.

During the time that the girls were getting ready for their county championship and last game with Annandale, the boys were going to the state basketball tournament where they played in the finals at Carleton College, Northfield. The girls lost to Annandale by one point and it ended their season.

The 1926-27 photo of County Champions includes: Marie Peterson Dickson; Lois Keeler Bauer, Mildred Elsenpeter, "Babe" Vivian Robarge, Emma Flynn Stuhre, Mildred Johnson, Mary Swanson Hastings.

Buffalo 1927

The 1929-30 photo lists – Front: Eloise "Honey" Anderson Mattson, Lois Keller, Dorothy Burshek, Viola Thompson, Winifred Roth. Back: Delores Robasse, Catherine Pouliat, Elmyra Hayes, Joyce Courrier. The team finished second in the county championship.

Buffalo 1930

In the 1930-31 photo, team members are – Front: Miss Turbak, Maureen Johnston, Eloise "Honey" Anderson Mattson, "Babe" Hayes, Ronald Fredericks. Back: Olive Flynn, "Babe" Anderson, Catherine Pouliot, Bernice Peterson, Joyce Courrier, Leona Elletson, Delores Robasse. The team was the County Champions.

Eloise "Honey" Anderson Mattson played from 1929-32. In 1932, the Buffalo girls basketball team achieved notoriety by being the team to end the 73 game winning streak of the Litchfield girls basketball team. The *Litchfield Independent Review*, 1932, headlined the loss, "Girls Drop First Game in Six Years of Play. The Litchfield High School girls basketball team, after playing nearly six years of basketball in which every game was a victory for the Green and White, failed to win what would have been their 74th victory at Buffalo last night."

Buffalo 1931

Special Stories

Vera described a practice outside with the team wearing bloomers, middies, anklets and athletic shoes. The male coach had the team doing their warm-up exercises. A woman across the street watched them doing their exercises. They learned that she was a member of the school board, reporting to their next meeting that the girls were out there 'half-naked jumping up and down in front of that man.' And she strongly recommended that it be stopped. The result was the team had to wear long stockings after that incident.

When the Litchfield team lost its first game in six years, the *Litchfield Independent Review* noted that the Buffalo squad was "led by 'Honey' Anderson, the scintillate star forward."

Vera described how, prior to a game, she was experiencing a lot of pain in her side. Vera said, "When Dr. Catlin examined me, he said, 'Oh my word, you have to have surgery and get that appendix out or it's going to burst.' I protested that I had a game." Vera said the doctor removed her appendix, taped her up with bands of tape like a tight corset so she could hardly breathe. The doctor said to Vera's mother, "Now, we've got her ready." Her mother said, "Ready for what?" The doctor replied, "To play. We need her too much." Vera recalls that she played that game and the rest of the season with tape wrapped tightly around her.

Vera said after she played basketball, "Self-confidence carried over into the rest of my schooling. I felt if I could do that (basketball) I could get up and do anything in class too, and I did."

Eloise "Honey" Anderson Mattson, 1929-32 recalled that her team played the last season before the team was discontinued by school authorities because it was said that "basketball was too much for females."

Newspaper excerpts reprinted with permission by the *Wright County Journal-Press*, Buffalo, and the *Litchfield Independent Review*

Byron High School

7 miles west of Rochester on #14
Years Represented: 1922-24

Leona Siewert Gray played her freshman and sophomore years on the Byron girls basketball team and her junior and senior years at Dodge Center. During Leona's playing years, the team played three-court, two-court and full-court rules.

"The gym in Byron was about the worst with benches around the side and people packed the two stairways that came down from the upper hallways." Leona Siewert Gray

Teams played were Mantorville, Pine Island, Kasson, Hayfield, Medford, Eyota, Elgin, and Stewartville. The coach was female. The team members received school letters.

Teams traveled by car when roads were open and by sleigh or train during bad weather.

On occasion, the girls' team stayed overnight in homes of the other team's players.

Leona said "the gym in Byron was about the worst with benches around the side and people packed the two stairways that came down from the upper hallways."

The uniform was black wool serge bloomers, a white middy blouse with sailor collar. The school bought the boys' uniforms but the girls bought their own.

Leona reminded us that the rules didn't permit players to take the ball away and they weren't to be too close to the other player. She preferred the half court game better to the original three-court game.

Byron 1924

A postcard of the 1924 team shows: Front: Leona Siewert Gray; Joyce Cutting Knutson. Middle: Miss Denmire, Coach; Stachea Mathew Manual; Ethel Whitcomb Fuchs; Helen Smith Benson. Back: Mabel Siewert Lienau, Lucile Parker Whitcomb, Mary Conway.

During her sophomore year, they played 16 games and won them all. On one Friday night, they traveled to Mantorville with a team of horses and sleigh and went cross country seven to eight miles. They had foot warmers and blankets and sat in the hay.

The host school determined the game rules for the night. Leona said, "One Friday, we went by train to Eyota and played girls' rules. We stayed over night and went by train to Elgin and played boys' rules." Leona recalls, "In Elgin with boys' rules, we lost one of the five off the team with fouls.

Byron guarding drill

There were only four of us and we were one point behind. My sister was a pretty good sized gal and she had pretty good-sized hands. There were two guarding her. She came out with the ball in one hand, threw it up and it went in and we won the game."

"One Friday, we went by train to Eyota and played girls' rules. We stayed overnight and went by train to Elgin and played boys' rules."
Leona Siewert Gray

Leona said there were no buses and they sometimes traveled by car with parents driving the team. One time her brother was to take the team in their car. Her brother had to milk the cows and was late getting started to Hayfield. He decided to go cross-country to save time. Leona remembers that the car slid off the road and the girls had to get out and push the car back onto the road. When they got to the school, they were so cold the coaches sent someone out to get them hot egg sandwiches to eat before they played.

The girl's team played as many games as the boys and they helped earn money for the school. Leona thought the girls' team should be able to go to state too, but there was no tournament for the girls.

When Leona shared her memories in 1999, she was 90 years of age.

Cambridge High School

50 miles north of the metro area on #65
Years Represented: 1928

The 1928 Cambridge High School yearbook included an article with a headline, "Girls Win District Championship."

The article pointed out, "After a lot of earnest effort on the part of the girls out for basketball and a considerable survey on the part of the coach, Miss Selander, the final selection made was as follows: (see photo)"

Members on the photo were – Front: Ordella Beckstrom, Captain. Middle: Nadine Forsberg, Ruby Chelberg, Ruth Klemz, Aina Jacobson, Mary Doyle. Back: Evelyn Lewis, Olga Loman, Miss Mildred Selander, Coach, Marjorie Goodwin, Dorothy Stroberg.

The article went on, "The girls' team found the path of victory in the first game of the season this year by defeating North Branch and it was but once that they were forced out and that was the fateful return game with Braham. Ruth Klemz is the one girl who can be given the credit of being an individual star this year. She averaged 18 out of every 25 points made in the average for each game. She had a good basket-eye which kept the team from defeat. The other two forwards are not to be forgotten, however. Ruby Chelberg filled the place at center and she was usually able to get the tip-off. Aina Jacobson was small, but she was always at the right place at the right time. The forwards are to be complimented on their splendid team work. The guards were steady and alert on the defense. They are to be especially complimented for their strong defense in the last game of the season with St. Francis. The St. Francis girls were unable to make a field goal but they got two points on free throws. The team will lose two players this year, Ruth Klemz and Ordella Beckstrom."

Cambridge 1928

The team uniforms had a large letter "C" on a v-neck top. The bottoms appeared to be pleated skirts or bloomers pulled above the knee.

The team played 10 games against North Branch, St. Francis, Braham, Anoka, and Princeton.

Cass Lake High School

Northern Minnesota, 25 miles north of Walker on Leech Lake; Highway #371
Years Represented: 1924-1926

Information from Jim Michaud, St. Cloud Apollo High School, indicates that his mother-in-law, Irene Koll Brennan, coached at Cass Lake High School.

Two photos were provided of the Cass Lake girls basketball teams.

The 1925 team players are shown in white pullover sweaters, bloomers and athletic shoes. Players listed were - Estelle Tedford; Mary Duffy; Buelah Potter; Helen Caswell; Lauretta Mettel; Rosalyn Smith; Nellie Marshall; Cleone Roth, Mabel Wright.

Cass Lake 1925

Cass Lake 1926

The 1926 team players are wearing uniforms with v-neck tops, shorts and knee high socks with athletic shoes. This uniform is an example of the change from bloomers to shorts. Players listed - Front: Lauretta Mettel; Estelle Tedford; Doris Johnson; Agnes Mettel. Back: Mary Duffy, Nellie Marshall, Helen Caswell, Marian Watts.

Clarkfield High School

12 miles west of Granite Falls on #67
Years Represented: 1911-1933

Clarkfield before 1920s

The first photos were printed in the centennial publication, *Clarkfield, Minnesota 1884-1984*.

Elnora Burke Budde and her twin sister Elvera Burke Lindborg played from 1924-1928. It was a two-court game. Their team played Hanley Falls, Dawson and

Clarkfield 1920s

Fourth Quarter 135

Montevideo. The players furnished their own uniforms, black bloomers and middies. Her coach was a female teacher. The girls' team traveled in their own bus and played the first game of the doubleheader. Elnora recalls that the community was supportive of the team.

The school newspaper provided many reviews and stories of the basketball season.

The Clarkfield High School paper, the *Clarkette,* February 8, 1924, "Clarkfield Super-Six Downs Wood Lake." It reported,

"The Super-Six of the Clarkfield Basket Ball Girls went down to defeat in the hands of Granite Falls Saturday night January 26 by a score of 21 to 14. The Conflict started with a scramble, Clarkfield scoring, but in a short while Granite was in the lead. They succeeded in remaining in the lead, holding Clarkfield down until the last quarter when Clarkfield made a desperate attempt to build up their score. Clarkfield was at a disadvantage owing to unfamiliarity with the floor and their defeat was perhaps due in part to lack of team work.

The yelling and noise furnished by the small groups of Clarkfield supporters was really an inspiration to the fighting team, and, although the yelling cannot perhaps be compared with Granite's highly organized and well-led gang of boosters, we know they had a large part in spurring the team on to play, the way they did. Hats off to the Girl yellers.

After the games Granite served the visiting teams a delicious lunch."

The Clarkfield High School paper, the *Clarkette*, February 8, 1924, "Basket-Ball Teams Entertained."

"The Boy's and Girl's Basket Ball teams were hospitably entertained at a Progressive Somerset and Whist party by Mrs. Belle Anderson Saturday evening, February 2. Other guests were Miss Kraft, the girls' coach and the Misses Haugen, Ellingson and Longfellow.

The evening was spent in a most enjoyable manner, every one striving desperately to win, the prize, a delicious box of home-made candy, being awarded to the whist shark, Harold Peterson. Wallace Wilson received the booby prize.

At midnight a delicious lunch was served after which all joined in a hearty expression of appreciation and thanks to their kind hostess for the delightful evening."

The Clarkfield High School paper, the *Clarkette,* March 7, 1924, "Super-Six Ties Madison."

"The game between the Madison girls and the Super Six, played Saturday, February 23, resulted in an uneven break for the two teams. The Clarkfieldites were full of pep and started out in fine style. They got away with two baskets and two foul shots the first half, while Madison got only one point. In the last half, however, the Super Six, confident of winning, slackened their pace; the visitors at once taking advantage of the fact by making a basket. Fouls called on Clarkfield gave Madison the rest of their points and at the sound of the whistle the score stood 7-7."

The Clarkfield High School paper, the *Clarkette,* April 4, 1924, "Basket Ball Banquet Social Event of the Season."

"A sumptuous 6:30 o'clock banquet was given in the Library of the High School, Saturday, March 22nd, in honor of the Girls' and Boys' Basket Ball Teams. This banquet marked the close of the Basket Ball season and the thought that it would perhaps be the last time we would be assembled in this manner made us all a trifle more serious than the occasion demanded. After the guests had been seated they were very much impressed when little Dorothy Arneson and James Galbraith, dressed in Basket Ball uniforms entered the room to the strains of 'In the Gloaming' and placed a Basket Ball upon a pedestal in the center of the room." Several speakers were listed with several musical performances by a boys' quartet, a piano solo, and soloists. The article concluded, "Altogether the Banquet was marked a success and a fitting climax for the season."

On May 19, 1925, the school newspaper reported that a combined banquet was held to include all athletic teams, girls and boys, the debate team and the Clarkette staff. "The theme of the program centered around football." The program, menus, comments were all football terms.

The school newspaper reported the girls and boys basketball games on the front page in adjacent columns. It is noted that the cost of the newspaper was 75 cents per year.

The photo identified as the 1925 team shows Elnora Burke Budde holding the ball. Her twin sister Elvera is in the photo, but not identified.

Clarkfield 1925

Elnora recalls that their team played a two-court game where they couldn't cross the center line.

Teams played were: Wood Lake, Granite Falls, Madison, Dawson, Canby, Minneota and Montevideo. A female teacher was the team coach.

In January 27, 1925, an article from a local newspaper reported a game with Dawson, "Because of a very slippery floor and the fact that the Super Six were all under the weather, more or less, Clarkfield was defeated."

Rosalind Knutson Cherkezian shared memories of her team in 1928-33. Her team played Dawson, Madison, Montevideo and Boyd. The boys' and girls' teams traveled together in a school bus and returned after the game. The girls' game was held first; boys' game second. Travel expenses were provided by the school.

The team played their games in the school gymnasium. The uniforms were red knit tee shirts with red cotton bloomers furnished by the school. The letter "C" was gray. The school colors were cardinal and gray.

Their female coach was a teacher who taught biology, general science and history. Basketball was not the only sport for girls. District competition was also held for girls in track and field.

Rosalind indicated that her team continued to play after her graduation.

Rosalind Knutson, right, and teammate, Dolores Kirkeby, Clarkfield, 1931

Special Stories

The 1924 page from the Clarkfield newspaper included an article, "Girls in Miss Kraft's Gym Classes Teach the Class."

"Miss Kraft has been giving girls in her gym classes about ten minutes each day to instruct the class. They seem to enjoy "giving orders" and watching the rest go through the exercises. If there are any who would like in the future to be a physical training teacher, join Miss Kraft's class and she will give you a chance to prove whether or not you'd be an efficient teacher."

Another partial article on the same page described a ceremony in which the superintendent awarded emblems to the captains of the boys and girls basketball teams.

The issues of the *Clarkette* are located at the Minnesota Historical Society

Cloquet High School

20 miles southeast of Duluth on #33
Years Represented: 1903-1930

The earliest photo located of a Cloquet girls' basketball team is dated 1903. The photographer for the 1903 photo was Octavie Morneau, a well-known photographer from Duluth. The photo is printed with permission of the Carlton County Historical Society, Cloquet, MN.

Cloquet 1903

Cloquet 1921

The 1921 Cloquet High School yearbook, the *White Pine*, said, "There may have been a High School team (before 1920), but it never met the opposition of other schools. In the year 1920-21 the attempt was made to renew the interest in Girls' athletics."

The school organized a GAA (Girls' Athletic Association) with practice in the "Y" gym (YMCA). Classes played each other and then a school team was selected. The team played Carlton and Proctor.

The 1921 team photo shows six players in white middies and dark bows, and bloomers. Members were Gladys Scheibe, Captain Lillian Eilers, Mildred Arf, Corinne Seim, M. Dixon and M. Olesen.

138   Daughters of the Game

Edith Anderson Bergan provided an interview of her playing years from 1922-25. They played YWCA, Carleton, Proctor, Alumni team, Lincoln, Barnum, Superior, and Coleraine

Members of the 1922-23 team were Lempi Laaksonen, Helvi Peterson, Marguerite White, Mildred DePoe, Lola Rine, Mildred Stolberg, Mary O'Neil, Edith Anderson, Mary Olesen.

Cloquet 1923

In 1923, the *White Pine* said that the season began with use of boys' rules, but changed because the State Athletic Association ruled that girls' teams must play girls' rules.

"This was a shock to all concerned as girls' rules were practically unknown. The changes seemed as tho' it would be for the worst but some of the fastest games ever played on the gym floor were played with girls' rules."

The yearbook noted that players also could play on the "Y" team.

The team practiced every night for about three months, playing ten games, losing two. The teams played Lincoln, Carlton, Proctor, Coleraine.

In 1923, the team played their last game against Coleraine at Coleraine. The school yearbook proudly stated, "This was the biggest game of the season. Coleraine claimed the Northwest Championship. Cloquet contended it. A record crowd came out for the game, the biggest crowd Coleraine had ever had at a basket-ball game. It was estimated at about seven hundred. The city band came out to lend excitement."

In 1923-24, the photo in the *White Pine* shows girls in white middy blouses and dark bows and scarves; some with dark blouses and dark bows, and bloomers. The team played eight games, losing two.

Cloquet 1924

The 1924-25 team received new varsity uniforms. Edith Anderson Bergan described them, "Our school colors were purple and white. The first two years we wore a red sailor middy blouse and big black bloomers and socks that came over our knees. We each had our own stockings so they did not all match. During our senior year we got new uniforms, purple with white trim. The top had a v- neck and capped sleeves with a "C" on the front of the shirt; the bottoms were purple shorts, a big change from our other uniforms. We had purple and white stockings. The uniforms were furnished by the school."

The 1924-25 team photo lists – Front: Sheean, Lillian Everson, Lucille O'Marro, Hebert. Middle: Berg, Elinor Scheibe, Captain Edith Anderson, Rebecca Collins, Eleanor McCarthy, Peterson. Back: Helvi Wiiret, Matkala, Weston, Coach Holcombe, Siltanen, Margaret Longsyo, Bertha Smith.

Cloquet 1925

The 1925 *Cloquet Pine-Journal*, included a game summary,

"The Cloquet high school girls' team won from the Carlton high school girls' team 34-16 in a game played last Friday evening in the local high school gym. Capt. Edith Anderson of the Cloquet team, played a stellar game, caging 15 baskets and 2 free throws, thus making 32 of her team's 34 points. This was the last game Miss Anderson will play with the local aggregation as she is a senior and will graduate this spring."

Edith's teams traveled by train, sometimes staying overnight. For schools closer to Cloquet, they traveled by cars. The boys' and girls' teams traveled together if they were playing the same team. In 1923 the team traveled to Carlton in a sleigh with several other sleighs following filled with rooters.

Nancy Melby wrote about her mother, Edith Anderson Bergan, "When we talked about her playing days, she never mentioned her 'stellar game!'"

The coaches were Herbert Drew for three years and Miss Inez Holcombe for the 1924-25 year.

Edith's favorite memory was "when I was a sophomore and Coach Drew chose me over a senior to travel to Coleraine on the train with the boys' and girls' team. We got to stay overnight. There was a large crowd and we played on a gym that was built up something like a stage. I got to play a lot. The city band came out to lend excitement. We lost to Coleraine, but it was very exciting!"

Edith's teams received a stripe for each year played which were worn on their purple and white school sweaters.

The 1926 team included Lillian Everson, Bertha Smith, Elinore Scheibe, Marie Bjorkland, Margaret Nilsen, Eleanore McCarty, Evelyn Loff and Margaret Matteson.

Girls' Basket Ball

Matteson, Smith, Holcombe Coach, Loff, Nilsen, McCarty, Everson, Scheibe, Bjorklund

Cloquet 1926

The 1927 team players were Alice Johnson, Ragnhild Johnson, Margaret Matteson, Captain, Helen Olson, Jean Vibert, Evelyn Thornblad, Elsa Anderson, Sylvia Sheean, Lorraine Brown. Coach Miss Sanford. The team played six games against Moose Lake, Proctor, Thompson, Carlton, winning five.

The 1930 team played four games with the White Pine noting: "There are few schools of our size in the district having girls' teams and so there was a handicap in scheduling games."

Cloquet 1927

140   Daughters of the Game

Team members were Lorraine Brown, Captain, Ruth Blake, Margaret Vibert, Alvilda Evenson, Evelyn Yelle, Florence Johnson, Martha DePoe, Dorothy Thorpe, Bernice Danielson, Kathryn Pollard, Myrl Wick, Ethel Strom, Irene Laaksonen, Mary Toland, Mildred Borsheim, and Cathryn Cormier.

Cloquet 1930

Cloquet 1932

The 1931-32 team photo shows the teams wearing white blouses or v-neck tops with dark shorts. Shown in the photo are Coach Hickisch and players Hattie Peterson, Dorothy Thorpe, Kathryn Pollard, Martha DePoe, Bernice Danielson, Martha Eilers, Helen Hendrickson, Catherine Cormier, Mary Toland, Irene Laaksonen, Ethel Strom, Carol Sandstrom, and Bernadene Tetu.

The yearbook proclaimed that the team completed an undefeated season. The team played the "Y" team and the yearbook article emphasized, "The game with the "Y" was the kind of a game that puts basketball on the map. Nobody could call that girls' game uninteresting."

Cromwell High School

Northeastern Minnesota; 40 miles west of Duluth on #210
Years Represented: 1925-1933

Several members of the Cromwell girls basketball team provided interviews and personal memories of their years together on the team.

Alice Dahlman Carter played from 1924-28 and shared that, "Our school bus was a box-type thing with canvas curtains. It had wheels in the spring and fall, and runners for wintertime. Many times the snowdrifts were so big that we tipped over. The boys' team always liked that as they had to help set it back up. The bus was pulled by a team of horses."

Blanche Line Kingsley, 1926-31, started playing in eighth grade. Basketball was her favorite sport. She added that her dad, Jasper Line, drove the first motorized school bus.

Their games were played in a small gym in the school, and later at the Farmers Hall, then the I.O.O.F. Hall in 1927. Blanche said of the I.O.O. F. Hall, "It was much easier having a place near the school for practice. Both halls were equipped with a barrel stove for heating the building and were located in one corner of the hall. A rope fence was placed around them for protection. The I.O.O. F. Hall contained a stage which extended across the front end of the building. A balcony above the other end of the hall added seating space for the school activities."

The girls' and boys' teams traveled together by bus, playing double-headers with the girls' game first. They played Wrenshall, Carlton, McGregor, Floodwood, Duluth Central, Barnum, Meadowlands, Moose Lake and Esko. The boys' team was supportive as were parents and the community. Publicity was carried through the *Carlton County Vidette*. Blanche says, "Most of all, I loved to play!"

Anna Karppinen Kohn, 1926-30, was a member of the team that won the 1926 district tournament. Team members received school letters. Their games were played in the basement of the school. The girls played with five on a team, but guards couldn't go across the court. Uniforms were black bloomers and white blouses. In 1926, they wore red and white uniforms furnished by the school. Anna said that her parents didn't understand basketball but got her athletic shoes. She says, "All the interest they showed was my mother would ask, 'Who won?'"

The game was half court with six players, one dribble allowed. Uniforms were a v-neck top and bloomers furnished by the school. The team had a female coach. Blanche said that in 1928-29, the uniform was black bloomers. She said, "We pulled them up to here and then they flopped down to here."

Teams played included Meadowlands, Wrenshall, Barnum, and Carlton. The games were played in a hall as the school did not have a gym.

Cromwell 1926

The school yearbook, the *Cromwellian*, provided photos and information about the teams.

The 1927 team won 10 of 11 games. They played Carlton, Moose Lake, Barnum, Wrenshall, McGregor, Isle and Chisago City. The team won the Carlton County Championship, the sub district championship, the District No. 5 championship, including over 20 high schools, and the championship of 14 counties from Proctor to Brainerd, and from Hibbing to Minneapolis. The Cromwell team scored 221 points to their opponent's 128. The school newspaper summarized, "All games except two were played on standard gyms, away from Cromwell. We had the very best of friendly relationships with all schools and teams played this year. We overcame the handicap of our small gym and low ceiling."

Cromwell 1927

The 1927 team photo lists the Cromwell District Champs – Back: Alice Dahlman, Sally Soukila, Mable Krogh, Grace Reynolds, Supt. Gustafson, Dorothy Johnson, Emilia Larson, Ellen Larson, Ellen Olsen, Valeria Kazunas. Front: Esther Klavu, Elva Lundstrom, Ina Larson, Martha Larson and Mary Gearnes. Substitutes who earned letters but were not in photo: Emelia Larson, Mable Krogh, Grace Reynolds and Anna Karppinen.

142   Daughters of the Game

The Sports Section of the *Pine Knot*, Saturday, December 12, 1998, included an article, "Cromwell girls basketball program has deep roots," The first photo of the 1930-31 photo lists: Blanche Line, Captain; Laura Dumas, Edythe Kibert, Alice Gearnes, Narma Jalonen, Eileen Maxner, Violet Palm, Mae Besman, Gladys Dahl, Hulda Larson. The team won all of its games. The second photo includes five women who attended a reunion of their team: Mae Besman White, Gladys Dahl Clark, Blanche Line Kingsley, Eileen Maxner Grove and Alice Dahlman Carter.

Cromwell 1929

The 1932 photo includes: Ercel Weimer, Narma Jalonen, Alice Gearnes, Rosemary Kubat, Esther Kuitu, coach; Lyla Larson, Gladys Dahl, Signa Illstrup, Mae Beasman and Lydia Kamunen. Holding ball: Hulda Larson, captain and Eileen Maxner. Uniforms were v-neck with shorts.

Cromwell 1931

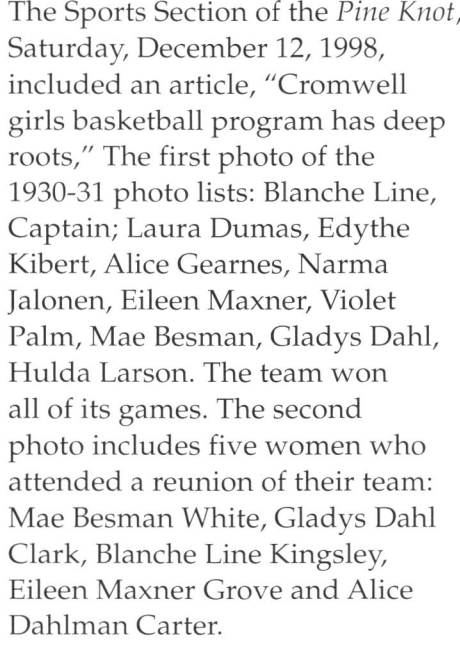

Cromwell 1932

1933 photo- Front: Lydia Kamunen, Eileen Maxner, Hulda Larson, Gladys Dahl, Jessie Line, Back: Lyla Larson, Mary Jerokovsky, Miss Kuitu, Coach, Rosemary Kubat.

1935 photo - Front: Mae McLain, Lydia Kamunen, Lyla Larson, Helen Reinhold, Betty McLain. Back: Dorothy Johnson, Darrel Houck, Marlys Groth, Marie Hill, Jessie Line, Helen Jerikovsky, Eleanor Johnson.

Eileen Maxner Grover, 1930-33, recalls tournaments with trophies held in Duluth and Carlton.

Cromwell 1933

Cromwell 1935

Jessie Line Houck and her future husband were both high scorers for their teams. Eileen said that one of her memories was that "I liked that they gave us oranges during the halftime. I thought that was so good because we didn't have oranges at home."

Special Stories

Blanche and Eileen believe that the last girls basketball team in Cromwell was in 1933. Eileen said, "They said the 'state' said they couldn't play competitive basketball anymore, due to the fact that women weren't strong enough to do things like that and that it was too hard on women's health."

Gladys Dahl Clark said,

"I don't remember if we were told anything in the year of 1931-1932 that we would not have any basketball the school year of 1932-1933. We were told in the fall of 1932 that there would be no more basketball games for the girls. Excuses were plenty: girls did not have the stamina, wasn't good for our health, not ladylike, and more. In the fall of 1932-1933, a group of the remainder of 1931-1932 basketball team plus some of the girls that played in 1930-1931 decided that we were going to play basketball. The boys were practicing basketball in the Odd Fellows Hall, Cromwell. We decided to boycott the boys' team. As soon as the boys were through practicing, we girls marched into the hall and demanded that we should practice and have a team for the year of 1932-1933, *which we did*!! That was the last girls basketball team for many years, almost a half century. What a shame!"

Eileen Maxner Grover, 1931-33, said that one of the boys was their cheerleader throughout high school. He was the first cheerleader at Cromwell High school.

Mae Beseman White recalled,

"Back in the 1930s, the Cromwell boys and girls basketball teams would travel together to all their games within a 50 mile radius of the Cromwell High School. Except for a few main roads that had a hard surface, every road was gravel and usually poorly maintained. Snow in the winter was their main concern because the roads would not be plowed or if they were, it could be anywhere from one to five days before the roads were passable. Since the school buses were homemade and built on old truck frames, they lacked the modern conveniences, like heat, lavatories, soft seats, etc. Everyone had to dress warm enough that if something happened on the trip, they could keep warm. Sometimes it was almost as cold inside the bus as it was outside. Mr. Jasper Line was usually the bus driver for the basketball trips. He was always concerned about the longer trips. Going to Meadowlands, they got turned around on the country roads and finally had to stop at a remote farm for directions. The farmer was in the barn doing chores and came out carrying a kerosene lantern to see who was coming. After getting detailed directions, they were off again. A good driver had to make up for the poor maps in the 1920s and 1930s because many of the back roads were not on the map."

> "We girls marched into the hall and demanded that we should practice and have a team for the year of 1932-1933, which we did!"
> Gladys Dahl Clark

> "Since the school buses were homemade and built on old truck frames, they lacked the modern conveniences, like heat, lavatories, soft seats, etc."
> Mae Beseman White

Blanche Line Kingsley said,

"At times, a little diversion from the usual occurred on our trips. One night while returning from a Floodwood game, the school bus stalled on the railroad crossing and needed some repair work before we could go on. We waited in the bus until the work was completed. I didn't arrive home until four in the morning. Bill was the driver and he brought me home. One night following a Barnum game, the bus slid into the ditch. My father was driving and the roads were glare ice. I never understood why we had the game that night when the roads were so bad. A farmhouse was located up the hill from the accident. We waited there until they had the bus on the road again. I arrived home at five in the morning and my brother, Jack, was just starting the fire. We played Central in Duluth one night when my father was the bus driver. The bus broke down in the middle of Duluth. My father stayed with the bus while the players jumped in a street car to get to the school for the game. I didn't have any money to pay the dime for the street car, but luckily, another girl had an extra dime and she took care of it for me….very embarrassing."

Blanche said, "I received a lot of acclaim from the team members and other students in the school. It took the whole team's effort to accomplish what we did. I never felt any jealousy during the years I played. This was a fun sport and I enjoyed all the effort and time spent involved in it. It made my high school years more enjoyable."

Eileen and Blanche said there was inter-school competition in track, volleyball and softball, but not as organized as basketball. Their team won several trophies in track and field.

The 1926 Cromwell yearbook, the *Cromwellian*, lists the Girls Track Team, "During the last four Carlton County High School Track Meets, our girls won the relay silver cup three times. The girls expect to enter the track meet again this year at Moose Lake. The principal runners this year are Gearnes, Kibart, Markula, M. Larson. The girls also expect to enter the County High School Indoor Baseball Tournament at Lincoln. This is our first attempt at the indoor baseball tournaments that are held every spring."

Legacy
Blanche's athletic abilities were shared by her daughter and granddaughters. Daughter June Collman coached her daughters, Tammy Hill, April Collman and Julie Collman on the Cromwell girls basketball team in the late 1970s and early 1980s. Julie broke many school records in basketball, earning state and national recognition. Blanche said, "I gave my school letter to Julie because she was the last grandchild who played, and she loved the game so much."

Teammates and Lifelong Friends
Basketball produces teammates who later become friends for life. Teammates gathered for a reunion to recall fond memories of their years together: Mae Beasman White, Gladys Dahl Clark, Blanche Line Kingsley, Eileen Maxner Grover, Alice Dahlman Carter.

Cromwell Reunion

Newspaper excerpts reprinted with permission of the *Pine Journal*

Crookston High School

Northwestern Minnesota; 20 miles east of East Grand Forks on #2.
Years Represented: 1910-1912

The 1910 Crookston High School yearbook reported

"The girls of the Crookston High School, about twenty-five in number, organized last fall, with Beatrice Treadwell as manager and Bernice Roemer as captain. With Miss Cornish and Miss Lofthouse as coaches, they practiced somewhat irregularly through the winter, gaining a fair degree of skill, but as the field is small and the ceiling so low as to prevent skilled goaling, it was thought best not to play any contest games until next year. They did, however, have three interesting games between classes, two at the gymnasium, and a third at the Hall, where they acquitted themselves with credit.

The girls certainly deserve praise for the excellent work shown, considering the limited amount of practice. Next year we hope to start out in the fall with a goodly number and plenty of enthusiasm, so that we may get the real joy and fun that comes with a recreation that should have a firmly-established place in our school."

Special Stories
The photos provided by Dr. Robert C. Wright were of his mother, Jeannette Page who played in 1911-1912.

Jeannette Page Wright, Crookston, 1912

Dr. Wright wrote, "My mother was in many ways a woman who seemed to live a life truly ahead of her time. Many of the things she did as a girl and as an adult became common for women in the 1970s and later, but were pioneering or at least rare in her day."

Crookston 1912

Dr. Wright wrote, "My mother was in many ways a woman who seemed to live a life truly ahead of her time."

Jeannette's mother died in 1898 and her father in 1907 in a famous train wreck. A commuter train that was attempting a speed record near New York flipped off the tracks, killing many of those on board, including her father. In the summer, Jeannette was raised by aunts on a farm near Edgerton, Wisconsin. During the school year, she attended high school in Crookston. In 1911-1912, at age 16, Jeannette was captain of the girls' basketball team. She finished high school at Oberlin Academy, Ohio in 1914. Jeannette later took training to become a kindergarten teacher and taught in Ohio and St. Paul. She joined the army as a trained nurse in World War I. Her service as a nurse came during the great flu epidemic of 1918-1919 that killed millions worldwide. Jeannette herself nearly died of the flu. After the war Jeannette returned to her teaching in St. Paul. She married and was very active in community and civic groups in Crookston and Thief River Falls. With the onset of World War II, her two sons volunteered for the U.S. Army, so Jeannette, age 47, reenlisted into the Women's Army Corps of the U.S. Army. She was sent to Ft. Knox, Kentucky, a tank training school, where she remained for the rest of the war. Jeannette returned to assume the responsibility for the family business and once again devoted her energies to her passion of organizing plays, musicals, parades and dozens of other events for the communities in and around Crookston and Thief River Falls.

Legacy

Dr. Wright, Jeannette's son, said, "In 1981-82, the youngest of our five children went to 'State' in volleyball and basketball. Our daughter, Lori, was co-captain of the St. Charles girls basketball team in 1982, 70 years after her grandmother also was a basketball captain."

Crosby and Deerwood High Schools

15 miles northeast of Brainerd on #210
Years Represented: 1901

The *Brainerd Daily Dispatch*, Sept. 21, 1999, included a photo which read:

"In 1901, playing girls basketball no doubt meant being quite hot in heavy sweaters and long skirts. It is not known what the apparently homemade Cs and Ds stood for, perhaps Crosby and Deerwood. But the photo was no doubt indicative of the basketball era for girls in the region"

Newspaper excerpt reprinted with permission of the *Brainerd Daily Dispatch*.

Crosby-Deerwood 1901

Fourth Quarter

Cyrus High School

Southwestern Minnesota; 10 miles east of Morris on #28
Years Represented: 1921

Cyrus 1921

Beverly Reque says that the team photo includes her aunt, Vivian Solvie, who is in the middle of the second row.

The photo describes the team as the "First Girls Basketball Team – 1921". Team members were: Charlotte Buesing, Margaret Quammen, Esther Solvie, Alice Barsness, Vivian Solvie, Lillie Hatlelid, Helen Squire, Coach, Haugen, O. Birkeland, Supt., Lillian Nelson, Marian Lee and Ruth Hanse.

Dawson High School

Southwestern Minnesota; 18 miles west of Montevideo on #212
Years Represented: 1910-1934

A 1910 photo postcard of the Dawson girls basketball team shows six players in dark bloomers, dark stockings and shoes. Anne Jerde is the third player from the left.

The postcard photo of the 1926 girls basketball team includes Cora Carlson Weisbrod.

Dawson 1910

Dawson 1926

Anne Jerde's daughter, Audrey Moe Froiland, played on the Dawson girls basketball team from 1931-34. At the age of 88 years in 2005, Audrey was pleased to recall memories of her playing days, as she said, "I loved basketball." She says, "I was not a great player; my main asset was height which was needed when every play returned to a center jump." She identified two of her teammates as Ellen Hoff, Richfield and Audrey Pederson, Minnetonka.

Their team played a two-court game, three guards on half the floor and three forwards on the other half. Practice was held in the National Guard Armory. Games were also played in the Armory.

The uniform was short bloomers, a black sleeveless tank top with orange letters. The uniform and a warm-up jacket were provided by the school.

Opposing teams included Montevideo, Appleton, Ortonville, Madison, Clarkfield, Boyd, Milan and possibly Marietta.

The team traveled by cars driven by parents, coaches or teachers. The girls' and boys' teams traveled together and the girls' team played the first game. The boys helped the girls' team and supported them. The girls' games received the same news coverage as the boys' games.

Audrey said that they participated in a tournament, won trophies and the players received athletic award letters.

Audrey added that, "In the early l930's, there was not much excitement out there. Basketball provided a little of that. We met kids from other towns, enjoyed our trips, even the practices. There was the thrill of competition and sometimes even the thrill of winning!"

Audrey recalled that the last team in Dawson was in 1934. Audrey said, "Appleton had discontinued girls basketball in 1934 and the reason was that jumping on the hardwood floors was damaging to the girls' reproductive organs."

Special Stories
Audrey adds that, after graduation from Dawson in 1934,

"I went to what they called a 'Depression College' in Appleton and a group of us who had played in high school got together to organize an 'independent team.' We had lots of fun going to play similar teams at junior colleges, etc. We usually played the preliminary game for a National Guard team. Our independents' played a preliminary game against my old Dawson team when the Appleton boys' team played Dawson."

Our 'college' was a large college if you took everything. We had teachers sent out from the University of Minnesota and a proctor came from the University at the end of the period and administered a University test. The teachers were all fresh graduates but everyone worked hard and got their credits at a cost of $24.00 tuition for the year!"

Legacy
Anne Jerde, 1910, and Audrey Moe Froiland, 1931-1934, provide a generational link of a mother and daughter playing on teams at the same high school.

Audrey reflected, "Dawson again has a basketball team. My daughters all missed it. Mary especially would have loved it. Everything is more elaborate and organized now but I think perhaps we had just as much fun and enjoyment as they do now, almost 70 years later or, as my mother did 90 years ago."

Deer Creek High School

West central Minnesota; 55 miles west of Brainerd
Years Represented: 1924-29

Irma Nelson Post started playing in eighth grade and played five years during the early 1920s. The team played the two-court game against high school teams from Parkers Prairie, Bertha, Hewitt, Battle Lake, Sebeka, New York Mills, and Wadena. They played one game against the Frazee Cane Women, an independent team.

Parents took turns driving the team to games held on Friday nights. Irma noted that sometimes they traveled by the local trucking company, the Rodekuhr Brothers. After they cleaned out the truck, they put straw in the truck bed and both boys' and girls' teams rode in the truck. If it was cold, they put a tarp over the top. Irma said, "Those trips were usually a riot. I wondered sometimes if the R. Brothers would stop and put us out."

The girls' game was played first in a doubleheader.

The team wore either a white or black blouse with bloomer type pants, tennis shoes and socks to match. Edna Mickelson, teacher, was the coach.

Irma wrote that "at long last I've found my favorite basketball picture, 1924-1925. It has a flaw but it's old too!" The photo shows Elizabeth Davis, Una Rector, Clara Rodekuhr, Violet Rodekuhr, Irma Nelson, and Lola Hompe. Other team members included Dolly Nelson, Alma Nelson, and Esther Nelson.

Deer Creek 1925

Special Stories

One of the schools, either New York Mills or Frazee, Irma recounted, had a wooden beam just off center of the hall where they played. She said, "None of us ran into it but the girls that played and practiced there really took advantage of that mean old beam!"

Irma remembered a big snowstorm when even the trains weren't running. Parents volunteered to take the team even though the roads weren't plowed.

"Una Rector and I were to ride with Rev. Keefer. He took a different road than the rest and I wish I could remember how many times we were stuck. He shoveled, we shoveled, he drove and we pushed. When we came to Battle Lake, our girls' game was in the fourth quarter. Una played. I didn't. I was so cold my hands were numb. That was the worst time we ever had. The others all got there on time. You can just guess show how much we were kidded. The minister was young, single and handsome, to boot!"

Irma remembered that a Deer Creek scorekeeper never missed a game. The man wore a small toupee and in one game, the ball hit him on the head and his hairpiece flew out on the floor. She said, "The laughter almost cracked the windows but he was a good sport about it. He was not hurt."

> "The scorekeeper wore a small toupee and in one game, the ball hit him on the head and his hairpiece flew out on the floor."
> Irma Nelson Post

Irma recalled that they played a "famous" game with the Frazee Cane Women.

"The Frazee gal was tall, maybe 2-3 inches over me. She got right on the center line. I couldn't go ahead of her because I couldn't go over the center line. Deer Creek was not getting the ball. Miss Mickelson, our coach, called a time out. She told me to guard her from behind. When the ball came to her I was to go under her arms and push the ball back to our forwards. I hit it with my open hand, as I didn't dare to bat it a good one. Well, it worked a couple of times, then 'Miss Tall' came down real hard on me with her elbow. I had good luck, and I wasn't hurt too bad. I didn't go out of the game, but I sure had a shiner. To tell you the truth, it was a master piece! I still think to myself, I must have been real proud of that 'mouse' even if they did beat us good. They were a nice group of girls."

In one game, Irma was called out of bounds because she fell near the line. She had a long braid and her hair went over the line and the other team got the ball. Irma said, "I was upset but kept still. Because of my long hair, the Battle Lake girls called me 'Anna Green Gables.'"

The benefits of playing basketball to Irma was, "Basketball kept some of us girls from quitting school, I'm sure, as I was one who worked at the Drug Store and Café. We had to keep our grades to passing."

In her interview letter, Irma wrote, "My mind goes into gear sometimes. As I washed dishes the other day, a couple of game cheers came to mind: 'Hit 'em high; Hit 'em low, Come on Deer Creek, let's go! Another was: 'Vas ist dis, Vas ist das, Deer Creek, Das ist vas!' Every time we scored, the cheer was, 'Atta' girl!!' Those were the days!"

"A couple of cheers came to mind: 'Vas ist dis, Vas ist das, Deer Creek, Das ist vas!!'"
Irma Nelson Post

Special Stories
In 2003, Irma said, "that's all for now unless I wash my dishes again and think of something more."

Irma Nelson Post
Deer Creek

Delano High School

Central Minnesota; 20 miles west of Metro Area on #12
Years Represented: 1921-1925

Ella Mae Bauer Pease was a member of the Delano girls basketball team during her four years of high school, 1921-25. She was captain during her senior year.

Ella said that she was the shortest player on the team but was still the jumping center in a two-court game. She could play the entire court. She could recall playing Watertown. Ella recalls that when other schools didn't have girls' teams, their varsity and second teams would play one another.

The team uniform was a middy blouse and bloomers made of cotton. Each player furnished her own uniform.

Ella recalls, "The boys used to kid us about our girls' game, so we challenged them to play with us under girls' rules and we beat the pants off of them. They couldn't play like we did."

The team was coached by a woman and they traveled in family cars.

1923-24 photo - Anna Meyers, running center; Margaret Raul, forward; Anna Riep, guard; Mary Kuka, guard; Geniveve Hellman, forward; Ella Mae Bauer Pease, jumping center.

Delano 1924

Ella Mae Bauer Pease

1924-25 photo - Armello Cramer, Esther Rieder, Isabell Horst, Geneiveve Hellman, Ella Mae Bauer Pease, Signe Overby, captain.

Ella said that her parents never came to the games. They lived on a farm. She would stay in town overnight. "For awhile," Ella said, "there were a couple other girls that lived in Maple Plain in a housekeeping room. They went to Delano High School and they had housekeeping rooms where they could cook their meals and sleep. I used to stay there."

Delano 1925

Delavan High School

Southern Minnesota; 10 miles north of Blue Earth on #109
Years Represented: 1922-1930

The 1922-23 team was coached by Alice Brack and won nine of their 12 games. The uniforms were white middy tops with rolled up sleeves, and woolen serge pleated bloomers. The team played Winnebago, Alden, Elmore, Kiester, and Blue Earth. Team members - Bernice Rorman, Esther Trembley, Adelaide Stiles, captain, Genevieve Fitzgerald, Grace Wheeler, Gladys Nessett.

Delavan 1923

The 1926-27 team photo listed - Bernice Halvorson, Rose Claude, Shirley Harper, Julie Howe Christopherson, Coach; Marceline Perrizo, Cleota Porath, Beatrice Stroble.

Delavan 1927

Bernice Halvorson Wheeler said that the court was divided into three parts and players had to remain in their own section. They had a jumping center, a running center and each end had two forwards and two guards. One dribble was permitted. Bernice played running center. They had plays. Bernice said, "I was quite short so I had to work hard to get the tip-off at center and get the ball to our forwards."

The uniforms were green middy shirts, v-neck with a school letter on the front and wool serge pleated bloomers. The team members wore green and white socks with black and white tennis shoes that cost, according to Bernice, "maybe $2.98." Bernice said the bloomers were non-washable. "Can you imagine?" she asked.

Girls' and boys' games played as doubleheaders; girls always played first. The girls' team had a female coach.

She stated that Winnebago was "the worst rival." Bernice said, "Those games got rough." The girls' and boys' teams rode together in the bus, or went by car, and in the winter, they occasionally traveled by train. The community was very supportive.

Bernice's mother died when she was thirteen. Bernice lived five miles from town and didn't drive, so she had, "many sleepovers after the games." Because she had three brothers, she was committed to basketball at an early age. Bernice said, "I loved the game and still do."

Derham Hall High School

St. Paul, Minnesota
Years Represented: 1939

The 1939 Derham Hall yearbook, the *Hour Glass*, contained an article titled, "Basketball."

It reported: "Basketball season is the high point of the sports year. Besides the inter-class tournaments, there were the games played with Oak Hall, Holy Angels Academy, University High School, and Saint Joseph's Academy. Every game was filled with excitement and fun, and we will long remember all of them. Every member of the team is to be congratulated for fine play and sportsmanship.

The cheering section did a fine job, and one of its outstanding accomplishments was the rendition of the "song of welcome".

Even those of us who took no active part in the basketball games will long remember the season for the lovely teas after the games."

Dodge Center High School

13 miles west of Rochester on #14
Years Represented: 1924-1926

Leona Siewert Gray played her freshman and sophomore years at Byron and her junior and senior years at Dodge Center.

During Leona's playing years, the team played three-court, two-court and full-court rules. Leona recollected that the rules didn't permit players to take the ball away and they weren't to be too close to the other player. She preferred the half-court game to the three-court game.

When she moved to Dodge Center, there was no gym so they played above the hardware store. In the winter, they had to change clothes in the school and go two blocks to the hardware store and back after the game to change clothes again. Leona said, "In the winter time that wasn't very nice."

The girls' game was played first, followed by the boys' game. "The girls' game," said Leona, "was every bit as popular as the boys' game." Leona says that the girl's team played as many games as the boys and they helped earn money for the school. She thought the girls' team should be able to go to state too, but there was no tournament for the girls.

When asked about her life during the 1920's, Leona said,

"We didn't live on a farm. My folks ran a hotel and livery stable. They kept cattle out on a farm that we rented, and kept the cattle in a barn in Byron during the winter. Our well couldn't water all the cattle so after school, my sister and I had to drive them to the stockyards and pump water for the herd. If the pump was frozen we went to the neighbors. They had water on their hard coal heater. We would take the tea kettle out and thaw the pump out. Then we would go home and sometimes husk corn for an hour or so. I also waited on table, and then in the summertime, there were about 6 of us that went out to the nursery and picked strawberries for the nursery men for 3 cents a quart. There was a lady that could pick 100 quarts, and I thought, if she can do it, I can. So I did pick 100 quarts one day. That was enough for me! There was an elderly lady and they hired me to come on Saturday for 25 cents an hour to wash their (cream) separator and to brush up around the house. When we made hay, Dad would cut and someone else drove the team of horses. I had to drive the team on the hay loader and then drive the team to pull the fork up. I helped load and unload the oat grain. Dad made eight stacks one fall. Later, they thrashed with a steam engine. I even took milk to the factory sometimes if something was wrong at home and my dad couldn't. We had one horse and a dray buggy. One day when I was driving the horse and buggy to school, the 'fills' broke. There was a girl that walked to school. Emma came by and I said would you stop at Schaffers and tell them to call the folks and tell them I'm stranded. So then they came and I got to school a little bit late, which I never liked to do."

Leona said, "I never got above 5 foot 3 inches and I never weighed over 138 lbs. After I was married, I could swing a can of milk into the tank and I could swing a hay bale."

At the age of 90 years, Leona couldn't understand the reasoning when her high school girls' basketball team was discontinued. She said that the reason was, "girls' organs would be damaged." It didn't make sense to her.

"My sister and I had to drive the cattle to the stockyards and pump water for the herd. If the pump was frozen we went to the neighbors. They had water on their hard coal heater. We would take the tea kettle out and thaw the pump out."
Leona Siewert Gray

Duluth High Schools

Northeast Minnesota on #35
Years Represented: 1896 1936

The Duluth High School yearbook, the *Zenith*, included the following information on girls athletics conducted through a Girls Athletic Association:

1896 – Girls Athletic Association was organized to play tennis.

1897 – GAA reorganized to play tennis and croquet. Physical culture planned for next year.

1900 - GAA reorganized to include track, football and co-ed tennis.

1917 - Reported on Girls Basket Ball, "A few old players were there, but most of the material was new. Although for the last few years it had been the custom for the girls to play boys' rules, it was decided to follow the example of the leading normals and colleges and to play girls' rules."

The 1920 Duluth Central yearbook, "*Zenith*," reported,

"For some unexplainable reason, the girls in Central during 1919-20 have not participated in any school athletics. It seems a mistake if the girls of our school intend to drop athletics for other things, because there is no dodging the fact that the girls of today need these athletics more so than do the boys. It is not expected that the girls should enter all branches of athletics but still there are many branches open to them. We cannot say that the girls have been lacking in "Pep" and enthusiasm because they have supported the athletics of Central for '19-20 in grand style. They turned out in big numbers for all of the football games and packed the galleries to witness the basketball contests. We are sure that the girls themselves upon thinking this over will agree with me that the girl's athletics should be developed to a greater extent rather than dropped, although it is too late this year, we hope that the girls of following years will revive this needed activity."

Interscholastic basketball was reported in the 1924 Duluth Central *Zenith*. It recorded that, "Interest in girls basketball was shown more this year than ever before. The girls themselves showed enough interest to organize a team, which was successfully coached by Miss Klaus. Early in the season the team started practice, under Miss Klaus and soon developed into a strong combination. Games were played with Cathedral and Morgan Park girls, and both of these schools fell before the playing of our girls. Our first defeat of the season was encountered when the Superior Central girls swamped us in their gymnasium by a one-sided score. The following week we again played the girls from over the bay and again Superior succeeded in defeating us. This last game with Superior closed our season which can be called successful in every way. The lineup of our team follows: forwards, Mary Alice Gale, Eva Erickson, Wilma Annand; centers, Bina Lignell and Esther Karon; guards, Katherine Wasson, Susan Gale, Janet Graham and Helen Seashore."

Duluth Central 1924

The following schools indicated that they played a girls' team from Duluth: Two Harbors played Denfeld, 1919-1920; Cromwell, 1925-1931.

The Girls Athletic Association Years
From 1923–36, the reports focused on GAA activities and class teams for basketball.

The Duluth schools reflect the early movement from interscholastic teams to the organization of Girls Athletic Associations typical in the larger school systems. Physical education teachers conducted a variety of sports and recreational activities that were open to all interested girls in the school. The GAA period lasted until the 1960s and the resurgence of interscholastic programs for girls.

Dundee High School

Southwestern Minnesota, 20 miles north of Worthington on #62
Years Represented: 1915

A photo shows six players in black middy tops and black bloomers. No identification provided.

Dundee 1915

Elkton High School

Southeastern Minnesota, 15 miles east of Austin, a mile east of #90
Years Represented: 1927-1931

Bernice Swenson Hokeness played on the Elkton girls basketball team from 1927-31.

The girls' game was a three-court game. The team played Adams, Lyle, Rose Creek, Le Roy, Spring Valley, and Grand Meadow. The team traveled by school bus. They usually played in school gymnasiums, sometimes in a hall.

The uniforms were furnished by the school. The uniform was a one piece, sleeveless, and with elastic on the legs. Color was green and white trim, the school colors.

Coaches were female for two years and males for two years.

1930 team photo – Front: Laura Corbet Bianchi, Alice Tiedemann Marks, Doris Voorhees Drake,

156   Daughters of the Game

Esther Schwerin Elness, Bernice Swenson Hokeness, Myrtle Rabine Hoppin, Edna Schwerin. Back: Elna Rubin Rabine, Louise Klaehn Littlefield, Veryl Kennedy Bundy, Coach Miss Florence Wilbrecht, Rosena Kraft Nelson, Hazel Harrison, Pearl Hanson Tufte.

Elkton 1930

Bernice Swenson Hokeness recalls that the boys' teams and coaches were very supportive and that they had big crowds at their games. The teams traveled on the same bus.

Bernice said that they won many games except Grand Meadow which had "real tall players." She noted, "We didn't have many activities in those days. We looked forward to the games." The community was very supportive. Bernice said, "Very much so. We had big crowds at our games."

One of the news clippings in Bernice's scrapbooks recorded, "Elkton Girls Boast Win Over Lyle Team. Elkton, Jan. 21. Elkton high school girls boast a decisive victory over the Lyle girls in a basketball contest in which the swift and undefeated Elkton cagers outplayed their opponents completely."

A second clipping from the local newspaper in 1931 summed up, "Girls Play Last Game of the Season." The last paragraph read, "It's going to be pretty hard for any girl to work up to the position that Bernice played as forward this year. We all know that the graduating class of this year is going to wreck almost completely the squad, but we know that there are still girls that have very good basketball ability. Let us hope that they will work hard and keep as clean a record as the girls did this year. We would all like to see them have the record that Grand Meadow has."

"It's going to be pretty hard for any girl to work up to the position that Bernice played as forward this year." Newspaper article

Ellendale High School

South central Minnesota; 15 miles south of Owatonna on #35
Years Represented: 1923-1926

The *Ellendale Eagle* newspaper, February 28, 1924, reported that the 1923-24 season was the first for organized girls and boys basketball in Ellendale.

"The work of the girls has been even more effective as to the number of games won and actual scoring ability. Miss Sorlie has made very good use of a wealth of unusually good material and has developed a scoring machine that can give any of the surrounding teams a very busy evening. While the girls lose quite heavily by graduation this year, still there is plenty of good material to fall back upon to form a strong team for next season."

The game was a three-zone court, with two players from each team in each zone. The team won four of seven games. Admission to games was 15 and 25 cents. The team won four of seven games.

The 1923-24 team members were Myrtle Thompson, captain, Iris Wayne, Olive Lewison, Helen Johnson, Lillian Larson, and Helen Newgard. Miss Sorlie was the coach.

For the 1924-25 season, the *Ellendale Eagle*, October 23, 1924, reported that Coach Bergeson would coach the girls' and boys' teams. Coach Bergeson, school principal, had previously coached a strong girls' basketball team in Manly, Iowa. The team photo lists – Front: Helen Johnson, Verna Gruetzmacher, Olive Lewison, captain. Back: Genevieve Toland, Vivian Randall, B.E. Bergesen, Coach, Iris Wayne, Violet Jensen.

Ellendale 1925

The *Ellendale Eagle*, February 18, 1925 stated that Ellendale defeated Freeborn 114-5. "Good use was made of the time between halves in allowing the baskets to cool and in ordering another gross of pencils for Wesley Steele (scorekeeper), and a new arm and a few boxes of chalk for J.C. Jensen, the honorable keeper and chalker of the abacus." Helen Johnson scored 64 points.

The article was headlined: "Girls Made 3½ Points a Minute: Helen Johnson (of the winners) managed to make a record individual score by shooting 32 baskets, 16 in each half for a total of 64 points. The *Minneapolis Journal* recently printed an article to the effect that an Iowa girl made 27 baskets in a game for an Iowa record. Thirty-two should be a good start on a Minnesota record."

On April 1, 1925 the *Ellendale Eagle* reported in a headline, "High School Star in Rotogravure." The article affirmed, "The rotogravure section of the Sunday *St. Paul Pioneer Press* this week gave a little well deserved credit to the Ellendale high school's star basket ball player. A very good picture of Helen Johnson in uniform in characteristic pose getting ready for one of her dead-sure free throws appears in this pictorial section. The text explaining the engraving reads: 'Miss Helen Johnson, Ellendale, star of the Ellendale high school girls basket ball team, who scored 290 of her school's 504 points during the past season. She produced a bigger score than the total made by opposing teams, 230 points and made 64 of these while Ellendale was winning from Freeborn by a record breaking score of 114 to 5.'"

"High School Star in Rotogravure" *Ellendale Eagle*, 1925

The *Ellendale Eagle* on February 25, 1925, noted that the Alden floor "which was the best and largest the local teams have played on this year, necessitated the use of the three-division game for the girls and this hampered them in getting started."

The March 4, 1925, *Ellendale Eagle* article indicated that in a game against New Richland, "the first half was played with three zones and the second half was played with the two-division game." Teams played included: New Richland, Waldorf, Freeborn, Alden, Blooming Prairie and Hayfield. The team won eight of their nine games.

The Invitational Tournament was considered the highlight of the 1924-1925 season. Five of the best area teams were invited: Hayfield, Kenyon, Waldorf, New Richland and Pemberton. The tournament games were played as two-court games, which the annual article said was new to most of the teams entered.

As tournament champions, Vivian Randall Harpel said that the players received a small basketball about 2 inches in circumference, and school letters for their season play.

On February 25, 1925, the *Ellendale Eagle* reported: "Ellendale 62, Freeborn 13. On Friday night, the Ellendale girls, returning to the two-division game defeated Freeborn 62-13. A large crowd had assembled to see the team that had defeated Freeborn the preceding week by the record score of 114-5. On every hand people were inquiring as to the authenticity of rumored and published reports. The Ellendale girls obliged by giving a good exhibition game. Not a field goal was scored on them the first half. In the second half Ardis Hatle of the losers tossed in five baskets. Helen Johnson was high scorer with 17 baskets."

In the 1925 invitational tournament, held March 6-7, some games were played three-court and others played with the 'new' two-court game. The tournament included Hayfield, Kenyon, Waldorf, New Richland, Waldorf, Pemberton and Ellendale. On March 11, 1925, the Ellendale newspaper reported that the tournament was won by Ellendale. The team received a loving cup and the players received individual medals. The officials selected Helen Johnson and Violet Jensen for the All-Tournament Team. The article was titled: "Are We Proud? Well! Well!" It stated, "The High School Girl's Basket Ball Tournament has come and gone and it left a mighty good taste in the mouths of the people of Ellendale. It is such a good taste that it has left them hungry for more and any time the schools undertake a similar enterprise they may count upon the enthusiastic support of the citizenry. As for our girls, we were proud of them before, but now we are simply all swelled up with pride. The girls not only played a skillful game, but they appeared so winsome and modest, clean and wholesome, that they couldn't help being attractive to everyone, which they were."

The 1925-26 season record was six games won and six games lost. The team included Verna Gruetzmacher, captain, Vivian Randall, Nellie Kiley, Idella Ohnstad, Iris Wayne, Violet Jensen, Genevieve Toland, and Mildred Ellingson. Coach: Raymond Nelson.

Ellendale 1926

Special Stories

The January 24, 1924 *Ellendale Eagle* reported,

"The New Richland high school girls' and boys' basket ball teams journeyed over here in bob sleighs for a doubleheader with the Ellendale high school boys' and girls' teams. Citizens of this village were just in the midst of admiring the unusual display of the northern lights in the heavens that evening when all of a sudden the air was rent with a bedlam of noise that along with the weird illumination suggested an invasion of Eskimaux and was unaccountable until it was recalled that Professor Lewis was around that noon painting up the town about a basket ball game with New Richland and that this unusual disturbance was undoubtedly the announcement of the visiting players' arrival on the field of battle."

In a publication, "Early Ellendale Basketball," the cover features the girls' and boy's basketball teams in 1925. One story related,

"An interesting side light of those early years was transportation. Ralph Wayne recalls that when they went to New Richland to play, they went by horses and sleigh. He also recalls that for a scheduled Saturday night doubleheader (girls game and boys game) at Medford it was very cold –way below zero. Ralph drove his father's team and sleigh to Ellendale and left the horses in Miller's barn. The teams assembled at the depot for the 3 o'clock train. They had supper at Medford and played both games. They had a long wait at the depot for the late train home! As there was no heat in the depot, the boys got to scuffling and one fell into the window and broke it. When they got back to Ellendale, Olive Lewison had no ride home so Ralph took her home. He said, 'When I got her home, I was farther from my home than when I left Ellendale. It was 3 a.m. when I got to bed.' The following Monday morning Mr. Lewis came around and collected 15 cents from each player for Mr. Todd to send to Medford to pay for the window."

The *Ellendale Eagle*, March 25, 1925, reported:

"Mr. and Mrs. E.M. Thompson entertained the 25 members of the girls' and boys' basketball squads. The hosts had planned several interesting events and one very strenuous and exciting contest beforehand, thus keeping the guests busy in entertaining themselves. Preceding the several contests was an exceedingly spirited basketball game. For the harrowing details consult anyone present. Suffice it to say that in the finals, the blowers led by Captain Helen Johnson out winded the die-hards led by Ernest Ellingson. Arthur Christensen carried away the individual honors. His technique was impeccable. The major fatality was caused by Emery Ellingson carelessly dropping his jaw on the prolate oblate spheroid, species egg, which served as the ball. Later in the evening a very complete lunch was served to the satisfaction of all, accompanied by unique favors consisting of miniature basket balls. The party broke up with rousing cheers for the hosts. Every one maintained that the party was the most successful one ever held in Ellendale for such a large group, so many, thanks and much credit is due Mr and Mrs. E.M. Thompson, our loyal fans."

Newspaper excerpts reprinted with permission by the *Ellendale Eagle*.

Excelsior High School

West metro on #7
Years Represented: 1917-1921

Clara Mae Donlin was 95 years of age when she shared the memories of her Excelsior High School girls basketball team, 1917-1921. Clara recalls the names of two team members: Ruth Hudson and Gladys Newman Peck. Gladys had a twin named Glee.

Clara said that the game rules changed every year. They started with three courts and she was a forward. Then they played two courts and she was a center and, "I could run all over the place. As a running center, you could run down on one end and be a forward and then you could run down and be a guard." The other team members had to be either a forward or guard during the game.

Her team played Waconia, South St. Paul, Hopkins, North St. Paul, and possibly Stillwater. Miss Montgomery and Lee Hutton served as their coaches.

Their uniforms were black wool. Clara says, "The uniform was made of beautiful black wool. The pants were so big that it was like a skirt. We wore a middy blouse. It was a real nice uniform. The wool was warm. We had a lot of underwear on." The school provided the uniform. Clara says, "If my mother had to buy it I wouldn't have had one. They (my parents) didn't have money; my father earned a dollar a day and didn't have money to throw away on stuff like that."

Clara's team played in Excelsior in the school that is now a grade school. When asked about traveling to games, Clara said, "Oh boy, that was something! One time we were going up to Waconia, and they got a livery stable that had a small truck for moving furniture and they put eight bales of hay in there. It was cold winter time and we all piled in there and went to Waconia and played basketball. They didn't have a school with a gym or anything. You were in a school room. We had one girl who was so bashful you had to stand in a ring with your back to her so nobody saw her in her long underwear that she wore."

The team traveled to South St. Paul by streetcar. It took a couple hours to get there. If it was chartered for the team, Clara said, "We were the only ones on it." In winter weather, the team traveled by sleigh/bobsled with the boys' team. They had a lot of fun traveling in the truck with the boys' team. Adults always went along to watch the teams play.

> "We had one girl who was so bashful you had to stand in a ring with your back to her so nobody saw her in her long underwear that she wore."
> Clara Donlin

The team also traveled by truck to some games. She said that one night they were out all night because when they got "out there in the boondocks" and we couldn't get any place and it was so cold. I didn't get home until 5:00 in the morning and my mother said, 'it's the last time you do that!' It was the year we went to Waconia."

When Clara was interviewed, she was very interested in sharing her memories. She had a team picture and scrapbook of her high school years. On the wall of her room, a poster-sized picture hung of her on a motorcycle. Clara said, "I went out the back door and the motorcycle was sitting there. I plopped on it and someone took my picture. That year, everybody got a Christmas card with me sitting on the motorcycle. I was always the clown."

Clara worked as a volunteer in Minnetonka classrooms until she was 88 yrs of age. Clara was awarded a Service Award from the Minnetonka School District.

Faribault High School

Central Minnesota, 40 miles south of metropolitan area on #35
Years Represented: 1920-1923

Faribault 1923

Faribault is listed on the schedule for Montgomery and New Prague in 1920.

The 1923 Faribault High School *Athenian* identifies the girls basketball team members – Front: Esther Schultz, Elenora Schlaet, Muriel Leach, Helen Shirk. Back: Eleanor Thompson, Sarah Schochet, Irene Taylor, Coach, Ruth Thompson, Phyllis Code.

Legacy
Marian Bemis Johnson, daughter of Elenora Schlaet Bemis, said that her mother was her inspiration.

Franklin High School

Central Minnesota; 12 miles east of Redwood Falls on #19
Years Represented: 1907-1929

The *Redwood Gazette* provided information on the early days of the Franklin girls basketball team. The first team was organized in 1907. Uniforms consisted of black bloomers, a middy blouse with a large sailor collar, a full-pleated skirt, long black stockings and black tennis shoes. The teams played a three-court game, one section for the two guards, one for two forwards and one for two centers. Only forwards could shoot and players were limited to one dribble.

The following article appeared in the *Franklin Tribune*, January 11, 1934:

"Basket Ball Was Popular Sport in Franklin Way Back in Days of 1908

Basket ball enjoyed popularity in Franklin 25 years ago, just as it does today, according to a toast which Mrs. Rudolph Diekmeier, of the class of 1908, gave at the recent high school alumni banquet at the hotel.

Published herewith is Mrs. Diekmeier's toast in its entirety:

'President, members and guests of the alumni: When asked to give a toast I said I had talked every year so somebody else ought to assume the duty this year.

I hardly knew what to choose as a topic, but basket ball being the real school sport then as it is now, I thought perhaps I could tell you a little about girls basket ball as it was played 25 years ago. This is ancient history of sports.

There were five on our team, sometimes six, if we could scare up one more—two guards, two forwards, and one or two centers. Our guards were Mrs. Berklund (nee Clara Lund) and Myrtle Amtsbauer; forwards, Jennie Foss and Eva Newton; and I was jumping center. (I didn't have quite so much avoirdupois to carry around then, as I was called 'Toothpicks.')

Our floor was divided into three sections, one for the forwards, one for the centers and one for the guards. Our rules at the time were a little different from what they are now.

Our suits were black, consisting of wide bloomers, a middy blouse with large sailor collar, and a very, very full pleated skirt, long black stockings and black tennis shoes. The only dash of color we had was a bow of blue and white ribbons, which were our basket ball colors.

When we were to play other towns, we drove with horses or went by train. We often had to stay until the next day at the place at which we played, and when visitors came they did the same.'

It is needless to say that Mrs. Diekmeier's interesting discourse on a popular game as it was played in the early days of Franklin high school was avidly accepted by all those present at the banquet."

The 1923-24 team was undefeated in seven games. The photo lists – Front: Clara Gerstenkorn. Middle: Florence Sherman, Coach Edith Foss, Ellen Kelly. Back: Valeria Kirwin, Orda Olson, Helen McFarland. Alice Stonelake not in photo.

The 1928 team photo listed: Front: Alice Schroeder. Middle: Grace Rieke, unknown, Evelyn Brandjord, Wynifred Kerwin. Back: Esther Schroeder, Bertha Schroeder, Mabel Erlandson, coach.

Franklin 1924

Franklin 1929

In 1999, at 88 yrs, Alice Schroeder McFarland provided information on a questionnaire and in the article dated February 25, 1999, in the *Redwood Falls Gazette*. The article was written by Wayne Cook. Alice was a forward and one of the stars at Franklin from 1926-1929.

The teams played the nearby schools. Alice said, "There was the jumping center and the running center. The centers passed the ball. With only one bounce, you better know where you're going to be. With the one-bounce, it hindered you. The referees would call you for running." Alice's father drove her and others to games by car. Her two sisters, Bertha and Esther, also played on the team. Alice said, "There were quite a few players packed in the car." Games were played in a city building. The coach was a "male professor." The games were officiated. Teams traveled together with the girls' team playing first.

Fourth Quarter

Alice said, "I didn't want to play one time. The coach said, "We might as well give up the game if you don't play." Alice said, "I really liked shooting. I kind of shot over my shoulder. I was one of the first ones to do that. There were no long shots. I never kept track of how many baskets I made or missed." The news article reports that her shot resembled a hook shot of today and was hard to block.

The *Franklin Tribune*, February 21, 1929. "Alice Schroeder and her fast-traveling cohorts were out for sweet revenge for the game they lost to Morton earlier in the season by one point (and it was not their fault that they lost it) Taking the game in hand, from the first tip-top, the Schroeder sextette began their glorious march to victory. With an early lead, they forged steadily forward and made a total of 26 points while the Mortonites were held at bay to be satisfied with only 11 tallies."

Alice said, "In my mind, the community liked the girls better than the boys. I don't know if it was because we had the better team."

Track and field was a sport at Franklin, but didn't compare to basketball. Alice remembered going to Bird Island to compete in the broad jump and high jump. Alice said, "We didn't have sawdust pits to land in." Alice set records at the county meet in 1925.

A photo of the 1931 team listed the following members – Front: Charlotte Homme, Mary Revier, Phyllis Ploof, Genevieve Homme. Back: Irene Scott, Rachel Jacobson, Helen Breffle, Harriet Nesburg, Esther Schroeder, Vera Strom, Coach.

A photo of the 1936 team listed the following members – Front: Quanita Sampson, Alvera Larson, Hazel Neunsinger, Lucille Neunsinger, Clare Grimes. Coach Vera Strom. Back: Marie Schroeder, Delores Honl, Beulah Sampson, Leora Rydland.

Franklin 1931

The 1936 team was the last team until 1970.

Legacy
Alice's legacy includes three granddaughters who share her love of basketball: Stephanie Hall Moran played for Mound; Lynn Trochlil Crist played for Willmar, and Michelle McFarland Bursch played for Jordan.

Newspaper excerpt reprinted with permission of *Redwood Gazette*

Franklin 1936

Frazee High School

Western Minnesota, 10 miles southeast of Detroit Lakes on #10
Years Represented: 1938-1939

The *Wannegan '39* was published by the Senior Class of Frazee High School. It included a photo of the 1939 girls basketball team – Front: Kathryn Aldrich, Marian Haas, Violet Mattfeld, Marilyn King, Margaret Corkery. Back: Kathryn Dengler, Marjorie Graham, Arliz Pfeiffer, Mr. D.A. Fraser, coach, Betty Iten, Virginia Brooks.

Frazee 1939

Teams played were-Lake Park, Audubon, and Underwood.

The team's uniforms were a green satin fabric, with short-sleeved tops with belted shorts. Green was the color for the Frazee Hornets. Kathryn's daughter, Deb Hoyhtya, remembers seeing her mother's green satin uniform when she was a child.

The yearbook revealed, "As a result of the excellent coaching of Mr. Fraser, the girls had a good fast team this year. Because a captain was not elected, the senior girls took turns at this honor." Kathryn Aldrich Schrom graduated in 1939.

Freeborn High School

Southern Minnesota; 15 miles from Albert Lea, on #29
Years Represented: 1910-1927

Freeborn 1910

Freeborn 1927

The 1910 Freeborn girls basketball team consisted of Edna Brooks, Ruth Miller Cherrington, Hannah Sorenson, teacher; Ella Hunte Miller, Lorna Purdie, Gladys Callahan. The team photo shows players in black tops with bloomers and long dark stocks and black laced leather shoes. Team members are wearing large dark bows in their hair.

The Freeborn High School yearbook, the 1927 *Tempest*, provided the names of the girls basketball team: Mildred Peters, Captain Carmen Johnson, Ruby Bates, Esther Thompson, Elizabeth Schultz, Alma Jacobsen, Olive Tukua, Laura Jacobson, Evelyn Christianson, Dorothy Schultz Schuster. In the team photo, Dorothy Schultz Schuster is in the back row, second from left.

The season summary recapped, "Much time has been spent by the girls in hard and earnest practice to make a better team than that of last year. Just two of last year's regulars were back to play with the team this season. Though not very fortunate in winning games we feel that the year has been successful. Mildred Peters played a consistently strong game throughout the season as jumping center. Captain Carmen Johnson and Ruby Bates are deserving of much credit for their playing at forwards. Esther Thompson and Elizabeth Schultz acted as substitute forwards. Five players — Alma Jacobsen, Olive Tukua, Laura Jacobson, Evelyn Christianson and Dorothy Schultz, — divided the duties of guards in a satisfactory manner."

Dorothy Schultz Schuster provided the following information in an interview. Dorothy remembers her first game as if it were yesterday. The team played the teachers and she had to guard her own coach, Miss Landus.

The game was two-court, with the offensive team consisting of two forwards and a center playing one half of the court. The defensive team was made up of two guards and a center guarding the other half of the court.

The uniforms consisted of middies and black bloomers. The girls made the bloomers at home or in home economics class, and purchased the middies. They wore long stockings and soft tennis shoes. Freeborn's school colors were orange and black and they wore an orange "F" on the front of their middies. The team played six games, two each against St. Clair, Pemberton and Alden.

The team rode the train from Freeborn to the game at St. Clair. There were no motorized buses at that time. The buses were horse drawn and too slow for distant games. Either families with cars took the girls or George Hinkley with a truck took them. They would ride in the back of the truck with no top on the truck box.

Special Stories
Their coach, Miss Landus, taught home economics, Caesar and biology. She was responsible for preparing one hot item for school lunch for the entire student body. Dorothy said it was potato soup, hot cocoa, and similar items. The students brought their own lunch buckets for the remainder of their meal.

Dorothy's father died when she was 7 years old and her mother died when she was in eighth grade. She lived with her two sisters and three brothers on the family farm between Freeborn and Wells.

After graduating from high school, Dorothy attended a year of Normal Teachers Training in Wells. She taught a year of country school at District 85, located north of Kiester across the road from the cemetery. The second year she returned to her home country school district No. 126, northeast of Wells. Her three children and nine of her 12 grandchildren all graduated from Freeborn High School. There was no varsity basketball available for her daughter but her granddaughters again had the opportunity and played. Dorothy, and her husband, Andrew, of 65 years, farmed southwest of Freeborn.

In 2004 Dorothy was 98 years of age.

"Their coach, Miss Landus, taught home economics, Caesar and biology. She was responsible for preparing one hot item for school lunch for the entire student body."
Freeborn 1927

Gaylord High School

Central Minnesota; 50 miles southeast of the metro area on #5
Years Represented: 1907-1924

Three members of the Gaylord teams participated in interviews about their teams of the 1920s: Margaret Huffman Thompson, 91 years; Clara Corcoran Lawrenz, 94 years; and Leona Briard Hanson, 93 years.

In 1907 the first Gaylord girls basketball team took the train to Arlington for the first game, which they lost 9-6. Team members included Myrtle Barger, Ella Schnobrich, Flora Fritzner, Mandy Fiss and Laura Timm. On December 7, 1907, the team defeated Henderson 20 to 0, the only shutout in Gaylord High School girls basketball history.

The game became popular again just before 1919 when Mrs. Alma Tohrer became the coach. Games were played in the old, red brick city hall.

The *Gaylord Hub*, March 25, 1999, headlined, "Margaret Thompson honored at girls basketball tournament." The women were honored by the Minnesota State High School League for their early playing days. Margaret explained their games of the 1920s, "There were six girls on a team, two forwards, two guards, a running center and jumping center. Forwards, the only players that could shoot, were not allowed to go past half court. They depended upon the guards to get the basketball." Uniforms consisted of middy blouses and loose fitting bloomers that came to the knees.

Belinda Corcoran Eckert provided information that she played from 1919-22. They played a three-court game, playing Winthrop, Arlington, Gibbon, Green Isle, Fairfax, Hutchinson and Excelsior. Belinda explained they traveled by train and car, sometimes staying overnight. She said they did not play double-headers with the boys' team. She said, "We were the big game." Her favorite memory was the enthusiasm of the crowds. At the time of her interview, Belinda was 96.

Gaylord 1920

Clara Corcoran Lawrenz said that she played from in 1919–22. Her team played three courts with officials, against Arlington, Green Isle, Gibbon, Fairfax, Winthrop, Excelsior, St. Peter and Hutchinson. Clara recalled that they did not play prior to a boys' game as the boys had no team at that time. She emphasized, "We were the big game." Her nickname was "Corky."

Gaylord 1922

The 1920 team photo lists - Belinda Corcoran Eckert, Gladys Dougal Hagen, Dela Kusske, Myrtle Werges, Clara Corcoran Lawrenz, Lucy Hoershgan.

A 1921-22 photo of the Gaylord Team lists – Front: Margaret Stowell, Leona Briard Hanson, Daisy Lindall. Back: Margaret Briard, Coach Naomi Wiedenmann, Clara Corcoran Lawrenz, Gertrude Briest. The team won 8, lost 3.

A 1922-1923 photo lists – Front: Bertha Hyzer, Julia Huelscamp, Captain Leona Briar, Edna Lichtenegger, Elsie Schueler. Back: Marie Spaude, May Reilly, Coach Naomi Wiedenmann, Helen Corcoran. The team won 8, lost 3.

Gaylord 1923

A 1923-24 photo – Front: Ruth Borchert, Edna Lichtenegger, Leona Briard Hanson, Bertha Hyzer. Back: Marie Spaude, Cora Warnke Lemberg, Coach Margaret Scheman, Thusnelda Doering, Julie Huelskamp, Margaret Huffman Thompson.

The 1924 Gaylord yearbook, the *Gaylee,* provided information that the girls' and boys' teams started practice late because the hall was being decorated. The girls' team played Arlington, Glencoe, Hutchinson and Winthrop. Some games were played as doubleheaders. Low-scoring games were typical of girls' and boy' games. In the boys' first game with Redwood Falls, the score was 12 to 9. In a doubleheader at Arlington, the girls' score was 12-10 and the boys' score was 10-7. At another doubleheader with Winthrop, the 1924 school yearbook reported, "On February 29th, the teams returned the games with Winthrop. The girls, however did not prove so successful this time, and lost by a score of 17 to 13. The boys' game was very exciting, as it decided whether the boys would go to the district tournament at St. Peter. The boys won by a safe margin, the score being 12 to 7."

Gaylord 1924

Margaret Thompson, 1919-24, stated that, "Uniforms were middy blouses and loose fitting bloomers that came to the knees, so we were called "the Bloomer Girls."

There were six on a team, two forwards, two guards, a jumping center and a running center. Margaret says, "My nickname was 'Skinny' as I weighed only 100 pounds. I was in the class of 1924." Their coach was Miss Bloom, a teacher at the school.

Leona Briard Hanson provided the following information in her questionnaire. She played from 1920-24. Her teams traveled by "touring car or train." Sometimes they came back on the midnight train or stayed overnight and returned the next day. Leona said that Everett Reimer had a big car, a Reo, so they would hire him to drive the team to many of the games. They went on the train to Excelsior.

Games were played at the two-story brick City Hall. Leona and her sister played running center and jumping center and were nicknamed "The Briard Battery." Leona said she was called "Little Donuts" and her sister was called "Big Donuts."

Leona enjoyed remembering when they played St. Peter and staying overnight in the players' homes. In Hutchinson, the team stayed at a hotel. They paid some of their expenses with tickets sold at the door. They traveled by train to Excelsior.

Leona said their games drew a crowd and the city hall was full with fans standing in the back by the movie equipment and on the stage. In some schools, there were radiators in the way. Fans sat along the wall. At Arlington, the space was so small that fans would have to stand up. If players threw a long shot, it would hit the ceiling. She said, "We liked our home court because we had a high ceiling in the City Hall. We always had to pay our own expenses. We even brought money to pay the light bill at the city hall, and brought wood to build the fire. There was a stove in the corner, and we had to sweep. The boys wanted to come in and watch us play and play before we did. So they would sneak in to carry in the wood and do all kinds of things for us."

The team received letters and Leona bought herself a sweater.

The women indicated that "Armalore" was their first coach. She was a teacher. They believed that the coaches "did it out of the goodness of their hearts; they didn't get paid for it." A woman teacher named Bell officiated games at Gibbon.

Records indicate that the girls' team was discontinued in the late 1920s. It was reinstated as an interscholastic team in 1973.

Special Stories
At the age of 91, Margaret Thompson participated in the reception for basketball pioneers at the 1999 MSHSL State Girls Basketball Tournament. At the reception, Margaret said, "My nickname was Skinny. I only weighed 100 pounds. Another player was called "Little Donuts." We were part of the class of 1924, 75 years ago when I was 16 and now I am 91."

Leona's daughter, Susan Hanson, assisted with the interview and Susan said, "It still makes me angry to think that I missed that experience. "

Newspaper excerpts reprinted with permission by the *Gaylord Hub* newspaper

Glyndon High School

Western Minnesota; 7 miles east of Moorhead on #10
Years Represented: 1934

A photo identifies the members of the 1934 Glyndon High School girls basketball team – Front: Lucille Griffin, Loretta Brandt, Ethel Alfe, Helen Griffin. Middle: Assistant Coach Dorothea Ward, Rosemary Andrews, Florence Koops, Barbara Driscoll, Violet Richards, Bernice Lamb. Back: Alvina Bekkerus, Dorothy Stempf, Maxine Headland, Viola Ekanger, Coach Douglas Sommerville.

The team was undefeated in 18 games, starting its winning streak in 1932.

Glyndon 1934

Team uniforms were light shirts and light shorts. A second photo of the team showed the players in dark, two-piece warm-ups.

Coach Sommerville was a teacher of many subjects in the school.

Glyndon 1934 in team warm-ups

Goodhue High School

Southeastern Minnesota, 20 miles southeast of Cannon Falls off #52
Years Represented: 1910

The Zumbrota Area Historical Society located one photo of the 1910 Goodhue girls basketball team. No names were available.

Goodhue 1910

Grand Meadow High School

Southeastern Minnesota, 25 miles south of Rochester
Years Represented: 1911-1939

Grand Meadow 1911

The first record of a girls basketball team in Grand Meadow is a photo of five girls with one holding a ball dated "1911." The team members from left to right are: Clara Ferris Lewis, Edith Gilman Rogers, Verna Warner Drinkall, Bernice Nolan Lindelien and Ruby Burrington Card.

The next piece of the team's history skipped to 1929 when the Grand Meadow girls basketball teams from 1929 – 1939 did what no team has done before or since: they won every game that they played during those ten years – 94 straight games!

The team averaged over 38 points a game and held the opponents to an average of just over 12 points a game. The winning streak began during the Great Depression and gave the community of Grand Meadow something to enjoy during those difficult years.

The *Spring Valley Tribune* writer David Phillips, March 19, 1986 "Girls basketball isn't all that modern. People talk about dynasties in high school sports, but there'll probably never be one like the Grand Meadow girls basketball team in the 1930s. The team went through 10 seasons and never lost a game. Back then, there were no post-season tournaments so the team didn't get a chance to see if it was state champion material. It also never got a chance to see how many years it could continue its win streak, for the state banned competitive sports for high school girls in 1940."

"As a former girls' basketball coach, I am thrilled to see the early history of Minnesota girls basketball brought together in this book. Since the 1970s, we have persevered to a point where our state could not even imagine the absence of girls' basketball in our schools. I am proud of the role that the Grand Meadow school system, and the entire southeastern region, played in the very early days of the sport. I hope the reader will enjoy this history and come to appreciate those who laid the foundation for today's outstanding program in Minnesota."
Bruce Klaehn, Superintendent of Schools, Grand Meadow ISD #495, 2005.

The 1939 team played the last season for a memorable team. It became a disappointing victim to the shut-down of competitive girls basketball teams across Minnesota and most of the country.

The coach for the first seven years was Lila Reiersgard of Ulen, MN. She was a graduate of Concordia College in Moorhead. Team members disclosed that their coach wore a red coat, wasn't very athletic-looking, but had tough practices several times a week. Ruth Bratrud Jacobson, 1930, divulged that their coach "didn't get after us for anything. We respected her so. No one would ever criticize her. She made you want to practice, and nobody ever missed practice. She expected us to be there for our practices always and do the right thing all the time. We kind of worshipped her, I think." Ruth added, "Everyone got along so well on the team."

The second coach for two years was Marion Nestande. The third coach was Carolyn Rem. Her coaching tenure ended when the school dropped the girls' team.

Grand Meadow was one of the few teams to have regular practices. Ruth Bratrud Jacobson, a senior on the first team in 1929-30, shared that they practiced and played in the Opera House where there was a big floor. There was a court painted on the floor and baskets on backboards. The Opera House was also used for dances, movies, county poultry shows, talent shows, graduation exercises, school operettas and plays, stereopticon slide shows, magic lantern shows, silent films, talking pictures and roller-skating.

Marie Tommerson Berg, 1929-1934, said that their game was the two-court game, the same as in Iowa where girls couldn't cross the center line and three girls stayed in each half of the court. Players were allowed three dribbles and then had to pass the ball. There was a jump ball in center court after every basket.

Boys' and girls' games were played the same night and the team members said that the fans came to see both teams. Ruth Bratrud Jacobson explained, "Our games were played prior to the boys' games. Many times the gym (i.e., the Opera House) was packed for the girls' game but many people left before or during the boys' game." Even so, the girls had no cheerleaders and the school administration determined that the girls couldn't ride in the bus with the boys to the games. They had to arrange their own transportation with parents driving the team to games. Ruth said that she lived in town, but the girls who lived in the country frequently had to walk home or stay in town with friends.

The girls provided their own uniforms. Marie Tommerson Berg said that they purchased the wool shorts and noted that the team members, 10 years later, were wearing the same shorts. They purchased or made their team shorts and sweatpants for warm-ups.

Marie Berg recalled that her father gave her one dollar for the games. It was to be used only in case of an emergency.

Alvena Travis Glynn of the 1934 team disclosed, "We'd dress in the school and regardless what kind of weather it was, stormy, icy, we would run to the Opera House. We just ran in our shorts. Then, we'd run back all sweaty. That was worse." Alvena also noted that she had one dress to wear to school. She said that it was a navy blue wool dress. One day she burned a hole in the back by warming up too close to a hot stove. Her mother patched it and she wore it for the rest of the winter. She said, "There was no money to buy another dress, so you used what you had."

Dorothy Allen Blanchard, 1936-39, remembered walking home after basketball practices to her home in the country. Her father cut the field fence line one year and drove through the field because the snow wasn't as deep as in the driveway. Dorothy said they went to school in a horse-drawn sled with heated bricks to keep her feet warm.

Ruth Bratrud Jacobson declared her favorite memory as being "Every part of it practicing, playing the game, discussions afterwards and winning every game......I loved basketball!!"

Teams played included Rose Creek, Kasson, Lyle, Lime Springs, IA, LeRoy, Adams, Elkton, Chester, Dover, Peterson and an independent semi-professional team from Mason City, Iowa. The win record included the game with the semi-professional team. The team played 14 games that year. On average, their teams played 10 to 12 games per season. They outscored their opponents 591 – 153. The team averaged 10 players.

Ceil Stier Schneider, a 1938 graduate, said there was some pressure because no team wanted to go down in the record books as being known as the first team that lost a game.

Mildred Berg Gilbert scored 50 points in a game during her senior year. DeVera Bratrud Proeschel, star of the 1939 team, once scored 51 points in a game. Her accomplishment was highlighted in the *Minneapolis Star Tribune*.

Grand Meadow 1930

There are three trophies in the school's trophy case when the team won the Mower Conference League by their season record. No tournament games were played.

The 1929-30 team – Front: Phyllis Rother Torgrimson, Mildred Berg Gilbert, Helen Gunderson, Gladys Nelson Travis, Marie Tommerson Berg. Back: Supt. Hugh Jones, Ruth Bratrud Jacobson, Pearl Tommerson Jacobson, Madeline McDonough Perry, Mildred Wakefield Olson, Gladys Peterson Fruth, Miss Reiersgard, Coach.

Grand Meadow 1931

1930-1931 team - Ruth Kuhn Goodrich, Pearl Tommerson Jacobson, Ruth Kelley Ramsey, Marjorie Elliott Namock, Agnes Peterson Olson, Alice Kuhl Coleman, Gretchen Harvey Peterson, Phyllis Rother Torgrimson, Marie Tommerson Berg, Gladys Nelson Travis.

1931-32 team – Front: Constance Torgrimson Stephenson, Klenora Olson Page, Gretchen Harvey Peterson. Middle: Coach Reiersgard, Ruth Kuhn Goodrich, Agnes Peterson Olson, Miriam Elliot, Alice Kuhl Coleman, Tess Nelson Jahns. Back: Opal Skaran, Gladys Nelson Travis, Marie Tommerson Berg, Margaret Forbes Peterson.

Grand Meadow 1932

Grand Meadow 1934

1933-1934 team - Rosella Jensen Necsik, Opal Skaran, Mabel Bates, Mercedes Doherty, Alvena Travis Glynn, Theresa Nelson Jahns, Edith Peterson Price, Captain Alice Kuhl Coleman, Alta Berg McCullough, Helen Terlinden.

1934-35 team – Front: Kathryn Iverson, Lillian Terlinden, Helen Terlinden, Ardis Peterson, Rosella Jensen Necsik. Back: Dorothy Quickstad Olson, Edith Peterson Price, Cecilia Stier Schneider, DeVera Bratrud Proeschel, Beulah Travis Ankeny and Coach Lila Reiersgard.

Grand Meadow 1935

Grand Meadow 1936

1935-1936 team — Ardis Peterson, Hazel Peterson Blanchard, Irene Mahoney Bye, Norraine Thorson Handke, Dorothy Quickstad Olson, Kathryn Iverson, DeVera Bratrud Proeschel, Rosella Jensen Necsik, Cecilia Stier Schneider, Beulah Travis Ankeny, Coach Lila Reiersgard.

1938-39 team – Front: Norraine Thorson Handke, Kathryn Skaran Losey, DeVera Bratrud Proeschel, Irene Mahoney Bye, Dorothy Allen Blanchard. Back: Daniella Thompson Peterson, June Wright Kramer, Winifred Goodsell Peterson, Mae Harvey Gross, Alice Jensen Evling, Coach Carolyn Rem.

Grand Meadow 1939

When the School Discontinued Girls Basketball in 1939

In 1997 The *Meadow Area News*, carried an article written by Sue Doocy, "The Grand Meadow Girls' Basketball Teams of 1929-1939." She had researched the time when the school administration decided to discontinue the girls basketball team. She reviewed articles in the *Grand Meadow Record*, state statutes and the minutes of the Grand Meadow School Board meetings. Assistance was provided by the Mower County Historical Society.

Her article read: "The *Record* made its comments (about the team) in black and white after all but one game – the last one – when Grand Meadow couldn't seem to find the words to say goodbye to their girls basketball team of the '30s. Maybe there was nothing left to say to answer the questions about "The Ban," the day Superintendent Dahlin received a letter banning girl basketball."

Kathryn Skaran Losey was a student working in the school office the day news of the ban arrived, and when asked in recent years (1992) by Dorothy McIntyre of the Minnesota State High School League what Superintendent Dahlin did with the letter, Kathryn responded, "The Superintendent threw the letter in the trash."

Austin Community College offered the Minitex Reference Service to conduct a search in Mason's Minnesota Statues from 1927 to 1941 for the law that "banned" girls' sports. No such article existed.

In a copy of Mason's Minnesota Statues of 1927, one article required all public schools to provide physical and health education courses for all students, boys and girls, with modified courses for those with physical or mental handicaps.

The Grand Meadow school board members took time to consider this law on October 6, 1938. The school board records stated, "The matter of complying with the State requirements regarding Physical training for all of the 7-8-9 and 10 grades of our school was considered and finding this to be practically out of the question if we continue our present courses of study without hiring another teacher, and in order to meet requirements it was moved and seconded that Superintendent Dahlin be authorized to personally interview and hire another teacher for such work as may be assigned her to relieve the situation. The motion carried." Other than the hiring of a physical education teacher, no mention is made of the discontinuation of girls' basketball at the end of the 1939 season."

In the Doocy article, Margaret Forbes Peterson, of the 1931 team, said, "Well, in those days, the teachers and the school superintendent, they were the law. They were the highest educated people and you just went along with what they said. You didn't interfere. You treated them with respect."

"We were told that it was state law that we couldn't play," said Mae Gross. "We were sick, we were angry. But we were in that age when we still were expected to respect decisions. The state said, 'That's it,' and we didn't think there was any choice but to accept it."

Special Stories
The Grand Meadow teams were honored on February 6, 1992, at a rally from noon – 1 p.m. at the State Capital Rotunda as part of the sixth annual National Girls and Women in Sports Day.

Marie Tommerson Berg played on the first team in 1929, as a guard. Her mother, Lillian Tommerson, had played for an independent team in South Dakota. Marie later taught physical education at Grand Meadow. Her two daughters and their generation never got to play on a team because of the ban on competition for girls. Marie became a spokesperson for the team at the National Girls and Women in Sports Day in 1992 and organized reunions of the players. Marie Berg told the audience with a laugh, "They said the girls weren't physical enough to stand it, not knowing it didn't hurt them a bit. We all felt bad when they cut it out. Who knows how long the win streak would have been if that hadn't happened."

Marie became a physical education teacher in Grand Meadow and Elkton. The Marie Berg Award is now presented annually at the National Girls and Women in Sports Day to a physical education teacher who has made positive contributions to girls and women in sports.

Newspaper excerpts reprinted with permission by the *Meadow Area News*

Marie Berg, Grand Meadow

Grand Rapids High School

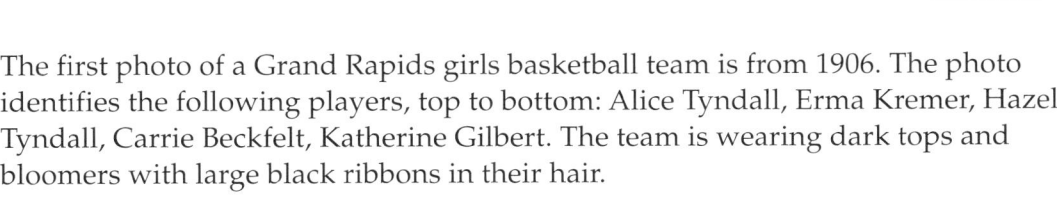

Northern Minnesota, 70 miles northeast of Duluth on #2
Years Represented: 1906 - 1930

Grand Rapids 1906

The first photo of a Grand Rapids girls basketball team is from 1906. The photo identifies the following players, top to bottom: Alice Tyndall, Erma Kremer, Hazel Tyndall, Carrie Beckfelt, Katherine Gilbert. The team is wearing dark tops and bloomers with large black ribbons in their hair.

The 1906 school yearbook contained an article, "The Girls' Basket Ball Team," that contended, "The girls' basketball team had a desperate time to establish its identity as a school organization. The same difficulty that the boys' team experienced in getting a game was had by the girls. Finally Cass Lake's invitation was accepted. The girls with hearts all aflutter accompanied by Miss Parker and chaperoned by William McAlpine departed for the Indian City. From the time of arrival to the moment of departure they were the guests of their rivals. No more delightful time could have been furnished a visiting team than that which they enjoyed. The game was not so interesting as the entertainment, and although it was lost to the Lakers by a score of 13 to 8, our girls were happy, the good time afforded taking off the entire sting of defeat. It is hoped that during the next season it will be the pleasure of the Rapids' girls to entertain their hosts above the line."

A photo of the 1907 team lists - Mary Hepfel, Carrie Beckfelt, Gina Hatelili, Captain Alice Tyndall, Hazel Tyndall, and Margaret McAlpine. The 1907 yearbook summarized the efforts of the players. The opening paragraph stated, "Alice Tyndall, center and present captain, has played her high school course on and off as basket ball teams have been organized and then fallen to pieces again for lack of proper interest in them. She has always played in her present place at center and put up a creditable game, being everywhere at once and having always an eye for the ball. The team is fortunate in having her for another year."

Grand Rapids 1907

The 1908 yearbook included a photo of the girl basketball team. It included 13 players not identified by name. The team lineup was Edna Bonarher, Alice Tyndall, centers; Molly Donavan, Mary Hepfel, right guards; Rose Wiegle, Gunia Hettly, left guards; Georgia Powell, Hazel Tyndall, left forwards; Cora Williams, Carrie Beckfelt, right forwards; substitutes – Irene Davy, Margaret McAlpine. Note: The page on boys' basketball said that the boys could only find a game with Cloquet that was outside of town. The Grand Rapids team won 11-6.

The yearbook article noted, "Of course, the prowess of the Cass Lake girls was remembered, and the experience of last year served to unnerve our girls for the time being. But when the game was called, the Grand Rapids girls went to their task like Caesar's immortal 'twelfth.'" The team won, 27-7. In a game with Eveleth, the game was played with fifteen minutes halves.

The 1909 yearbook included a photo of the "Girls Basket Ball Team," six players in dark middy tops, headed, "High School Champions of

Grand Rapids 1908

Grand Rapids 1909

Northern Minnesota." A second photo, "Our Pride," included seven players and a male coach. The article recorded that the team organized on October 8th, electing Annabel Hermes as team captain and Margaret McAlpine as business manager. The lineup included – Margaret McAlpine, Lucy McCormick, Ruth Beckfelt, Rosemary Logan, Annabel Hermes, Emma Frederick and Henrietta Kremer.

The team won the first game against Hibbing, 30-0. The visitors won the respect of the Grand Rapids team for "being good losers," and, "they entered heartily into the spirit of the reception, which was given after the game."

Their second game against Floodwood was not a regular high school team because there were several teachers on the team. It was a difficult game with a slippery floor and high baskets. The article indicated "But, because of a number of enthusiastic rooters, who certainly helped 'some,' and also, because of 'rubbing a little rosin,' which helped some more, and of course, because of good, scientific playing, the final score was 15 – 1, in favor of the black and the orange. After the game, there was 'dancing in the hall' (should anyone desire further information on this point, just ask our captain), and we tore ourselves away barely in time to catch the midnight train. It was a tired but happy crowd which Miss Burlingame marshaled back to town to the tune of 'Lo! The Conquering Heroines Come.'"

The third game was a return game with Hibbing. The article affirmed,

"Notwithstanding the severe cold, there was a very good crowd out to watch Hibbing get her second defeat at the hands of the Grand Rapids champions. Well, they got it, but let us say to their credit that they took it quite as gracefully as could be expected. The article went on, "Both teams were playing to win and neither side scored again until the last minute, when Rosemary made a basket." The final score was 7-4. "It was the most hotly contested game of the season; and we were a weary, forlorn and bruised bunch when 'the ball was over.' But with every groan of 'oh, my lip!' or 'Don't touch my arm, Kid!' went a breath of thanksgiving that 'we beat them.'"

The next game on February 6th was a double game of boys' and girls' teams at Cass Lake. The yearbook reported,

"We found a friend on our way – the jolly conductor – who attended our game, and proved himself possessed of almost as much voice as heart, both strangely enough on the right side." The teams were shown around the village during the afternoon and had supper at different homes prior to the game. Both teams were victorious. After the games, the article summarized, "After removing all traces of our strenuous exercise, we were invited to trip the 'light fantastic' to strains of sweet music. Not until the hour when ghosts begin to walk, did we return to the high school, where a sumptuous banquet was prepared for us. There we ascertained that Cass Lake had domestic as well as athletic girls. After all had done justice to the banquet, Superintendent Larson addressed us, saying some very pleasant things for the Rapids, among others, that he believed 'the Lord was on our side;' he asked our referee and our captain to explain our victories otherwise, if they could."

Lester Lofberg acted as referee for the games.

Grand Rapids 1910

The article finished, "By this time, other matters of graver importance were demanding attention and no more games were prepared for."

The 1910 team consisted of – Ruth Beckfelt, Annabel Hermes, Margaret McAlpine, Gertrude Luther, Miriam Cordes, Blanche Gaard, Henrietta Kremer, and Pearl Gole. The team played two games against Hibbing. Grand Rapids lost the first game to Hibbing, 6-3. The article in the yearbook began, "Well may Hibbing be proud of her victory, for it was the first time the Grand Rapids Basket Ball Association had lost a game since its organization. 'It boots not' to explain how or why the disaster befell." The article went on, "After the game, the Hibbing girls took us to the grand opening dance at the new Armory, where we danced until the wee tiny hours of the morning. Happy, and yet unhappy, we boarded the Merry Widow for home, where we were warmly welcomed, though we had failed to completely sustain the reputation of the school along athletic lines." The Grand Rapids team won the second game at home against Hibbing, 15-3. The team concluded, "On account of the lack of girls' teams in this part of the state, we were unable to secure more matched games; but we feel justified in calling ourselves Champions of the Range."

The 1911 team was organized in November but began practicing in mid-December "But owing to the fact that all but one of the regulars of the team were old players, a strong team was soon coached up to fast team work." They played Hibbing, Chisholm and Aitkin. The team defeated Chisholm 80 – 1. "But it might be well to pay Chisholm a compliment for their courage and for the brave fight they put up to the end of the game. We out-matched the Chisholm girls in every respect in age, height, weight and training; they had iron wills to keep their wits about them as they did, having to play against a bunch of girls twice their size."

Grand Rapids 1911

After the Aitkin game, the host team provided a banquet and entertained the team at their homes. The yearbook article disclosed, "At 6:30 the following morning our beloved chaperone, Miss Thomas, boarded the train with a happy and victorious crowd of girls."

The team lineup was – Ruth Beckfelt, Miriam Cordes, forwards; Margaret McAlpine, center; Blanche Gaard and Mary Brandon, guards. Henrietta Kremer was substitute. Galen Finnegan was coach and referee.

The records of the Grand Rapids teams moves to 1926.

An interview conducted in August 1998 with Lily Parks Tinquist revealed that Lily played on the Grand Rapids girls basketball team for three years, graduating in 1930. It was a three-court game with three dribbles permitted. Lily's team played Proctor, Coleraine, Cass Lake and Cloquet. Lily's sister, Elsie Parks Conat, also played on the team.

Grand Rapids 1928

Arbuta Hendricks Wisuri was a member of the 1926, 1927 and 1928 teams.

The games were held in a gymnasium and were officiated. Players could bump others but not push them. There were two guards, two forward and one center on each team. The centers stayed in the middle court and were the tall girls. Sometimes the games were doubleheaders with the girls' teams playing before the boys' game.

The 1928 team wore what Lily described as "short bloomers." The 1929 team photo shows a uniform with shorts with v-neck tops, and short sleeves. The team's coach was Miss James.

The 1929 yearbook, *Pine Needles*, included a summary of "Girls' Basketball." It asserted "Girls' basketball has come into its own in Grand Rapids High School. During the past four years there has been an unusual development in the interest and competitive spirit among the girls, which have resulted in splendid basketball teams. The game is now played on practically the same par as the boys."

The 1929 team was coached by Miss Dittes and led by Captain Irene Bentz. The team played Proctor, Coleraine, Proctor and Cass Lake.

The 1929 team photo lists – Front: McKee, Peavey, Ranfranz, Irene Bentz, Snyder, Elsie Parks Conat, R. Cochran. Middle: Hursh, Lily Parks Tinquist, Pogue, Fox, Wright. Back: Arscott, Stevens, Sherman, Trask, G. Cochran.

Grand Rapids 1929

Lily commented on the fun of playing basketball. She said she didn't earn all "A"s like some did, but "basketball was my fun time."

Granite Falls High School

Western Minnesota; 110 miles west of the metropolitan area on #212
Years Represented: 1910-1915

Carol Fuller found old correspondence that pointed out, "Pearl was a good athlete. She had played basketball in high school. She taught her girls to swim, play softball, ice skate and appreciate nature. She fanatically encouraged higher education." The letter was from a cousin named Griebler.

Pearl Fuller was born around 1895 and was likely in high school between 1910 and 1915.

Greenbush High School

Northwestern Minnesota; 20 miles southwest of Roseau on #11
Years Represented: 1920-1924

Oline Christianson Erickson played on the Greenbush girls basketball team from 1920-1924.

The photo of the 1924 team lists - Shallborg Hildahl, Ruth Lillemon, Lucille Thomas, Ella Forsness, Mabel Aamodt, Oline Christianson, Hilda Johnson, Ruth Swanstrom, Coach Holzinger

Greenbush 1924

Fourth Quarter

The team played Badger, Holt, Middle River, Warroad and perhaps Roseau.

Oline's team played 'real boys rules' and there were officials. Oline said, "We traveled by train to most of the games. We stayed overnight, returning the next day. Most of the games were played on Friday night. The girls played the first game and the boys played afterwards."

There were no problems for the girls' and boys' teams to travel together. Oline said, "There were only eight girls and eight boys when we went to other towns."

Greenbush had a gymnasium in the school as did the other teams.

The uniforms were not furnished by the school. Travel expenses were paid by the school.

Special Stories
Oline's family lived on a farm eight miles from Greenbush so she had to find a place to stay in town during the school days and go home on weekends.

Oline reflected that, "Our school and the community were very supportive. I remember my parents came to town with horses and sleigh to watch my sister and me play ball. That was something special for me."

Greenway High School, Coleraine

Northeastern Minnesota; 7 miles northeast of Grand Rapids on #169
Years Represented: 1921-1929

The Greenway High School yearbook, the *Blast*, included a summary of the 1921-26 and the 1929 seasons for the girls basketball team.

The 1921 *Blast* stated, "Though Greenway has had girls' athletics for only three years, a great deal of interest has been shown and great strides taken toward more and better athletics for Greenway." The team won five and lost one game.

Greenway 1921

The team included Allie Koski, Helen Larson, Vivian Kinter, Vivian Franti, captain, Amelia Derzai, Margaret Smith, Margaret McGrath, Zenya Raisanen, Iva Bell. Teams played six games with Proctor, Nashwauk and Olcott. They won two games out of three with Proctor, and won the games with Nashwauk and Olcott.

The *Blast* stated, "We expect Greenway to capture not only the Range Championship, but also the State Championship. In one of the hardest fought games ever seen, Greenway took the Championship away from Proctor after three ties. The final score was 18-22."

In the 1922 *Blast*, "Girls' Basket Ball" section," it was reported "Our last year's victorious basket ball record must have had something to do with our difficulty in arranging the schedule of girls' basket ball for this year. At first no one seemed to have a desire to play us, but finally a few games were scheduled."

The first game with Proctor ended with a loss of 15 – 12.

"Maybe the Proctor girls' colors, dances 'n everything stunned us girls, but just wait——!" The second game was with the Marble City Team at Marble. The Marble team won an easy victory of 22-9. A return game with Marble was "a real fight." The article went on, "It nearly ended a tie, but one basket could not be counted as someone in the balcony touched the ball, so that Marble received the laurels of this night by a score of 15 to 3." At a following game with Proctor, the Greenway team won, 21-18.' The game certainly proved that 'where there's a will, there's a way.' The next day we went to Duluth raiding the Ten-Cent Stores and nearly making the Athletic Association bankrupt with our banquet bill at the Spalding."

Greenway 1922

The 1922 team included - Helen Larson, captain, Zenya Raisanen, Anna Tok, Margaret Smith, Iva Bell, Alma Koski, Vivian Kinte, and Allie Koski. Coaches: Miss McNally and Miss Brumeister.

The 1923 *Blast* summary indicated that the team played Proctor with the promise that if they won both games, they could play Cloquet. The game with Cloquet was played before "the largest crowd that had ever assembled in the Greenway gymnasium to witness a game." Bill Hare, former athletic director at Greenway, said that the game was for the Northwest Championship with over 700 fans at the game. A band concert was held before the game started. Greenway won a closely-contested game. A party was held in the school gymnasium where games were played and a delicious lunch was served.

At the end of the season a "grand banquet was given by Dr. Dutter for the basketball and debating teams in the school cafeteria. Speeches were made by the captains, coaches, and seniors." The team was coached by Miss Tobin and assisted by Miss Reid.

Team members were Alma Koski, captain, Vivian Kinter, Saima Purra, Della Bluntach, Catherine Murphy, Anna Tok, Rose Tok, Neva McKeeby, and Luverne Lynn.

The 1924 *Blast* indicated that "The season of '24 came to an end with a victorious girls' team for Greenway." The team played two games with Proctor and the Cloquet YWCA team. The team won all three games.

Greenway 1923

The *Blast* further pointed out "Our coach, Miss Alway, and Miss Reid went with us and saw that we didn't raid the 'Bakery Shops' and 'Candy Stores' before the game. Proctor was very certain of winning the game but to begin the fight we told them that we were told to bring home the bacon, and that we would. When the referee's whistle blew, the numbers 31 to 17 shone out brightly in our favor. Sunday afternoon we started home with the bacon."

The 1924 *Blast* lists team members as Anna Tok, Angeline Gaffney, Rose Kidd, Neva McKeeby, Rose Tok, Anna Krmpotich, Vivian Kinter, Alma Koski, captain and Saima Purra. The coach was Miss Alway, assisted by Miss Reid.

Greenway 1924

The *Blast* recorded the 1925 season as follows. "The school year closed another victorious season for the Greenway girls basketball team." The team won all of its four games with Proctor and Grand Rapids. The highest scoring game was 53-17 against Grand Rapids.

The 1925 team photo showed – Front: Amy Tregillis, Rose Tok, Alma Koski, Neva McKeeby, Yentka Tok. Back: Audrey Hall, Charlotte Mangseth, Florence Mayer, Lillian Fremont, Rose Kidd, Miss Always, coach.

The 1926 *Blast* showed that 50 girls came out for the team. In two weeks, the squad was cut down to 12. The team lost both games to Grand Rapids.

Team members were Amy Tregillis, captain, Genevieve Patnaude, Viola Radosevich, Yentka Tok, Rose Radosevich, Frances Adlesick, Florence Mayer, Bernice Lavalier and Lillian Fremont. Coach: Miss McKenna.

Greenway 1925

The 1929 *Blast* claimed that, "Although the defeats were greater than the victories, much credit must be given to our coach, Miss Johnson, who tried her best to make this team a success."

The 1929 team photo: Back: Margaret Enstrom, Hilda Purra, Hazel Ecklund, Captain Viola Radosevich, Mary Rafinski, Violet Secker, Miss Johnson, coach.

Greenway 1926

Front: Rose Bedi, Evangeline Adlesick, Velma Arpan, Dorothy Treboyvich, Alzada Titus, Mary Bedi.

The team played Grand Rapids, Olcott and Proctor. It won two games and lost three.

Greenway 1929

Grove City High School

Central Minnesota; 7 miles west of Litchfield on #12
Years Represented: 1924-1926

Anna Martinson Neuman played at Grove City from 1924-26. Her team played a two-court game. Anna played the guard position.

Teams played were Belgrade, Kerkoven, Atwater and Eden Valley.

The Grove City team traveled by car, with dads of players usually driving. When they played Kerkoven, they took the train, leaving at 4:00 p.m. and coming back the next day. They stayed overnight in the school. The host team would provide food and different games until another train early in the morning would take them back to Grove City. Only the girls' team traveled to Kerkoven for this game.

The school paid train fare. When they traveled by car, drivers volunteered their vehicles.

Home games were played in an old town hall. For games with Eden Valley, they played upstairs over a grocery store. The community was supportive of the girls' team.

The team's mothers made the uniforms, black sateen bloomers and white middy blouses.

Anna recalled that she played "because they needed another player. I enjoyed being part of a team and sharing experiences with the girls and the other teams."

"On one hand I'm very envious of the opportunity the high school girls have today to play basketball. On the other hand, I'm very proud that through hard work and dedication over the years, the girls and coaches have built a high caliber basketball program. High school girls' basketball builds teamwork, sportsmanship and brings family and community together."
Elvera "Peps" Neuman, 2005

Special Stories
Anna's daughter, Elvera, said, "Mom lived to the wonderful age of 94. Even though she couldn't see very well, she always looked forward to high school basketball on television. She would have a piece of paper and wrote down who was playing and who won the game. In March Mom never wanted people to come over unless they came to watch the games with her."

Anna Martinson Neuman is the mother of a professional basketball player, "Peps Neuman" of Eden Valley. During the 1960s, most schools did not have any girls basketball teams because sports for girls were discouraged during those decades. Elvera "Peps" Neuman was born in 1944. She was a 1962 graduate of Eden Valley High School and did not have the opportunity to participate in high school girls' athletics. However, Neuman organized a Girls Athletic Association at Eden Valley High School and the basketball team played against Paynesville and Grove City.

Hancock High School

Western Minnesota; 10 miles southeast of Morris on #9
Years Represented: 1916-1928

The Hancock girls basketball team was started in 1916. In 1920 the team won all their games.

Beverly Reque interviewed her mother, Marion Halvorson Solvie (age 89) and Irene Angier Jensen (age 92).

The team traveled in cars and returned home after games. The school had a gymnasium for games. The uniforms were maroon bloomers and white blouses. Players furnished their own uniforms.

Irene played from 1924-26. Irene remembered that it was fun "going to other towns and the tournaments in Breckenridge. Irene said, "I graduated in 1925, but went one more year to take more classes and to play ball an extra year."

Marion played from 1925-28. Their team played a two-court game. Marion stated that they played Benson, Murdock, Morris, Willmar, Ortonville, Alberta, Breckenridge and the "Aggies."

Marion said, "I worked one whole summer to earn money for a letter sweater by milking cows and taking care of babies for a local family."

"I worked one whole summer to earn money for a letter sweater by milking cows and taking care of babies for a local family."
Marion Halvorson Solvie.

The 1923-24 team – Front: Christine Van Cura, Erma Ray, Gladys Johnson. Middle: Jessie Benn Clark, Agnes Daberkow Erickson, Ethel Fenton Lundman. Back: Joyce Smokstad Fernelius, Margaret Conroy O'Leary, Coach Lawrence Van Cura, Violet Gregor Arntz, Ruth Erickson Kielb, Irene Angier Jensen.

The 1924-25 team – Front: Joyce Smokstad Fernelius, Erma Ray, Irene Angier Jensen. Back: Marjory Borland Corbert, Margaret Conroy O'Leary, Ruth Krenz Nelson, Coach Lawrence Van Cura, Ruth Erickson Kielb, Erma Sommer.

Hancock 1924

The 1925-26 team - Irene Angier Jensen, Erma Ray, Marion Halverson, Doris Snyder, Alvina Garlie, Genevieve Gjevre, Ruth Krenz Nelson, Millicent McArthur, Margaret Conroy O'Leary, Coach Lawrence Van Cura.

Hancock 1925

Hancock 1926

The women said that the community was very supportive and the local newspaper covered their games. Players received school letters.

The women were proud that their teams were the district champion in 1924-25 and 1925-26.

Hartland High School

South central Minnesota; 10 miles north of Albert Lea on #13
Years Represented: 1910

Hartland 1910

The Freeborn County Historical Museum provided a photo of the Hartland girls basketball team of 1909-1910. The coach is identified as Art Aarder who taught at Hartland and later at Albert Lea High School. Members of the team are unidentified.

Fourth Quarter

Hayfield High School

Southeastern Minnesota, midway between Rochester and Austin.
Years Represented: 1921-1925

Dorothy Iversen Viker played on the Hayfield girls basketball team from 1921-25.

Dorothy provided information and a photo of the 1925 Hayfield girls basketball team. The photo lists – Front: Dorothy Iversen Viker, Frances Blaisell, Agnes Oyen, Ella Mathison, Lucille Janes. Back: Coach; unidentified player; Alvina Kording, Josephine Evjen, Edith Ellingson.

Hayfield 1925

The photo was in the possession of a friend's relative whose home was nearly destroyed by a fire. This photo was one that was saved from the fire. The photo was given to Dorothy at an all-school reunion 75 years later. Dorothy described the photo as "Hayfield's 1925 pride and joy!"

Dorothy played from 1921-25. She said, "I think that there was a good girls' team playing boys' rules at least two years before I entered high school in September 1921."

The team played neighboring towns and traveled in cars, and if necessary by train, with an overnight stay. Dorothy's team also hosted visiting teams overnight. She says, "What fun!"

Her team played Kasson, Kenyon, Blooming Prairie, Dodge Center and Byron. Hayfield had a gymnasium for their games though they played some games in a hall.

"Our girls' team was as popular as the boys'," Dorothy confided, "and was outfitted by the school, as was the boys' team. In 1924, we had reason to be very proud of our uniforms. Gold cotton sateen middy blouses and bloomers, wool socks and beanies (not to be worn while playing) with purple trim." Dorothy said they were "ordered from a catalog."

"We were enthusiastically backed by the townspeople," Dorothy said, "and the business men showed their approval when we played well with boxes of candy."

Dorothy contended, "I don't think anyone questioned our ability physically to play the game."

In one tournament at Ellendale, the Hayfield team was named the "best-appearing team both on and off the floor."

Her coach for all four years, Dorothy said, "was a fun-loving teacher from Kenyon. We were so fortunate to have her."

At the time that Dorothy wrote a letter of her high school years, Dorothy was 91 years.

An article appeared in the *Austin Daily Herald*, February 3, 1999, written by staff writer Jana Peterson.

The article, "Breaking down the barrier," featured Dorothy Viker as a basketball player from the 1920s. The article was announcing the local program to celebrate "Girls and Women in Sports Day."

Excerpts from the article reported, "When Dorothy Viker played high school girls' basketball for Hayfield, she was on the court with five other players and they were all dressed in blue and gold bloomers with a middy blouse – it had a sailor-style collar – and wool socks in the same colors up to the knee. The bloomers were supposed to go below the knee, but Viker said the girls usually rolled them higher up. They also had matching beanies to wear off the court. The years were 1922 through 1925."

"They changed over to the old Iowa system my freshman year," Viker said. In the Iowa system there were three offensive players and three defensive players per team on the court. Neither group could cross the center line. Before that year girls had played by the men's rules.

Throughout her playing time at Hayfield, Viker stated that the girls enjoyed excellent support from the school and the community. The team would travel to other schools, sometimes in cars and sometimes by train. They even came in second in a girls basketball tournament in Ellendale. However, despite its popularity, the program was discontinued the year after she graduated. "They felt it was too strenuous for us," Viker said.

Hendricks High School

Southwestern Minnesota on the border with South Dakota, 50 miles northeast of Pipestone, on #75
Years Represented: 1928

The *Hendricks Pioneer*, January 6, 1998, contained an article written by Violet Nelson, "Local Woman Recalls Her Days with 1928 Hendricks Basketball Team."

Clara Digre Johnson played on a winning team in 1928. Her team played Tyler, Ivanhoe, Lake Benton and schools from South Dakota, Flandreau and Clear Lake. The team's favorite official was a banker from Elkton, S.D.

The 1928 team photo lists Clara Digre Johnson, Clara Hanson, Frances Luman, Gertrude Luman, Alyce Ness Trooien, Claryce Ness and chaperone Julia Granger. Other members were Della Danielson, Iona Danielson and Bernice Stufferd.

Clara Johnson has her basketball uniform, #14, at her home. The uniforms were orange and black, cotton bloomers and a short-sleeved, v-neck top. The team wore dark cotton stockings with cream colored athletic shoes.

Hendricks 1928

The article reported that, "The girls basketball team went to Tyler on the train one time because the roads were blocked. They did not clear the roads as fast as they do today. Hans Hanson and Slim Buseth of Hendricks often took the team by bobsled to the various towns. Clara said the sleds were quite long and that once when they were transporting the boys' team to one of their games, the girls sneaked in the sled also."

Clara said, "Since the girls had such a winning team, the town was very proud of them. Not every home had a radio to listen to the broadcasting of the games, so they would all congregate at the homes with the radios."

After Clara's sophomore year, the school discontinued the team which left the girls only inter-class games. Clara always enjoyed reminiscing about her playing days.

Excerpts of article reprinted with permission of the *Hendricks Pioneer*

Herman High School

Western Minnesota; 40 miles west of Alexandria
Years Represented: 1913

Herman 1913

A photo on a 1913 postcard was addressed by Irene to Aunt Clara and Uncle Henry Tiedt who lived in Argyle, Minnesota. The postmark is from Herman, May 12, 1913. It is believed that Irene's name was "Knudsen" or "Knudson."

Irene wrote on the postcard, "The picture is one of our basketball team." The ball includes the word "Champs."

Information from Mrs. Myron William Tiedt indicates that Irene's name was "Knudsen" or Knudson," Mrs. Tiedt's husband is the son of "Aunt Clara" and "Uncle Henry." In 1998 Mrs. Tiedt wrote a letter to the editor, asking if anyone could identify the girls in the photo. There was no response to her request.

Heron Lake High School

Southwestern Minnesota; 25 miles northeast of Worthington on #60
Years Represented: 1910

The photo shows six players on the team of 1910. The players are wearing dark bloomers, white blouses of varying styles and large black bows in their hair.

Heron Lake 1910

Hibbing High School

Location: Northeastern Minnesota, 60 miles northeast of Duluth on #169
Years Represented: 1909, 1910

The 1909 Grand Rapids High School yearbook, *Pine Needles*, provided a summary of the Grand Rapids games with Hibbing as follows.

In the first game, Grand Rapids won 30-0. "Hibbing, moreover, won our highest respect and admiration, for they proved themselves good losers, and entered heartily into the spirit of the reception, which was given after the game."

The third game of the season was a return game with Hibbing.

"Arriving in Hibbing, we found a goodly number of our opponents waiting to receive us, and we were escorted immediately to their high school. Notwithstanding the severe cold, there was a very good crowd out to watch Hibbing get her second defeat at the hands of the Grand Rapids champions. Well, they got it, but let us say to their credit that they took it quite as gracefully as could be expected. In the first few minutes Hibbing scored, and applause ran high among the local rooters until Grand Rapids scored, about two minutes later. Then Hibbing fouled, and Annabel threw and made it! Thus the first half closed 3 to 2 in our favor. Early in the second half both sides scored once. That meant 5 to 4. Both teams were playing to win, and neither side scored again until the last minute, when Rosemary made a basket. That left a final score of 7 to 4. It was the most hotly-contested game of the season, and we were a weary, forlorn and bruised bunch when 'the ball was over.' But with every groan of 'Oh, my lip! or 'Don't touch my arm, Kid!' went a breath of thanksgiving that we beat them."

"But with every groan of 'Oh, my lip!' or 'Don't touch my arm, Kid' went a breath of thanksgiving that we beat them."

Fourth Quarter

The 1910 Grand Rapids school yearbook reported on a game with Hibbing in its summary of the girls basketball season.

"Only two matched games with other schools were played during the winter, both with the Hibbing girls. The first game was played on the 18th day of December at Hibbing. Sad to relate, we were defeated, the score being 6 to 3 in our opponent's favor. Well, may Hibbing be proud of her victory, for it was the first time the Grand Rapids Basket Ball Association had lost a game since its organization. 'It boots not' to explain how or why the disaster befell. Hibbing won, and Hibbing rejoiced, but we took our defeat in silence, for we knew our day was coming. After the game the Hibbing girls took us to the grand opening dance at the new Armory, where we danced until the wee tiny hours of the morning. Happy and yet unhappy, we boarded the Merry Widow for home, where we were warmly welcomed, though we had failed to completely sustain the reputation of the school along athletic lines.

Anxiously we awaited the arrival of the 11th day of February, for on the evening of that day we were to play a return game with the Hibbing girls. 'Our day' came, and we showed our friends and classmates we could play basket ball if we were given half a chance. We won a decisive victory over the Hibbing girls by a far greater score than they made against us - 15 to 3."

Hutchinson High School

50 miles west of Minneapolis on #7
Years Represented: 1919-1922

Mary Hajicek Berry played on the team for four years through 1922. She said that several of the girls on the team were her best friends, and they remained friends throughout their lives. Mary recalled how heavy their bloomer uniforms were as they played the game.

Charlotte Johnson Johnson played on the Hutchinson girls basketball team for three years, graduating in 1922. Charlotte informed us that the team received felt letters.

Hutchinson 1921

The 1921 team photo – Front: Bertha Filk, Mayme O'Fallon, Edna Carrol, Mary Hajicek, (N/A) Thompson, Charlotte Johnson. Back: Coach Madsen.

1922 team – Front: Willma Hopper, Mary Hajicek, Charlotte Johnson. Back: Helen Fratzke, Helen Krantz, (N/A) Nelson, Coach Lillian Poppitz, Mayme O'Fallon, Bertha Filk.

Teams played were: Litchfield; Glencoe, Norwood/Young America, New Ulm, Olivia, Fairfax, Cokato and Morton. Many towns were on the same railroad line, the Milwaukee.

Hutchinson 1922

Games were officiated. The game rules and number of players would vary depending on the other team. Litchfield played with five players and Hutchinson had six on their team. Charlotte was a running center so she did not play when they had a game with Litchfield.

Charlotte Johnson played on Hutchinson's girls' team in 1921 and 1922. Johnson, who was born in 1905, lived in Litchfield when she shared her stories with her grand-niece, Candace Barrick. Charlotte recalls that when she was a senior in high school, her mother left the farm and came to town where she rented a house and stayed all winter. Charlotte said that her mother "had boarders and rooms for school kids."

Going to games in cars was becoming a common mode of transportation. When the roads were full of snow, Charlotte recalled that they went by bobsled. Both the girls and boys would ride in the sled to the other towns like Glencoe. Charlotte remembered sitting in hay or straw with lots of blankets over them. For other games, Charlotte said, "we traveled by train, the Milwaukee, to the teams 'down the line.'" The school provided the tickets rather than hire cars to take the teams to the game.

Charlotte Johnson, Hutchinson

Uniforms were the typical bloomers with a middy top. Charlotte said that the parents provided the uniforms. Some of Charlotte's relatives had sailor suits, and they wore them. Charlotte was happy to have a uniform made by her mother. Some uniforms worn by the other girls had more cloth to them than Charlotte's uniform. She said, "We lived in the country and were hard up, you know, so I was just happy to get that."

At the time that Charlotte shared her stories, Charlotte was 94 years of age. Charlotte said that people were surprised when she said she had played basketball in high school. She said, "Well, how would they know?!" Charlotte added, "It's been a long time ago and I never bragged about myself like I do about my great-grandkids and things like that."

> Charlotte was happy to have a uniform made by her mother. She said, "We lived in the country and were hard up, you know, so I was just happy to get that."

Legacy

The Hutchinson girls basketball team began to play again in the 1970s, once more providing opportunities for the young women in Hutchinson. One of its players, Lindsay Whalen, added to the heritage of the early teams during her high school years at Hutchinson. Lindsay graduated in 2000 and went on to play at the University of Minnesota where she led the women's basketball team to its first Final Four appearance in 2004. In 2005 Lindsay was playing professional women's basketball.

On December 26, 2004, Lindsay said to the Minneapolis *Star Tribune*, "Players now have to understand their place on the timeline. The first players put themselves on the line when they didn't have the opportunities we have today."

International Falls High School

Location: Northern Minnesota on the Canadian border next to Fort Francis on #53
Years Represented: 1924 1925

The first International Falls girls basketball team was established in 1924-1925. The photo was contributed by Agnes King McIntyre. Players are identified as follows – Front: Emily Day Olson, Roberta Fritz Hanson, Hazel Wilson, Ellen Emlaw, Elizabeth Brown. Back: Coach Elvira Ehnbom, Evelyn Linden, Agnes King McIntyre captain, Loretta Nelson, Hjordis Liljeblad.

The team was unbeaten in nine games. They won their games against the teams from Littlefork, Blackduck, Baudette, Warroad and Northome. Their game was two-court. Their highest score was 53 – 14 over Northome.

International Falls 1925

The toughest game was a 16-14 win over Warroad.

Agnes King McIntyre provided information on the Basketball Pioneers Questionnaire. Agnes was team captain in 1925 as a junior. Agnes was the only one from the first year's team to play on the second year's team. Agnes shared with us that the second year coaches were Goldthorpe and Marie McIntyre, Agnes' sister-in-law.

The team traveled by personal autos. It played in the high school gymnasium in a brand new high school. The players' mothers made the uniforms which were full-pleated black bloomers and an orange top with purple trim.

There was no connection with the boys' team and little or no support from them or the community. Expenses were not paid by the school, and the girls' and boys' teams traveled separately to games.

In 1925, the *Northern Light* wrote of the final game against Northome. "This game was the poorest of the season as the girls broke the rules of training by eating sweets all day."

> "This game was the poorest of the season as the girls broke the rules of training by eating sweets all day."
> *Northern Light*

When Agnes was dribbling onto the court before a game, she threw a basketball from behind the center line and made the basket. She recalled that there was no sound from the audience.

Agnes believes that sports gave the girls self-confidence and self-esteem. She was also a player on the first girls softball team, called 'kittenball.' She was active in anything that improved "my active life and good health."

One of Agnes' favorite stories was a game when her future sister-in-law, Marie McIntyre did not like a call by the official. "She slammed the ball to the floor and it bounced up and hit the low ceiling of the gym and back down and part-way up again. She didn't like the official's next call either!"

At the time of completing her questionnaire, Agnes was 92 years of age.

Jeffers High School

Southwestern Minnesota; 12 miles north of Windom on #30 off #71
Years Represented: 1927-1930

Avis Hofslund Piper played basketball for Jeffers High School, graduating in 1929.

The team players in 1927-1928 are identified in a photo as – Front: Carol Swartz, Marcella Grabert, Lillian Tasler, Marjorie Englund, Anna Goeman, Neda Vold, Leota McCloud. Back: Ella Swenson, Miss Nelson, Verna Schimnoski, Mildred Anderson, Avis Hofslund Piper, Coach Harold Carlstrom, (N/A) Snook.

Jeffers 1928

The team uniforms in the photo appear to be shorts with a v-necked top, knee high socks and athletic shoes.

The Jeffers team played surrounding towns including Storden, Westbrook, Lamberton, Sanborn, and perhaps Walnut Grove and Comfrey.

The highlight of the 1930 season was a victory over the Windom team, the largest town of the area.

The team colors were black and scarlet. They had no cheerleaders, but cheers were led by members of the squad. The 1930 coach was Louis Diedrichs.

Legacy
Roberta Takle noted that her own athletic opportunities were as a member of the Girls Athletic Association in the late 1950s at Windom High School. Avis was 93 years of age in 2005.

Roberta's daughter, Teri, followed in her grandmother's footsteps by playing basketball at Elk River Area High School from 1980-1983 and at Hamline University from 1983-1986.

Jordan High School

25 miles southeast of Minneapolis on #169
Years Represented: 1907-1932

The *Jordan Independent* newspaper, March 1907, headlined "Basket Ball Girls Play New Prague. The girls basketball team of our high school went to New Prague Saturday and played the New Prague school team. The glory of winning went to the New Prague lasses, 10 to 3, in a very pretty contest, not so one-sided as the score might indicate. New Prague was lucky again Sunday, when the Whitesox team came down from 'Beantown' and played the Jordan Turners in Harmonia Hall. The element of luck seemed to be with the jolly Praguers. Final result, 16 to 10." The team lineup included Courtney, Sanborn, G. Herder, F. Herder, and Brockway.

The earliest photo submitted of a Jordan girls basketball team was from 1911. The team is wearing the traditional dark bloomers, and white middy tops with bows.

Jordan 1911

Jane Varner Breimhorst and Lucille Beckman played on later teams Beckman from 1924-28 and Breimhorst from 1928-32. Margaret Bieder Levander played from 1929-1932.

Games were played in the gymnasium of the high school in Jordan, currently the Schule Haus site. The school was fairly new, built in 1921. Jane fondly remembered that "Jordan's gymnasium was one of the nicest. We played basketball at one school where we had to play around a stove in the center of a hall. At Montgomery, we played in a hall too because they had no gym." Lucille added, "In Henderson we dressed in the basement. I'm sure it was a coal bin. We had to walk outside around the building to get to the stairs to play on the top floor. But I enjoyed every bit of it."

Jane said that her team played with two forwards, two guards and a jumping center. It was a two-court game. Practices were held nightly after school. Their games were officiated.

Jane said her team had the distinction of being the first girls basketball team at Jordan to wear shorts. "Before that they wore bloomers, a split skirt gathered with a cuff below the knee. We were considered pretty risqué with our shorts and t-shirts."

> "In Henderson, we dressed in the basement. I'm sure it was a coal bin."
> Lucille Beckman

Margaret Bieder Levander described her 1932 team's uniforms as gold shirts with maroon shorts of a knit material. The uniforms were provided by their school.

Jane said that the team had an excellent woman coach and support from their school and community. The local newspaper provided coverage after all of their games.

The Jordan team played in a district which included Belle Plaine, New Prague, Montgomery and Jordan. They occasionally played non-district teams such as Henderson and Carver.

Lucille said, "When we played at Carver, we often took the 'dinky' (a small train) after school. The train's schedule was so that it could then pick us up and deliver us home by 11 p.m. that night." The team also traveled in automobiles driven by coaches or teachers.

Jane's fondest memories were in 1932 when her team won the District Championship. They defeated Belle Plaine and then New Prague. "It was really great to win the trophy for your school. School spirit was so great back then. It was a big confidence builder. We thought we were so important."

An article in the *Jordan Independent*, March 24, 1932 read, "The championship cup is now in possession of Jordan High School. This is the second time the cup has been in The Hub, as the school won the honors in 1929." The trophies were often traveling trophies, usually given to the school after the third win.

The 1932 District Championship team photo – Front: Jane Varner, Marion Morley, Margaret Bieder Levander, Evie Killian. Back: Mary Krautkremer, Norma Greenwald, Coach Verna Dahl, Ruth Walm, Amy Casey. The players received gold basketballs engraved with their initials and "JHS Champions 1932." Jane Varner Breimhorst wore her basketball as a necklace and brought it to the recognition ceremony held in 1999.

Jordan 1932

All-District First and Second Teams were selected. Jane Varner Breimhorst and Marion Morley were selected for the All-District First Team. Evie Killian and Amy Casey were named to the All-District Second Team.

The local newspaper provided the following coverage of games.

The *Jordan Independent*, January, 30, 1930

"The Jordan girls played a fine game to hold Montgomery to a score of 30 to 17. The girls' game was a good one to watch. Montgomery's veteran team was somewhat surprised at the fighting Jordan team. Had the local girls been better shots they might have had a much closer score. Jordan girls flashed a dandy offensive to gain many close-in shots. However they were weak on putting the ball through the hoop."

The *Jordan Independent*, March 17, 1932

"Silver Loving Cup Brought Back to Hub for First Time Since 1929. All-District Team Announced." "Jordan took first honors at the girls basketball tournament held in New Prague last Thursday and

Friday evenings. They defeated Belle Plaine, 26 to 12 and Montgomery, 23 to 16. Following the tournament, W.F. Kritta, president of the New Prague Commercial Club, presented Marion Morley, captain of the Jordan team, the silver loving cup, emblematic of the title of champions, held by the Jordan girls."

The *Jordan Independent*, November 26, 1998

In the (1932) district championship game between Jordan and Montgomery, the report said, "Fans were there with automobile horns, razzers, and Pete Schmitt of The Hub assumed the cheerleader's role with ultimate success. The stands were eager and anxious to lend vocal support to the teams and every time a basket was made on either side, enthusiastic applause rang forth for several minutes."

Special Stories
Margaret said that her school provided a variety of sports opportunities and required physical education classes. The only interscholastic sport was basketball.

Jane told a story about a teammate, Evie Killian, who was so excited after winning a game that "She jumped into a person's arms, throwing her arms around his neck and her legs around his waist. When she looked down, she realized it was Superintendent Wurst. We had a lot of laughs about that."

Lucille told the story about a Montgomery game. "Johnny Graeff was the coach at Montgomery. During one of our games he was kind of ribbing me all the while. Finally, I just turned around and told him off. When I looked up, there was my mother standing. Boy, did I get it. I was a little bit mouthy at that time. You had to be a little meaner and a little tougher to play guard. But you didn't get by with being disrespectful to adults."

Newspaper excerpts reprinted with permission of the *Jordan Independent*

Kasota High School

South-central Minnesota, near St. Peter; 10 miles north of Mankato
Years Represented: 1930-1931

Players were not identified in the 1930 photo.

Kasota 1930

The 1930-31 team is identified as Anna Abel, Leveta Halverson, Anne Cole, Miss Larson, Coach, Benita Marquette, Vera Whiting, and Laura Marquette.

Kasota 1931

Lake Crystal High School

12 miles southwest of Mankato on #60
Years Represented: 1931-1932

Mary Champlin Tonkin played in 1931-1932. Mary's favorite memories were, "Great exciting memories, being one of the younger sophomores; everything and everyone was larger than life to me!! I ran and played my heart out. I weighed 110 lbs and was not one of the stars – yet!!" The team was dropped the following year, and Mary was never able to reach for her star.

Her team played the two-court game, three forwards and three guards. Their games had officials. Teams played were St. Clair, Pemberton and perhaps Rapidan.

The boys' and girls' teams played doubleheaders. The girls' team traveled on the basketball bus with the boys' team. The school paid for team expenses when they traveled to away games

Lake Crystal 1932

Lake Crystal had a gymnasium at the school, and games were played there.

Team uniforms were blue and white that, according to Mary, "were beautiful," and she added, "Almost like the boys!" The school provided the uniforms.

The 1932 team photo lists – Front: Mary James, Wilner Foster, Frances Bartlett, Geraldine Othoudt Johnson, Ima Larson. Back: Supt. I.R. Anderson, Emma Lee Anderson, Pearl Sizer Goodell, Margaret Bate, Mary Champlin, Helen Billet, Coach Auretta Wing. Other teammates included Pearl Sizer Goodell and Geraldine Othoudt Johnson.

Mary recalled, "There was terrific community support with standing room crowds!!"

Mary said, "We always played the first game, and as we almost always won, we had every soul in Lake Crystal screaming in the stands. The only second-rate part of it was that we always had to wait until the boys' team had practiced before we could have the gym. It contributed to many late suppers for basketball families."

Mary also participated in county-wide track and field days and on a softball team where she was the shortstop.

One of Mary's teammates was Emma Lee Anderson. At a high school reunion in 1999, Emma told Mary that basketball had been her whole life when she was in high school. Emma said, "I dreamed, ate, slept, thought and lived basketball. In fact if I had worked as hard at my studies as I did my basketball, I would have been a 4.0.

Special Memories
Mary vividly recalled, "Of course, the saddest moment of all was when we came back to school in the fall of 1932 to hear the news that girls basketball was canceled as it was "too hard" for us. What a travesty!"

Mary attended the reunion of basketball pioneers in March 1999 at the MSHSL State Girls Basketball Tournament. Later, when her school held a 100th anniversary of their school district, Mary shared her experience with three of her team members. Mary wrote, "They were all thrilled to hear the story of the event at Williams Arena. Also, when the video came, I invited Mrs. Ruth Rawn, the 100-year old, (Willmar, 1914) and her daughter to our house to see the video. While she was sitting on the davenport hearing about the event, I put the basketball we received at the reception in her hands. It was a very charming picture. She is such a beautiful woman and she smiled as she turned the ball over in her hands. I could almost see her dream of putting that up through the hoop as she held it. She enjoyed the reference to her in the video as did her daughter."

Le Roy High School

Southeastern Minnesota; 30 miles south of Rochester on #56
Years Represented: 1939

The *Le Roy Independent*, February 1939, stated,

"The Le Roy Girls Defeat Chester 22-17." The article reported, "The Le Roy girls basketball team gained their second victory over the Chester team last Tuesday evening, the final score being 22 to 17. The red and whites started out in the lead but the blue and whites were soon gaining steadily. The Le Roy girls were handicapped by not getting their passes through whereas the Chester team passed much more efficiently. During the second half Le Roy ran up their score 14 points but were also called for several fouls which gave their opponents a gain. Maxine Quade was high scorer for the Le Roy team with Goldie Larson for the Chester team."

The *Le Roy Independent*, March 17, 1939 recapped,

"The Fairer Sex Wind Up Basketball: Seven will be Lost by Graduation. The Le Roy Girls Basketball season ended with a victory over the Rose Creek team. Their season has been fairly successful, winning seven games out of the eleven played. The Red and White's defeats were the two games with Grand Meadow and McIntire (IA) and one game with the Spring Valley squads. The following girls were on the traveling squad this year: Forwards, Marjorie Engstrom, Gwen Sawdey, Arlene Quade, Maxine Regan, Marilyn Moe and Maxine Quade. Guards, Aline Desparde, Esther Eastwold, Esther Bhend, Thelma Nauman, Lorrie Volkart and Mary Crowe."

Le Sueur High School

20 miles north of Mankato on #169
Years Represented: 1920-1925

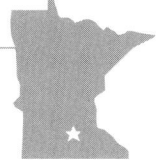

The LeSueur High School girls basketball team was active in the 1920s. Blossom Renneke Schwartz played on the 1919-20 and 1920-21 teams.

The 1919-20 team photo shows eight players. Blossom Renneke Schwartz is standing on the right end of the back row.

LeSueur 1920

LeSueur 1921

A photo of the 1920-21 team included – Front: Fern Frantz, Blossom Renneke Schwartz, Frances Johnson. Middle: Ruth Anderson, Ruth Klanke. Back: Maisie Hanson, Minnie Schneider, Frieda Von Lehe, Gertrude Hartung, Alice Martens, Coach Margaret Blanchard.

Blossom often spoke to her family of her opportunity to play games and the trips by train that frequently entailed an overnight, returning the following day.

The *LeSueur News-Herald*, March 22, 1984, published a photo of the 1925 team and asked the public for assistance in identifying the players. In the following week's edition, March 29, 1984, staff writer, Margaret Block, published the photo of the 1920-21 team and wrote an article about the team. After the March 22nd article, Blossom Renneke Schwartz called from her home in Sleepy Eye to say that she thought her team "deserved remembering." Blossom declared, "The fun we had. Basketball was, for us, the highlight of the winter, practicing in the old city hall, going to other towns for games by car, train or bobsled, sometimes staying overnight and eating at a hotel. This was high adventure for us."

Fourth Quarter   199

Blossom told the *LeSueur News-Herald*, March 29, 1984, that their team "defeated all the neighboring high school teams that we played and Mankato Teachers College. We finally lost to the girls of Hamline University." The team played its home games in the gym of the Washington School at Risedorph and Third.

A small article noted, "Juletta Nelson remembers the girls." Mrs. Juletta Nelson of LeSueur was the first to identify the team because she taught English at the old Washington School from 1923-26. "'They were good,' Juletta said of the team. She also remembered they played in a gym called 'the crackerbox' because it was so small and she chuckled as she made note of the bloomers the players wore back then."

The 1924-25 team was identified as – Ruth Nelson, Grace Sunderman Bauman, Grace Zachor, Helen Von Lehe, Hazel Bauman, Luella Zachor, Mary Kampen, and Coach Katherine Sherwood, home economics teacher.

Special Stories

Lucy Schwartz Sontag said, "As a student from 1943-47 at Sleepy Eye High School, I was envious of my mother's stories about traveling to other schools while we were restricted to intramurals."

Newspaper excerpts reprinted with permission by the *Le Sueur News-Herald*

> "Basketball was, for us, the highlight of the winter, practicing in the old City Hall, going to other towns for games by car, train or bobsled, sometimes staying overnight and eating at a hotel. This was high adventure for us."
> Blossom Renneke Schwartz

Litchfield High School

70 miles west of Minneapolis on #12
Years Represented: 1903-1932

Litchfield 1903

The first record of the Litchfield girls basketball team was reported in an eight-page tabloid, printed by the Crow River Press, Inc., owned in part by the *Litchfield Independent-Review*. It was researched and written by Ray Lenhard, Class of 1917. Vern Madson, Class of 1950 provided the layout and news for the LHS Alumni Association.

The article concluded, "The 1903 Litchfield Girls' Basketball team is one of the earliest on record. Team members are listed as – Front: Bessie Peterson, Nina McMonagle. Back: Elizabeth McLaughlin, Hildur Lundeen, Blanche Heiny, Anna Olson, Mary Flynn."

The article recounted: "Girls Basketball Began in Early 1900's. In 1904 and 1905, the girls of the Litchfield High School put on two lively basketball seasons. They played a regular schedule at home and in adjoining villages. The point farthest west they made was Benson, and the farthest east was Howard Lake. The 1904 and 1905 teams included

Anna Olson Determan, Blanche Heiny Peterson, Nina McMonagle Burns, Hildur Lundeen Tonning, Elizabeth McLaughlin DeMotts and Mary Flynn."

The 1915 Litchfield High School yearbook lists the team members as Sybil Davis, Ada Kopplin, Captain Mildred Anderson, Martha Werner, Beryl Burfening, Linnea Linner, and Ruth Sexton. The coach was M. Jones. The annual featured a game with Dassel, "In the last two games of the year, Litchfield showed a marked improvement over the kind of basket ball exhibited earlier in the season, especially in the game at Dassel, the visitors out-playing their hosts in every respect but making scores, and their inability to do that was due to the fact that the baskets were twelve inches higher than the regulation height." The team won one game; tied one, and lost three.

Litchfield 1917

The 1917 Litchfield team includes one player identified as Sarah Mortenson. She is the second player from the right in the team photo.

The 1924 team included Blanche Gamer, Eunice Mellquist, Elaine Sather, Marian March, Ina Cassidy, Cora Evenson(s), Edna Tostenrud, Martha Danielson, Coach Peterson, Luella Smith, and Gladys Parsons. The yearbook stated of one game, "The return game with Dassel proved to be a turn of the tide. The girls went down to defeat with a smile at Dassel but came up to victory on our own floor with a more radiant smile." The season ended with three wins, one tie and two losses.

The history moves to 1927 and the article in the *Litchfield Review*, 1930. It profiled the teams from the beginning of the winning seasons in 1927 and described their record-setting 73 wins in 1932.

Litchfield 1927

The 1927 team photo lists – Front: Frances Risdon, Myrtle Grendahl, Marian March, captain; Elva Sederstrom, Ila Peterson. Back: Harriet Harmann, Myrtle Anderson, Coach Horton, Agnes Grendahl, Hazel Bendickson, Beatrice Palm, Charmion Baker. Edith Anderson not pictured.

The 1928 squad: Hazel Bendickson, Captain; Myrtle Grendahl, Edith Anderson, Elva Sederstrom, Harriet Harmann, Luverne Rosenquist, Marian Nelson, Wilma Johnson, Olive Hahnke, Geraldine Longworth, Rhoda Anderson, Cora Nelson.

Edna McGraw Burns played as a sophomore in 1928. She recalls getting in the game occasionally and did score a basket. She was the center of the three forwards that played half court. The three guards played on the other half of the court. Edna vividly recalls that the team went to St. Paul to play a game. The team stayed in a hotel. Edna said, "It was the first time I ever stayed in a hotel and I had a bed all to myself. With three sisters and two beds, sleeping by yourself was a real treat." Edna recalls that the school burned on March 11, 1929. Iris, Jeannette and Phyllis McGraw were all her cousins. Edna graduated in 1930.

1929 Squad: Geraldine Longworth, Captain; Helen Berens, Ferne Bendickson, Wilma Johnson, Luverne Rosenquist, Joan Peterson, Olive Hahnke, Mildred Rielly, Gertrude Crosby, Florence Urdahl, Harriet Peterson, Muriel Sederstrom, Mildred Cassidy.

1930 Squad: Olive Hahnke, Captain; Ferne Bendickson, Helen Berens, Geraldine Longworth, Joan Peterson, Luverne Rosenquist, Florence Urdahl, Tilda Marstad, Muriel Sederstrom, Harriet Peterson, Wilma Johnson, Carrie Grendahl, Hazel Cassidy, Mildred Cassidy, Grace Horton, Doris Peters, Ethel Johnson, Pearl Anderson.

"It was the first time I ever stayed in a hotel and I had a bed all to myself."
Edna McGraw Burns

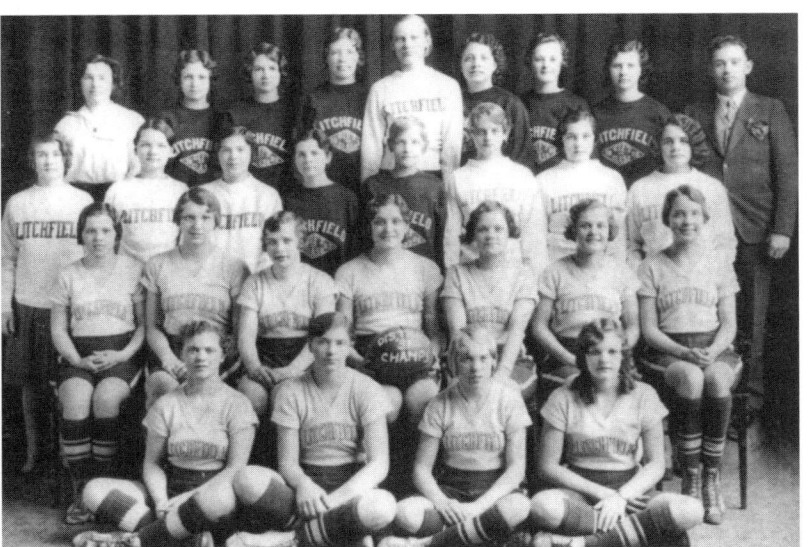
Litchfield 1931

1931 team photo lists – Front: Grace Horton, Annette Draxton, Doris Peters, Hazel Casidy. Second: Harriet Peterson, Ferne Bendickson, Tilda Marstad, Captain Florence Urdahl, Muriel Sederstrom, Joan Peterson, Carrie Grendahl. Third: Ila Peters, Frances Peterson, Barbara Brown, Phyllis Murphy, Lucille Mortenson, Phyllis McGraw, Hazel Lenhardt, Jeanette McGraw. Back: Coach Becker, Vivian Caylor, Beatrice Hillman, Ethel Johnson, Elizabeth Nelson, Edna Booth, Marguerite Nelson, Margaret Anderson, Coach Millard R. Horton.

The 1932 photo lists – Front: Frances Peterson, Pauline Shoultz, Captain Hazel Cassidy, Joan Peterson, Muriel Sederstrom, Harriet Peterson. Middle: Coach Becker, Lucille Mortenson, Phyllis McGraw, Lorraine Nelson, Jeannette McGraw, Barbara Brown, Coach Horton. Back: Erickson, Delke, Stoner, Elizabeth Nelson, Berens, Lahr, Longworth.

The winning streak came to an end at Buffalo on February 12, 1932. The *Litchfield Independent-Review,* 1932, wrote about the ending of the winning streak. The headline said, "Girls Drop First Game in Six Years of Play. The Litchfield High School girls' basketball team, after playing nearly six years of basketball in which every game was a victory for the Green and White, failed to win what would have been their 74th victory at Buffalo last night." The article went on to say, "Buffalo has a great team and as the Litchfield girls already have the nation's high school girls' team record in consecutive games won, they preferred to lose to the Buffalo team rather than to any other

Litchfield 1932

in the country. And from now on they will play for fun and not have worries about maintaining the unbeaten string of victories."

The article noted that the victorious Buffalo squad was "led by 'Honey' Anderson, the scintillate star forward, and her five teammates who have been playing together for four years as a team."

Special Stories

After high school, Florence Urdahl Lundmark taught in a one-room schoolhouse for two years. Later, she began working for the Grain Exchange in Minneapolis. During her 40-year career at the Grain Exchange, she rose from being a board marker, who manually changed the prices of wheat and grain on a big board, to become the group's supervisor.

"Buffalo has a great team and as the Litchfield girls already have the nation's high school girls' team record in consecutive games won, they preferred to lose to the Buffalo team rather than to any other in the country."
Litchfield Independent-Review

Iris McGraw Campbell provided an interview about her junior high basketball team at Litchfield, 1931-1932. They played intramural basketball and did not play out of town, but they anticipated playing on the high school teams. Iris distinctly recalls that the community was very supportive of the girls' teams, and she believes, "that the girls' team in Litchfield was more popular than the boys' team." Iris said, "It was a great honor to be on the Litchfield girls' team because of its incredible winning record. It could give a girl self-confidence and certainly contributes to one's health and fitness."

Iris shared her personal loss. She said,

"Litchfield discontinued girls' basketball at the end of the 1932 season, thus depriving me of playing on the varsity as I was only in the eigth grade. I had dreams of being a basketball star. The whole town was outraged by the ruling and I never got my chance."

Newspaper excerpts reprinted with permission by the *Litchfield Independent-Review*

Luverne High School

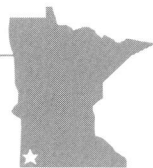

Southwestern Minnesota on Interstate #90, 25 miles south of Pipestone
Years Represented: 1933-1939

The 1934 Luverne girls basketball team was a winning team. Members included Ihlan and Rolfing, forwards; R. Brooks, running center; Chizum, jumping center; Loose and Nesguthe, guards. Substitutes were English, Pack, F. Brooks, Petersen and Goolsbey.

The 1935 Luverne girls basketball team won the District 8 Championship. They had a season record of 10 victories, two defeats and one tie. The team defeated Pipestone, Hills, Jasper, Edgerton, Fulda, Beaver Creek and Flandreau, S.D. In the championship game, they defeated Edgerton.

The team members lists – Front: Jessie English, Patty Nelson, Ruth Brooks, Verna Chizum. Middle: Shirley Ohlen, Elizabeth Jones, Lois Kroeger, Hazel Canfield, Lorraine Stroeh, Arlene Johnson. Back: Helen Norelius, student manager, Bonnie Holmied, Phyllis Horne, Agnes Christiansen, Ruth Vande Velde, Janice Edmonds, Marion Berg, Coach Magdalene Hughes.

Luverne 1935

The 1937 Luverne girls basketball team also enjoyed a successful season, also winning the District 8 tournament. Team members included Ruth Norelius DeLapp, Arline Johnson and Ruth Brooks, forwards; Lois Kroeger and Verna Chizum, centers; and Hazel Canfield and Jessie English at guards. Their coach was Miss Crabbs.

Teams played included Fulda, Hills, Jasper, Edgerton, Pipestone, Worthington, Adrian, Marshall, Flandreau, S.D., Tracy, Blue Earth, Windom, Beaver Creek, Mt. Lake, Jackson, and Lakefield.

The team played three-court basketball with officials from Sioux Falls, including Dana Fleming, the Superintendent of Schools at Hills, Minnesota.

During the winter season of 1937, the *Rock County Star-Herald*, Luverne, headline read,

"Little Ruth Bags Winning Points for Luverne Girls in Championship Thriller." The article began: "Luverne's undefeated girls' basketball team stood on the brink of disaster in the closing minutes of the district championship game with Hills here Tuesday night, when Ruth Norelius, carrot-topped reserve forward, was injected into the game. Hopes for the championship and for a clear season's record were fast fading as the visitors held at 17-15 lead with only four minutes left to go. But little Ruth had her own ideas about the game and pulled the fans out of their seats when she dropped in the basket tying the score. Bedlam reigned as both teams tried desperately for the winning counter. The game was

Luverne 1937

"In the 1930s, Ruth (Norelius DeLapp) and I both loved to play basketball at Luverne High School. The boys could play in district tournaments all the way to a state tournament. Ruth's team won their district tournament and their season ended there. During the many years of raising our family together, we both continued to support opportunities for girls and women in sports and throughout our society."
Roland R. DeLapp, Administrator,
Minneapolis Public Schools, 2005

204 Daughters of the Game

clinched in the last two minutes, when Ruth was given the opportunity to make a free throw. The gift shot was converted and Coach Kuske's charges clung to their one-point margin until the final whistle was blown."

In 1937-1938, the team included Ruth Norelius, Arlene Johnson, Ruth Brooks, Lois Kroeger, Verna Chizum, Hazel Canfield, Jessie English.

The teams traveled by cars provided by parents and the superintendent. The team was popular in the community.

Special Stories
Ruth Norelius DeLapp remembered some of the challenges that teams faced in other gymnasiums. At one game at Pipestone, the snow in the ceiling ventilators began dripping on the floor at the free throw line. During the girls' game, Ruth took the nicest tumble on the slippery floor. The boys' game had hardly gotten underway when another vent began to drip. So the janitor was forced to stand on the court and mop vigorously when that area was free from play.

> "Our parents respected the school authorities who were among the most educated people in our community. So, if that is what they said should happen, our parents accepted it."
> Ruth Norelius DeLapp

Ruth Norelius DeLapp said in her interview, "I believe that playing basketball developed my confidence and self-esteem."

Ruth lamented that her team was discontinued when she returned for her senior year in 1938-1939. She said that the team was extremely disappointed but there wasn't anything they could do. Ruth said, "Our parents respected the school authorities who were among the most educated people in our community. So, if that is what they said should happen, our parents accepted it."

In 1916, H.C. Bell, Superintendent of Schools in Luverne, was the first president of the new organization for high school sports, now named the Minnesota State High School League.

Newspaper excerpts reprinted with permission by the *Rock County Star Herald*, Luverne.

Lyle High School

South central Minnesota, near Iowa border, 12 miles south of Austin on #218
Years Represented: 1929-1931

Helen Speckel Allen was a coach of the Lyle girls basketball team from 1929-1931.

Helen said, "I've never played basketball in my life but I was a basketball coach." Helen said of her stint chaperoning for the girls basketball team on bus trips, "The boys and girls would leave on different buses, but somehow they'd always end up coming back together."

She recalled that the Lyle team played Grand Meadow among others in their area.

Mabel High School

Location: Southeastern Minnesota on Iowa border, 10 miles east of Harmony on #44
Years Represented: 1927-1931

Mabel Thompson Erickson played on the Mabel High School girls basketball team for five years from 1927-31. Mabel provided information during an interview and later made a presentation wearing her own uniform at the 1999 MSHSL Women in Sports Leadership Conference.

The game was a three-court game. Mabel played running center. At 5 foot, 1 inch, her responsibility was to get the ball to the forwards so they could make a basket. Running centers stayed in the center part of the court and could not shoot for scores. One player was the jumping center. Two players were forwards and two were guards.

The team traveled by bus with the boys' team and sometimes traveled in cars. Games were played as doubleheaders in gymnasiums. Spring Grove had a new gymnasium, that Mabel said, "was awesome."

Teams played included Caledonia, Harmony, Canton and Spring Grove.

Mabel Thompson Erickson from Mabel with her school letters

Team uniforms were bloomers when Mabel was a freshman in 1928. Mabel said they were the first team to change to shorts in 1929. She said it made her "feel so free." Mabel recalled,

"Once when we were playing in Spring Grove, I got my foot caught in the pocket of the jumping center. We had to laugh and our coach was madder than a hornet. She said, 'get up, get up, get up.' We got up right away, but of course it was funny because it opened up the placket. That was when we wore bloomers. Then we switched to shorts and sleeveless tops in 1929. Our mothers made the entire outfit. We were the first team to have shorts in Fillmore County. Our school colors were purple and white.

Mabel's mother made her uniform. Mabel received several chenille school letters for her participation on the girls basketball team. She has kept them throughout her life.

Mabel provided the photos of the teams in 1929 and 1931. In the 1931 photo, she is on the top of the pyramid. Other players are not identified.

Mabel said that at first her parents didn't want her to play because they thought it was too hard.

When asked about physical examinations, Mabel said the town had two doctors and one was lenient in his examinations of the players. She said, "He put the stethoscope outside their clothes and said, 'fine, fine, fine.' We got a charge out of it, I'll tell you.

Mabel 1929

Team-building, Mabel 1931

We came out of the office laughing because we had no real exam."

Mabel recalled that they didn't want players to drink water during the game. She said, "They'd give you a mouthful of water and you'd have to spit it out."

Mabel said that "Basketball made me strong. I played volleyball, softball, everything, even marbles. Only two girls in school played marbles. Another girl and I had a bag of shooters and brassies, *and we had all the marbles.*"

In 2005 Mabel remains an active woman at 93 years, and she says, "I walk the Mall of America all the time."

"Only two girls in school played marbles against the boys. Another girl and I had a bag of shooters and brassies, and we had all the marbles."
Mabel Thompson Erickson

Madison High School

Western Minnesota, 35 miles northwest of Granite Falls on #75
Years Represented: 1916-1919

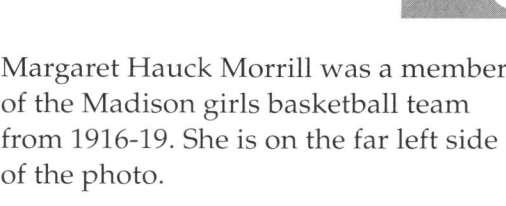

Madison 1919

Margaret Hauck Morrill was a member of the Madison girls basketball team from 1916-19. She is on the far left side of the photo.

In her Basketball Pioneer's Questionnaire, Margaret wrote that they played six players on a team. Margaret said, "I was little but I was fast!!"

She recalled that one school they played was Dawson. They traveled there by train. The team played in the gymnasium, but Margaret lamented, "We only got to play when the boys were finished."

"I was little but I was fast!!"
Margaret Hauck Morrill

Margaret said her favorite memories were the "fun parties with hot cocoa after the games. They played games at the parties. We did a lot of cooking for the parties. Everyone who came to the game came to the party."

Mankato High School

South central Minnesota, 60 miles from metro area on #169
Years Represented: 1913-1921

The 1913 *Otaknam*, the Mankato High School yearbook, recorded that two games were played with outside school teams; the first with the Normal School on their floor and the Normal School on their home court. The Normal School won both games. The coach was Lillian Hughes.

The 1921 *Otaknam* section on "Girls Basket Ball."

"For the first time in the history of the Mankato High School, a girls' varsity team in basket-ball has been organized. The second week in January, the tryouts for the first team squad were held. The girls were enthusiastic and the rules of training were lived up to with as much interest as those of the boys. As the team was not allowed to play games with outside High Schools a schedule of games was made with the Loyola Club, Bethany College and the Normal School. The team has held a clean record having won three games straight. Now that a varsity team has been started it is to be hoped that objection to interscholastic games may be overcome and a schedule of games with other high schools in the district may be arranged for another season."

Mankato 1921

The team was coached by Mrs. Blakeslee. The yearbook article extended praise with, "The girls of the squads think themselves very fortunate in having for their coach such a splendid leader as Mrs. Blakeslee."

Mary Thomas Dickmeyer Todnem was a student under the coaching of Mrs. Blakeslee. She recalled that the games were three-court games and that the teams traveled by car to the other schools. The uniforms were bloomers and middies furnished by the players. Mary said, "The boys respected us and when Mrs. Blakesley wanted the gym, she got it." She said, "All the kids' mothers were supportive."

Mary has memories of playing New Ulm against a girl who was "at least a head taller than I am. I know I barely came up to her shoulders. She had a braid that she could sit on. I was her guard and we'd run for the ball and that braid would go around my neck. Then, of course, we'd just have convulsions."

Special Stories
Mary taught and coached at Cohasset High School. Her teams played Big Fork and Blackduck. In the 1960s Mary was a leader in the state's physical education associations and an advocate for the return of girls' sports in Minnesota.

Mary's sister, Evelyn Bradford, LaCrosse, WI, taught and coached swimming at Nashwauk.

In 2005 Mary is living in a care facility in Minnesota. When a visitor asked how to find Mary, the receptionist said, "Mary is 'holding court' in the solarium." Mary was still a leader, guiding the group's activities, telling stories and playing games. Mary is 98 years of age; her sister, Evelyn, lived to 100 years of age; and her sister Bess had died earlier at age 106 years.

Mantorville High School

15 miles west of Rochester off #14
Years Represented: 1930s

Lorraine Stussy was a member of the Mantorville girls basketball team. Her team in the 1930s played other towns in that county. Lorraine said, "Kasson was our arch enemy."

Lorraine can recall playing Hayfield, Claremont, and she believes they played West Concord and Dodge Center. Her teams played games once a week.

Marshall High School

Southwestern Minnesota, 30 miles south of Granite Falls on #23
Years Represented: 1923-1924

The 1923 Marshall High School yearbook pointed out, "Marshall High School had the best girls' basketball team this year that it has ever had. The regular lineup was Sheffield, Hammer and Adler, forwards; Johnson, Meehl and Hunter (JC) guards. Captain Hunter and Doris Sheffield have made a wonder record. They have played in nearly every game for the past four years, always playing an excellent game, and showing the best of sportsmanship." The article lists additional players: Kiel, Marshall, Nelson and Madden.

Marshall 1923

The team photo lists - Back: D. Sheffield, H. Marshall, G. Kiel. Middle: G. Johnson, Mr. Peterson, coach. Front: I. Meehl, D. Hunter, Capt; F. Adler.

The team won 8 out of 10 games played. Teams played were Granite Falls, Ivanhoe, Tracy, Lamberton, Canby, and Minneota.

The 1924 high school yearbook reported in the "Girls' Basket Ball" summary:

"One noon, just before the holidays, Miss Drummond summoned all the girls who were interested in Basket Ball into the Assembly Room. She told them that soon after vacation they would begin their practices. Naturally their minds were greatly relieved for it had been rumored that Marshall was not to have a Girls' Basket Ball team this season. Coach Peterson spent a great deal of time every week teaching and training the girls on the principles of basket ball. The foundations are laid for a good fast team for the year of twenty-five. The team of twenty-four was practically a new team, Adler being the only player who had the complete experience with the first team last year. F. Adler, H. Marshall, captain, and M. Rathjens played forward, E. Nelson, jumping center, R. Cartier and G. Kiel, guards. The second players were E. Bladholm, F. Skieriski, F. Seward and B. Madden."

The 1924 team photo lists – Front: E. Nelson, H. Marshall, captain; F. Adler. Middle: M. Rathjens, H. Peterson, Coach; R. Cartier. Back: F. Skierecki, G. Kiel, E. Bladholm. The team won one and lost five games. Teams played were: Canby, Granite Falls, Minneota, and Tracy.

"It had been rumored that Marshall was not to have a Girls Basket Ball team this season." Marshall High School yearbook, 1924

Marshall 1924

The Beginning of Girls Athletic Clubs

The 1924 yearbook ended with, "We have hopes for a good fast team next season that will make a record similar to the team of twenty-three." However, basketball was replaced with "Girls Athletic Clubs (GAC).

The 1925 yearbook reported, "Seven Girls' Clubs were organized at the Marshall High School during the second semester of the school year of 1924 and 1925. The purpose of these organizations is to promote physical development through exercise and personal hygiene talks, also to promote a better spirit of fellowship and service among the girls of the high school to aim at higher ethical and moral standards and by these means to prepare the girls for the responsibilities which they will have to assume after they are graduated from high school. Among the sports that have been indulged in are hiking, basket ball, golfing, skating and folk dancing."

The history was gathered from high school yearbooks by Matt Irvin, student at the University of St. Thomas. Matt was part of a class project to gather history on the first era of girls' basketball. The instructor was Thomas A. Hodgson, Ed.D., Adjunct Professor, School of Education.

Mazeppa High School

Southeastern Minnesota, 20 miles north of Rochester on #60
Years Represented: 1905

Mazeppa 1905

A 1905 photo shows the Mazeppa High School girls basketball team. Lorraine Huffmeier has identified her mother, Hattie Pehl, as the second player from the left.

Milaca High School

East central Minnesota, 25 miles northeast of St. Cloud on #169
Years Represented: 1915-1921

Winifred Swanson Stromberg was a member of the 1920 Milaca girls basketball team.

The *Mille Lacs County Times*, 1994, contained an article written by staff writer Jeffrey Hage.

It featured an interview with Winifred Stromberg of Milaca. At the time of the interview, Stromberg was 90 years of age. Her memory was as "sharp as a pin" when she recalled days as a player on the 1920's Milaca girls basketball team.

The game in 1920 was a two-court game, with three guards and three forwards, each restricted to their own section. Stromberg was a jumping center and a guard. Players could dribble twice to advance the ball. Defenders couldn't touch the ball unless it was in the air. Winifred recalled, "No grabbing or trying to get the ball away was allowed."

The 1920 girls' and boys' team photo listed the girls' team members as – Front: Myrtle Almlie Abrahamson, Beatrice Nelson, Lois Cramb. Middle: Gladys Young Davis, Edna Leveau Lindstrom, Winifred Swanson Stromberg, Stella Hedges, Doris Heilig. Back: boys' team members with Coach Wysochi (boys) and Coach Ann Benson (girls).

Milaca had built a new gym in 1915 and was one of the finest facilities for basketball. The girls' team traveled to Hinckley by train. The train left Milaca at 9:00 a.m. and arrived in Hinckley before noon. Games in Hinckley were played on a slippery dance floor. After the game, the team went to the homes of Hinckley team members where they spent the night. They returned to Milaca on the morning train. The same hospitality was returned when the Hinckley team came to Milaca.

Milaca 1920

Winifred recalled,

"Road games to Princeton were a bit easier to make than those to Hinckley, but not by much. In 1920 the girls rode in cars on bad, muddy roads.' Stromberg told of one return trip from Princeton when she had to ride back with the coaches because she had been running late. The car carrying the team broke down south of an area called Wendell Brook. The girls were forced to spend the night in an old school house and in the morning a farmer close by brought the girls into town. Stromberg didn't get stranded that night but didn't get back home until after midnight. She was dropped off at the school and had to walk home a couple miles on a sprained ankle she injured in the game."

> "The girls were forced to spend the night in an old school house and in the morning a farmer close by brought the girls into town."
> *Mille Lacs County Times*, 1994

Fourth Quarter 211

Winifred recalled how Hinckley tricked Milaca into disclosing what positions each Milaca player would play in the game. She said, "When it was time to assign sleeping quarters to the Milaca girls, Hinckley said that a forward sleeps here and a guard sleeps here etc. Pretty soon each position had been assigned a place to stay and Hinckley knew who was who."

In 1921 the girls' team traveled to Princeton in pickup trucks that had been converted to buses. The back ends were covered and benches were installed which sat six people. Winifred said, "The basketball team crammed eight girls into the so-called buses."

The team wore bloomers, as did most teams during that era. Joy Moore Brekke enjoyed basketball several years later at Milaca, graduating in 1931. She liked playing the game but did not recall if they played other schools. Joy recalled, "I was the first girl to play basketball in shorts instead of bloomers. My mother, Florence, went to Minneapolis and got them for me. My future husband, Al Brekke, coached girls basketball at Riverton."

Special Stories

Jeannette Stromberg Helmen wrote about her mother in 1998, "We were listening to the MSHSL State Girls Basketball Tournament and they were asking for information about the early girls basketball teams. I interviewed my mother and found her memory clear and full of her experiences on the Milaca girls basketball team. At present she resides in our local nursing home and will be 95 years of age in July. She enjoys talking about her high school days – especially basketball!"

Milan High School

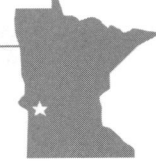

Western Minnesota, 40 miles west of Willmar on #40
Years Represented: 1923-1935

Ella Olson Gandel, 1923-27, completed the Basketball Questionnaire. Edith Dalen Bjornlie, 1924-1927, and Ruth Olson Kleven, 1925-29, participated in an interview.

The 1927 photo showed Captain Ella Olson Gandel, Verna Dalen Struxness, Ruth Olson Kleven, Mavis Halvorson Larson, Rhoda Nordgren, Edith Dalen Bjornlie, Leola Huseby Solheim, Ella Nelson Opjordan. Coach Iverson, a grade school teacher.

The following information of their playing days was provided by Gandel, Bjornlie and Kleven, 1923-29. There were six players on a team with substitutes. They recall playing Holloway, Correll, Odessa, Bellingham, Watson, Clarkfield and Madison Normal.

The coach was a female grade school teacher. Sometimes the men from the town team would help the girls' team with coaching pointers.

Left to Right: Ella Olson Gandel, Verna Dalen Struxness, Ruth Olson Kleven, Mavis Halvorson Larson, Rhoda Nordgren, Edith Dalen Bjornlie, Leola Huseby Solheim, Ella Nelson Opjordan

Milan 1927

Ella Olson Gandel played from 1923-27. She recalled that Milan "has always had a girls basketball team." Sometimes, the boys would help coach the girls' team. Ella said that they never lost a game. At one game in Correll, she and another player were struggling for the ball when a Correll fan grabbed her by the hair to prevent her from making a basket.

Edith Dalen Bjornlie, 1924-27, related how they traveled in cars to games. Edith recalled, "We traveled in a Case Car" with a lot of seats so the more the merrier. One night it was snowing and the driver followed the car ahead of us right into the ditch. We sat and laughed and got out and pushed the cars back onto the road. It wasn't much of a ditch, but it was off the road." Home games were played in a gym that was a separate building behind the schoolhouse.

> "We traveled in a Case Car with a lot of seats so the more the merrier. One night it was snowing and the driver followed the car ahead of us right into the ditch. We sat and laughed and got out and pushed the cars back onto the road."
> Edith Dalen Bjornlie.

The opposing teams were Holloway, Correll, Bellingham, Odessa, Marietta, Watson and Lutheran Normal School in Madison. Players covered their own expenses when they traveled. The girls' team did not have tournaments but the boys' team did.

Edith remembered one game in Correll where "they had a heat pipe that came right close to the basket, so we had to shoot up and around like that to get it into the basket. You know it wasn't much of a gym and I'm sure all the baskets weren't that high, exactly the same. The basket was on a backboard. Sometimes the other schools had places like a tin shop, i.e., a repair shop, not always intended for basketball games." Ruth's sister, Annie, played games in a tin shop that had to be cleaned out. The girls helped clean it too.

The boys played in the same facilities as the girls' team. The boys' games were also played in the tin shop. When their game was over, they would run in their suits to the barber shop and shower. Edith said, "The girls didn't have a chance to shower."

Before 1927 the girls' team played with white middy blouses and black sateen bloomers. Black stockings were worn so no skin would show. The girls provided their own uniforms.

Ruth Olson Kleven, 1925-29, related that the school had only one janitor to keep up with everything. Ruth said, "Sometimes the floor was pretty dirty and all of the girls on the team decided they should wash the floor. We were on our knees washing the gym floor before our game."

Ruth said that Milan was a sports town and there was no need to take a train. The girls' and boys' teams would travel in separate vehicles. They would return home again after games.

> "Sometimes the floor was pretty dirty and all of the girls on the team decided they should wash the floor. We were on our knees washing the gym floor before our game." Ruth Olson Kleven

Edith said, "We had our own little suitcase for our suit, etc. We put our suits on in girls' restrooms or some vacant office." One time, the girls found a filling station that had a big office with a room behind it and they used it to change into their uniforms.

In 1927, the team had new uniforms with shorts replacing the bloomers. At the first game with the new uniforms, there was a big crowd with chairs all the way around the gym where the fans would sit. The out-of-bounds line was right at their feet and players would occasionally fall into someone's lap.

Their new uniform had red shorts with white trim, red v-neck shirts and high top tennis shoes. The girls wore red bloomers underneath the shorts to ensure that they were properly covered. The team also wore cloth headbands with "M" on the front.

Edith explained that in her senior year, "This was the first time knees were visible to the public." Ruth said, "My mother got another mother to go to a game. They shook their heads and looked mostly at the floor."

Parental support was not unanimous. One of the women said that her mother thought it was fine to play, but usually didn't go to games. Her father would go to her brother's game, but not her games. Her brothers and one sister and her husband always attended her games.

The women didn't recall much publicity for their games. The team members received letters for each year of playing.

> "This was the first time knees were visible to the public. My mother got another mother to go to a game. They shook their heads and looked mostly at the floor."
> Ruth Olson Kleven

Special Stories
The women reminded us that their high school classes were small, 14 students total, 6 boys and 8 girls.

When the team played Madison Normal, their hosts made lunch and invited them into their kitchen. The women clearly remembered, "The smell of that good food was something!"

The women said, "Those kids were from our area that went to school in Madison so we knew most of them there. We would go down to the café and have a hamburger after the game, but we paid for our own. We had a good time."

Ruth stayed from Monday through Friday in town with her married sister. She stayed because that was when they practiced basketball and had games, and that was 'my special time.' She said, "I got to be in town and after living in the country that was something special."

The women said they gained, "fellowship, the being together. I think you learned that if you lost a game that you couldn't pout about it or anything like that. You just had to be stronger for your next game."

Milan 1935

The 1935 photo was identified as being the last girls' team in Milan during that era. The 1934-35 team photo named the players — Front: Doris Sweno, Ione Dalen, Junice Dalen, Violet Nelson, Adelaide Blom, Evelyn Mikkelson. Back: Norma Winje, Ellen Undlin, Coach Hollichek, Verna Larson, Margaret Mikkelson.

Ella provided the information in her questionnaire in 1999 at 91 years of age. In 2002 when Edith and Ruth participated in the interview, Ruth was 90 years of age and Edith was 93.

Four Generations of Basketball

The *West Central Tribune*, Willmar, carried an interview on February 12, 2004 by Rand Middleton, staff writer. The headline read, "Four score and eight decades ago." It featured the playing days of Ruth Olson Kleven and the four generations of basketball players in her family: Ruth, her son Jim, Jim's daughter Missy Struxness, and Missy's daughter Lauren. It is a rare four-generation family, especially when the first generation began with girls basketball. Ruth returned to her Milan gymnasium, now part of the Lac qui Parle Valley school district. There she watched and cheered as two great-granddaughters, Lauren Struxness and her second cousin Ali Unger played one another's teams. Lauren played for Lac qui Parle Valley and Ali for Willmar.

Ruth with two great granddaughters

The article concluded,

"Ruth and her sister Ella aren't the only strong Norwegians surviving from that unbeaten 1927 team. Edith Dalen Bjornlie also lives in the nursing home in Dawson, while Ella Nelson Opjordan, also 95, is at the Appleton nursing home."

Newspaper excerpts reprinted with permission by the *West Central Tribune*, Willmar

Minneapolis Schools

One of the Twin Cities, east central Minnesota
Years Represented: 1899-1908

Joel Rippel, Minneapolis *Star Tribune*, was researching the history of the women's basketball team at the University of Minnesota when he found information that the University teams played area high schools:

In 1899-1900: On February 24, 1900, an article appeared in the University of Minnesota *Ariel*, a student publication that was the predecessor to the *Minnesota Daily*. It pointed out, "The 'U' girls' basketball team will play a team from Stanley Hall in the North wing of the Armory this afternoon at 2:30 p.m. Ladies only will be admitted, a fact in itself, which insures an exciting game. An admission of twenty-five cents will be charged to cover expenses." The final score was: 'U' 12, Stanley Hall 6.

Games scores were listed for each year:

1900-1901:	2/19 - 'U' 3	Mpls. Central HS 2
	2/23 – 'U' 4	Mpls. Central HS 4
1901-1902:	1/27 – 'U' 13	Mpls South Side HS 4
	2/03 - 'U' 23	Mpls. East Side HS 1
	2/22 - 'U' 13	Mpls. North Side HS 8
	2/24 - 'U' 4	Stanley Hall 9
1902-1903:	1/17 - 'U' 12	Mpls. North Side HS 0
	1/31 - 'U' 13	Mpls. Central HS 11
	2/21 - 'U' 36	Mpls. South Side HS 4
	3/14 - 'U' 12	Stanley Hall 3

1903-1904:	1/19 - 'U' 51	Drummond Hall 15
	1/23 - 'U' 16	Mpls. Central HS 9
	1/30 - 'U' 20	Mpls. South HS 3
	2/17 - 'U' 41	Drummond Hall 2
	3/11 - 'U' 15	Stanley Hall 3
1904-1905:	1/25 - 'U' 58	Drummond Hall 15
	2/03 - 'U' 56	Mpls. South HS 6
	2/10 - 'U' 30	Mpls. Central HS 12
1905-06:	… … 'U' 53	Drummond Hall 2
	1/20 - 'U' 72	Mpls. South HS 2
	2/14 - 'U' 39	Mpls. Central HS 10
	'U' 62	Stanley Hall 2
1906-1907:	2/23 - 'U' 20	Mpls. South HS 1
	3/23 - 'U' 14	Stanley Hall 1
1907-1908:	3/07 - 'U' 12	Mpls. South HS 14
	3/14 - 'U' 9	Mpls. Central HS 1
	3/28 - 'U' 7	Stanley Hall 4

FRANCES M. KIDD
Administrator

A *Minneapolis Tribune* article dated February 3, 1901 showed a photo of the "Girls Basketball team of the Central High School." There are 12 players in the photo. The article states,

"Basket Ball as a Game for the Girls. No game yet devised has, or will for some time to come, take the place of basket ball as a popular game, and the popularity is growing every year. The game was first adopted by the different Young Men's Christian Associations, and were the only ones to play it for a number of years.

After a time, however, the athletic directors and coaches in the colleges began to realize the value of the game to athletes in foot ball and base ball men and now every college and school in the county has one or more teams. It has given better results than any indoor winter game yet devised.

And still more important, it has become a permanent and popular game among the school girls of the West. There is no time in the girl's life when exercise is so necessary to her physical welfare as during the period when she is in high school.

For a long time it was considered improper for girls to participate in sports of any kind, at least if not improper, unwomanly. The girl could attend the indoor meets and see her brothers and companions play, run and jump, and the only part she was permitted to take would be to wave her school colors.

The game was introduced among some of the more advanced and it might be said, audacious schools, and girls' teams were formed. The sport grew in popularity, and now there are many teams among the school girls of the country.

The game is excellently adapted for them. While the play is fast and sometimes furious, it never becomes rough, and there is little danger of serious injury. It does not require a strong girl to play well. It rather requires agility and wits.

The play itself is an excellent physical developer. It brings many muscles into play that otherwise would seldom be called upon to perform any save the most ordinary functions. It makes the girls straight and strong, gives them an independent bearing, a good color and confidence in themselves that a girl or woman who has not full control of her body cannot feel.

In Minneapolis the game is exceedingly popular at the high schools, and there are several excellent players on the different teams. The East Side, North Side and Central high schools all have teams. Last winter the different teams met and played, and much benefit and pleasure resulted. Stanley Hall also has a team that played against Central last year.

One of the most enthusiastic players in the city is Miss Hattie Van Buren, captain of the Central high team. She plays well herself and is an ardent advocate of the game as an exercise for school girls. The Central team this year is a good one and their rivals will have to work hard to defeat them.

Miss Hosmer and Miss Brown still play guard again this year and they are both fast developing into expert players. Miss Bogart and Miss Wales are playing forward this year and are doing good work. Miss Brazee, at center, shows a wonderful understanding of the game and is among the best on the team. Among the other players at Central are Misses Mollie Hartley, Bessie Cox, Bessie Dansmore, Alice Bracket, Mabel Smith, Elsie Craig, Sadie Preston. They have a game scheduled with Carleton College, New Richmond, Red Wing, Madison and West Superior normal school. "

Special Stories
In 1925, Frances Kidd graduated from Minneapolis Central. Fran played on teams sponsored by settlement houses that served as the gathering places for new immigrants to the United States and as places for their children to play. Girls played basketball in the settlement houses. Fran played three-court basketball and recalled one game when a "feisty player" by the name of Emma gave an opposing player a "poke in the face," Then Emma ran out and around the building, re-entering on the opposite end of the court. Fran laughed as she recalled, "And no one said a thing."

The 1925 Minneapolis Central yearbook, the *Centralian*, included a one-page review of "Girls' Athletics." It summarized, "Girls' athletics in Central are conducted by the Girls' Athletic Association. Because of the large membership of the association, an executive board, representing the active members, is appointed by the president to aid the officers in performing their duties." Their advisors were Miss Clare E. Bell and Miss Evelyn Bowen.

The article listed eight activities, including "tennis, hiking, volley-ball, skating, track, golf, folk dancing and swimming". Points were earned for participation in an activity. The hiking activity included 72 girls that took trips ranging from four to eight miles. Some walked during the winter. Twenty-one girls earned 50 points by hiking 32 miles. In skating at Powderhorn Park, 52 girls participated in skating, winning points in "plain and fancy skating." Competition between classes was held in tennis, volley-ball, track, golf and swimming; but not in folk dancing. "Folk dancing is a sport with no competition which every girl can enjoy and win points for. This year 174 girls took part in this activity."

In the 1950s, Fran Kidd would become the Supervisor of Physical Education for the Minneapolis Public Schools. She was a pioneer in providing competition in several sports for girls in the Minneapolis high schools. Fran was active professionally in state and national organizations. She was selected to attend the 1958 Conference in Estes Park, Colorado where discussions would begin to talk about expanding sports opportunities for girls. In 2005, Fran at age 98 years, says, "I'd do it all over again!"

Montevideo High School

West central Minnesota, 35 miles southwest of Willmar on #7
Years Represented: 1913-1935

Montevideo 1913

A postcard with five girls in bloomers and dark tops is identified as the Montevideo High School girls basketball team of 1913. It was sent by Edna Linnee Jorvig to her Aunt Martha in 1913. Edna is the second player from the left. It is believed that the player second from the right is Edna's friend, Elenore Amundson.

Montevideo 1918

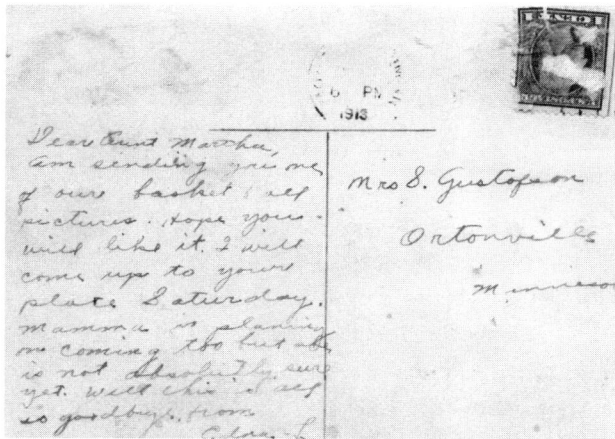

Montevideo postcard 1913

On February 24, 2000, the *Montevideo American-News*, Bruce Olson, Staff writer, headlined his article, "High school girls basketball: You've come a long way baby." Olson wrote that the Montevideo High School girls basketball team in 1918 began with 22 girls out for practice, coached by Miss Malmen. The six players in the starting lineup consisted of Minnie Schultz, Martha Amendson, Ariel Levoy, Grace Nicholson, captain, Esther Tollefson and Charlotte Haugland. The 1918 Montevideo High School yearbook indicated that the team played boys' rules for the first two games and then switched to the girls' rules of that era. The team defeated the local Windom College 9-1 in the first game.

The 1919 team shows 10 girls with no identification.

According to Bruce Olson's article, the 1925 team was led by Katherine Brabec and won six of its seven games. The team won the District 11 Championship.

The 1928-29 team photo lists players as – Front: Evelyn Rhoades, Dorothy McHugh, Solda Nyre, Helen Himley, Fergus Lynch, Alice Andres. Back: Clara Thomtom, Julia Mason, Dorothy Wilson, Winifred Goar, Coach Victor Lanning.

Montevideo 1919

Montevideo 1929

The 1929-30 team photo lists: Front: Winifred Goar, Marholz. Middle: Glenna Fuhs, Clara Thomton, Evelyn Rhoades, Julia Mason, Hamilton. Back: Dorothy Wilson, Lois Canton, Alice Andres.

The 1930-31 photo identifies a limited number of players – Front: Julia Mason, Clara Thomton.

Back: middle player, Alice Andres; middle row, first player on left, Harriet Larson.

Montevideo 1930

The 1931-32 photo identifies – Front: Mary Lou Goar and N/A. Middle: Ruth Monroe, LaVon Thomas, Monroe, Marvel Sundem, Marcella Van Fleet. Back: Thea Sletkolen Stay, DeEtta Nemitz, Mildred Meilke.

Montevideo 1931

1932-33 photo – Right front: Anna Mae LeRoy. Middle: Inez Molde, Ruth Monroe, Marvel Sundem, N/A, Mildred Mielke. Back: Coach Delores Allen; Thea Sletkolen Stay, Loretta Nemitz, Lorraine Nemitz. Other members of this notable squad were Mary Lou Goar, Captain Evelyn Olson, and Irene O'Conner.

1933-1934 photo – Left front: N/A. Right front: Anna LeRoy. Middle: Ruth Monroe, Mildred Meilke N/A, N/A, Marvel Sundem. Back: Coach; Thea Sletkolen Stay; Loretta Nemitz; 4th – N/A.

Montevideo 1932

Thea Sletkolen Stay played from 1931-35 and "was a one-girl scoring machine." Olson wrote, "Thea scored 15 more points in her senior season than Montevideo's opponents."

Montevideo 1933

Teams practiced in the school gymnasium and played at the armory. Uniforms were maroon and gold. The school provided the uniforms that were wool pullover jerseys and bloomer-type pants. Thea said that the uniforms were hot and scratchy.

"Thea scored 15 more points in her senior season than Montevideo's opponents." Bruce Olson, *Montevideo American News*

Montevideo 1934

The team played a two-court game. A jump ball was held after every basket but rules changes removed it during Thea's years to speed up the game. The games were officiated. Teams played included Appleton, Ortonville, Madison, Dawson, and Clara City.

Sometimes the boys' team played against the girls' team in practice. The two teams would travel by bus and return home after the games. The girls' team played the first game of doubleheaders.

Thea exclaimed that when the two teams traveled by bus together, the boys' coach would say, "Girls on one side and boys on the other." She said, "We always had a good laugh over that expression."

In 1933 the girls defeated a highly respected Ortonville team 33 to 15 to win the district crown and finished with an undefeated season. In this finale Thea Sletkolen, center, and Anna Mae LeRoy, a forward, accounted for 31 points between them. Thea snagged ten field goals and Anna Mae five field goals and one free throw.

Two team members were Anna Le Roy and Amy Anderson who played forward. Thea averaged 24.6 points per game, shooting 197 of her team's 331 points in 1935. She never failed to score at least 20 points in any game.

Playoffs included the top two teams and the champion received a large trophy.

In 1934, with Anna Mae LeRoy, Thea Sletkolen, Ruth Monroe, Mildred Mielke, Marvel Sundem and Loretta Nemitz back from the 1933 championship squad, Miss Mildred Oelke came up with a successful team. New members of the squad were Phyllis Waldron, Avis Nordquist, Rachel Michaelson and Amy Anderson. They played 10 games and lost two during the season. In the district tournament, Montevideo again won the title by defeating Ortonville 31-21.

Montevideo dominated the district from 1926-1935, winning the title every year except 1930 and 1932.

Montevideo 1935

The 1935 District Champion from Montevideo lists the following players - Front: Amy Anderson, Anna Mae LeRoy. Middle: L. Mielke, Z Berg, Captain Ruth Monroe, Marvel Sundem, L. Averill. Back: Thea Sletkolen, Rachel Michaelson, Loretta Nemitz, Coach Mildred Oelke.

The following players were prominent over the years of the Montevideo girls basketball team:

Thea Sletkolen was Monte's high cage scorer. It was said that she rarely missed an opportunity to score and opponents failed to come up with a defense to stop her. Outstanding players included: Anna Mae LeRoy, the Goar sisters, Clara and Winnie, Ruth Wilson. In earlier years, outstanding players include: 1916, Naomi Leroy and Gladys Biegert; 1917-18, Grace

Nicholson and Ariel Levoy; 1926, Mildred Pedlar, Louise Norman, Myrtle Botten; 1924, Evelyn Lynch; 1927, Fergus Lynch; 1930, Clara Thomtom, Evy Rhoades and Alice Andres.

The team was discontinued after the 1935 season. In 1936 the school began sponsorship of its Girls' Athletic Association.

Special Stories

In Thea's interview, she said that she went to a small country school, grades 1-8, with about 25-30 students. There was only one teacher. The room was heated by a round pot belly stove. There were outdoor toilets and students had to ask permission to go outside. Her dad would take them to school by horse and sleigh in the winter. She left the country school to finish seventh and eighth grade in Watson where they had their own teacher. She then went to high school where her parents rented a room for five dollars a month for her. The house had four bedrooms with eight girls going to high school, and one bathroom. They cooked their own breakfast and dinner on a kerosene stove in the basement. They brought most of the food from their homes. Thea's high school years were during the Great Depression. She said, "There were times that I didn't have money that I could go have a coke after the game; there wasn't that kind of money. It was hard for me because a lot of these girls lived in Montevideo; their folks had a good business going. We lived on a farm and didn't have any crops all those years."

In 1985, Ruth Wilson Martin, 1925, and Thea Sletkolen Stay, 1935, and were inducted into the Montevideo Hall of Fame. It was Thea's 50th class reunion. She said, "They had a large parade in Monte and we rode in a red convertible! What a thrill!!"

Newspaper excerpts reprinted with permission by the *Montevideo American-News*

Montgomery High School

South central Minnesota, 10 miles south of New Prague, 15 miles west of 35W
Years Represented: 1926-1932

Irma Malone Foley shared many stories in an interview and for a panel presentation at the October 1998 Minnesota State High School League's Women in Sports Leadership Conference.

Irma graduated from Sherman High School in Montgomery, MN in 1932, playing basketball from 1928 through 1932. Sherman High School was re-named Montgomery High School in 1936.

After high school, Irma went to Montgomery "Normal School" one year and then taught in a one-room country school in Montgomery.

Bernice Malone Pexa and Eunice Wolfe Washa provided interviews and provided many stories about their teams. Bernice played four years, 1926-1930. Eunice played from 7th-12th grade, graduating in 1932.

Their games were played with two-courts and officiated by men from Belle Plaine. Other officials were from Northfield Colleges and Minneapolis.

The team played New Prague, Jordan, LeCenter, Belle Plaine and Henderson. The girls' and boys' teams played doubleheaders, traveling in separate cars or going by train. One of Irma's favorite stories was of a stormy winter day when they were to play New Prague. The roads were closed, so a friendly train engineer in town offered to take them to New Prague in his caboose.

One of Irma's favorite stories was of a stormy winter day when they were to play New Prague. The roads were closed, so a friendly train engineer in town offered to take them to New Prague in his caboose.
Irma Malone Foley

The team played in a dance hall that was three blocks from school. The team changed clothes at school and then ran three to four blocks to the town hall on Main Street. Irma indicated that sometimes, "Br-r-r, it was cold!!" "We had very nice uniforms," Irma said. "They weren't bloomers as my grandchildren asked about!"

The teams had male and female coaches, including the superintendent. The female coach was Miss O'Connel. The male coach was John R. Muraski.

Irma asserted that "The entire community was supportive. My father never missed a game."

The annual district tournament included a silver loving cup which was won once by Montgomery, twice by New Prague and twice by Jordan. The team winning three times would be given permanent possession of the cup.

Montgomery won the District 7 Championship in 1930. In the February 28, 1980 *Montgomery Messenger*, Coach John Muraski wrote, "The girls basketball team won the league championship, also, the girls basketball tournament held at New Prague. This was the best basketball team I ever coached, and the girls worked very hard to achieve the championship in 1930."

The 1930-31 high school newspaper reported, "The girls met with some real 'hard luck' during the tournament which was held in the gymnasium at New Prague March 4th and 5th when they lost to Belle Plaine and Jordan. They will never forget when Eunice sprained her ankle and finally when Irma was carried from the floor. This situation called for some real fight and spirit and the girls were there to give it up to the last minute of play. This same attitude was shown throughout the year – both at practice and regular games – and it is because of this that we can all say, we are truly proud of the girls and wish them the greatest amount of success during the season of 1931-32."

Bernice was a high scoring forward. Eunice was the center forward.

Montgomery 1930

1930 team photo – Front: Catherine Westerman, Irma Malone Foley, Florence Kubat, Julia Jindra, Bernice Malone Pexa, Eurnice Wolfe Washa. Back: Coach Muraski, Gertrude Hezs, Evelyn Vitha, Mildred Hezs, Rosalia Havel.

1931 team photo - Irma Malone, Charlotte Oren, Harriet Washa, Eunice Wolframstorf, Florence Kubat, Evelyn Vitha, Bernice Malone Pexa, Marcella Kotek, Coach Muraski.

Montgomery 1931

1932 team photo – Front: Irma Malone, Rose Dietz, Eunice Wolframstorf, Evelyn Vitha, Catherine Westerman, Rosalia Have. Back: Alma Bradash, Helen Vitha, Mildred Hezs, Ione Mladek

On March 17, 1932, the *Jordan Independent* provided coverage of the district tournament. It headlined, "Jordan High School Girls Win District Championship Honors." Silver Loving Cup Brought Back to Hub for First Time Since 1929. Jordan took first honors at the girls basketball tournament held in New Prague last Thursday and Friday evenings. They defeated Belle Plaine, 26 to 12 and Montgomery 32-16."

The article went on, "Montgomery, and that means Miss Wolfe, returned the victor in the other Thursday night elimination contest. Eunice Wolfe plays a hard game. She had a capable running mate in Irma Malone (Foley), who although much smaller, was equal to the task of playing hard driving type of basketball. Eunice Wolfe carries the scoring punch of the Montgomery team. She is fed the ball under the basket by her two forwards, Havel and Malone and has a good eye for the basket. She shoots like a man and apparently does not tire under the strain."

Montgomery 1932

After the presenting of the trophy the all-district team was announced. Montgomery was awarded two positions on the All-District First Team, Wolframsdorf being placed at center and Irma Malone winning a forward position. Vitha was named to the All-District Second Team."

Special Stories
Karen Norell, then Principal at Montgomery High School, organized the first Wall of Fame in 1999. Irma Malone Foley was one of its first inductees.

The *Montgomery Messenger*, February 4, 1999, included an article with the headline, "Honorees to be inducted into the Wall of Fame Friday."

The article stated, "On Friday, February 5, at half time of the boys basketball game, the distinguished group of honorees will be inducted into the Wall of Fame at the Montgomery-Lonsdale High School. Nominations were taken and among them the following were selected to be honored: Irma Malone

Foley. Foley presently lives in Bloomington but has been a life long advocate of the community of Montgomery and an outspoken advocate for girls' sports. She played on the 1930 District Girls Championship Basketball Team from Montgomery and was the second Kolacky Queen. She was also active in drama and speech during her high school career. Foley graduated in 1932."

In 2005, Irma is 91 years of age. At her assisted-care home, an alcove outside her room holds special memorabilia. Irma has selected photos of her Montgomery girls basketball team and the plaques she received at the 1999 reception for basketball pioneers at the MSHSL State Girls Basketball Tournament as well as those received when she was honored as a Sports Pioneer at a Minnesota Lynx game. She is affectionately called "our little basketball player."

Newspaper excerpts reprinted with permission by the *Montgomery Messenger* and the *Litchfield Independent*.

Monticello High School

30 northwest of Minneapolis on #94
Years Represented: 1923-1924

The 1923-24 Monticello High School girls basketball team photo identifies several players as - first player unknown, 2nd girl from left: Dorothy Bradford Lilja, captain, Helen Bryant, next three unknown, Ethel Carlson Fitzgerald holding the basketball, Alice Eggena, Florence Fish, Gladys Gehrenbeck.

Monticello 1924

The team's coach was Miss Williamson.

Mary Bollman reports that her mother, Dorothy Bradford Lilja, was a forward on the team. In 1992, Dorothy was 85 years of age. In 2002, her aunt Ethel Carlson Fitzgerald, was 95 years of age.

Moose Lake High School

35 miles southwest of Duluth on #35
Years Represented: 1929-1933

The 1930 Moose Lake High School yearbook, the *Minicahda*, reported that,

"It was a large, but untried squad that reported to Miss Trydal during the last week of October. Keen competition for positions on the team produced a caliber of basketball seldom displayed by girls' teams here before. The majority of games played were quite close, the girls piling up the margin of victory in the final quarter. Outstanding during the season were the two victories over Barnum."

The article pointed out, "The team lined up as follows: Marie Westholm, captain and center forward; Wanda Blasyk, right forward; Vernette Peterson, left forward; Marcella Westby, center guard; Thora

Almquist, right guard; Dorothy Skelton, left guard. Substitutes for the team were Emma Lu Westholm, Gladys Upgren, and Marion Bergquist." Their team played 12 games. The team won eight games, lost three and tied one.

Members of the 1930-31 Moose Lake girls basketball team were: Thora Almquist, Marie Westholm, Evelyn Couillard, Emma Lu Westholm, Dorothy Skelton, Coach Trydal, Luvane Olson, Vernette Peterson, Grace Gay, Ruth Upgren and Hulda Lampi. The season record was 7-1.

Moose Lake 1930

The Moose Lake High School yearbook reported in an article,

"An Undefeated Season. To the team of 1931-32 goes the distinction of a perfect record, a season without a defeat. In turning back their opponents in the eight games played the girls amassed a total of 351 points to 130 for the opposition. Members of the successful squad, coached by Miss Lynda Trydal, are Captain Dorothy Skelton; Hulda Lampi, Captain-elect Evelyn Couillard, Marie Westholm, Emma Lu Westholm, Mable Palon, Marguerite Van Camp, Vernette Peterson, and Grace Gay. The majority of games were won by clear cut margins of victory and in no contest were the girls forced to extend themselves to win. It is to be regretted that four of the players listed above have played in their last game for Moose Lake. The writer makes no effort to list the outstanding players for truly this was a team in the fullest sense of the word."

Moose Lake 1931

Teams played included Willow River, Cromwell, Pine City, and Barnum. The highest scoring game was a win over Willow River, 71-3.

Moose Lake 1932

The Moose Lake High School yearbook of 1932-33 reported:

"Another short but successful season has been closed with five games played. Much of the credit for success goes to Miss Lynda Trydahl, coach. Moose Lake lost one game, tied one and won three Team members included: Captain Hulda Lampi; Captain-elect Evelyn Couillard, Eldora Johnson, Grace Gay, Dorothy Skelton, Ruth Abrahamson. Substitutes were: Marion Bergquist, Loretta Burns, Helen Zasoski, Dena Holte, Ethel Amundson and Helen Millimaki. In the past three years the girls have won 19 games, lost two and tied one."

Moose Lake 1933

Teams played included Willow River and Barnum.

The 1939 school yearbook included a "Boys' Athletic Club," and a "Girls' Athletic Club." There is no mention of a girls basketball team playing other schools.

Morgan High School

25 miles northwest of New Ulm on #71
Years Represented: 1924-1928

In 1923-24, Luretta Parker Trobec played on the Morgan High School girls basketball team. Luretta provided information on a questionnaire in 1998 when she was 91 years of age.

Elsie T. Berdan played at Morgan High School from 1924-28. Elsie reported it was a five-member team with officiated games. She was a defensive player and couldn't shoot for scores.

One official was Sam McNall, a mail carrier.

Teams played were Redwood Falls, Sanborn, Springfield, and Lamberton. The coach was a male chemistry teacher.

The team traveled by car, returning home after games. Practices and games were held at City Hall. Uniforms were middies and bloomers furnished by the school.

Morgan 1925

The community and parents were very supportive. The *Morgan Messenger* carried articles of the girls' games.

The photo identifies players as - Inez Root, Margaret Haney, Luretta Parker Trobec holding the ball, Hiacynth Brosch, Elsie Berdan, Grace Albrecht.

Elsie and Hiacynth went to nursing school in Minneapolis in 1925. Elsie lived an active life as a nurse and was in the Army.

Morris High School

West central Minnesota, 30 miles southwest of Alexandria on # 9
Years Represented: 1934-1939

Orell May Judd Jensen, in a 1999 letter wrote, "I was so glad to see the article about girls' basketball. So many younger women don't believe me when I say I was on a team. Morris is my home town and the high school had a full intramural program, competition and all for girls. In those days, we didn't need physical conditioning. We were girls after all. Now, I can't exactly recall if we competed with other schools in the area. I have no remembrance of bus trips to play ball at other schools. Perhaps you'll get news from other women about that from towns in the area (Benson, Herman, Chokio, Glenwood).

I graduated in 1938 and the yearbook notes that I'm in #2 place as the most athletic girl. Which only means that basketball was very important in my life at that time, as well as swimming. It was the beginning of a way of life which has been very healthy for me – active, paying attention to diet, etc. "I hope good results come from your efforts."

Morton High School

Southwestern Minnesota near Redwood Falls
Years Represented: 1928-1932

Leone Revier Schell graduated in 1932. She played guard and never got the chance to shoot. "People wanted to shoot," she said. "That's what you practiced, shooting all of the time. You liked to be the forward." Leone played in the girls' game and then played flute in the school band for the boys' game that followed.

Her teams practiced after school. Games were played at the city hall across from the school as her school had no gymnasium.

> "Everybody in the town and the farmers came to our games. It was the biggest school event during the winter."
> Leone Revier Schell

Leone reminisced about pep rallies where pep songs were sung and players and coaches talked. "Basketball was important in those days. Everybody in the town and farmers came to our games. It was the biggest school event during the winter. I remember people coming from the farms, especially if they had kids playing. Farm kids were the strong ones."

Mountain Lake High School

Southwestern Minnesota, 10 miles northeast of Windom on #60
Years Represented: 1923

Mountain Lake 1923

The town's centennial publication, *"Mountain Lake 1886-1986,"* was written by the Centennial Committee. The publication stated that Mountain Lake's first girls basketball team played a schedule of games in 1923.

Team members included – Front: Marie Kintzi, Frances Kintzi, Esther Porish, Lydia Miller. Middle: Alice Stenke, Ruth Johnson, Ann Thiessen. Back: Coaches Victor Jansen, Harold Tallakson, Miss Ekberg.

The publication contained a section, "Girls basketball," that stated:

"Girls played basketball as a preliminary to the boys' game in the first years of basketball in Mountain Lake. Why this was discontinued is not known."

New Prague High School

South central Minnesota, 30 miles south of the metro area on #21
Years Represented: 1907-1932

New Prague 1918

The *Jordan Independent*, March 1907, headlined an article, "Basket Ball Girls Play New Prague." It reported, "The girls basket ball team of our high school went to New Prague Saturday and played the New Prague school team. The glory of winning went to the New Prague lasses, 10 to 3, in a very pretty contest, not so one-sided as the score might indicate. The New Prague team was lucky again Sunday, when the Whitesox team came down from "Beantown" and played the Jordan Turners in Harmonia Hall. The element of luck seemed to be with the jolly Praguers. Final result, 16 to 10. The New Prague lineup was Hennen, Jelinek, Vanasek, Bates and Sery."

A photo of the New Prague team of 1917-18 showed 17 girls and a male coach. The players are wearing dark bloomers and black stockings with white middy tops and dark colored bows.

In 1999 four women living in New Prague provided information and descriptions of their teams.

Ida Picha Welter played from 1927-1931. In 1999 Ida reported that three teammates lived in her apartment building: Marietta Sharkey, Lorretta Musil and Ann Juni. Other teammates included Monica Janda Simon, Irene Slavic Nordvedt, and Anna Shambour.

Ida contended, "The first game I played in as a freshman was at a church in Le Sueur and we were taken by friends of the athletes. There were no dressing rooms, no showers, no toilets. One of the girls couldn't wait until we got home so she used a coal bucket that was in the sanctuary of the church." Ida added, "Too bad it leaked!"

Ida said, "When we played for the championship of our district, we played against Belle Plaine. It was still a two-court game with forwards and guards staying on their half of the court. I was a forward and I had the ball very near the center line. The court was sided by bleachers. It happened that Belle Plaine fans were to my right. One of the Belle Plaine fans yelled at me to shoot; what was I waiting for?! I shot and made the basket which won the game for us. The Belle Plaine fans let out a few cuss words but our team was happy."

Ida reported that the team received letter sweaters, and a letter with the logo and date.

> "One of the Belle Plaine fans yelled at me to shoot, what was I waiting for?! I shot and made the basket which won the game for us."
> Ida Picha Welter

Monica Janda Simon played in 1929-1930.

The New Prague girls basketball team played Jordan, Montgomery, St. Peter and Belle Plaine. They traveled in cars, returning home after games. Margaret Fredrickson was the coach.

Monica played in tournaments with other schools, including one hosted by New Prague because the other schools had nice gymnasiums. Monica said that the girls' team frequently played the first game, prior to the boys' game. She felt that the girls' team was well supported by the community.

Their uniforms were t-shirts with NP letters on the front, with bloomers with elastic bottoms on the legs.

Adeline Kamish Musil and Evelyn Vales Kraus reported that they played in 1928, 1929, and 1930. It was a two-court game. Their first games were in a dance hall, and later in their high school gymnasium. Their team wore black bloomers and a red wool short-sleeved sweater.

The *Jordan Independent*, March 17, 1932, reported on the District Championship. New Prague hosted the tournament won by Jordan. The article showed that the president of the New Prague Commercial Club presented the captain of the Jordan team with the silver loving cup, "emblematic of the title of champions." New Prague had lost a first round game to Montgomery, 21-18. L. Maytas, freshman, carried by the "scoring punch for Beantown. She was assisted by Sachs and Ambrose." In an upset of the tournament, Belle Plaine defeated New Prague on Friday night by a score of 14 to 12 and won consolation honors. The team lineup was Sachs, Panek, Ambrose, L. Matyas, M. Matyas, Kamish, Kodadek, McKenny. New Prague placed Matyas on the All District First Team, and Kamish on the All District Second Team.

New Prague, Jordan and Montgomery were all district champions during the era.

Newspaper excerpts reprinted with permission by the *Jordan Independent*

New Richland High School

South central Minnesota, 13 miles south of Waseca on #13
Years: 1925-1927

Evelyn Sponberg Young played on the New Richland girls basketball team during her junior and senior years, 1925-1927.

Evelyn explained that her team played a two-court game and she was a running guard.

Their games were played in a metal building heated by a round stove in the corner.

The team's uniforms consisted of a white middy top with black bloomers, black stockings and athletic shoes.

Special Stories
Herb, one of Evelyn's brothers, wanted to play basketball. The family lived on a farm and the sons were expected to work. Herb talked to Evelyn about joining the girls' team and they both approached their parents to request permission for both of them to play. The parents approved and both Herb and Evelyn played basketball.

When weather permitted, they would travel five miles each way from the farm to New Richland with a horse and buggy, a cutter or wagon.

When the winter weather arrived, they would stay for days at a time with family friends in town, Herb with one family and Evelyn with another. Herb's brothers would do his farm work during the basketball season.

After high school, Evelyn remembered playing basketball at Gustavus Adolphus College, St. Peter. Evelyn became a legendary figure as head of the food service at Gustavus for 35 years.

Legacy
Evelyn's granddaughters Sara Sampsell-Jones and Laura Sampsell Hoffman share her love of basketball. Sara and Laura both played for Edina.

New Ulm High School

25 miles west of Mankato on #14
Years Represented: 1919-1926

The *Owatonna People's Press*, March 19, 1992 contained an article headed, "Girls' team best in state in 1919." Staff writers were Brenda Guderian and Loren Nelson.

The article reported, "In 1919 the Owatonna High School girls' basketball team had played just five games when it boldly proclaimed it was the state's best. And it was – unofficially – after beating New Ulm 24-18 in a winner-take-all challenge game at the old Owatonna Armory." The article went on, "The girls will play any recognized high school on a regulation court under girls' rules of the game," the *Journal Chronicle* reported, adding that OHS had sent letters to the state's other 25 high school girls' teams challenging them to a title game. Owatonna, which hadn't finished the regular season when it issued its challenge, beat Albert Lea in its final scheduled game before playing New Ulm. The rest of the state's teams reportedly refused to contend for the title."

"In 1919, the Owatonna High School girls basketball team had played just five games when it boldly proclaimed it was the state's best."
Owatonna People's Press

For this game, the girls' rules provided for a two-court game with guards and forwards playing at opposite ends of the court and restricted from crossing the center line.

The school newspaper had a photo of the 1926 New Ulm girls basketball team. Players are not listed in order and some names are incomplete. Coach Louise Fritsche Menzel, Ann Sperl, Louise "Katsy"

New Ulm 1925

New Ulm 1924

New Ulm 1926

Esser, Lorraine, Lola, Cora Meidl Siel, Helen Hintz, Verna, Polly Polie Fenske, Lydia; Ruth, Lavera, Hildegard Amann Christenson, Statistician.

Newspaper excerpts reprinted with permission by the *Owatonna People's Press*

Nielsville High School

Northwestern Minnesota, 25 miles south of Crookston on #75
Years Represented: 1928 -1931

Alice Aanenson Lervold played at Nielsville and Climax from 1928-31. Alice reported that her team was unique in that era by playing the full court game with five players.

A photo identified the team members as Belle Haugan, Ethel Pederson, Alice Aanenson, Carol Howland, Alice Waale and Coach/Principal Wylie.

Her team played schools in Caledonia, North Dakota, and Reynolds, North Dakota. The team had a

Nielsville 1928

male coach who was also the principal.

The team traveled to games in cars and only stayed overnight if there was a snowstorm. The girls' and boys' teams played on different days.

A tournament was held in Climax that included teams from North Dakota.

Team uniforms were black bloomers with a white sailor top. Alice kept her uniform with her high school memoirs.

Alice emphasized that the community was very supportive of both the girls' and boys' teams.

Alice said her favorite memories were having the chance to play basketball which she enjoyed so much. She played guard most of the time. The team played in a gym heated by a potbellied stove. A couple of the men would stand by the stove so players wouldn't run into it.

> The team played in a gym heated by a potbellied stove. A couple of the men would stand by the stove so players wouldn't run into it.
>
> Alice Aanenson Lervold

Legacy
Alice began a three-generation family of female basketball players.
After high school, Alice played one year of intramural basketball at Concordia College. Her daughter, Kathy Lervold Goodrich, played in college at Moorhead State from 1968-72. Kathy was the coach of the New York Mills girls basketball team from 1972-77 and coached the team to the Class A State Championships in 1977.

Alice's granddaughter, Heather Goodrich Schrider, played at Woodbury High School, 1996-98, and participated in the 1997 and 1998 MSHSL State Girls Basketball Tournaments.

Kathy wrote, "My mother passed away in the fall of 2001. She really enjoyed the recognition as a basketball pioneer at the 1999 MSHSL State Girls Basketball Tournament. She kept the basketball and plaque she received at the tournament in her room at the nursing home. They are now part of my basketball keepsakes."

North Branch High School

35 miles north of St. Paul on #35
Years Represented: 1930-1932

The *North Branch Review*, April 2, 1908, indicated that 13 girls were out for basketball - Emilene Wilkes, Nancy Bjorklung (sic), Delia Bergdahl, Effie Bergwell, Dora Fagerstrom, Allie Olson, Grace Rogers, Ruth Grahn, Delia Aney, Mildred McIllveen, Nanny Magnusson, Florence Hendrickson, and Adelaide Waldhoff.

The girls practiced on the second floor of the old school on the corner of Seventh Avenue and Maple Street.

North Branch 1929

The 1929 North Branch yearbook, the *Branch*, reported that,

"Though losing game after game by the narrowest of margins the girls' team never relinquished their fighting spirit and every start found them giving their best to win a victory for their school. The three veterans, namely, Gladys Carlson, Myra Thurner, and Maurine Otto, played excellently throughout the year and were responsible to a great extent for the fine work of the newer members of the squad. Verna Krueger, Bernice Anderson, and Fanny Livingston, the three girls to win regular positions, were always found in the thick of the fray, every minute fighting for possession of the ball and starting a rally for North Branch. The substitutes disported themselves nobly when called upon to replace one of their mates."

The 1931 team photo lists the following members - Front: Marjorie Stephens, Bernice Anderson, Josephine Otto, Verna Krugar, Kathleen Anderson. Back: Ruth Swenson, Dorthey Sederberg, Coach Doris McCrady Alvin, Lydia Krugar, Frances Kueckler.

The 1932 team photo lists - Front: Marjorie Stephens, Ruth Swenson, Kathleen Anderson, Katherine Stephens, Lorraine Peterson, Jeanette Stephens. Back: Norma Nordstrom, Lydia Krueger, Helen Peterson, Lola Anderson, Alta Anerson, Coach Marge Smith.

North Branch 1931

North Branch 1932

Lorraine Peterson Olson, 1932, believes that her team was the last team of the era. The next information in her files identified her participation in the GAC (Girls Athletic Club) and play days with Cambridge.

Fourth Quarter 233

Northfield High School

35 miles south of Minneapolis; 7 miles east of 35W
Years Represented: 1904

In 1892 Max Exner, friend and roommate of James Naismith at Springfield College in Springfield, Massachusetts, came to Carleton College in Northfield, Minnesota. Max Exner introduced the game of basketball to the college women and it quickly moved into the high schools of Minnesota.

The first Northfield girls basketball team was formed in the spring of 1904, according to the NHS Athletic History by C.E. Sandberg, Red Wing. The first games were played against Carleton College and St. Olaf College in Northfield.

The following excerpts are reprinted with the permission of the *Northfield News.*

On May 14, 1904, *The Northfield News* stated,

"Co-Eds Play Ball. There is a lively interest being taken at present in the formation of a girls' basket ball team at the Central High School building.

There is plenty of good material for a fast team and the co-eds are working hard for places on the school team. The girls are being coached by Paul Albert and expect to have a game in the near future with a team from Gridley Hall (Carleton College women's team). Among the young ladies who are out for positions are Ida Hendrickson, Edith Street, Katherine Lee, Gertrude Greaves, Clara Lathrop, Alice Lee, Laura Reilly, Lucile Crary, Lavina Wilson, Laura Black, Velma Black, Helen Ballou, Lelia Hall, Francis Giffney, Virginia Kilmore, Ennis Seltun and Sena Bark."

The first basketball game against another high school was on November 4, 1904. The opposing team was St. James. The *Northfield News* reported "There will be a basket ball game on the high school grounds this afternoon at 2:30 between teams representing the St. James and the Northfield high schools. The former team claims the championship of southern Minnesota and the game promises to be one of interest. The Northfield team will play as follows: forwards Alice Lee, Helen Hoppin; centers Katherine Lee, Margaret Blodgett; guards Edith Street, Beth Street."

The *Northfield News*, November 12, 1904 reported on the game between St. James and Northfield. The headline read, "High Girls Defeated. St. James Representatives Win Friday's Game by Large Score."

This article stated, "In the first matched game of basketball ever played by the high school girls' team the young ladies met with defeat. The game, which attracted much attention, was played last week Friday afternoon on the high school grounds. The opposing team was from the St. James School. It was composed of veteran players and from the beginning the outcome of the contest was a foregone conclusion. The visitor's team work was par excellent and the individual playing was very good. Baskets were thrown by them almost at will and their confidence in their officials added not a little to their alertness. The representatives of the Northfield school played very well under the circumstances and in the last half held the visitors down evenly. The score of the game was 39 to 6. Both the umpire and referee of the game were from St. James and their decisions at times were not very satisfactory to the spectators."

The *Northfield News*, November 22, 1904, pointed out that:

"The young ladies basket ball team of the high school defeated the St. Olaf team last Saturday afternoon in a well-played and interesting game. The score was 19 to 10. The members of the victorious team are Margaret Blodgett and Helen Hoppin, forwards; Alice Lee, center; Mildred Ware, Laura Black and Katherine Lee, guards."

100-Year Commemorative Game Held

On January 8, 2005, the Northfield Schools invited St. James to Northfield for a 100-Year Celebration to commemorate their first game held on November 4, 1904. The teams and captains were presented with commemorative basketballs and the traditional reception of the early 1900s was held after the game.

The Commemorative Program for the "Game of the Century", January 8, 2005, noted that, "It was November 4, 1904. Rough Riding Teddy Roosevelt had just been re-elected president in a close election. The Russian-Japanese conflict dominated international news. The World Fair was in progress in St. Louis, MO., and straw hats for men and taffeta hats for women were the fashion statements of the day. Then the first ball went up, it was the beginning of a rich and storied century of basketball at Northfield High School."

Northfield News stories reprinted with permission by the *Northfield News*. Copyright *Northfield News*. All rights reserved. Excerpt reprinted with permission of Scott Richardson, Northfield, "Commemorative Program, Game of the Century," January 8, 2005.

Northome High School

North central Minnesota; 40 miles northeast of Bemidji on #71
Years Represented: 1934-1937

Mildred Wick Gorden played on the Northome girls basketball team from 1934-37. The game was a two-court game played in gymnasiums. Games were officiated.

Teams played included other schools around Northome, and the team also traveled to International Falls and Fort Frances for games. In 1936 the team lost only one game all season.

Their team was playing during the years of the Great Depression so players made their own uniforms. They were able to play wearing shorts and blouses.

The 1936 team photo showed – Front: Freda Pierson, Mildred Wick, Margaret Bloom, Clara Sarasin, Charlotte Schomberg. Back: Coach Benny Dixon, Dorothy Draheim, Evelyn Logdahl, Margaret Sjostrom.

Mildred said,

"We had a male coach." Schools played included the nearby county schools and Ft. Frances,

Northome 1936

Canada. The girls' and boys' teams traveled on the same bus to games. They returned home after games. Mildred added, "I remember especially one game when we played Ft. Francis, Canada. They always had an excellent sports program and were a much larger school than ours. We won both games that year and the score was 7-6. One needed good defense."

The teams were well supported by their community. Mildred says, "We had big crowds." There were no tournaments. Players received school letters at the end of the season.

The 1936 team was the last school-sponsored team of that era.

Mildred reported that her favorite memories included:

"Very close relationships with team members. I'm still in touch with some of the girls. I learned to be in the public eye. It gives one lots of confidence and it never bothered me to be in front of people to speak or take part in any activity. The exercise kept weight off and keeps one healthy, I think. I'm so happy that girls basketball is back in my school and all schools."

Mildred said that she remains an avid sports fan and "I believe my interest in sports all goes back to my participation in high school."

Olivia High School

West central Minnesota; 22 miles east of Granite Falls on #212
Years Represented: 1906-1937

Olivia 1906

Shelly Moudry, a student at the University of St. Thomas, conducted a research study into the history of girls basketball in her hometown of Olivia.

Olivia High School sponsored a girls basketball team as early as 1906. A photo shows six players and one coach. The girls are wearing matching uniforms. The shirts and bloomers were a very dark color. The letter "O" representing the school was sewn on the front of the shirts. The shirts are long sleeve and tied tightly around the neck. The bloomers appear to be long and heavy. Shelly noted, "No skin is showing anywhere. The players are very proper. Also the coach is dressed very sophisticated."

The 1906 team photo included – Front: Blanche Weischelbaum, Anna Morgan, Myrtle Hedlund. Back: Flora Windhorst, Coach Myrtle Heins, Clara Schroeder, Iva Schoregge.

Another photo is of the 1920 team, seven players and one coach. The uniforms continued to be bloomers, but they appeared to be shorter and lighter. The uniform tops appeared to be old navy

Olivia 1920

236   Daughters of the Game

shirts, commonly referred to as middies. The players were wearing matching high-laced shoes.

The girls' team was invited by other towns to come and play when the boys had a game there. Travel was by horse and buggy or by train. Sometimes the teams would stay in a hotel overnight and then take the train to Fairfax for another game. Teams later traveled by Model T Fords, nicknamed the 'Tin Lizzies." Lizzie was a name commonly given to horses and to the "horseless carriages."

Games were first played in the local armory and later in a gym located in the high school. The name of one coach was Miss Sassy.

Games were officiated by the hometown team for the first half and the visiting team the second half.

> Teams later traveled by Model T Fords, nicknamed "Tin Lizzies." Lizzie was a name commonly given to horses and to the new "horseless carriages."

Neighboring teams included Bird Island, Danube, Sleepy Eye and Fairfax.

Olivia 1937

The third photo is from 1937. Shelly noted that the players seemed to be more relaxed and 'free-spirited.' The 1937 photo lists - Kate Dodds, Janet Bordewich, Dorothy Einerson, Bette McDowell, Dorothy Cuta, Vonnie Walleen, captain. Behind the players is Miss Pike, Coach

The last team on record was in 1937.

At the conclusion of her study, Shelly realized, "I have a greater appreciation for the history of women's sports, especially in my town. I have learned that the town is full of amazing treasures waiting to be discovered."

Onamia High School

North central Minnesota, located on south end of Mille Lacs Lake, #169; 22 miles north of Milaca
Years Represented: 1929-1932

Nell Lane graduated from Onamia High School in 1932 and played on the Onamia girls basketball team for three years. The schools in the area had about the same enrollment as Onamia. Her team played Wahkon, Isle, Pierz, Lastrup, Milaca and Ogilvie.

Their game was a two-court game with players limited to their half of the court. The team traveled by school bus, returning home after games. The players covered their own traveling expenses.

Nell recalled that the boys had tournaments but the girls' teams did not. The boys' team and community were all very supportive.

Games were played in a gymnasium. "But," Nell said, "It was not a regulation gym." The team wore bloomers and blouses with capped sleeves. Their coach was female. Players covered any expenses incurred for travel.

Nell recollected that her favorite memories included, "it was great fun even though some of the cheerleading squad had some 'uppity' gals.'

Nell also participated in track and field. She entered the shot put and high jump.

Owatonna High School

South central Minnesota; 60 miles south of Minneapolis on #35W
Years Represented: 1919-1924.

The 1919 Owatonna girls basketball team played and defeated Austin, Kasson, Albert Lea, New Ulm, Osage and the State Public School. The photo identified players were Marie Tomsche, guard; Frieda Kottke, running center; Edna Jahreiss, jumping center; Estelle Johnson, guard; Eloise Hanson, forward, Marjorie Leach, forward.

Owatonna 1919

The *Owatonna People's Press*, March 19, 1992, included an article written by Brenda Guderian and Loren Nelson that proclaimed,

"Girls' team best in state in 1919." In 1919, the Owatonna High School girls basketball team had played just five games when it boldly proclaimed it was the state's best. And it was – unofficially – after beating New Ulm 24-18 in a winner-take-all challenge game at the old Owatonna Armory. The team did exceptionally well considering that it had to practice in the old armory, which was not sufficiently heated during the season."

The *Owatonna Journal-Chronicle* reported in its April 19, 1919, edition, "The girls will play any recognized high school on a regulation court under girls' rules of the game." The *Owatonna Journal-Chronicle* added that OHS had sent letters to the state's other 25 high school girls' teams challenging them to a title game.

Owatonna 1919 game announcement

Owatonna had not finished the regular season when it issued its challenge, beat Albert Lea in its final scheduled game before playing New Ulm. The rest of the state's teams reportedly refused to contend for the title.

Girls basketball was young then, having started in Owatonna in about 1912." It was poorly organized," said Frieda Kottke Coleman, a "running center" on the 1919 team.

The girls' team played a different kind of basketball than is known today. According to the newspaper stories, guards and forwards played at opposite ends of the court and were not allowed to cross mid-court. A "jumping center" also played although her role is unclear.

The girls' games, usually played once a week as part of a doubleheader with the boys' team, were split into 15-minute halves. Admission for the championship game against New Ulm was 15 cents and 25 cents. Coleman, now 91 and living in Fargo, ND, either didn't recall her role or is modest about it, but the April 11 *Owatonna Journal-Chronicle* claimed, "The playing of Frieda Kottke and Eloise Hanson was always the pride of the high school fans who depend on those two players when the opponents seemed threatening."

The sport wasn't very established, so the team didn't have a loyal following, Coleman said, 'The boys had much more,' she said with a laugh.

But, it was still exciting for the girls. Frieda recalled. She said. "It was wonderful…to get that much notoriety, it was exciting."

Owatonna 1924

Besides Kottke and Hanson, a forward, the team included Estelle Johnson, guard; Marie Tomsche, guard; Marjorie Leach, forward; and Edna Jahreiss, jumping center. Coleman kept in touch with Hanson, who has since died, but she doesn't know what happened to the other girls.

> "The playing of Frieda Kottke and Eloise Hanson was always the pride of the high school fans who depend on those two players when the opponents seemed threatening."
> *Owatonna Journal-Chronicle*

A photo of the 1924 OHS girls basketball team identified the players as - Ruth Wilkinson, Emily Ripka, Leona Johnson, Tillie Allard, Maxine Sperry, Berniece Costigan, Ethel Darby, and Coach Evelyn Mann.

Special Stories

Sandy Boss, early girls' sports pioneer and coach at Owatonna, wrote, "In 1989 when our girls basketball team went to state, the town was abuzz with 'first time ever.' It reminded me of when I was first teaching in Owatonna and I had a call from a woman who called me to come to her house. She had a wonderful scrapbook of memories from that 1919 team. She was so excited that girls again had the opportunity to play sports and knew that I would be interested in her stories. I only wish I had kept in better contact with her."

Sandy said, "When the 1989 team was to go to the state tourney, I dug through old newspapers and came up with some articles which our local press re-published. One of the 1919 'state champs' players, Frieda Kottke, was living in Fargo. I had the chance to visit her via phone. She, too, had some great memories of her basketball days."

At the time of their conversation, Frieda was 103 years of age.

Newspaper excerpts reprinted with permission by the *Owatonna People's Press*

Paynesville High School

30 miles southeast of St. Cloud on #23
Years Represented: 1926-1929

Letta Farnum Swedelius provided an interview of her playing days from 1926-29. Their game was a two-court game in which she played the position of guard.

Team members on the 1928 photo were – Front: Miranda Wendtland, Pat Garding, Jean Haines, Eileen Sandborn, Ione Buehe.
Back: June Buehe, Letta Swedelius, captain, Edna Goodman.

Her team played Litchfield, Brooten, Belgrade, Cold Spring, Eden Valley, and Sauk Rapids.

Travel was by car. Letta said, "We rode with anyone that had a car. There were no buses."

The team returned home after night games. Games were played in gymnasiums. The girls' and boys' teams played on the same night, with the girls' game played first.

Paynesville 1928

The team uniform was paid for by the players and consisted of a top and bloomers with long stockings.

The coach was female and was responsible to be the team chaperone.

Letta indicated that the parents, community, and the boys' team and coaches were supportive. She said, "We all looked forward to playing and had a good time."

Pelican Rapids High School

Western Minnesota; 40 miles southwest of Moorhead on #59
Years Represented: 1911-1914

Pelican Rapids 1912

Pelican Rapids High School sponsored a girls basketball team in 1912. The photo shows a team photo with what appears to be the first and second teams.

One player was identified as Ethel Lyden Anderson who graduated in 1914. A white "X" marks Ethel on each photo.

Ethel kept her uniform throughout the years and it was displayed at the Minnesota State High School League's 1998 Women in Sports Leadership Conference.

Ethel's daughter, Pat, said that her mother frequently told her that this uniform also served as her swimming suit. Her daughter added, "And Mom was a good swimmer!"

Legacy
In 2005 Heidi Robbins of Illinois modeled her great-grandmother's uniform, preserved by the family since 1912.

Pine Island High School

Southeast Minnesota; 10 miles north of Rochester on #52
Years Represented: 1904-1908

The *Pine Island News-Record*, March 6, 1985, included an article, "Old Time Basketball," written by staff writer, Loraine Vettel. "The indoor sport of basketball was invented (in 1891) by James B. Naismith, an instructor of the International YMCA Training School in Springfield, Massachusetts. There was a need for a competitive game that would fill the winter vacuum after the summer baseball and autumn football games."

The article went on:

"Basketball, as a sport for high school, began in Pine Island in 1904. In October the Boys' and Girls' Athletic Association prepared an oyster supper to raise funds for equipment for the new gymnasium. The supper cleared $20. By late October the equipment for the boys had arrived. The girls were still waiting for theirs. The Opera House had been wired for basketball and the boys were practicing there every night. In November a special exhibition game was played at the Opera House to enable local people to see 'what a lively and skillful game it is.' Admission was ten cents. The boys' team played the Red Wing team on Thanksgiving Day at 3 p.m. Due to the large crowd expected, a large scoreboard was hung up in the hall. The official score was given after each goal made. Another game was played on Christmas Eve.

> "In October the Boys' and Girls' Athletic Association prepared an oyster supper to raise funds for equipment for the new gymnasium. The supper cleared $20."
> *The Pine Island News-Record*

In January 1905 the girls basketball team played an exhibition game, defeating the teachers. Several exhibitions involved both the boys' and girls' teams, each playing their opponent the same night. One night both boys' and girls' teams were to play Stewartville. The boys had their game, but as the Stewartville girls failed to show, the local girls played the teachers again.

Usually teams traveled by train to their games; spending the night at the town before returning home the next day. One game in February against Pleasant Valley should have had the players arriving here on the 5 p.m. train. The train was delayed until 9 p.m. The players had been left in Rochester and had to drive here. In another game, Pine Island took the train to Lena arriving 1½ hours late. They then drove to Mazeppa, arriving there at 9 p.m. to play their game.

In 1908 it appeared the boys' opponent played a rough game. One account referred to the 'football tactics.' At another game, "the players and referee were bombarded with lemons and other missiles,

Pine Island 1908

some of which inflicted serious bruises, and one struck referee Billings in the face, loosening several teeth. The Opera House had the spectators crowded to the limit. They experienced difficulty keeping the crowd off the floor."

Under a photo of the 1908 team, the *Pine Island News-Record* reported that, "In February 1908, the Pine Island girls' quintet defeated Kasson and Rochester 14 to 6 and 18 to 6."

Newspapers excerpts reprinted with permission by the Pine Island *News-Record*

Preston High School

Southeast Minnesota, 35 miles south of Rochester on #52
Years Represented: 1940-1941

Marjorie Nelson Johnson played one year and then sadly learned in 1941, "The new superintendent and school board voted to discontinue girls' basketball." Marjorie graduated in 1944.

Marjorie's team played Harmony and Lanesboro. They traveled to out-of-town games by school bus, returning the same night.

Games were played in the school gymnasium. The team wore blue one-piece suits with elastic hem on bottom. Marjorie said they were called the "Bloomer Team."

The coach was their physical education teacher, Ruth Telander.

Marjorie related that she fell during a game, injuring her knee, but she said, "I regained control of the basketball in my fall and made a basket and our team won!!"

"I regained control of the basketball in my fall and made a basket and our team won!!"
Marjorie Nelson Johnson

Special Stories
Marjorie Nelson Johnson provided an interview via the questionnaire for her years as a member of the Preston girls basketball team, 1940-41. She wrote her response with an apology, "I'm sorry my handwriting is not very good right now. I have a chemo pump on my right hip and a tube in my right arm." Marjorie wanted to ensure that the Preston team was included in the history of the sport in Minnesota.

Princeton High School

North central Minnesota; 40 miles north of Minneapolis on #169
Years Represented: 1921

Princeton 1921

The *Princeton Tiger* yearbook included a photo and article about the 1921 team:

"During the past year, the P.H.S. basketball girls met with great success. Although they lost three letter men last year, there were many capable girls picked from the many that appeared the first night. The girls established a world-wide reputation on winning six out of eight games and thus gained the championship of this district. As they had no regular lineup, it cannot be definitely stated, but the leading players were Blanche Oakes, Marjorie Chapman, Florence Miller, Mae Howard and Madge Chapman. Although they will again lose three letter men, the girls who are left hope to keep up this reputation. Time will tell. Wait and see."

The team played Elk River, Milaca, Anoka, and Cambridge.

The team photo showed the team members wearing a light middy top with a scarf, dark bloomer-type bottoms, dark stockings, light athletic shoes and head bands.

The team coach was Miss Allen.

Proctor High School

Northeast Minnesota, 5 miles southwest of Duluth
Years Represented: 1917-1926

Proctor 1917

The photo of the 1917 teams identified it as the first Proctor high school girls basketball team. Players were identified as Brenda Stewart Beaulier, Katie Rappold, Ruth Barncard, Ruth Carlson Wombacher and Thelma Stewart Hendricks.

In 1919, the coaches were Mr. and Mrs. Jedlicka. The team was undefeated after playing two games against Duluth Denfeld and one game with Duluth Normal. The 1919 team photo shows - Front: Thelma Stewart, Vivian Davis, Captain Eleanor Brayden. Middle: Mabel Emberg, Edith Ryan, Laura Spearman. Back: Superintendent and Coach A.I. Jedlicka. Superintendent Jedlicka was the longest-tenured Superintendent in Minnesota history.

The 1920 *Proctorian* yearbook reported that the team won its games against Duluth Normal, Nelson Dewey at Superior, and

Two Harbors. Then the team suffered its "first game ever" loss to Two Harbors losing 18 to 14. The last game against Superior Central ended with a score of 60 to 4 in Proctor's favor. The game was refereed by Miss Smith of Duluth Normal.

Proctor 1920

The 1920 team photo shows Eleanor Brayden, Edith Ryan, Mildred Sathers, Vivian Davis, Ruth Stewart, Bessie Anderson, Ada Rossetter, Doris Quick, Coach Miss Higgins.

The *1921 Proctorian* wrote of its girls basketball team, "Proctor High has one possession indeed which other schools cannot boast of. What is it? The champion Girls Basketball team. Champions of the Head of the Lakes and St. Louis County."

Proctor 1919

The 1921 team photo lists players as – Front: Bessie Anderson, Mildren Sathers, Eleanor Brayden, Laura Spearman. Back: Madeline Mahoney, Doris Quick, Ruth Stewart, Laura Yount.

The 1922 Proctorian wrote that it was a successful season though fewer games were played. The coach was Miss Gillesby.

The 1922 season opened with a pep banquet with a toastmistress, and the season was underway. The first game was played against Carlton at Proctor. Coach Gillesby was the referee. The next game was with Cathedral with Miss Allen of Superior as referee. Proctor won 12-3. In February, a game was played at Coleraine, the only team to have previously defeated a Proctor team. After a hotly-contested game, Proctor returned home the victor by a score of 15-12.

Proctor 1921

Proctor 1922

The third game against Carlton was won by a score of 33-5. The next game against Cathedral was a challenging game with "Cathedral playing in a style that fully equaled the boys and consequently most of our team was rather stiff for a few days." Proctor won 4-2. The last game was played against Greenway of Coleraine and resulted in the only loss of the season, 18-21.

Proctor invited Coleraine to play a third game to decide "the better team," but Coleraine refused. The yearbook stated, "So we claim the Northwestern Championship."

The team was awarded heavy white sweaters as a reward for their "hard work and good showing in basketball." The article concluded, "We also wish to thank the townspeople for their loyal support and for the encouragement they have given us at all of our games."

In 1923, the yearbook reported that the girls' team practiced in the YMCA gymnasium because the new gymnasium was not ready. Miss Gratzek, coach, selected the following players for the team - Marjory Stewart and Doris Davis, forwards; Mildred Ferguson and Eva Zebott, centers; Bertha Darrach and Catherine McCurdy, guards; Evelyn Bemel, Lucille Morgan and Edith Peterson were the substitutes. The first game was won by Proctor against Carlton, 39-4. A new coach, Miss Carss, took over the team. The second game with Cloquet was a loss for Proctor, 18-15.

Proctor 1923

The new gymnasium was opened with a "moving picture shown from five o'clock until eight. It was followed by a dinner served by the Parent Teachers Association. Following the dinner was a doubleheader game with Carlton. The Proctor girls won, the score being 22-6."

Proctor lost to Greenway, won against Cloquet, and lost to Greenway a second time. That loss removed Proctor from contending for the district championship.

Proctor 1926

The 1926 team members were Laura Yount and Flora Stewart, forwards; Irma Greene and Eulalia Haar, centers; Ilda Emberg, captain and Thelma Yount, guards. Additional players included: Colleen Stewart and Gladys Zebott, guards; Helen Jollymore, center; and Annie Stipka, forward.

The 1926 school newspaper, *The Mallet*, featured an article with a headline, "Girls' Team Undefeated Has Remarkable Season." The article stated, "The girls basketball team of 1926 has provided what Proctor High School can do in girl athletics. A long list of victories is indeed something to be proud of, but when every game on the schedule has been a victory it is a record which any school should envy." The article went on, "The school is proud of them and not only for their good playing but for their admirable sportsmanship. Is it not at times harder to show good sportsmanship with their opponents when they themselves have won a victory? Those who have played the game know that it is. Never once, however, have our girls done a thing which was an action of a poor sportsman. Too many good things cannot be said of our girls' team."

The 1926 Mallet reported on the impending closure of girls basketball teams in Proctor:

"A Girls Athletic Association has been started headed by Miss Everts. The purpose of it is to get every girl interested in some form of athletics. Laws and by-laws have been drawn up by a committee for that purpose. Every kind of athletics available in Proctor will be introduced.

This GAA does not promise to be much this year but by all indications it will be an organization to be proud of next year.

Proctor 1929

There will be a Girls Basket Ball Captain elected this year as it is not decided yet whether there will be girls' inter-scholastic basketball next year or not. Rumors are that a law providing against girls' inter-scholastic basketball was passed by the Minnesota State Legislature recently. It will be definitely decided next year and we hope the decision will not be as harsh as it seems."

The 1929 Proctor team members are not identified.

"Thank you for giving 'new' life to our girls who have been forgotten in recent years. New life, with new excitement to girls who were true pioneers and rose to the level to be fine examples of the Spirit of the Proctor High School."
R.A. Silverness, school board member, Proctor Public Schools, 2005.

Special Stories
"The original Proctor High School was painted Duluth Missabe and Northern Green. This dark green paint was in abundance on the railway as it was used on all of the passenger cars. Dark green was selected as the official school color along with white. The school colors, Missabe green and white, continue on at Proctor High School, located on the original Summit School location." R.A. Silverness

Rapidan High School

South central Minnesota; 10 miles south of Mankato
Years Represented: 1922 - 1930

In 1973 the Rapidan High School held its 50th year reunion. A booklet was made for each graduate about the history of the school from its beginning in 1922-23. Included was a picture of Aileen Just Luther titled, "outstanding girl basketball player of the state of Minnesota."

Aileen made a presentation at the reunion and provided an overview of the Rapidan girls basketball teams from 1922-30. The team was discontinued by the school after the 1930 season.

In the early years, their court was divided into three sections with two guards, two forwards and two centers, each staying in their section of the court. By the late 1920s, the rules changed to two-court basketball with guards and forwards limited to half of the court.

The girls' team wore black gabardine fully pleated bloomers which extended below the knee. The white middies had black collars and long black bows. As the Rapidan team increased in notoriety, the girls' uniforms changed. In 1926-27 Miss Pear Ware was the coach and dared to change the traditional black and white uniforms to the school colors of medium blue with white trim. They were basic bloomers but with a yard or two less material, made of broadcloth. They continued to be pleated and worn to come below the knees. Blue and white stockings were worn with them. The uniforms were made by the mothers of the team members. In 1928-29, Gladys Wandersee Mohr,

Rapidan 1924

Rapidan 1925

Rapidan 1926

coach, went "modern" with all white suits with blue trim. The uniforms were small unpleated bloomers. Players were also permitted to wear them above the knees and to roll the stockings below the knees or to their ankles.

The first team in 1922-23 did not have a very successful season so the players recruited new players for the next year.

In 1923-24, the team members were Stella Johnson Reedstrom, Clara Olson, Pearl Daughterty, Lydia Kriel Reedstrom, Mildred Pettis Skewes, and Louise Just Dewey. Substitutes included a fifth grader, Lorna Lochmiller Phillips, and a sixth grader, Aileen Just Luther. The school principal, Carl Pothoff, was the coach. Players not identified on the photo.

In 1924-25, Ruby Strand Quigley and Cameon Hawes joined the team. Mr. Potthoff remained as coach.

In 1925-26, the team consisted of Ruby Strand Quigley, Lorna Lachmiller Phillip, Aileen Just Luther, Hilda Schwanberger Mennaga, Marjarie Crase Farmer, Mabel Plumb Bernhart, Ellen Berger, Verna Miller Hanson, and Eva Hanson Hennissey. Lewis Raberton, principal, was coach. Players not identified on the photo.

The 1926-27 team consisted of Minnie Plumb Owens, Lorna Lachmiller Phillip, Aileen Just Luther, Hilda Schwanberger, Marjorie Crase Farmer, Mabel Plumb Bernhart, Ellen Berger, Verna Miller Hanson and Eva Hanson Hennissey. The team was coached by Miss Pear Ware. Players were not identified on the photo.

Aileen recalled that the girls' and boys' teams frequently traveled together with the boys' game played first. The team had a light lunch before each game under the supervision of their home economics teachers. The menu was usually creamed eggs on toast and fresh fruit.

Pep fests were held before each game with skits and yells. One of the girls would lead cheers for the boys and a boy would lead cheers for the girls.

"Seldom did we return to Rapidan without a little harmonizing," Aileen reminisced. "Remember the one we sang? "'Oh Rapidan's, a go-er, all others are slow-er. Our team is the cream of the country, HoRay! Yum, ya, ya'"

Aileen received a lot of support from her family. "My mother, Marie Just, would sit in the balcony which surrounded the gym floor right above the basket.

Every time I'd come in for a basket I could hear her shout "Make it, Aileen."

> "Every time I'd come in for a basket I could hear my mother shout, "Make it, Aileen!"
> Aileen Just Luther

Aileen told the class reunion, "We always looked forward to stopping at an ice cream joint on our way home for a 10 cent soda or sundae. That was about all most of us could afford but then it usually turned out that our dear Superintendent, Mr. Strobel, would pick up the tab for all as a reward for games well played.

Aileen recalled, "When the Rapidan school was built, it seems that they did not anticipate a girls basketball team, so they did not provide for a girls' locker room and shower. The girls were permitted to use the boys' room and shower when not in use by the boys' team. One evening we were all waiting our turn for a shower after a game. Hilda Schwanberger saw a bar of soap on the upper ledge of the shower she could not reach. She climbed on the lavatory to get the soap but fell to the floor with the bowl, plumbing and all. By the time we could all get dressed so the custodian, Mr. Dougherty, could get in, the room was full of steam and water. The Athletic Department got the bill for the repairs and it was the last time the girls were permitted to use the room. However this prompted the school district to construct a locker room for the girls in the basement on the west side. By this time the interest and enthusiasm for girls basketball had grown to new heights in Rapidan."

The places where games were played sometimes had obstacles. Aileen recalled, "At Waldorf there was an area screened off for the heating unit. If the ball happened to bounce just right, it would land down in the boiler room. Then a time out was necessary to retrieve the ball. Pemberton had support beams on the edge of the playing floor which we were warned not to run into. At Nicollet we played in a hall with the spectators sitting near the edge of the playing floor. Many times we were accidentally tripped by some, and the time the floor was heavily oiled, it took a lot of Fels Naptha and P and G soap to get the oil off our light suits."

The District 7 schools played included St. Clair, Nicollet, Lake Crystal, Garden City, Vernon Center, Waldorf, Good Thunder and Pemberton. Other teams played were Bethany College, Loyola of Mankato, and Tam O'Shanter of Mankato.

In 1927-28, the Rapidan team competed in a two-day District 7 tournament in the gymnasium at the Mankato Teachers College. Teams included Rapidan, Garden City, Pemberton and Waldorf. Good attendance followed. Aileen Just, Marjorie Crase and Eva Hanson were named to the All-Tournament First Team. Aileen Just was the star of the game with Garden City, defeating them 28 to 17 to win the district tournament. Aileen scored all but one point. A crowd of 500 attended the final contest. Rapidan ended its season with 15 straight victories.

Rapidan 1927

The 1927-28 team photo included – Front: Ellen Burger, Eva Hanson, Marjorie Crase, Elsa Lachmiller, Verna Miller. Back: Anna Flo, Minnie Plumb, Coach Herbert Hartshorn, Mabel Plumb, Aileen Just.

Aileen indicated that team members received medals for winning the district tournament. The team received a trophy and all players received school letters.

After winning the district tournament, Aileen said, "Winning the trophy called for a celebration. Mr. and Mrs. Strobel furnished cookies and some Kool-aid which we all drank from the trophy cup." The team won the tournament in the following year and in Aileen's final year, the team placed second. The team was given a basketball but their athletic association had a bill at Mohowalds, so the team turned in the basketball to help defray the bill.

Rapidan 1928

Rapidan 1929

The 1928-29 team lists: Verna Miller Hanson, Pauline Knutsen True, Doris Councelman Raub, Harriet Summers, Evelyn Miescke Huebsch, Eva Hanson Hennissey; Aileen Just Luther, Ellen Berger, and Elsa Lachmiller. Gladys Wandersee Mohr was coach. Players are not identified on the photo.

Rapidan trophy 1928

Aileen had many favorite memories: "I loved to play my best and be the top scorer but disliked the large number of interviews (and there were a lot of interviews). We really wanted to beat Garden City and we did!" She adds, "The game gave me a lot of confidence from competing with the different schools, the teamwork, and getting along with others. I enjoyed tremendously working with the different girls that played on the team year after year."

Newspapers
Local newspaper headlines included: "Aileen Just Continues To Better Her Point-A-Minute Average; Rapidan Winner;" "Aileen Just Out for More Score Honors – Sensational Rapidan Girl Forward Plays Against St. Clair Tonight;" "Aileen Just Gets 30 of 32 Points – Brilliant Girl Forward of Rapidan Stars in High Win Over Alumnae."

Rapidan 1930

In 366 minutes of play during the season, Aileen Just scored 410 points and became known as "Point-A-Minute Just."

The 1929-30 team photo lists – Front: Dorothy Lachmiller, Evelyn Miescke Huebsch, Aileen Just Luther, Elsa Lachmiller Olson, Pauline Knutson True, Virginia Sandon. Back: Earl Engbritsen, Coach, Leona Just, Leila Friedrichs, Viola Krueger, Dorothy Washburn, Mabel Nassif.

Several articles credited the presence of Aileen Just as the reason for the large crowds following the team.

A picture of Aileen Just was sent to all corners of the U.S., appearing in papers in Chicago, Massachusetts and Denver, among others. The caption read, "Aileen Just, Outstanding Girl Basketball player of the State of Minnesota. A 16 year old and a sophomore at Rapidan, Aileen has brought her team through to 40 victories in 43 games played in three years. Thirty to 35 points scored in a game are a common occurrence for her."

The *Minneapolis Journal*, December 15, 1927, wrote, "Girl Cager Scores 73 of Rapidan's 86 Points in 2 Games. Aileen Just, 16-year-old sophomore at Rapidan high school, could find a position on any boys' quint, if it were possible under the rules to have girls playing on boys' teams. Miss Just has created a furor in basketball circles of Southern Minnesota. The Rapidan girls have won two games thus far, and Aileen has accounted for 73 of the 86 points scored."

"Newspaper reporters would give numerous paragraphs describing the actions of the girls' game followed by a single sentence or at the most a paragraph for the boys."
St. James Plaindealer, Marsh 12, 1980

The *St. James Plaindealer*, March 12, 1980, included an article by staff writer, Angie Proctor,

"In the 1920s, Rapidan girl scores point a minute. Between the years of 1922-1930 girls basketball drew more attention than boys basketball. Usually boys and girls doubleheader games were scheduled on the same evening with the girls' game first. Newspaper reporters would give numerous paragraphs describing the action of the girls' game followed by a single sentence or at the most a paragraph for the boys. Her picture appeared nationwide in the newspapers with the caption 'Aileen Just, Outstanding Girl Basketball Player from the State of Minnesota.'" After that she received fan mail from all over the U.S. 'One day I got 16 letters in the mail. It was mostly from young people who wanted to be my pen pal. I loved basketball but I hated all the publicity,' she continued. 'Once sport writers get on your trail they are after you all the time. I could only do my best but they expected me to play well continually.'"

Toward the end of one basketball season a newspaper clipping summed it up,

"Play in the district departmental girls basketball tournament at the Mankato Teachers College will start tonight. The fact is that the Rapidan team with its star forward, Miss Aileen Just, the outstanding girl player of the Northwest, has done much to stir up interest in our tournament. With its undefeated record and its string of 14 straight victories, all by large scores, Coach Herbert

Hartshorn's Rapidan team ranks as the favorite to win the district cup. Aileen Just, of the Rapidan basketball team, made one of the best records in girls basketball this year in this state when she scored 453 points in 416 minutes of play. The total number of points scored by the team of which she is a member was 614 as against 224 scored by its opponents in 16 games."

The Rapidan girls were scheduled to play the First National Bank (FNB) women's professional team out of Minneapolis in the armory at Mankato. The FNB team was the champion of the northwest. On a return trip from Canada the professional team was involved in a bus accident so the game was cancelled. "We wonder what would have happened at that game," Aileen said. "It would have been interesting to see how we would have done against professionals."

The professionals had asked Aileen to play on their team after her graduation from high school but she had other plans. "I had my mind set on home economics," she stated. After two years of training at the University of Minnesota she became a county club agent working with 4-H groups. However, she never lost her interest in sports.

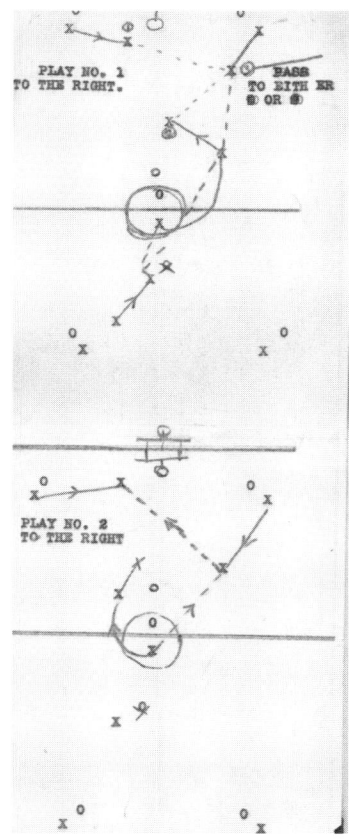

Rapidan basketball play diagram

"The girl basketball team was the big show in the town of Rapidan. We boys played the second game of a doubleheader with the girls playing the first game. Very few spectators would have come to the boys' game if we had played the first game. Everyone came early to see the girls play. We used to scrimmage the girls team and they would always win. My sister Aileen was an outstanding player. There was no comparison between Aileen and the boys and girls who played basketball at that time. She had long arms and great reach so no one could out jump her. Some teams put two defensive people guarding Aileen and then would try to foul her to slow down her scoring. I never missed one of Aileen's games. Even with all the publicity she received Aileen was very humble and modest about her success. I could never understand why they dropped girls basketball in the early 1930s."
Richard Just, brother of Aileen Just Luther

The year after Aileen and her class of eight graduated from Rapidan, high school girls basketball was phased out. "I never did find out exactly why it stopped," she said.

Two of the trophies won by the Rapidan girls basketball team are on display in the Rapidan Village Hall along with other girls basketball memorabilia.

Basketball was about the only organized sport in the 1920s but each year Rapidan and surrounding schools had a Blue Earth County Field Day with all schools participating in a number of sports including competitive running, relays, softball and athletic games.

Rapidan High School consolidated with Vernon Center and Garden City to become Wellcome Memorial, and later to Lake Crystal-Wellcome Memorial.

Newspaper excerpts reprinted with permission of the *St. James Plaindealer*

Red Wing High School

40 miles southeast of the Metro Area on #61
Years Represented: 1917-1926

A photo of the 1917 Red Wing High School girls basketball team includes Ruth Rehder who is in the front row, second from the right.

The 1926 Red Wing Seminary yearbook reported that Red Wing High School played Red Wing Seminary High School in February and that Seminary won 20-12. In the return game Seminary again defeated Red Wing, 13-0.

Red Wing 1917

Red Wing Seminary High School

Location: 40 miles southeast of the Twin Cities on #61
Years Represented: 1920-1926

A serious student at the Red Wing Seminary, Margarethe (front center) was the captain of the basketball team.

Red Wing Seminary 1921

Margarethe Romo Thoreson played on the Red Wing Seminary girls basketball team in 1920 and 1921. Margarethe described the school as a co-ed Lutheran school.

The game was a two-court game with five players on a team. Margarethe played center. She was the team captain and only the captain could play over the entire court. Their games were played in the gym of the main building.

The team was coached by Edwin Swanson that Margarethe described as "a student who was very handsome and very helpful with our wraps, etc."

252   Daughters of the Game

The players provided their own uniforms. Margarethe said, "My mother sewed my blue serge bloomers and a white middy blouse with a blue tie."

When the team played Zumbrota, Margarethe recalled that after the game, the team was invited to a Zumbrota player's house for lunch. She said, "And it was very good!"

The team traveled by cars and returned the same evening. The school paid for any expenses on the trips to other schools. The girls' and boys' teams played on the same evening. The girls' game was first. The boys' team traveled separately.

Margarethe said that the students at the school were from all over the state so there was little parental support at their games.

According to Margarethe, "Games were fun." She said, "We never had much time to practice so the scores were low and only the forwards and captain could score."

Margarethe provided information from the 1926 yearbook, *LAHODEWAAN*. The article, "Girls Basketball," reported that the team played Wanamingo on January 9, 1926 and won 19-14. It reported, "The girls showed plenty of speed and a good eye for the basket."

The article said the second game was with a "local team" and the Seminary team won 31-17. The third game was the "Seminary girls" against the Red Wing All Stars. They won 19-8.

The following game was lost against Ellsworth, Wisconsin, 17-12. On February 26, the team "motored to Wanamingo, MN. At this time they hung up another victory by defeating the Wanamingo girls 11-10. It was a closely contested game throughout, and kept the spectators on edge from start to finish."

The next game was against the local high school (Red Wing High School). Esther "Speed" Nelson scored all 20 points in the 20-12 win.

The last two games against Red Wing High School and an alumni team were both wins and culminated a successful season.

Red Wing Seminary 1926

The photo identifies the team as - Front: Esther Nelson, Selma Norbeck. Middle: Mae Langeness, Stella Swensen, Lillian Rowo. Back: Stella Skurtvold, Esther Njus, Coach Saul, Luello Vikesland, Linka Njus.

Special Stories
Margarethe's sister, Lillian Romo Aakre, played in Wanamingo. Margarethe provided the history of her teams in 2005, shortly after celebrating her 100th birthday.

Redwood Falls High School

Southwestern Minnesota, 45 miles northwest of Mankato on #19
Years Represented: Early 1930's

The Redwood Falls girls basketball team played Morton, Franklin, Wabasso, Morgan, Vesta, Belview, Fairfax and Clements.

The railroad alongside Highway 19 was the common mode of transportation for basketball teams. Cars were used provided by coaches and parents.

The first teams played a three-section game with a section for two guards, two forwards and two centers. Players were limited to one bounce. The jumping center could hit the ball to the forwards who were the only players that could shoot the ball. A jump ball was held to begin play after every basket.

Uniforms were black bloomers, middy blouses with a large sailor collar, full-pleated skirt, long black stockings and black tennis shoes. The uniforms were not numbered.

The Redwood Gazette Progress, February 25, 1999, included an article written by Wayne Cook, titled, "Shooting hoops, Girls basketball survives, prospers. Lois Eckhart Ahrens played in the early 1930s, attending school through 11th grade. It was during the Depression and 'you had to get out and work.' She remembers a Wabasso game very well. 'I recall getting knocked out once,' Ahrens said. 'I played forward because I was short and had a guard guarding me from Wabasso. I was shooting for a basket and she hit me and I went over backwards. I remember laying there and seeing the lights going in and out in the ceiling of the gym.' Dr. Flinn came to check out the extent of the injury. Ahrens was put on a tumbling mat and carried out.

'The referees wanted to make sure I was OK before I got up. I was angry because they wouldn't let me get up and show them that I could play. I turned out OK but I had a bad back for quite a while,' she said. Now 81 years of age, Lois said the players cherished the friendships they made with other players."

Special Stories
Rowena Ceplecha played high school basketball in Louisiana in 1934-1935. In her town, the three schools, two public and one non-public school played one another. Parents came to watch but there was no fanfare, no bands. Later in Minnesota, Rowena had the opportunity to watch her daughter, Isabella Ceplecha, play on the 1976 Redwood Falls girls basketball team.

Isabella's team won the first MSHSL State Class A championships in 1976. Isabella was the high scorer on the team. Rowena recalls that after her daughter's team won the state championship, "All the way from Fairfax on down, there were flags along the roads. Farmers had 'hurrah, girls,' on their mailboxes."

Newspaper excerpts reprinted with permission of the *Redwood Gazette*

After Redwood Falls won the 1976 Class A Girls State Championships Rowena said, "All the way from Fairfax on down, there were flags along the roads. Farmers had 'hurrah, girls,' on their mailboxes."
Rowena Ceplecha

Rochester High School

90 miles south of the metropolitan area on Highway #52
Years Represented: 1921

The photo shows eight players with a ball, "R.H.S. 1921." The third player from the left is Ethel Kalb, known as "Sis," mother of Bob Nangle, Pipestone.

The team members are wearing the traditional white middy blouse with dark bloomers, long black stockings and white athletic shoes. They are also wearing a stocking cap with a white tassel.

Names are handwritten on the uniforms and appear to be the following – Front with ball: Marg Richman. Back: Dot Cooke, Blanche Ward, Ethel Kalb, Min Graham, Gen Kvale, Feim Kieren, Furty Furtuey.

Special Stories
The 1926 Rochester school yearbook contained an article titled "Girls' Athletics" that describes the type of activities provided after the competitive activities were dropped:

"Miss Townsend, director of Girls' Athletics, has provided to be a very capable and enthusiastic promoter of girls' athletics.

Rochester 1921

She was graduated from the State Teachers' College of Cedar Falls, Iowa. She is very fond of her work and enjoys being with young girls. Under her instruction, many girls have passed various athletic tests. Her plan, to further the ideals of good sportsmanship, has proved very successful during her first year in R.H.S. "Class attention! Ready for roll call!" It's a gym class and we are going to have a triple test. Much emphasis has been placed in posture work this year, with a triple test each semester. A Posture Contest added much enthusiasm to the work. The most perfect posture in each grade was chosen and finally the most perfect posture in Junior High and Senior High. Aside from the regular calisthenics, folk dances and games, the high school girls have had two tournaments to play off.
The Basketball tournament was won by the two upper grades: The freshman in Junior High, and the seniors in Senior High. The volleyball tournament followed later with stiff battles for all grades.
A Gym Demonstration in March, giving the public an idea of what we do in gym was the formal ending of the gym work this year. In swimming, many of the girls passed their swimmers' test, and fourteen of them went on to take extra work in the special Life Saving Class to become either a junior or senior lifesaver. The work in Swimming ended in an Inter-class Swimming Meet. Four senior girls, all-prominent in girls' athletics, won their R.H.S. monograms this year by earning the required number of points. The points were earned in swimming, hiking, skating, skiing, and tennis; and in

being, in general, good all around athletes. These girls were: Grace Foster, Edna Maass, Helen Thomas, and Harriet Quale. This year, athletics for girls, more than ever before, have been recognized as having an important place in the school curriculum. Interest in this phase of school work is growing, among the girls who participate and among the student body in general, as illustrated by the enthusiastic turn-outs for the basketball and volleyball games."

Rose Creek High School

Southeastern Minnesota about 5 miles south of Austin on Highway #56
Years Represented: 1919-1936

Helen Johnson played in 1919. Her coach was Miss Bergney from Adams. The coach contracted pneumonia and died that winter. Helen remembers playing against the Lyle team. Other team members were Ada Mae Hall, Alice Pulver Taylor, Erma Jacobson Hawkins and Mae Kasten.

Rose Creek school letter

Nora Johnson Rasmussen played from 1926-1928. She was awarded a school letter in 1928.

The next information on a Rose Creek Girls' Basketball team is a 1928-29 team photo – Front: Muriel Reagan, Mable Johnson Miller, Frances Eppley, June Young. Back: Erma Jacobson, Florence Larson Freed, Coach Thor Haugland, Josephine Peterson, Monica Reagan.

Florence Larson Freed played from 1932 –1936. The team played Adams, Elkton, Grand Meadow, Lyle and Little Cedar, Iowa. Florence recalls tournaments usually held at Austin.

The team traveled by school bus. The team wore black stockings, blue bloomers and blue middies. The school provided the uniforms. The coach was female.

The team uniform consisted of black shorts with yellow trim, and a V-necked top, white long stockings to the knee, and black shoes.

The girls and boys' teams traveled separately. The girls played the first game. The team traveled by bus; parents came in their cars and supported the team at every game.

Rose Creek 1929

"Each week, whenever a game was scheduled, the superintendent made a 'big deal' and special event and recognition for it."
Florence Larson Freed

Florence remembers, "Each week, whenever a game was scheduled, the superintendent made a 'big deal' and special event and recognition for it. "

Roseau High School

Northwestern Minnesota on Highway #11, about 25 miles from Warroad
Years Represented: 1917-1937

Roseau 1917

The 1917 Roseau girls basketball team members are identified as – Velma Hamlin Hanson, Anita Dahlquist, Ethel Oie, Inez Oveson, Iva Franklin. The school colors are green and white and sometimes have a gold accent.

Roseau 1919

The 1919 team photo showed seven players in dark bloomers and middy tops with black ribbons. No names were available.

The 1923 team photo listed: Ruth Berentzen, Nellie Bassett, Marie Martin, Nina Bassett, Helen Rice, and Selma Peterson.

The 1925 Roseau girls basketball team members were Inga Holdahl, Maxine Hegland, Helen Negland, Margaret Rice, Maurine Parr, unidentified, Bergetta Sorenson, Hannah Norlander and Harriet Overby. The coach was Lillian Jelstrup. The team uniform was a dark top with a v-neck and a large "R" on the front. The bottom of the uniform was dark bloomers.

Roseau 1923

Roseau 1925

Paula Bruss Bauck, Moorhead, attended Roseau High School from 1934 1937. At that time, there were no girls basketball teams in her school or in the area. Paula reports that she and Muriel Quanbeck Turritin organized their own games against the boys' second team, but did not play other schools. The girls' team played the Roseau boys' second team, the "B" team, when the visiting school only had a varsity team.

Fourth Quarter

When the girls played games against the boys, Paula noted, "We wore our terrific green physical education uniforms."

Paula said, "The girls' team consisted of the 'best' basketball players from our gym classes. Miss Day was our coach although we weren't coached as you do today. We used the 'one forward could go across the center line' rule at first. Then we switched to the boys rules of complete floor usage. We played about four times each year during the boys winter basketball season, winning two games each year.

Paula said that a passing/shooting drill that her high school team used was very successful when they played against the boys. When Paula went to Augsburg and played intramural basketball in 1938-39, they used the same drill. Later as the physical education teacher at Moorhead High School, Paula said her students were surprised that she knew the same drill from her high school years.

Special Stories
Paula Bauck was one of the early pioneers in the 1960's as the movement began to re-establish girls' high school sports. She developed teams at Moorhead High School and helped to teach other teachers how to organize and coach their female students. Paula was active at all levels of professional organizations and a member of the ad hoc committee that would prepare the first Bylaws for Girls Athletics adopted by the Minnesota State High School League in 1969.

Royalton High School

Central Minnesota on Highway #10 about 10 miles south of Little Falls
Years Represented: 1904-1905

The *Royalton Banner* newspaper, January 18, 1905, announced that the girls basketball team would play at home against the St. Cloud Normal team at the Opera House on Saturday night, 8:00 p.m.

The *Royalton Banner*, January 26, 1905, reported under "School Notes," that the Royalton girls basketball team played the Normal team with the visitors winning 12-8. The article stated, "Although the basket ball game of last Saturday evening resulted in defeat for the home team, yet we must acknowledge that the girls played a very good game, and had they had the advantage of experience in match games, the result would have been changed to a score in their favor."

"The Normal girls stated frankly that they had met no stronger team than that of the Royalton high school."
1905 *Royalton Banner*

Royalton 1905

The article concluded, "The Normal girls stated frankly that they had met no stronger team than that of the Royalton high school. They also spoke very complimentary in regard to the fine way in which they were received and entertained by the Royalton people. We can assure them of as good treatment upon any future visit, and judging from the girls away from the Normal, we can well look forward to a pleasant time when we go to meet them on their home grounds."

On March 25, 1981, the *Little Falls Transcript*, now the *St. Cloud Times*, included a photo of the 1905 team with an article that noted, "Contrary to popular belief, girls' basketball is not just something of the '80s. A close look tells you it's been around for awhile."

The 1904-05 Royalton Girls Basket Ball team lists members as Theresa Kobe, Julia Sjoberg, Otella Kobe, Vernette Lambert, Susan Batzer, Carrie McDougall, and Lydia Batzer.

Newspaper excerpt reprinted with permission of the *St. Cloud Times*

Rush City High School

50 miles north of St. Paul on #35
Years Represented: 1914-1936

Rush City 1914

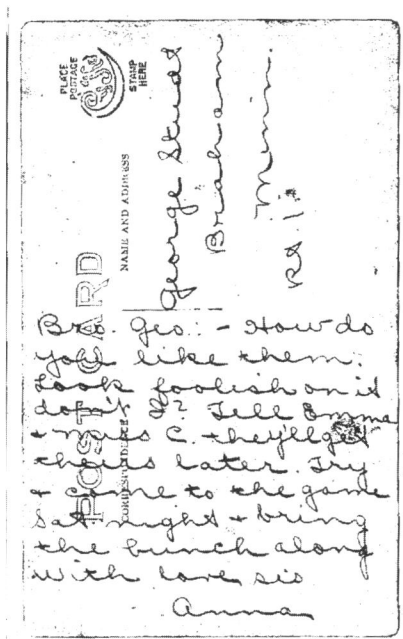

A 1914 postcard provided by Marion Larson, Braham, shows a Rush City team that competed against other towns on Saturday nights. The postcard shows nine players wearing bloomers, light middy tops with bows, and white shoes.

Games were played in a building called the Eagles Hall. Marian's aunt, Ann Studt, sent the postcard to her brother, George, urging them to "try to come to the game Saturday night and bring the bunch along."

Ann Studt went on to play basketball at Winona Normal School, a two-year teacher training school, graduating in 1916. She coached at Buffalo High School in 1919-1921.

In 1934-35 and 1935-36, the girls in Rush City had two teams that played before the boys' games. They didn't travel out of town but competed against each other. Those games were discontinued after 1936.

"Try to come to the game and
bring the bunch along."
Ann Studt

St. Cloud Cathedral

Central Minnesota on Highway #10, about 60 miles NW of Minneapolis
Years Represented: 1927

The St. Cloud Cathedral girls basketball team played a game reported in the *St. Cloud Times*, January 6, 1927. The headline read, "Cathedral Girl Quint to Play."

The article said, "The St. Cloud Cathedral girls quint will play its third game of the season against Sauk Rapids Friday night on the Sauk Rapids floor.

The game should be an even contest, as the local quint won from Holdingford and the Sauk Rapids girls won one game and tied one with Holdingford.

So far the Cathedrals have had an even break on games, winning from Holdingford and dropping a game to Melrose. They will have two practice sessions before the Rapids contest."

Newspaper excerpts reprinted with permission of the *St. Cloud Times*

St. James High School

Southwestern Minnesota on Highway #4, about 4 miles southwest of Mankato
Years Represented: 1904-1918

The St. James girls basketball team played Northfield in 1904. The *Northfield News*, November 12, 1904, headline read,

"High Girls Defeated. St. James Representatives Win Friday's Game by Large Score." The article summarized, "In the first matched game of basketball ever played by the high school girls' team, the young ladies met with defeat. The game, which attracted much attention, was played last week Friday afternoon on the high school grounds. The opposing team was from the St. James School. It was composed of veteran players and from the beginning the outcome of the contest was a foregone conclusion. The visitor's team work was par excellent and the individual playing was very good. Baskets were thrown by them almost at will and their confidence in their officials added not a little to their alertness. The representatives of the Northfield school played very well under the circumstances and in the last half held the visitors down evenly. The score of the game was 39 to 6. Both the umpire and referee of the game were from St. James and their decisions at times were not very satisfactory to the spectators."

Bill Nordgren, St. James historian, researched yearbooks from the local historical chapter and found the following scores: 1905: St. James 63, Wells 3; 1910: St. James 18, Worthington 11; 1911: St. James 14, Heron Lake 11; Mankato Normal 46, St. James 10; 1912: Mankato Commercial College 14, St. James 12; 1915: St. James 15, Worthington 1; St. James 48, Worthington 2.

St. James 1914

The 1913-14 St. James High School yearbook recapped that, "The girls' basketball team of 1914 was one of the strongest teams this High School has ever produced. They were beaten in but one game, with Windom, but as this was the first game in which Windom had been victorious, our girls easily claimed the championship."

St. James 1915

Schools played included Heron Lake, Lake Crystal, and Windom. Team members were Grace Copeland, Lilia Benson, forwards; Hilma Nelson and Mattie Peterson, centers; Cecilia Grogan, captain, and Veronica Wermerskirchen, guards. Hazelle Hanson, forward. The coach was Miss Palmer.

In 1914-15, the yearbook stated, "The outlook for a winning team in basket-ball was not very bright at the beginning of the season, as most of the members of the championship team of 1913-14 had either graduated or left school." The team won all but one game. Schools played were Heron Lake, Madelia, New Ulm, and Worthington. Team members were Mattie Peterson and Grace Copeland, forwards; Hazelle Hansen and Mable Otsea, centers; Veronica Wermerskirchen and E. Voss, guards. Evelyn Bermel and Ella Henderson were substitutes.

In 1915-16, the yearbook reported, "This year the girls were unfortunate in being allowed to play only two games, both with Windom. In these two games they showed remarkable speed, excellent team work and accuracy in locating the basket. This was in a large sense due to the efficient coaching of Miss Palmer, who, in her three years as girls' coach has never failed to turn out a team of championship caliber." The team won both games with Windom and also a game with the alumni.

Team members were Mattie Peterson, captain and forward; Mable Otsea, center; Ella Henderson, running center; Nora Rolf, forward; Dorothy Michel and Lucile Curtis as guards.

St. James 1916

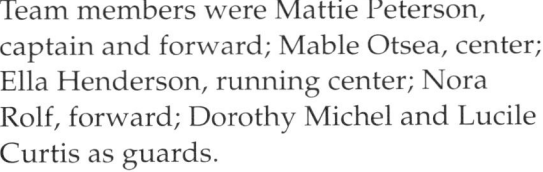

St. James 1917

In 1916-17, the coach was Miss Grace Moonan. The season began in January. The team played three games, winning one. Schools played included Owatonna, "one of the fastest teams in this part of the state." St. James won the game. The next game was at New Ulm. The yearbook reported, "The strange environment, coupled with the speed of the opponents, was too much for our girls. Despite defeat they returned home with a determination to practice more diligently than ever before for the final game of the season." The final game against Owatonna went against St. James

St. James 1918

"The speed and team work of the Owatonna girls, however, were so remarkable that they managed to wreak vengeance upon the localites for their former defeat. Team members were Mable Otsea and Hertha Uhlhorn, forwards; Nora Rolf, running center; Lottie Anderson, jumping center; Alvida Benson and Dorothy Michel, guards.

In 1917-18, the season got off to an early start. "There were a large number of girls present at the first practice on the last of October. There were some fifty girls in all, and some promising material from which to pick the school team. Miss Olson was selected as coach; she has proved herself well worthy of the position." After inter-class playoffs, the team was selected. Members were Lottie Anderson, jumping center, Nora Rolf; running center; Alvida Benson and Dorothy Michel, guards; Hertha Ulhorn and Mabel Otsea, forwards. The team lost both games to New Ulm and Kasota. The yearbook noted, "A number of the players of this year's team are in the graduating class, but there is some material left that ought to make a favorable showing next year."

Special Stories

The *St. James Plaindealer*, Feb. 1, 1996, included an article written by Bill Nordgren. Headlined "Coach from distant era sees fast-paced game."

"A special guest at Saturday night's St. James and Jackson girls basketball game saw the contest played in a much different manner from when she coached the sport almost three-quarters of a century ago.

The guest was Evelyn Wenstrom, 94, of St. James. Born in St. James and a long-time resident of the city, Miss Wenstrom coached girls basketball in Slayton for three years starting in 1923. Saturday night's exposure to the 1990s style of action was quite a revelation for her. 'It's a lot tougher,' she remarked about the way the girls handled themselves and, quite 'interesting,' she confided. 'I enjoyed it very much.'"

On January 8, 2005, the Northfield Schools invited St. James to come to Northfield for a 100-Year Celebration to commemorate their first game held on November 4, 1904. The game was called, "The Game of the Century." The teams and captains were presented with commemorative basketballs and the traditional reception of the 1900s was held after the game.

Newspaper excerpts reprinted with permission of the *St. James Plaindealer*. *Northfield News* stories reprinted with permission by the *Northfield News*. Copyright *Northfield News*. All rights reserved.

"Without the written word, the sports history of the day, a great deal of what is important especially in small communities, would get submerged in the tumult of time and not emerge again. I'm old enough to have seen the girls play basketball in their bloomer-uniforms and the girls of the 1970s regain admission to the hardwood floors."
Bill Nordgren, sports reporter and historian, *St. James Plaindealer*, 2005

St. Mary's High School, Waverly

Central Minnesota, 40 miles west of Minneapolis on #12
Years Represented: 1931-1933

Sister Ellen Joan Malone provided information regarding her participation on the St. Mary's High School Girls Basketball team in Waverly, MN, 1931-33.

The team played a two court game. The coaches took turns officiating the games. Teams played included the neighboring towns of Winsted, Rockford, Maple Lake, etc. The team traveled in private cars, returning home after games. The girls' team traveled with the boys' team and played the first game.

Games were held in the old town hall. Uniforms consisted of navy bloomers with a white blouse. The girls provided their own uniform.

The team's coaches were Ches Ogle and Norman Fuller, both St. Mary's alumni.

Sister Ellen Joan Malone recalls that the girls' team received "great support from the whole village." The teams enjoyed watching each other play 'all as one.' Games were covered in the weekly newspaper, the *Waverly Star*.

Sister Ellen Joan Malone said her favorite memories of playing basketball were the "practice and victories."

St. Paul Schools

The eastern city of the Twin Cities of Minnesota
Years Represented: 1896-1915

In 1896 the girls of St. Paul Central began playing basketball in the attic gymnasium for two hours every Friday afternoon. The first organized girls' team was in 1901-1902, the same year as the beginning of the boys' basketball team.

The 1902 photo lists the following members – Front: Gladys Barclay, Lillian Goodnough. Back: Louise Ohage, Ursula Pringle, Minnie Beyer. Teams played included the University of Minnesota. The team uniform consisted of jersey sweaters and bloomers. Team also traveled to Hudson and Menominee.

From 1902–1915, the opposing teams included Humboldt, South St. Paul, Johnson, Lincoln, Stanley Hall of Minneapolis, Agricultural College, St. Cloud, Mechanics

St. Paul 1902

Arts, Lyndale Independents and the University of Minnesota. Games were played in the Minneapolis YMCA, the "U" Armory and the Lexington Avenue Gymnasium. In 1909, St. Paul Central played the Agricultural College, Stanley Hall, South St. Paul and St. Paul Humboldt.

On March 21, 1909 the *St. Paul Daily News* headlined an article, "St. Paul Central Girls' Team Wins."

"The St. Paul Central High School girls' basketball team defeated the Stanley Hall girls' team of Minneapolis by a score of 16 to 10 in a well-played game in the YWCA Gymnasium in Minneapolis Saturday afternoon. The St. Paul girls outplayed their Minneapolis opponents in every department of the game and the Mill City basket tossers never had a look-in for victory. Central players included Goette, Giantvalley, Graupman, Coe and Horwitz. Stanley Hall players were: Sauer, Ellwood, Wing, McLean and Crane."

St. Paul 1915

The *St. Paul Daily News* article, March 28, 1909 reported that the St. Paul Central team won the Twin Cities championship by defeating Humbolt by a score of 30 to 1. Team members mentioned in the article were Irene Goette, Lillian Graupman, and Margaret Tupper. The coach was Mr. Heberling.

In 1915, the St. Paul Central team played St. Paul Humboldt, St. Paul Johnson and St. Paul Mechanic Arts High Schools.

The *St. Paul Daily News*, April 14, 1915, included an article: "Winners of Girls City Basketball Championship." The article reported,

"Central High School Girls' Basketball Squad. Standing, l to r – Catherine Keys, manager; Cecile Moersch, guard; Gertrude Hauser, cheer leader; Elsa Bernheim, center; Eleanor Fargo, center; Raymond Foote, acting coach; Martha Freeman, guard, Louise Nickow, forward. Sitting: Edna McLeod, forward; Eleanor De Vault, captain and center; Laura Medinnes, forward. The Central high school girls' basketball team won the city championship Tuesday afternoon at Mechanic Arts high school by defeating the Johnson high school girls' team 9 to 6. The Central girls lost their first and only game to Johnson 9 to 8, won from Humboldt twice, Mechanics Arts twice and after tying Johnson, captured the titular contest by a margin of three points."

Special Stories
Ryan J. Kavanaugh and Matt Jeppson were students at the University of St. Thomas. Their instructor, Dr. Hodgson, provided the class with the opportunity to conduct research on girls basketball teams and to share this information with this project. Their research papers provided information about the St. Paul girls basketball teams.

Ryan Kavanaugh noted that the language describing basketball in the early 1900s, was quite fascinating. "The way we speak and write today almost seems like a new language compared to the early 1900s. They routinely referred to making or missing shots with vocabulary such as 'basket tossing,' 'connecting with the net,' and 'hard luck in shooting goals.' Modern day trash talking and griping to the referee back then was referred to as 'rag-chewing.' Despite the language differences, girls basketball back then seemed to be both competitive and fun just as it is today."

Legacy
The first Minnesota State High School Girls Basketball Tournament was held in March 1976. The St. Paul Central team won the first Class AA championship.

St. Peter High School

11 miles north of Mankato on #169
Years Represented: 1924

A photo of the 1924 St. Peter High School girls' basketball team lists the following members - Gretchen Schmidt, Grace Annexstad, Margaret Holz, Helen E. Anderson, Leah Johnson, Helen Klocow, Lillie Petersen, and Genevieve Clark. Genevieve Webster is on the (right end of the middle row). Other players are not identified on the photo.

St. Peter 1924

Special Stories

Genevieve Webster kept a scrapbook with many tickets, programs, etc. One invitation is from President H.E. Wiest, of the St. Peter Association, dated March 28, 1924. The invitation reads:

"Madame: Enclosed you will find a ticket for the Athletic Banquet which will be given in honor of the athletes of St. Peter High School and Gustavus Adolphus College at the armory on Monday evening, March 31st, under the auspices of the St. Peter Association. You will be the guest of the person whose name is inscribed at the bottom of the ticket. Please bring it with you and be there promptly at 6:30 o'clock to take your place among your teammates at the table provided for the honor guests.

There will be 200 fans – men and women – present next Monday evening. Earl Martineau, All-American football star, will be the principal speaker. Expressions will be made by local citizens, members of the faculties and others. There will be music and a good 'feed' served by the ladies of the English Lutheran Church.

On behalf of the St. Peter Association, and the fans, I wish to extend to you this invitation."

Sauk Rapids High School

Central Minnesota just north of St. Cloud on Highway #10
Years Represented: 1908-1925

Information on the Sauk Rapids girls basketball team appears in newspaper clippings.

The *Sauk Rapids Herald*, March 12, 1908, described a doubleheader played by the girls' high school team against the "ladies' city team" and the boys' high school team against the "men's city team." In 1920, the newspaper mentions both the Sauk Rapids boys and girls winning a doubleheader against Monticello.

The *St. Cloud Times*, January 9, 1925, "In the girls' game, the Rapids *cagers* overcame a 7 to 14 lead for Big Lake at the end of the first half, and in the second half piled up four points while holding the Lakers scoreless. Sauk Rapids won by a count of 8 to 7."

Special Stories

Interclass tournaments were popular during this era. In this school, members of the varsity team were given training and opportunity to learn coaching skills.

The *St. Cloud Times*, March 18, 1926, described the class project, "Varsity Girls Coach Classes. Their knowledge of basketball is being tested in the coaching now being given participants in the girls' inter-class basketball tournament by the members of the girls basketball squad. Each girl on the varsity sextet is coaching one of the class teams."

"In the girls' game, the Rapids' cagers overcame a 7 to 14 lead for Big Lake at the end of the first half, and in the second half piled up four points while holding the Lakers scoreless."
1908 *Sauk Rapids Herald*

Newspaper excerpts reprinted with permission by the *St. Cloud Times* and the *Sauk Rapids Herald*

Sherburn High School

Southwestern Minnesota on Highway #4, approximately 20 miles west of Fairmont
Years Represented: 1922-1927

Two high school basketball players, Pauline Holmes Eiden, Dunnell, 1922-23; Sherburn 1924-25 and Ruth McCarron Dahlke, 1924-27, provided information about their participation on the Sherburn girls basketball team.

From 1923 – 26 the game was a three-court game. In the middle court were the jumping center and the running center, two forwards in one court and two guards in the third court. Only one dribble was allowed. In 1926-27 the game changed to a two-court with two dribbles.

"One time the car I was riding in went into the ditch on the way to Winnebago. The windshield was broken, and we were late arriving to the game. It was ten below zero and we had to return home without a windshield."
Ruth McCarron Dahlke

The team traveled by car provided by family and volunteers. The girls and boys teams played on the same nights with the girls' game played first. Ruth recalls, "Expenses were paid by the school. After we came home from an away game, both teams went to a local restaurant and were allowed 15 cents for lunch.

Ruth recalls that, "On Friday afternoon at school, the players went to the bulletin board in the gym to see what car they would ride in. One time the car I was riding in went into the ditch on the way to Winnebago. The windshield was broken, and we were late arriving to the game. It was ten below zero and we had to return home without a windshield."

Ruth said, "In 1927, we went to Winnebago on a Friday afternoon on the Milwaukee Railroad. Both the girls' and boys' teams stayed in the hotel. The chaperones were the two coaches. We returned the next morning to Sherburn."

The team uniform was a black satin bloomer with white middy blouses. Pauline recalls falling because she came down from a jump and got a foot caught in the big bloomers. Ruth said "the school provided the middies, but the players made the black basketball bloomers. In 1926, the school bought the short outfits for us. We were the first team in Martin County to wear shorts."

The teams played included – Jackson, Winnebago, Trimont, Ceylon, Welcome, Granada and Elmore.

The 1924-25 team members included Helen Holmes, Marie Janssen, Dorothy Meinhard, Esther Packard, Adella Mathwig, Ruth McCarron, Josephine Schultz, Pauline Holmes Eiden, Eunice Meilke, Illa Packard and Coach, Miss Zimmerman. On March 13-14, 1925, the Sherburn team won the Sherburn Invitational Tournament. The team received a large trophy with a silver basketball on the top. Teams in the tournament included Welcome, Triumph, Granada, Ceylon, Elmore and Jackson.

Pauline believed that the team was popular in the community.

Games were played in a gymnasium except in Ceylon where Ruth said "we played on a dance floor. During time out we stepped out the front door and stepped into resin. We walked on our heels back to the floor. We were down more than we were up. All of us had skinned knees and elbows."

Sherburn hosted an invitational tournament in 1925. It was won by the Sherburn girls basketball team. Team members received rings and the school was awarded a silver trophy.

Pauline Holmes Eiden kept an original copy of the 1925 tournament program in her basketball memory book.

The *Sherburn Advance Standard*, June 1975, headlined an article, "Remember the girls basketball team of 1925? It was a Real Winner!"

The article said, "Back in 1925 – a half century ago – Sherburn High School produced an outstanding girls basketball team. They clobbered all area towns during the season, and easily won what in those days was a big Sherburn Invitational Tournament, receiving a regulation size silver basketball trophy in the process.

Here is a picture of that team, posing proudly with said trophy (which incidentally cost $26.00); left to right, Back: Esther Packard, Helen Holmes, Dorothy Meinhard, Hilda Zimmerman (coach), Adella Mathwig, Marie Janssen, and Josephine Schultze. Front: Pauline Holmes, Ila Packard, Ruth McCarron Dahlke, Eunice Meilke. Miss Packard and Miss McCarron were juniors and the others seniors."

Sherburn 1925

Sherburn was chosen as the site of the tournament because they had a 48 X 64 gym with a 5-foot out of bounds all around. The Businessmen's Association purchased the trophy and provided other prizes, and Dr. Farrish volunteered his services to care for any injuries to the players. The rules were a kind of combination of both boys' and girls' rules. The quarters were shortened 'in order that the strain on the players will not be too great.' The tournament was in March. It snowed so much that Elmore couldn't get here, but Alpha substituted for them. Sherburn won three games on the way to the title, downing Alpha 22 to 4, Jackson 18 to 6 after holding Jackson to one lone free throw in the first half, and Ceylon 20 to 11 in the finals.

Sherburn players reunited with trophy

The newspaper reported that, "A week ago Sunday, June 22, the Class of '25 gathered at Etter's Fine Dining for a reunion. The old trophy had been resurrected and shined up and five members of the team were present, left to right: Marie Janssen Markus, Dorothy Meinhard Slaba, Adella Mathwig Theobald, Pauline Holmes Eiden, and Eunice Meikle Meyer."

One photo is of the 1927 Sherburn girls basketball team. From l to r: Marian Brundage, Dorothea Bradt, Margaret Landin, Helen Holmes, Ruth McCarron, Dorothy Peters, Thelma Clark. Leonore Greene not pictured.

Sherburn 1927

Special Stories

Ray Herman, athletic director at Martin County West (formerly Sherburn High School) contacted the League Office. He had located the large and beautiful silver trophy from 1925. Ray had found the trophy in a storage room as he was cleaning facilities for the new school consolidation. The trophy has been on display at several conferences and meetings.

Ruth Dahlke wrote this touching story to share with the MSHSL Women in Sports Leadership Conference in 1999:

"In March 1925, the girls basketball team won the district tournament. I was a sophomore and a member of the team.

Later, at the high school assembly the squad was awarded sterling silver rings. In the summer of 1925 I went swimming in Fox Lake and dove off a raft. When I came up for air I realized my ring was gone. My friends and I dove for some time but couldn't locate the ring. When I realized my ring really was gone, I cried many times.

Ruth Dahlke, Sherburn, 2005

The years went by and during 1995 my daughter, Carron Klukow, attended an auction. Later I called her to find out what she had bought. She had bid on two rings – one a 1925 class ring and a smaller one (she didn't know the story of the basketball ring). When she showed it to me I cried, realizing I now had an identical ring that had belonged to Adella Mathwig, our captain. Even though the sands and waves have been washing over my ring for 74 years, I have my teammate's ring to remind me of those enjoyable basketball days."

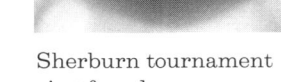
Sherburn tournament ring found

Ruth wears the ring to this day and has made it clear that the ring will not leave her hand and has said, "it will be buried with me."

Ruth added, "I played basketball four years in high school, two years at Mankato State and coached it two years at East Chain. In my adult years I have played softball and golf. I am now 96 years old so I am sure basketball never hurt me physically. At the time girls basketball was discontinued in Sherburn, we were led to believe that it was detrimental to our health. The real reason was that the schools were not producing good boys' teams. By getting rid of the girls they could then have a "B" squad for the boys, and eventually the "A" team would be better. We are 22 miles from the Iowa border where all these years they have had girls basketball."

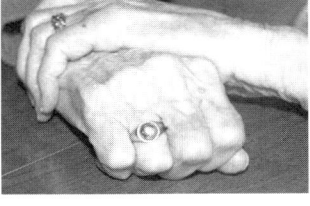
Ruth wearing Sherburn championship ring

In 2004 Pauline Holmes Eiden was 96½ years of age and so happy to know that the history of the Sherburn girls basketball team would be preserved.

Newspaper excerpts reprinted with permission by the *Martin County Star*.

Slayton High School

Southwestern Minnesota on Highway #30 about 25 miles east of Pipestone and the South Dakota border
Years Represented: 1901-1932

The 1901 photo of Slayton girls basketball team provided by the Murray County Historical Society lists the team members as Ada March, Mary Moon, Esther Burke, Nannie Thompson, and Ethel Hickman.

One photo has been identified as a team from the early 1900s.

The *Slayton Wheel-Herald*, November 14, 1912, reported that, "The girls of the Pipestone High School basket ball team came down last Saturday and played the Slayton girls. The latter won by a score of 10 to 9."

The Murray County Historical Society included an article from the high school yearbook dated 1915:

"With only three of last year's girls on the squad at the opening of the Basketball season this year, the outlook was not very promising. But with the playing and winning of the first two games prospects brightened considerably, considering the earliness of the season and the fact that for half the members of the team this was the first game ever played.

The season opened this year with a game with Westbrook, which we won by the score of thirteen to sixteen. As it was the first game, the team did not display the teamwork, pep and fighting spirit which were so evident in later games. A few weeks later we played a return game with Westbrook, followed by a game with Edgerton on the home floor. Both these games we won. After practicing for a few days, Windom visited us and we were defeated by the close score of twenty to twenty-one. Although this was rather unfortunate at this particular period, it did not dampen the girls' spirits in the least.

Our next opponent was Lakefield. We had gotten some good practice this week with the aid of the second team, and again we won. In the return game with Windom, which was played next, we had to work hard, and at the final close up of the game we lost, the score being twenty-one to twelve.

The team was now waiting patiently for the last game of the season, which was held at Lakefield. We had a team equal to that of Lakefield, and we decided to go them one better and beat them, the resulting score standing two to six in our favor.

In all the games played during the year, five were won and three lost. This makes a very good average for a team made up so largely of raw material at the beginning of the season. Coach Miss Nelson deserves much credit for putting out such a first class team, one of the fastest in the district."

Slayton 1901

A 1915 photo from the Murray County Historical Society showed six players wearing bloomers, dark tops with ribbons and a knit cap with tassels on the top. The coach was Miss Nelson.

The 1920-21 team played Heron Lake, Windom, Lakefield, and Pipestone.

The 1921-22 team schedule included Tracy, Bingham Lake, Pipestone, Worthington, and Westbrook. The team played 15 games, a high number for that era of girls' basketball.

In 1922-23, the team played nine 9 games. The article provided by the Historical Society stated, "The season opened with the game at Edgerton on December 8, 1922, and ended with the game at Fulda on February 21, 1923. The last game was the game of the season. The sidelines were crowded and the loud cheering greatly aroused both teams.

Slayton early 1900s

But the players were not the only active ones. The spectators were kept on the jump all the time, keeping track of the ball. We are glad to say that the game ended in a victory for Slayton, but we are even prouder of the fact that there was no crabbing."

The team of 1923-24 played 12 games. Players included Edna Erickson, Gladys Point, Captain Lenore Wornson, Ethel Tietema, Agnes Roetman, Marjorie Baker, Rita McNamara and Orpha Stevens. The photo showed the team with a female coach, Miss Evelyn Wenstrom.

The Slayton High School yearbook reported on the 1923-24 girls basketball team. The article stated,

"The girls' basket ball season opened November 19th when they won a warmly contested game from the fast Westbrook team. The Westbrook team has met with some fast teams this year and met their first defeat at Slayton, by a score of 15 to 17. The locals have but one veteran on the team this year, Mary Lamb. It was due to her splendid basket shooting that Slayton won the game. Eunice Hook, our other forward also played a good game and is to be commended for her splendid team work. Jeanette Hyslop and Olga Sheerin, although diminutive in size, played fast and guarded closely. Meree Larson and Elenor McNamara can hold their own with any two centers in High School Basket ball. Under the capable supervision of Miss O'Connor the girls have developed into a wonderfully fast team and are in line for the championship of this part of the state."

The 1924-25 yearbook pointed out that the team had a late start but "under the excellent coaching of Miss Wenstrom, they promised to make very good material." Players included Gladys Point, Marjorie Baker, Lenore Wornson, Clare Wise, Marjorie Minder, Orpha Stevens, Marguerite Knowlton, Ione Hegstad and Gladys Thompson. Evelyn Wenstrom coached the team for three years from 1922-25.

The Slayton High School yearbook, 1924-25 included this verse:

"The Basketball Team
Mr. Referee, where's your horn!
Gladys is over-guarded, see her scorn;
Marjorie's dribbling down the line.
Made basket, ain't that fine?
See our opponents, they look so forlorn.
As for the baskets they are torn.
Clare and Lenore, our guards sublime,
Keep them moving all the time.
Orpha and Marjorie, the ball have borne
'To Success,' we say while others mourn;
With Wenstrom as coach, it is easy to climb,
The Season is ended, so ends this rhyme."

Slayton 1915

Slayton 1923

Slayton 1924

The 1927 team photo includes Signa Johnson, Mildred Brewster, Connie Weld, Marjorie Minder, Lois Egerton, Lola Peterson, Lillian Schellenberg, and Jeanette Halverson. (no order provided)

An article and photo provided by the Murray County Historical Society, dated March 22, 1928, stated, "Slayton's Winning Basket Ball Team. Pictured above is the Slayton High School girls basketball team. Coached by Mr. Potthoff this team won an enviable reputation, not only for the ability of its individual members, but for the school as well. The team won every one of its eleven games in the district and was nosed out for the championship of the district by the Luverne sextette by the narrow margin of two field goals, on the Worthington floor."

Team members are identified as - Front: Lois Egarton, Gladys Rathlisberger, Lillian Schellenberg. Middle: Dorothy Knutson, Mary Lowe, Signa Johnson, Edna Stanley, Cora Mae March, Mildred Brewster. Back: Jeanette Halverson, Constance Weld, captain, Lola Peterson, Coach C.J. Potthoff.

The 1931 and 1932 team photos do not identify the players.

Excerpts from Newspapers
St. James Plaindealer: Feb. 1, 1996

"Coach from distant era sees fast-paced game" "Born in St. James and a long-time resident of the city, Miss Wenstrom coached girls' basketball in Slayton for three years starting in 1923."

Slayton Gazette, Dec. 9, 1920

Slayton High School Basket Ball teams went to Tracy Last Friday. Girls Lose 29-19; Boys Win 16-17. In a just and hard fought game the local girls went down to defeat at the hands of the Tracy delegation on Friday evening of last week. It took the local girls until the last quarter to find themselves, holding the Tracy team scoreless for that period. The girls were handicapped by a larger floor and the two-court division of the floor. Yet the better team won and the credit goes to Tracy."

Slayton Gazette, Dec. 16, 1920: The Girls' Basket Ball team played the Edgerton team on the night of Tuesday, December 14th.

Slayton 1925

Slayton 1927

Slayton 1928

Slayton 1931

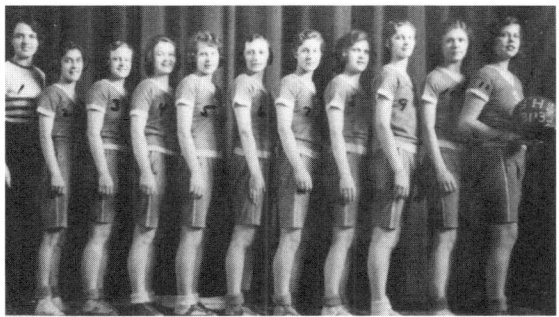
Slayton 1932

Slayton Gazette, Jan. 15, 1924:

"Both the girls' and boys' teams are practicing in the new Gym and making rapid progress as far as practice is concerned. Our teams are at a disadvantage in meeting other teams due to the fact that they have had a shorter period for practice and development than their competitors. It is only recently that our Gym has been available for practice and it is not yet available for contests. We hope to be able to invite the public to enjoy the athletic contests in the new Gym and auditorium. We also at this time suggest enthusiastic patronage when our season does open, as we have been more or less cut off from basketball patronage and revenue on account of the unfinished structure. When we do open, we would like the enthusiastic support and patronage of the entire community to make up for and offset this handicap and hope even yet to close the athletic season without a deficit financially, all of which can only be accomplished thru the combined efforts of the entire community. The boys' and girls' teams will travel to Luverne on the same evening that the debating team goes to Windom. We were splendidly received at Luverne last year and expect a fine reception this year, both as to the game and as to the cordiality of the Luverne High School in general. We expect to reciprocate the hospitality of the Luverne team for the past two years in our new Gym in the near future."

Special Stories

In 1999 Carleen Andert, student at the University of St. Thomas, participated in a research project to locate information on girls high school basketball teams. She focused on Slayton High School. Carleen summarized her research by saying, "We definitely need to know and value the history of women's sports because it is the past that allowed us to advance to where we are today."

Newspaper excerpts reprinted with permission of the *Murray County Wheel-Herald* and the *St. James Plaindealer*

South St. Paul High School

Southeastern suburb of the Twin Cities metropolitan area
Years Represented: 1901-1925

South St. Paul 1920

The South St. Paul girls basketball team played the St. Paul teams during the years 1901-1915. Specific years not provided.

Sarah Steichen researched girls basketball at South St. Paul as part of a class project at the University of St. Thomas. Sarah located several South St. Paul school yearbooks in the South St. Paul Public Library. They included photos of a girls basketball team in 1920, 1921, 1924 and 1925. From 1920–24, the girls played inter-class teams, i.e., freshmen, sophomores, juniors and seniors played as a team against the other classes.

In 1925 the school yearbook reported that the girls basketball team played against other schools. The article reported

South St. Paul 1924

"A vital interest has been shown this year in girls basketball. Formerly the girls expressed their appreciation of basketball by attending the general 'pep' meetings and the boys' games. This of course, was a good thing, but it was not helping girls' athletics any. This year, however, the Girls' Athletic Association, with renewed zeal started to promote girls' athletics.

South St. Paul 1921

Under the direction of Miss Kuehl, our gymnasium instructor, we have had a very successful basketball season. The girls have engaged in a number of games, winning all those played with other high schools on our home floor.

The girls have been very faithful in practicing every night throughout the season and have been willing to sacrifice their own pleasures in living up to the rules. This is the basis for successful basketball.

The girls on the first team are Seniors; while those on the second are Juniors. The lineup of the first team throughout the season has been as follows: Lauretta Gallagher, right forward; Gertrude Wilson, left forward; Florence Fender, shooting center; Evelyn Sandell, jumping center, Myrtle Bloemers, guard; Martha Woolsey, guard; Arlene Goltz, Sigrid Carlson, Astrid Ahlgren, substitutes.

All of these are to receive letters in honor of their successful work in basketball. We hope the present junior, sophomore and freshmen girls will continue another year to promote the good spirit and interest which have been made manifest in 1923 and 1924."

The 1925 school yearbook includes a photo of the girls basketball team – Front: Mildred Grunau, Irene McNulty, Arlene Goltz, Jeanette Johnson, Sigrid Carlson, Astrid Ahlgren. Back: Leona Wynn, Katherine Lynch, Thelma Canton, Dorothy Weir, Mabel Glewwe, Luella Gallagher, Miss Kuehl, Coach.

South St. Paul 1925

Starbuck High School

West central Minnesota on Highway #28, approximately 10 miles west of Glenwood
Years Represented: 1910-1930

In the 1980s, Matthew Pederson prepared a *Starbuck Basketball* booklet. In the section, "Early Years," he wrote, "Starbuck High School had their first graduating class in 1910. One year earlier, the *Starbuck Times* reported on the organization of basketball teams for the girls and boys. There wasn't any mention of games played, but it is most likely that they did not play against other schools."

The booklet indicated that, "The earliest known team photo is from the *Starbuck Centennial History Book*. It depicts the 1910 team."

The 1910 Starbuck girls basketball team members were - Coach N/A, Ruth Stenson, Evelyn Englund, Lyla Olson, Emma Brantsag, Charlotte Swenson, Nora Anderson, Olga Nordstrom.

The booklet continued, "Written newspaper recaps from 1919 provide the first evidence of

Starbuck 1910

Starbuck 1930

interscholastic play. Miss Andrews coached the girls. There were three games reported: a win over Villard, a 15-2 loss to Hancock, and a 15-5 win over Glenwood. Against Glenwood, Captain Mabel Johnson scored 'several baskets. Very little information is available from the next two seasons. What is known is that the coach in 1919-1920 was Miss Mildred Ortman, and that the one score given for the 1921 season was a 19-0 loss to Cyrus. Other opponents were thought to have been Morris, Elbow Lake, Benson, and Glenwood."

The article continued, "Games were played at the Town Hall, located where the Senior Citizen's Building is. The girls made their own uniforms which consisted of bloomers and blouses. They raised money to pay rent and to buy wire protectors for the lights. There were six girls on a team – three on each side of mid-court."

The next team photo is of the 1930 Starbuck girls basketball team photo – Front: Christie Baukol, Bonnie Markland, Lillian Tollefson, Jeanette Hagen, Clara Kjonaas, Jenny Hofstad, Jeanette Brenden, Ione Markland. Back: Olea Mickelson, Virginia Heegard, Alpha Scheflo, Coach Thelma Foss, Mabel Aaberg, Ethel Smedstad, Viola Pederson.

Stillwater High School

Eastern side of the metropolitan area on Highway 95, about 20 miles out of St. Paul.
Located on the St. Croix River
Years Represented: 1920-1929

Stillwater 1920

Stillwater 1922

The Stillwater High School yearbooks the *Kabekonian*, provided several articles on the Stillwater girls basketball teams.

The first article in 1920 indicated "The first Girls' Basket Ball Team came into prominence this year, under the supervision of our athletic coach, Miss Phillips, who showed great interest in the work of the girls." The team played seven games, winning four. The article reported, "These seven games were the first outside games ever played by a S.H.S. Girls' team. Teams played included North St. Paul, the YWCA team of St. Paul and White Bear Lake. The photo shows eight players and the coach. Players were not identified. The team uniform consisted of a dark middy top with dark bloomers, black stockings and athletic shoes.

In 1920-21, the team won eight games and lost only one. Stillwater played New Richmond (WI), Ellsworth (WI), North St. Paul, White Bear and Farmington. The team played five-player games as well as six-player games. The article indicated that "Helen McBeath was captain of the team and played forward with Doris Sinclair. Lenore Isermann played center and Lucy Salmoiraghi running center when six players were used. Hedwig Lund and Dorothy Welshons played guards with Catherine Kent as a substitute."

In 1921-22 the coach was Miss Abbetmeyer, assisted by Miss Cates, Miss Blair, and Miss Shotwell. The team

Stillwater 1923

Stillwater 1924

experienced its first undefeated season. Players included Lenor Isermann, captain, Doris Sinclair, Blanche Johnson, Catherine Kent, Ruth Spencer, Luella Johnson, Grace Newman, Genevieve Peterson and Lois Peterson. The team played North St. Paul, White Bear and South St. Paul. A banquet for the team was held in the Domestic Science room, hosted by the Athletic Association.

In 1922-23, the team won three of four games against White Bear, North St. Paul and Hudson (WI). Team members included Catherine Kent, captain, Ruth Spencer, Genevieve Peterson, Grace Newman, Louise Ulrich, Luella Johnson, Lois Peterson, Lillian Anderson, Viola Brenneer and Fannie Lott. The coach was Miss Abbetmeyer. The article stated, "The girls basketball team will lose five of its first six players and all of its substitutes at graduation this June; but let us hope that with the new gymnasium and a bigger and better school, that girls' athletics will take the place in Stillwater High School activities that it so justly deserves."

Stillwater 1925

Stillwater 1926

"Helen Slocum, Margaret Hall, Harriet Foster and 'Peg' Mohr the best scoring quartette ever developed in Stillwater High School."
1927 *Kabekonian*

Stillwater 1927

Stillwater 1928

1923-24 with one returning veteran, the team won two and lost two games. Team members included Captain Louise Ulrich, Helen Slocum, Fern Lundgren, Florence Naegele, Florence Holmes, Margie Groves, Julia Paganini. The coach was Miss Robertson.

In 1924-25 team members included Captain Helen Slocum, Margaret Hall, Marion Smith, Harriet Lescarbeau, Alma Schultz, Harriet Foster, Leona Bonin and Lucile Doran. No record of games provided.

In 1925-26 the team was coached by Miss Holton. Margaret Hall was captain and other team members included Helen Slocum, Margaret Mohr, Harriet Foster, Norma Knowles, Leona Bonin, Lucile Doran, Pearl Bangert, Marian Smith and Faith Robertson. The team played Hudson (WI), White Bear, Derham Hall, Forest Lake, Twin City Business College and Golden Rule.

In 1926-27, the captain was Harriet Foster and the coach was Miss Holton. The yearbook stated, "In most of the games Helen Slocum was the chief scorer, but without the aid of Margaret Hall, "Sloe" would have been lost….Helen Slocum, Margaret Hall, Harriet Foster and "Peg" Mohr the best scoring quartette ever developed in Stillwater High School." Other team members included Faith Robertson, Norma Knowles, Violet Hoppke. Teams played included Twin City Business College, Chisago City, Pine City, and White Bear. Stillwater won all games played.

In 1927-28, the team won eight games and lost one. Team members included Faith Robertson, Grace Hagstrom, Dorothy Salmore, Phyllis Slocum, Violet Hoppke, Ruth Newman, Margaret Ann Lammers, Lulu Grove and Olive Perry.

The 1928-29 team appears to have been the last team provided by Stillwater High School. The team won five and lost one game to the First National Bank. Other teams played included Unity House, White Bear and Forest Lake. Team members included Margaret Ann Lammers, Phyllis Slocum, Grace Hagstrom, Ruth Newman, Violet Hoppke, Dorothy Salmore, Margaret Loehr, Elinor Walker and Gertrude

Stillwater 1929

Janilla. The coach was Miss Pierce. The team played the First National Bank women's basketball team of Minneapolis. The yearbook article reported, "The Minneapolis team claimed the undisputed championship of the Northwest. The girls from Minneapolis had splendid teamwork and their fast playing made it difficult for the high school team to keep pace. The visitors' accurate shooting kept the score constantly climbing. The girls of Stillwater gave fine opposition and never gave up the fight once during the full game. Although they lost this game, they lost as though it was a victory, gloriously. The team was downed by a score of 19 to 12. It was the most exciting game that has ever been staged on the home floor."

The Girls Athletic Association

The team records end with the 1929 team. The *Kabekonian* in 1930 includes an article about the Girls' Athletic Association, GAA, with members earning points for participation in a variety of team and individual athletic activities. The organization held a Big Sister Party and participated in skating, skiing, and hiking. A banquet was held at the conclusion of the year with GAA awards given to those who had earned from 100 to 1,000 points. This is the type of organization that replaced the interscholastic basketball programs.

The article ends with, "The GAA has proved successful, and has taken the place of other girls' organizations."

Swanville High School

Central Minnesota on #28, about 20 miles southwest of Little Falls
Years Represented: 1922

Ann Truog Larson played on the Swanville girls' basketball team from 1919-22.

The girls' team played "boys' rules." She played guard. Games were officiated.

Teams played included Sauk Center, Grey Eagle, and Burtrum.

The team traveled by train and car to out-of-town games. The girls' game was played prior to the boys' game. The teams stayed overnight at Sauk Center with families of team members.

Games were played in a gymnasium. The team uniform consisted of navy blue bloomers with a middy top. The coaches were Miss Pritchard and Mrs. Olson.

Ann believed that the girls' team was supported by the boys and their coaches as well as the community. There was news coverage in the Swanville newspaper.

Ann recalled that it was fun to make friends playing basketball. Her brother played on the boys' teams until her last year when he was out of school.

Thief River Falls High School

Northwestern Minnesota, 40 miles from East Grand Forks on Highway #59
Years Represented: 1918-1920

Thief River Falls 1919

A photo of the 1919 Thief River Falls girls basketball team shows 11 players and a male coach. One player is identified as Eileen Herron. Eileen is in the middle row, first player to the right of the coach.

The uniforms were the middy tops with dark bloomers and a ribbon around the top. The uniforms vary in style with some collars solid colors, others striped and some white. The varied styles would indicate that the players provided their own uniforms.

Thief River Falls 1920

The 1920 photos include seven players and a female coach. The players are wearing similar white middy tops, dark colored bows, and bloomers with athletic shoes. Eileen Herron is the second player from the left end in the back row.

An insignia can be seen on the sleeve of the player with the ball.

280   Daughters of the Game

Toivola High School

Northeast Minnesota, 20 miles south of Hibbing
Years Represented: 1933-1938

The historical summary of the Toivola Athletic Club shows a photo of the 1933 girls basketball team. Players listed were - Laila Turkula Wegener, Irma Sorvari Beebe, Thelma Laine Lehtinen, Lillian Lahti Sorvari, Martha Sorvari Sandstrom, Elsa Jokinen Dunkle, Madeline Niemela Takala, Linda Turkula Kontola, Thelma Pellika Hintikka. Coach: Dan Dasovic.

Lillian Lahti Sorvari played from 1933-1937. They played other South St. Louis County schools including Cherry, Cotton, Cook, Alborn, Brookston, and Meadowlands.

The gymnasium where games were played was separate from the school. It had been built and owned by the Toivola Athletic Association.

Toivola 1933

Lillian's team wore a one-piece bloomer-type uniform with knee-high pants. Games were supported by the community. Each game was reported to the local newspapers by the coach and always printed.

Lillian recalled the fun of playing basketball, but she said, "We hated the old rules of girls basketball where you could not cross that center line. We wanted to play the whole court."

Saima Saari Savela graduated from Toivola in 1940 and played interscholastic basketball from 1936-38. Her class consisted of 11 students.

Saima's team played a two-court game with six players. Two dribbles were permitted. A history booklet, *Sports: The Toivola Athletic Club*, revealed "Scores from those days (girls and boys basketball) were very low, compared to those of today. In 1937, for example, Toivola defeated Cherry 26-13, and the girls won over Meadowlands 8-7. Of course, the rules required a much slower game, but just as exciting to spectators. Games always drew a good crowd."

The team played other St. Louis County schools – Cherry, Cotton, Cook, Alborn, Brookston and the independent school of Meadowlands. The girls' and boys' teams traveled by school bus. The girls' game was played first.

Players earned school letters in basketball. The gymnasium was in a separate building from the school and was equipped with showers, lockers, etc. The players wore regular gym suits, which were short bloomers, furnished by the players.

The coach was the school principal, Dan Dasovic. Saima recalled that he "worked the team very hard, but it sure was fun!"

Special Stories
During the Depression, the Works Progress Administration (WPA) employees helped to keep the winter sports facilities in good condition.

Toivola was a school within the St. Louis County schools, including its rural schools. Toivola developed an extensive intramural program for its students, including competitive opportunities in basketball, volleyball and softball. Trophies and letters were awarded. The principal, Dan Dasovic, established the program to "keep the students so busy, they didn't have time to think of mischief." The program included every single student in the school, high school and elementary.

Mr. Dasovic was considered a strict disciplinarian but a fair one. One of his rules was that the girls must not wear slacks to school. In the winter, some would wear them under their skirts. Occasionally a girl would forget her skirt at home and come to school wearing only slacks. She ended up in a conference with the principal.

Lillian Lahti Sorvari made a trip back to Toivola. She said,

"We dug around in the old school. We did find our 1937 basketball trophy!! It isn't in perfect shape after 60 years of air exposure, but I have taken a photo of it. The inscription reads: 'St. Louis Co. Champs, Girls, Toivola, 1937.'"

In 1998, at the age of 76, Saima Savela wrote,

"At the beginning of my senior year in high school in 1939, our girls' varsity basketball team had played two games, winning both of them, and we were all fired up thinking we would be having a great year, when suddenly we were notified that this activity would be dropped at the request of the state legislators because they felt it was too strenuous for girls. This didn't make any sense to me. I was aware of the fact that many of the legislators at that time were from farming communities, and they certainly should have known that girls raised on the farm worked hard during haying and harvesting seasons, took care of farm animals, feeding and watering them, and so consequently would have the stamina to do something as enjoyable as taking part in sports."

"Occasionally, a girl would forget her skirt at home and come to school wearing only slacks. She ended up in a conference with the principal."
Saima Saari Savela

Toivola trophies and letters

Tracy High School

Southwestern Minnesota, 25 miles southeast of Marshall on #14
Years Represented: 1909-1927

"The first Tracy High School girls' basketball team was organized in 1909," according to Seth Schmidt of the *Tracy Headlight-Herald*, in an article printed July 1, 1998. The article went on, "The first high school yearbook published in Tracy, the 1911 *Teton*, states that, 'In 1909, with the assistance of Miss Callaghan and Miss Desmond, two double basketball teams of girls were formed. This year the interest has continued and it is hoped that girls athletics in Tracy High will forge ahead and gain in value in the years to come."

There were six girls on the 1910-1911 team - Emma Pattridge, Kathrine Price, Zella Campbell, Blanche Campbell, Mary Nelson and Vera Pierce. The coach was Alyda Clark. Four games were played with Lamberton and Lake Benton. The team lost all four games.

Tracy 1911

The next reported segment of the team's history moves to 1925. Seth Schmidt wrote that the 1925 *Teton* yearbook had reported, "The prospects for girls basketball this year were very, very good…The girls' record for the last five years has been exceptional for a school of this size, being marred by only three defeats."

A 1925 photo lists the team - Coach Nibbe, Emily Schottenbauer, Florence Rawlings, Alice Opheim, Elsie Peterson, Alice Giroux, Christine Torp, Lucille Skuse, Florence Jasperson, Lorene Haugen, and Muriel Donaldson.

The article continued with a report of a game with Lamberton described as follows.

"There were shivers going down every player's spine and the following motto was constantly before them: 'Determination is the key-note to success.' Every time the whistle blew, she (Florence Jasperson) was in the air doing her best to get the ball where it should belong. Business!!!"

Emily Schottenbauer was described as: "Can shoot baskets as good as her name is long. Oh boy, how she does pivot down the floor." Another player was described as "The fighting Dempsey, always knocking the other fellow in the ribs and laying them on the floor. She is the champion free-thrower of the sextette."

Tracy 1925

An historical event occurred in 1927. The 1927 *Teton* sadly reported, "At the beginning of the year the news was spread that the girls would be out-of-luck as far as basketball was concerned. They would have class teams, but would not play out-of-town games. The girls were disappointed that they couldn't play the different towns, but they decided interclass games would be better than nothing."

"The girls were disappointed that they couldn't play the different towns, but they decided interclass games would be better than nothing."
1927 *Teton*

Seth Schmidt concluded his article,

"Local school officials in 1926-27 didn't understand that most athletes – male and female – enjoy sports competition. Competition helps make athletics fun and interesting. Unwittingly, by banning interscholastic girls' sports, school officials relegated girls' athletics to a second-class status that continued in Tracy for nearly fifty years."

Newspaper excerpts reprinted with permission by the *Tracy Headlight-Herald*

Two Harbors High School

Northeastern Minnesota on Lake Superior, 30 miles north of Duluth
Years Represented: 1920

Laurie Newtson provided an original copy of the 1920 Two Harbors High School yearbook, *The Agate*. Her grandmother was Athelyn Amundsen Truman, captain of the Two Harbors Girls Basket Ball team. Athelyn was also known as "Skinnay."

Teams played included Proctor, Duluth Denfield, and Duluth Normal.

Two Harbors 1920

A photo in the yearbook of the 1920 team lists the follows team members - Coach Edna Schropp, Edith Strand, Mildred Austed, Pearl Borak, Evelyn Sunder, Eleanor Lund, Captain Athelyn Amundsen, Pearl Du Moe, Irene Nelson.

The annual includes an article on basketball as follows.

"Basket ball was a regular epidemic here this year, and those who did not catch the disease could not have been human. Therefore the high school girls lived right up to grade and began an early season of what later became good, hard basketball practice. It was found all the more difficult because in previous years we had all been used to playing boys' rules, and because we wished to take part in interscholastic contests we found it necessary to change to girls' rules. Imagine our disappointment when we learned that instead of playing and traveling all over the floor we had to stay in our own little division or court as it is called. Of course, we all rebelled at first, but our desire to play outside teams won out and so we buckled down to learn girls' rules, that is, we tried to.

> "Basket ball was a regular epidemic here this year, and those who did not catch the disease could not have been human." *The Agate*

Our first game came after the Christmas holidays, in our own gymnasium; but, nevertheless, we were all rather nervous because so far the visiting team, Proctor, had not been defeated. Of course, it being our first game, we wished to make a good impression, so we purchased suits, or rather had them made, by ourselves, which consisted of red middies, black bloomers and the rest of the paraphernalia that goes with a suit. With this attractive attire and a 'bold front' which we managed to put on, we looked fit for either defeat or victory. The game started at last, and also the 'outside' umpire called only eighteen fouls on us for over-guarding, it ended in our favor. Later, we were rather indirectly informed that we played boys' rules instead of girls.' Of course, this was a thorn in our side so we began immediately to reform.

The next game we played was also played on our floor, and we sent Denfield, the visiting team, back defeated. Our next game was looked forward to with an extraordinary amount of enthusiasm because we were to play a return game with Proctor. The night we played them we met our first defeat and because we had promised our coach to smile, we smiled. Have you ever seen a person who was eating a lemon try to keep a 'straight' face? That is the way we looked. The following week we play the Duluth Normal girls in Duluth and we were also defeated by them. Now, we had one game left to play and we were determined to win it, because the Duluth Normal girls were playing a return game with us. So far we had won two games and lost two. We wanted our season to end with a seventy-five per cent victory. Strange as it may seem that is the way our first season of interscholastic basketball contests ended.

> "The night we played them we met our first defeat and because we had promised our coach to smile, we smiled. Have you ever seen a person who was eating a lemon try to keep a 'straight' face?"
> *The Agate*

On the whole, the season though short, was very successful and the towns-people may look forward to a sextet of champions next year because five of the old players will be back. Of course, good coaching is as necessary as good material, and if Miss Schropp decides to come back they will have it. By graduation, the team will lose their jumping center, and they will probably never find another one like her, because it is not possible for every class to produce a "Skinnay." Financially, much to the surprise of many, we were very successful, and therefore can start our next year's team out on a safe footing."

Underwood High School

Western Minnesota, 10 miles east of Fergus Falls on #210
Years Represented: 1936-37

The Underwood High School yearbook, *The Misquah*, has a photo of the 1936-1937 girls basketball team and an article that reported,

"The girls' team had a successful season winning all their games with other high school teams but losing two games to the St. John's team, one of which was lost by only one point. The girls defeated the strong Frazee team twice by a considerable margin. This year's captain, Evelyn Olson, with Adeline Throndson, Winnifred Browne, Ardis Mortenson, Betty Woldy, and Annie Aanden, took care of the guard positions. Willis Olson played at center, and Merelle Gronner, Mildred Kester, and Hazel Throndson played forward positions. Although three of the team are graduating, the team has good prospects in the grade players who have been along playing. Winnifred Browne has been elected next year's captain." Mr. Kloster was principal and coach."

Underwood 1937

Evelyn Olson Kukkola provided an interview, indicating that she played from 1934–1937. Their team played full court. Evelyn played guard two years and forward two years.

Her team played St. John's, Pelican Rapids, Frazee, and Glyndon. They traveled by school bus and by "teachers' cars."

"On one occasion, the team stayed overnight in Glyndon," Evelyn recalls, "Each girl took one of us home for the night. I ended up at one of those beautiful big farm homes. I was from a very poor family and really didn't know how to act, plus being shy. I had my own room and breakfast was outstanding. I'll never forget that place."

Games were held in the Woodman's Hall in Underwood. Sometimes they were double-headers with the girls' game played first. The coach was the school principal, Mr. Kloster. The team uniform "for the first two years was like a jump suit, but by my junior year, we got regular uniforms in red and white." Evelyn added that the benefits from her years on a basketball team were "confidence and self-esteem."

> "Each girl took one of us home for the night. I ended up at one of those beautiful big farm homes. I came from a very poor family and really didn't know how to act, plus being shy. I had my own room and breakfast was outstanding. I'll never forget that place."
> Evelyn Olson Kukkola

Verdi High School

Southwestern Minnesota, 18 miles north of Pipestone on the border with South Dakota; on #75
Years Represented: 1933-1935

Erling Johnson, Anoka, provided information on the Verdi High School girls basketball team. Mr. Johnson would later serve as the Superintendent of Schools, District 11 and also served as the Commissioner of Education for the State of Minnesota.

Mr. Johnson said that he coached in Verdi in 1933-1935. The girls' team played a two-court game. He said, "I enjoyed coaching the Verdi girls basketball team in the mid-1930s. The girls' team was very popular in the community and, in my opinion, was just as good as the boys."

Teams played included: Russel, Lynd, Lake Benton, Balleton, Hendricks, and Ivanhoe.

> "I enjoyed coaching the Verdi Girls Basketball team in the mid 1930s. The girls' team was very popular in the community and, in my opinion, was just as good as the boys."
> Erling Johnson, Anoka

Wadena High School

Northwest Minnesota, 50 miles west of Brainerd on Highway #10
Years Represented: 1910-1913

Wadena 1911

Three photos show the Wadena girls basketball teams of 1911, 1912 and 1913.

The *Brainerd Dispatch*, September 27, 1999, reprinted a photo from a postcard to commemorate the Wadena girls basketball team of 1911 - Back: Elma Abramson, Ruth Carroll, Ouida Van Dyke. Middle: Grace Harding, Theresa (Tracy) Mettel. Front: Nina Perkins, B. Miller.

The *Wadena Pioneer Journal*, Sports, Volume 86, 1963, featured the photo of the 1912 Wadena High School girls basketball team. It reported,

"Basketball for Wadena High School girls in 1912 is reflected in the picture above. There is no information now to indicate that the girls played games with outside teams but confined themselves with inter-squad games in the school. Modesty then decreed

Wadena 1912

that the young ladies wear long black stockings, bloomers of some dark hue and waists (blouses), all of which prevented exposure of a large part of their anatomy, a far cry from the relatively scant attire of today. Pictured above are Nina Perkins, Alma Abrahamson, Theresa (Tracy) Mettel, Ruth Carroll and Ouida Vandyke."

The 1913 team photo listed - Elma Abramson, Eva Hunt, Ouida Van Dyke, Ruth Carroll, Bessie Miller.

Newspaper excerpts reprinted with permission from the *Brainerd Dispatch* and the *Wadena Pioneer Journal*

Wadena 1913

Wanamingo High School

Southeastern Minnesota; 52 miles south of Minneapolis on #52 and west of Zumbrota on #57
Years Represented: 1924-1928

Hilda Satren Aaker played on the Wanamingo High School girls basketball team in 1924-25. Hilda played forward and remembered playing full-court basketball. Their games were played in gymnasiums. Hilda's uniform consisted of dark bottoms or bloomers and white middies.

Her team played Mazeppa, Zumbro Falls and West Concord. The team traveled by train and by car. Expenses were paid by the school when they traveled to other schools.

When Hilda's team traveled by train, they stayed overnight and returned the next day. Hilda vividly remembered that in the morning after the game, the team would often go sledding on hills in Mazeppa and Zumbro Falls before the train left for home in the afternoon.

> "They all dyed their hair with henna, a red color, so they all had red hair. As it got warmer and hard work playing, they got sweaty and the red dye dripped and ran down their faces."
> Sister of Lillian Romo Aakre

Celia Vangsness Hostager played on the Wanamingo team from 1925-28. Celia's team wore dark black long shorts and white tops. They played teams from West Concord, Zumbrota, Goodhue, Kenyon, Cannon Falls and Pine Island.

The team traveled to games on a school bus. Celia recalled that their parents did not come to the games. There were five players and the court was divided into three sections. Celia was a center and played in the middle court. The two guards were on one side and the forwards on the other side. The team did not play in tournaments. Players received a school athletic letter at the end of the season.

Lillian Romo Aakre played in the late 1920s. Games were held in the town hall heated by a stove.

Special Stories
Margarethe Romo Thoreson, who played at the Red Wing Seminary High School, shared a story about her sister who played for Wanamingo: "My sister, Lillian Romo Aakre, played in Wanamingo in the town hall. It was heated by a big old stove. They all dyed their hair with henna, a red color, so they all had red hair. As it got warmer and hard work playing, they got sweaty and the red dye dripped and ran down their faces. Quite a mess! This was about 1929."

Warroad High School

Northwestern Minnesota on Lake of the Woods, 7 miles south of Canadian border on #11.
Years Represented: 1919-1930

The *Warroad Pioneer* newspaper covered the games of the Warroad High School girls basketball team. An article, January 30, 1919, reported,

"Warroad Won Both Basket Ball Games," over Roseau. The article went on to state, "This being the first real games our players have taken part in we were a little doubtful as to the outcome." The girls' game was played in three ten-minute periods. The team lineup was: Franson, Wahlberg, Jensen, Roberts, McKenzie. There were two forwards, one center and two guards, i.e., five players on the team.

On February 13, 1919, "Our Girls Won but Our Boys Lost," the report said, "Being the train arrives (in Roseau) during the noon hour practically the whole student body was at the station to meet the visitors. The afternoon was spent in visiting school and in practicing. For supper, the visiting teams were given a banquet at the school house which put everyone on good speaking terms as two opponents of each team were seated at each table."

Warroad 1922

Warroad 1923

The games were played in the Opera House which was poorly heated and no place for the spectators.

The January 29, 1920 article reported on the games between the Badger and Warroad girls' and boys' teams. Both Warroad teams won. The article reported, "The Badger teams played at a disadvantage owing to our floor space being much larger than what they were used to playing on."

Warroad 1925

"Being the train arrives in Roseau during the noon hour, practically the whole student body was at the station to meet the visitors."
Warroad Pioneer 1919

A photo of the 1922 team lists - Florence Carlquist, Mildred McKenzie, Sylvia Akre, Vega Pearson, Rosalie Marschalk, Clara Wahlberg. Team members are wearing the traditional middy blouse and bloomers.

The 1922-23 team lists – Front: Maria Goulet, Clara Wahlberg, Mildred McKenzie. Back: Rosalie Marschalk, Vega Pearson, Coach Oscar Levine, Sylvia Akre, Esther Wahlberg.

The 1924-25 team included - Grace O'Donnell Comstock, Ida Norman, Evelyn Fox Peterson, Sylvia Akre, Florence Akre Sandberg, Mildred Carlquist Hohn, Lois Hamlin, Garnett Merrill, Coach Haubner. This team is the first photo of a uniform which has a v-neck, short-sleeved top.

The name of one player on the 1930 team was Dorothy Lewis.

Newspaper excerpts reprinted with permission by the *Warroad Pioneer*

Wayzata High School

Located on the west side of the Twin Cities metropolitan area on #12
Years Represented: 1924

The 1924 Wayzata girls basketball team photo identifies the players as Carrie Keller, Mildred Brandon, Charlotte Minnick, Harriet Spencer, Beth Lamb, Gladys Berg, Hazel Lamb, Anna Milbert Kamleiter, Rosella Keesling, Margaret Day, Cynthia Batson, and Elsie Day.

Wayzata 1924

Wayzata 1926

The photo provided by Marion Wise includes her mother, Anna Milbert Kamleiter. The 1926 team photo lists members as - Front: Charlotte Minnick, Cynthia Batson, Gladys Berg, Theadora Champion. Back: Harriet Spencer, Elizabeth Wise, Maxine Beer Dart, Beth Lamb, Mildred Brandon Cheese. Seated on left: Teacher Mildred Tronson, Supt. F.E. Heinemenn.

West Concord High School

Southeastern Minnesota, 15 miles northeast of Owatonna on #56
Years Represented: 1925-1929

Rose Robinson Wichser shared her love of basketball with students at Kasson-Mantorville school for a 'Women in History' class. She spoke for an hour and a half. The students had many questions. Rose attended West Concord High School from 1925-1929. She played basketball throughout high school as "Popsey" because, Rose said, "I would pop out of nowhere." Rose started playing in her freshman year.

The team played with three guards and three forwards. A jump ball was held after each basket. Rose was the jumping center. Signs were given by the jumping center. For passes, Rose said the ball was held chest high in both hands. For free throws, both hands were down low.

Games were officiated by one official per game. Other teams played were Dodge Center, Claremont, Kenyon, Hayfield, Kasson, Mantorville, and Randolph.

Rose recalls that the team sometimes traveled to away games by cattle truck. The boys sat on one side and the girls on the other side. They also traveled by train leaving West Concord on the 5:00 p.m. train and returning on the 10:30 p.m. train. The teams also traveled using a 'driving team' (very fast horses) and sleigh. During the cold nights, they would have hot bricks and robes to keep warm.

Games were usually played at 7:00 p.m.

On one occasion, Rose recalls, "we got stranded in Hayfield and got up at 4:00 a.m. and flagged down a train to get back on Saturday morning."

There was no gymnasium for games. They played at the movie theater in the City Hall. The baskets were in front of the movie screen and the front door. Rose said, "There were two stoves – one in the northeast and one in the southwest corners. The only seating was around the edges and in the movie projector area. Only a few attended."

West Concord City Hall

The 1929 West Concord yearbook wrote of the girls' basketball team, "The team was scheduled to play Kenyon early in 1929. In spite of the cold weather and snow storms many lusty throated supporters accompanied the teams to Kenyon. Our train was late due to the snow storm, but at last it puffed into West Concord. The game was called (started) at ten o'clock. As the old saying goes, "Weight broke the wagon reach", so did it in regard to our game, "and the W.C. team lost to Kenyon 17-14."

For another game, the yearbook reported, "On the following Wednesday night we journeyed to Dodge Center by cars and sleigh, we finally reached the metropolis. Not being used to playing in an 'ice-box', we lost 13- to 5."

Uniforms were provided by the school. Rose said, "In 1925, when I started playing we wore short uniforms. Two senior members and one junior talked the superintendent into the short uniforms and we were the only ones in Dodge County to have them. The pants came half of the way to our knees (a lot of bare skin) and we all felt very naked the first time. We pulled our socks up to below the knee to cover our legs. Word spread through town and the attendance at the next game was large – inquisitive males to see those short uniforms!!!"

The players dressed at home or in the hotel restroom. They wore high tennis shoes.

Teams changed into uniforms in the West Concord Hotel.

Teams changed into uniforms in the West Concord Hotel. The team's coach was the English teacher, Miss Peters. The superintendent served as chaperone. The two teams traveled together to games and the girls' game was played first. The boys and girls were very supportive of each other. Rose recalls, "We needed to be as spectators were very few."

When the girls were seniors, the school provided red sweaters with W.C. letters on them.

Players were not allowed to have water during the game. They were given a quarter of a lemon at halftime.

Team members in 1928-29 were: Edna Jaeger, Captain, Lorene Zeller, Rose Robinson, Elna Campbell, Marguerite Henry, Luella Fairbank, Carmen Spreiter, Mildred Wilson and Hazel Gochnauer. The team won 8 of 11 games.

Special Stories
Rose reminisced, "My parents were never able to attend, probably because of cost."

"Some of the memories are the excitement of being one of the students able to play and the good times, we had together. After some games we would stop at the local restaurant or bakery and have a 15 cent soda. If we traveled by sleigh we were given something warm to go back home like hot chocolate and cookies.

The team had a 9:00 p.m. curfew. Mr. Schofield checked the dance hall. Rose said that "one time when I was on my way to babysitting, I stopped by the hotel to see who was at the dance and the professor (superintendent) was there probably checking on the players. I couldn't go to the next game at Dodge Center and they lost!!"

The school song which the teams would sing was: "West Concord will shine tonight (3 times), all down the line. Ball goes up and basket made, West Concord will shine."

> Players were not allowed to have water during the game on the theory that they might get sick. They would have a quarter of a lemon at half time.

Westbrook High School

Southwestern Minnesota, 20 miles northeast of Windom on #30
Years Represented: 1914-1934

The *Westbrook Schools, 1910-1990* reunion book reported, "There was a girls basketball team as early as 1914, plus track, until 1932 when the state department decided that girls' sports were unladylike and not suitable for their delicate frames."

The 1924 team members were - Grace Peterson Sickman, Erma Christ Stebens, Irene Wellner Peterson, Marguerite Norstegard Bies, Dora Krueger Lindmeyer, Harriet Pederson Bergquist, Magdalene Wellner Nelson, Alvera Knudson Lien, Ethel Jaeger Anderson, Elsie Schmalz Weinrebe, Mrs. George Krueger, coach.

The reunion book had a photo of the 1924 Westbrook girls basketball team wearing bloomers, white middy top, white stockings and light athletic shoes.

Westbrook 1924

The booklet pointed out, "In the Twenties the girls played "three-court ball as a preliminary to the real event of the night – the boys' game. The attic served as a gymnasium until 1934; all games were played there with the large ventilator shafts adding an element of hazard to the many exciting events that took place. After the games, the host and guest teams had lunch together."

Clarine Knudson Takle played on the Westbrook team, graduating in 1929. Games were played in the Legion Hall.

The reunion book listed the 1930 team members as - Front: Bethel Marks, Evelyn Knudson, Lucille Hopkins, Edna Erickson, Daphne Rossing. Back: Irene Norstegard, Mable Eng, Coach Dorothy Knox, Myrtle Larson, Lucyle Schmalz.

Legacy
Teri Takle, granddaughter of Clarine Knudson Takle, played for Elk River High School, 1980 - 1983 and Hamline University, 1983-1986.

Westbrook 1930

Wheaton High School

West Central Minnesota on the South Dakota border, 60 miles west of Alexandria, on #27
Years Represented: 1933-1937

Muriel Jacobson, was a member of the Wheaton girls basketball team from 1933-1937. She had played with her sister until Vera graduated in 1935. Muriel said, "Vera was a really good player."

Muriel's team won the region championship in 1937. Muriel played all during her high school years and now wishes she could have played longer.

Their team played the two-court game against Herman and Graceville.

The girls' and boys' teams traveled together by bus, playing back-to-back games with the girls playing first.

The team uniforms were shorts and sleeveless shirts in maroon and black colors.

The following girls were members of the 1936 Wheaton girls basketball team - Hilma Simpson, Muriel Jacobson, Eunice Erickson, Ethel Schneider, Grace Johnson, Magel Peterson, Katherine McClellan, Mae Worner. Coaches: Miss Sprague and Vernon Danielson.

Wheaton 1936

The 1937 team players were - Mae Worner, Virginia Opp, Ethel Schneider, Muriel Jacobson, Coach Hanley, Hilma Simpson, Ruby Lindquist, Katherine McClellan and Dorothy Packenham. The ball is marked, "Champs."

Wheaton 1937

Special Stories

Muriel grew up on a farm near Wheaton. She had three sisters and a brother. During high school, Muriel would need no encouragement to try out for the team because her sister Vera was already on the team and, Muriel said, "Vera was the star forward on the team." Together they were a potent offensive and defensive tandem. Vera as a forward and Muriel as a guard were affectionately called "Big Jake" and "Little Jake" by the fans.

The following year, their team was discontinued. Wheaton was one of the last teams to be discontinued in the movement to drop competitive teams and replace them with intramural programs. They were also one of the first teams to begin playing again when teams were reinstated in the 1960s and 1970s.

Muriel went on after high school to explore her love of flying, taking lessons and reaching the point of flying solo. She went on to work for Northwest Airlines for the next 36 years, training reservation staffs throughout the world.

White Bear Lake High School

Ten miles northwest of St. Paul on #61
Years Represented: 1912- 1929

Correspondence with Mrs. Florence Holzheid Leversee brought the news that girls basketball was very popular at White Bear High School when she was in school from 1912-1914. Florence wrote of tryouts for the team and provided the names of the 1914 team - Freida Gall, Florence Reif, Anna Gilmore, Florence Holzheid Leversee, Margaret Hull, and Ruth Lapham.

The pictures she described never made it back to White Bear from California where she was living at the time. Florence spoke with great enthusiasm of the fun they had and how much she enjoyed playing on the team.

The White Bear High School yearbook, the *Matoskan*, provided valuable information and photos.

In the 1919 photo, the players were not identified by name.

White Bear Lake 1919

Until 1920, games were played in an attic gym on the top floor of Washington School, now a care center. Before the new school was built in 1920, players describe playing in various halls in the village. One player said they played in the building attached to the end of the armory which is now a dance studio. Florence described playing in the Legion Hall, on fourth east of Banning, and a place called Rodger's court. The new school is now White Bear Middle school.

Players in the 1920 photo are identified as - Front: Julia Finn, Grace Herbert, Martha Webber. Back: Eileen Bourquin, Mabel Ramsey, Helen Frantz, Pat Cook, Coach Skogland, Marva Bourquin, Elsie Long, Rose Auger.

In the 1921 photo, players are not identified in order - Miriam Farrar, Martha Webber, Mildred Houle, Margarite Therrien, Elsie Long, Mabel Ramsey, Eileen Bourquin, Edith Long, and Evelyn Rohlfing .

In 1922, the game was a three-court game, each playing one-third of the floor. In 1924, it was a two-court game. Guards and forwards were restricted to one-half of the court and the running centers played full-court.

White Bear Lake 1920

White Bear Lake 1921

White Bear Lake 1922

There were tryouts for the team and players were required to have physical exams. Uniforms and transportation were provided by the school.

Players in the 1922 photo - Eileen Bourquin, Elsie Malchow, Adelaide Parrhysius, Gertrude Freeman, Mildred Houle, Martha Webber, Mildred Post, Laura Peterson, Naomi Rohlfing (one name N/A)

The 1924 *White Bear Press*, had two-inch headlines, "Ladies Basketball Games." The article stated,

"Our ladies basketball team has been earning a very enviable reputation this season as expert players, and are a credit not only to themselves, but to our school and village. They have played No. St. Paul, and Mechanics, defeating them both. The high school expects to play Hamline, the University of Minnesota and Humboldt High next week."

The 1924 photo did not provide the names of players.

A second large headline in the *White Bear Press* said, "Season Closed." The article recapped the season,

White Bear Lake 1924

Fourth Quarter

"Our ladies basketball team, victorious this season, won laurels in nearly 90% of games. White Bear ended a successful season winning from the Humboldt champions of St. Paul by 13-3 and also by defeating the University of Minnesota, 24-8. Our team has won 9 out of 11 games this season. The largest score was 95-0 when White Bear Defeated North Saint Paul."

From 1920-1923, the players said they traveled with the boys' team on the trolley or streetcar. The girls' and boys' teams also traveled on a chartered bus from 1924-1927.

White Bear Lake 1925

Photos and players on the last four competitive teams are listed below:

1925 photo - Alice Lawton, Kathryn Schweitzer Fournelle, Adele (NA), Helen Schofield, Lorraine Bourguin Sansome, Delphine Smith, Mary Holmes, Marian Wyler, Coach.

1926 photo – Front: N/A, Mary Holmes, Alice Lawton, Lorraine Bourquin Sansome, Alexina Post Benson. Back: Coach Alvina Kraft, Harriet Rosamind Bloom, Louise Miller, Mildred Harper, Kathryn Schweitzer Fournelle, Coach Thora Langlie.

White Bear Lake 1926

1927 photo –Front: Helen Fisher, Mary Holmes, Lorraine Bourquin Sansome, Harriet Rosamind Bloom, Clara (Mary) Louise Blake. Back: Dorothy Tardiff Spreck, Kathryn Schweitzer Fournelle, Coach Alvina Kraft, Louise Miller, Mildred Harper.

1928 – Front: Janet Fournelle, Helen Fisher, Clara Louise Blake, Lilly Halley, Lucille Mehlhorn; Back: Jessie Moore, Margaret Dougherty, June Collison, Coach Nesbitt, Jane Harrington, Dorothy Tardiff, Lucille Brennan.

The last team in 1929 consisted of: Margaret Fulton, S. Holmen, Jean Shields, Lucille Mehlhorn, Aurora Bloom, Viola Christoffersen, Willa Bauer, Jean Holmes, Martha Holmes, E. Schultz, Marion Holmen, LeNora Auger, Jane Harrington, Marion Van Voorhis, Catherine Collette, Marion Holmen, Aldona Bohdanowicz, Myrtle Clewett, Helen Johnson, Jean Guttersen. Coaches Ziebarth and Redding.

White Bear Lake 1927

Teams played included Excelsior, Stillwater, North St. Paul, Y.W.C.A., St. Catherine's, Forest Lake, Oak Hall, Mahtomedi, Farmington, Twin City Business College, University of Minnesota, and Hamline University.

White Bear Lake 1928

"Today we attend a Bears girls basketball game and enjoy watching talented athletes who are well coached compete against other similarly talented athletes from schools across Minnesota. And yet this was not always the case. Our female basketball players are carrying on a tradition that began over 90 years ago when the young women of White Bear Lake demonstrated the same passionate desire to play basketball. Today, as the superintendent in White Bear Lake, I am able to enjoy the games from the stands. Instead of my hometown Muskies, I now cheer for the Bears. As I look back on over thirty years as an educator, it is one of the highlights of my career to be able to say that, as a young teacher and coach, I played an instrumental role in starting a girls basketball program in my hometown. Many years later, as I was driving back home to visit relatives, I found myself listening on the radio to the play-by-play as that same hometown school competed for a state championship. I can only imagine the pride the players of those initial teams felt as they watched the success of those who followed down the path that they so honorably and arduously created."

Dr. Ted Blaesing, Superintendent of Schools, White Bear Lake, 2005

Special Stories

Players interviewed in 1978 included: Kathy Swietzer Fournelle, Eileen Bourquin Buckley, Loraine Bourquin Sansome, Dorothy Bloom Kulkey, Evelyn Rolfing and Naomi Rohlfing.

The Bourquin sisters felt the girls' team was equally as important as the boys' team. "We were popular. There was no boy-girl competition as to who had the best team. The girls' and boys' teams cheered for each other. Sometimes the boys came to the girls' practices to help them. Girls' games were of equal importance and not considered 'preliminary' to the boys game."

Both sisters in 1978 remained in good physical shape, exercising, bowling, swimming, canoeing, playing golf and camping. Eileen remembered playing in the St. Paul city league after graduation in 1923. They wore shorts and played boys rules. She said the games were rough.

Kathy Swietzer Fournelle, 1927, had kept her letter sweater, her high school yearbook and team photos. She remembered playing Oak Hall, a private school, who provided lemon slices at halftime.

Naomi Rohlfing said of her physical exam, "One thing that I can remember is as a kid growing up, I had a heart murmur and it took a long time for my doctor, Dr. Clanahan, to let me play. He said 'alright you can play but I want to be there,' so he was there for my first big game. He was there many times. He had his office on the second floor and there were steep stairs to go up there. He would have me run up and down those stairs and then would check my heart again and say, 'oh go ahead and play,' because my heart wasn't any worse after running up and down those stairs than it was sitting."

Naomi Rohlfing's scrapbook was a wonderful book of memories. The players had made black arm bands with the letters WB in orange felt, and also the WBL emblems of an orange felt material that were worn on the front of their shirts.

Naomi shared stories of her high school years and said that her class had invented senior skip day at White Bear. The class took the train to St. Croix Falls, boarded a passenger boat down the St. Croix River to Stillwater, and then took the streetcar back to White Bear.

Dorothy Bloom Kulkey played from 1928-1933. She was on the first Girls Athletic Association Board that became the replacement for the interscholastic basketball teams.

Excerpts reprinted with permission of the *White Bear Press*.

Willmar High School

West central Minnesota, 30 miles northeast of Hutchinson on #12
Years Represented: 1913-1928

Ruth DeLaHunt Rawn played in 1913, and provided an interview at the age of 100 years.

Ruth played on the Willmar girls basketball team in 1913-1914. She played one year and then said, "When I was a senior I was too busy as editor-in-chief of the annual, besides my school work." There were 45 in Ruth's graduating class.

Ruth recalled that her sisters and friends were playing as late as 1924.

The team uniforms were middies and wool serge bloomers. The wool was 54 inches wide so there was a yard of wool for every leg. "The bloomers were baggy pants and after awhile," Ruth said, "the elastic in the legs got worn out and mine would keep falling down and I had to stop and pull up my pants all the time. I got fouled for that. I guess I took too much time."

The game was a three-court game with players limited to their own court. Ruth said, "We were running and we'd get that far, get to that big white line and we had to stop, and if you got your feet over (the line) the whistle blew. You fouled." Players were allowed only three fouls before they had to sit out of the game.

Forwards were the only players that could score. Guards got the ball to the forwards. After a score, a jump ball was held in the center circle.

The 1913 team consisted of - Sorenson, Grace Sperry, Esther Tallman, Pearl Curran, Mildred Smith, Ruth DeLaHunt, Mooney, Hawklund and Severinson.

Willmar 1913

Ruth shares that her school had a nice gymnasium where they played their games. Other teams came to Willmar to play. Players provided their own uniforms. Ruth said, "I imagine my mother made my uniform as I don't know how else I got them. My sister Eleanor got mine. We wore the middies to school. It was part of our wardrobe."

"I remember being on the court and playing and it was all very exciting." Ruth adds, "There were people on the sidelines watching. Once you are out on the court running around and playing, you don't pay much attention to anything else. I can remember the feeling of being there and I was always running and chasing after my forward and guarding her. That's my job. I couldn't make baskets or anything like that. You had rules of how close you could get to your forward. You had to try to keep her from throwing the ball. You had to be as fast as she was. If I stepped over the (center) line or if I got too close to her, they were very strict about that. Most of the fouls were on the guards. Three fouls and you were out."

Ruth's father was an express agent and they got passes on the train.

Ruth said, "I never heard of any disapproval of girls' playing. We were heroes." She said, "I felt running was good for me when I was young so I ran everywhere, all the time." Ruth started running because after waiting at home for the bathroom with seven siblings, she was always late and had to run to school in order not to be late."

"I never heard of any disapproval of girls playing. We were heroes."
Ruth DeLaHunt Rawn

Opposing teams played included: Raymond, Granite Falls, Madison and Howard Lake.

The 1914 team members were - Esther Tallman, Mildred Smith, Margaret Allen, Pearl Curran, Amy Severinson, Grace Sperry, Ruth Beck, Ruth DeLaHunt, Thelma Curran. Fern Doremus was the coach.

The yearbook reported, "On January 16, both girls and boys went to Howard Lake for a double header. Here we met a new and puzzling situation; the Howard Lake girls

Willmar 1914

had previously played 'boys' rules' only, while we had played according to girls' rules. For a time the outlook was dark, but finally a special edition of rules was put into use and the game was played according to girls' rules in the first half, and according to boys' rules in the second. The final score was Howard Lake 13, Willmar 26." Other teams played were Appleton, Granite Falls and Litchfield.

A photo from the Willmar H.S. yearbook, shows the 1915 team. The team won four games and had no losses. Uniforms were black bloomers with white middy blouses. No names were provided.

A photo of the 1916 Willmar girls'

Willmar 1915

Fourth Quarter

Willmar 1916

Willmar 1921

basketball team lists - Ruth Beck, Captain, Adline Marshall, Pearl Otterness, Ethel McKee, Emma Boyd, Elsie Styles, Ethel Bergeson, and Ruth Olson. No order given.

Eleanor DeLaHunt Strand provided an interview at the age of 95 years. Eleanor said, "We had to do without basketball our junior year because the high school was under construction and we had no gym." She lamented that the boys' team went to Seminary where they had a court but the girls weren't allowed to play, as "they told us that we might contract colds."

Eleanor played in 1917-21. There were eight players and Eleanor was the jumping center. She recalls that "the girls' team was dropped sometime after 1929 after they got that order."

Eleanor's team played a two-court game with six players. The running center played as one of the three forwards.

The 1921 team photo listed – Front: Mable Peterson, Ethel Munson. Middle: Ruby Otterness, Pearl Johnson, captain, Vella Lundquist. Back: Myrtle Johnson, Eleanor DeLaHunt, Anna Overgaard. The team won 6 and lost 2.

The team usually traveled by train, the Great Northern. It left Willmar early and they played teams "on the line." Eleanor said, "The Flyer, they called it, the one that went through to the coast was supposed to pick us up later on. There was one earlier than the Flyer that they scheduled us on. I remember the night that we played at Dassel, we all wanted to stay for the party after the game. But, no, we had to get down to the depot and get ready to take the train back to Willmar. So we all got down to the depot and our superintendent was there. It was his job to see that we got on the train. I can still remember how he looked when the train went by 'swoosh!!' It never stopped!! So we went back to the party and then we had to stay there until the later train that came from the coast that took us back to Willmar. That was really great!"

"We all wanted to stay for the party after the game. But, no, we had to get down to the depot and get ready to take the train back to Willmar. So we all got down to the depot and our superintendent was there. It was his job to see that we got on the train. I can still remember how he looked when the train went by 'swoosh!!' It never stopped. So we went back to the party."
Eleanor DeLaHunt Strand

Eleanor said that the town's whistle blew at noon. Students would go home for dinner. Willmar was a crossing point for trains coming from the north, east, south and west. The trains would stop, have lunch and transfer their express and freight, etc., and then take off again.

The girls' and boys' teams also traveled by car. There was a Buick car 'agency' in town.

The girls' game was played first. Then the girls were cheerleaders for the boys' game.

The girls' team members received school letters. Eleanor's granddaughter now has her letter. It was a ball with WHS on it, red with white letters.

Eleanor said that she wore her sister Ruth's uniform. Her shoes cost about $2.00 a pair.

Willmar 1924

"The coach," Eleanor said, "was more like a chaperone. Her name was Viola Redding, a teacher who taught science and math."

Helen Ohsberg Lindahl provided an interview. She played from 1924-1928. The girls' and boys' teams traveled together and Helen recalled that the teams supported one another. Uniforms were middy blouses with navy blue bloomers. Teams played included Litchfield, Grove City, and Kerkoven. Helen said, "At a game, there was a voice, 'Go Strong Heart!' Afterward, that was my nickname."

A photo of the 1924 team listed - Helen Ohsberg Lindahl, M. Schmitz, O. Overgaard, H. Arvig, B. Nelson, A. Bakken, O. Felt, L. Ackerman, G. Benson, Miss Stutsman, coach.

Willmar 1927

The school yearbook, the *Wilohi*, reported that the team won six games, tied one and lost none. Teams played included Atwater, Hancock, Paynesville, Litchfield and Kerkhoven.

In the 1927 photo, the player in the front row, left end is identified as Addie DeLaHunt Osterberg Larson, youngest sister of Ruth and Eleanor DeLaHunt.

Special Stories
Ruth said, "The best, smartest girls played basketball. The outstanding girls played. It was the thing to do."

Ruth taught in Burnstad, a small town in south central North Dakota. It was a very flat area except for what were locally described as 'the hills.' She went to teach

Willmar 1928

domestic science. However, the principal had to go to World War I and instead of teaching, Ruth found herself principal of the school. As the only high school teacher, she taught high school students for two years in English, Ancient History, Algebra and Latin; whatever they needed to pass their state exams.

"It was cattle country," Ruth said, "and one of my favorite students was a young kid named Theodore Roosevelt Thurston. His father and Teddy Roosevelt were good friends, and Ted was named after him. She said, "Ted was a good student. When spring came the boys quit as they had to take care of the cattle."

When Ruth's daughter, Florence, received a copy of the Willmar team information, it arrived on her birthday. "Reading my mother's words again was just the best birthday present I could have received."

Willow River High School

40 miles southwest of Duluth on 35 W
Years Represented: 1931

A letter from Donald Swartz said that he played on the boys basketball team at Willow River High School in 1931.

There was a girls' basketball team that played their game right before the boys during most of the season. Donald said,

"At our home games, the girls baked two cakes for each game; a devil's food cake and an angel food cake. If we lost, we had devil's food and hot chocolate after the game. If we won, we, of course, had the angel food."

Our Lady of Good Counsel Catholic School, Wilmont

Southwestern corner of Minnesota, 20 miles from Worthington on #16

Marie Hippert Larson played on the girls basketball team at Our Lady of Good Counsel Catholic School in Wilmont. When her son saw a news article about girls basketball, he remembered that she had talked about her playing days.

> "We lived three and a half miles from town so when we went to practice, either we walked the railroad tracks which cut down a mile or rode the horse."
> Marie Hippert Larson

Marie said, "When we first got the team started, I was to play on the first team and mother said I couldn't wear those bloomers in public. Then she consented so I was captain of the second team but played on the first team."

Marie recalled that "her church school was only allowed to play a home town, Lismore and Iona."

She said, "We only had a chance to play out of town a few times. We lived three and a half miles from town so when we went to practice, either we walked the railroad tracks which cut down a mile or rode the horse."

Windom High School

Southwestern Minnesota, 50 miles southwest of Mankato on #60
Years Represented: 1914-1929

The Windom School District opened a new school in 1912. It is believed that the first Windom girls basketball team was in 1913. School yearbooks documented teams until 1929.

The *Windom Reporter*, January 17, 1913, under a section entitled "High School Notes," stated, "The girls basket ball team will go to Worthington Saturday afternoon to play their team. The line-up is as follows - Grace Roberts, Geraldine Dickerson, Centers; June Seely, Tillie Grimstad, Forwards; Irene Hanson, Elsie Kettlewell, Guards; Mildred Crane, substitute."

Windom 1914

In 1914, the Windom team played Heron Lake, Slayton and St. James. They lost four games and won the last game against St. James, 12-8.

In 1915, the "W" Club selected the following players for school letters - G. Morgan, R. Myers, Edna Gillam, Agnes Lund, E. Tenjum, Helen Hebbel, V. Loveland. Teams played were Heron Lake, Worthington and Lake Crystal.

Members of the 1916 team were listed as - Helen Hebbel, Irene Elness, Gladys Jeffers, Edna Gilliam, G. Morgan, Ruth Dryden, Agnes Larson and Elvina Lund.

Windom 1915

The 1917 Windom yearbook, the *Cricket*, included a photo of each team member with individual descriptions of their play.

Under Myrtle Smith's photo, it read, "Myrt came out to play with the pretty big ball this year, despite the remonstrance of papa and mamma that little daughter would ruin her health playing that awful game. Nevertheless she still appears to be surviving the terrible ravages of basketball, and as far as we can see, Myrt's frail constitution has been little injured."

"'Myrt' came out to play with the pretty big ball this year, despite the remonstrance of papa and mamma that little daughter would ruin her health playing that awful game. Nevertheless she still appears to be surviving the terrible ravages of basketball, and as far as we can see, Myrt's frail constitution has been little injured."
The 1917 *Cricket* yearbook

Under Helen A. Hebbel's photo, it read, "'Heb's' main specialty is falling down at the crucial point in a game and the thud which results reminds one of the distant thunder. But in this way she forms a fine padding for the hard and relentless gym floor. She has a reputation for 'hanging on like a bull dog' and 'sittin' on her opposing center's stomach."

For Gladys Jeffers, the yearbook wrote, "'Jeff' always plays a mighty peppy game, but especially when she has a desirable audience. One can always reckon her by the shade of complexion which she develops. When she only is pink, she is just 'peeved'" when she turns red she is 'sore;' when she gets scarlet she is 'mad;' and by the time she gets purple there is nothing left of her opponent to tell the tale."

Windom 1917

Ogla Olson's description stated, 'Ole' hailed from Lakefield in the fall of 1916. They let her come here to school in order to play jumping center for Windom and to get a Normal certificate on the side. "'Ole's' little 'tootsie wootsies' have been a great factor in defense in our center field as she always managed to spill her opponent just at the critical point."

Under Ruth J. Dryden's photo, the following caption appeared, "I wish I could play boys' rules." It said, "Ruth is our dashing forward and captain from the little suburb of Bingham Lake. She never stops for anything, be it referees, stone steps or bleachers. Occasionally, it is rumored, she makes a basket just to tease the other team and to give the scorer something to do."

The 1917 team included Agnes Larson, Olga Olson, Myrtle Smith, Gladys Jeffers, Irene Elness, Ruth J. Dryden, Margaret Beise, and Helen A. Hebbel.

In the fall of 1918, the *Cricket* reported that the girls' team began practice early with enthusiasm. However, the basketball season was interrupted in Windom and other schools by a long influenza vacation. The girls could only secure one game against St. James which they lost. Team members were - Guards Grace Hansen and Ruth Drewry; Forwards Anna Jacobson and Irene Elness; Running Center Helen Weiser; Jumping Center Lucille Lanpop, Substitutes Arline Solem, Anna St. John. Coach: Miss Ella Johnson.

The 1920 *Cricket* recapped the girls' basketball season with a headline,"More Deadly Than the Male." The article described a successful season with Grace Hanson as captain and Miss Bryant as coach. "The initial game at Worthington, showed the results of conscientious practice and brought out the fact that we had a REAL girls' team. The enemy was far out-classed on floor work, but the jinx seemed to shadow the home team in basket shooting. The game stood 16-16 in the last few moments of play and it was in the final breath that Worthington slipped in the winning counter."

The team also played Slayton, and Fulda. The *Cricket* included the first names of the players as: Grace, Anna, Arline, Ruth, "Jake," Helen, Frances, Mary, Alma and Miss Bryant, coach.

In 1921, the Windom team won every game but one game with Worthington. The yearbook noted, "A peppy coach, interested superintendent and noisy rooters did half the work and the team strove to do the other half." The team defeated Slayton, St. James, Bingham Lake and Worthington. The yearbook said, "We challenged Worthington for a game deciding the championship winners on a neutral floor. They did not favor this nor did they offer any better method of gaining a decision thus giving Windom the right to claim the championship." The coach was Miss Grow. Team members were not identified in the yearbook.

In 1922, the *Cricket* reported another positive season. It said, "If there were such a thing as a district championship in this sport, it could well be claimed by Windom as the team was defeated only once in the race – by Worthington - while we are also credited with a victory over them." The following girls received letters through the "W" club - Alma Kraft, Frances Rogers, Arlene Solem, Orpha Christie, Lucille Thompson, Avis Cone and Vera Wallace. Other team members included Evelyn Silliman and Frances Judd, Ada Quam, Mildred Moser, Jeanette Cone, Lucille Peacock and Annie Sotaaen. No other teams played were listed.

Windom 1922

Windom 1923

The 1922 team photo lists- Front: Cone, Judd, Wallace. Middle: Silliman, Christie, Quam, Thompson. Back: Rogers, Solem, Kraft.

In 1923, the *Cricket* opened its report on girls' basketball with, "I, Mr. Basketball of the 1922-23 season, went into the Brewster-Windom fray on December 13th, with a somewhat doubtful expression on my broad countenance. For many weeks I had suffered much by being tossed violently to other people, and had been bounced around on the floor until I knew who were the ablest jugglers among the thirty some enthusiasts that came out for Girls' Basketball. A series of class games had decided that the Juniors were the champions and as a result two Junior forwards went into the Brewster battle, December 13th, besides three Seniors, a guard and two centers, and a guard from the Sophomore class. I came out of the fray with a more battered but a less doubtful countenance as the score board registered 5 to 12 in favor of Windom." The team won two games and lost two playing Brewster, Bingham Lake, Jackson and Worthington.

The 1923 team members were listed – Front: Moser, Peacock, Hakes. Back: Sotaaen, Cone, Coach Zollner, Quam.

The 1924 *Cricket* reported that the team won three and lost three games. The *Cricket* reported on the final game of the season and stated, "Then came the final game of the season, the thrill that we had been looking forward to, the Windom-Worthington combat. A great 'mob' of rooters was there to see us 'get Worthington's goat.' It was a good fast game, with the scores almost even throughout. Then a moment before the deciding whistle, the Worthington forward dropped a ball through the rim, winning from us by two points."

Other teams played were Slayton and Jackson. The 1924 team photo listed - Front: Moser, Wallace. Middle: Cone, Thompson, Judd, Sotaaen. Back: Coach Zollner, Carter, Sunderman.

The 1925 *Cricket* reported a very successful season with the number of games won and the sportsmanship exhibited during the season. Teams played were: Brewster, New Ulm, Slayton, Heron Lake, Wilder, Lakefield and Lamberton. The 1925 team members receiving "W's" were - Jeannette Cone, Ruth Carter, Avis Sogge, Mantie Hakes, Ann Sotaaen, Bessie Cowan and Lucille Sunderman. Additional team members included Helen L. Nelson, Mildred Estenson, Merle Hanefeld, Myrtis Wellman, Lucille Meade, Lucille Ryan. The coach was Miss Zollner.

The 1926 *Cricket* recapped, "When the schedule for girls' inter-school tournament was announced it was received with great joy for there had been a rumor that there would be no girls basketball this season." Games were played with Brewster, Jeffers, Wilder, Lakefield and Bingham Lake. The team only won the last game with Bingham Lake.

1926 photo - Front: Hanefeld, Mitchell, Peterson, Thake. Middle: L. Sogge, Cowan, Hakes, Captain; Totman, Lowrie. Back: Estenson, Mones, Coach Bjorklund, Sogge, Nelson

The 1927 squad was selected from 35 girls who reported to the first practice of the season. Sixteen were selected for the regular squad. The team played the 'Wilder Sextette' and defeated them 18-19. The next game at Lakefield was a defeat for the Windom team. The yearbook reported, "The remaining five games were played according to two court rules. This new method

Windom 1924

Windom 1926

Windom 1927

seemed to make the games snappier and more interesting." The team played Bingham Lake and Lakefield, completing the season with five wins, one loss, and one tie.

1927 *Cricket* team photo - Front: Spielman, Lowrie, Capt. Estenson, L. Sogge, Mitchell. Back: Mead, M.C. Hanefeld, Jones, A. Sogge, M.M. Hanefeld. Coaches: Mr. Ernest and Mr. Fuller.

Windom 1928

The 1928 team played an 11-game season. The team won nine and lost two. The yearbook reported, "Jeffers seemed to be their undefeatable opponent as they lost both games to them." The team scored 278 points to their opponent's 135. They were coached by Mr. Fuller and Mr. Ernst. Other teams played included: Lakefield, Westbrook, Comfrey, Fulda, and Bingham Lake. The team photo lists - Front: Annabelle Lowrie, captain; Kanne, Sogge, Mitchel, Speilman. Middle: M. Hanefeld, Thake, Johnson, Wills, A. Hanefeld. Back: Coach Fuller, Coach Ernest.

The 1929 team consisted of nearly all veteran players from the 1928 squad. The yearbook summarized, "Although they lost the majority of the games, the team was a success in its fine spirit of cooperation and willingness to fight against the odds. The public showed an increasing interest proving that the girls are learning to play a real game." The team played Lakefield, Fulda, Bingham Lake, Jeffers, and Springfield, winning four and losing five games. The 1929 team photo lists - Front: Kanne, Silliman, Annabelle Lowrie, captain; Mitchell, Sogge. Middle: Swenson, M. Hanefeld, Johnson, Thake, A. Hanefeld. Back: Coach Fuller, Coach Ernest.

Windom 1929

The *Windom Reporter*, January 26, 1929 reported on girls' and boys' double header games with Fulda and Mountain Lake. The girls' team lost in overtime to Fulda, 17 to 18. The return game with Fulda ended in a tie.

The *Windom Reporter*, February 1, 1929 headlined, "Windom Wins Four Fast Games," and described the girls' and boys' games in the Armory with Lakefield and Jackson. The article described the opening of the girls' game with Lakefield, "Tuesday night witnessed two of the most thrilling games of basketball history. As Lakefield beat Windom in the first game of the season, everyone knew this would be a close game. The Armory was filled with a cheering throng as the girls' game started." The end of the game was described as, "Windom tied the score. Then with only a few minutes left to play, Hanefeld scored the winning basket. The end came with Windom 17, Lakefield 15. M. Hanefeld made all of the Windom baskets." The newspaper reported that the boys' game was played first.

The *Windom Reporter*, February 15, 1929, reported on the last games of the season with three games to be played: "The first game will start promptly at 7:30 and will be between the Springfield boys' first team and Windom's fastest quint. This game will be followed by a game between Springfield girls and the Windom girls' team. Then the Windom first team will play the St. James boys."

"The boys' game was played first"
Windom Reporter, February 1, 1929

The 1929 Windom girls basketball team was the last team recorded in the high school yearbook or newspapers for that era.

Newspaper excerpts reprinted with the permission of the *Citizen Publishing Company*

Winona High School

30 miles east of Rochester on #14
Years represented: 1921-1928

Stacy Cordes was a graduate of Cotter High School in Winona and researched the school's history for her class at the University of St. Thomas. Stacy learned at Cotter that when Cotter and Cathedral combined in the 1920s, the old yearbooks and records were gone and no history was available. Yearbooks were available at Winona High School.

Winona 1921

The Winona High School yearbook was called the *Radiograph*. Yearbooks were located with reports on the girls basketball teams in 1921, 1927, and 1928

The 1921 the Winona High School girls basketball team had a successful season. They were coached by the Physical Director of the Young Women's Christian Association, (YWCA), Miss Macomber. Fifteen girls were on the team and practiced on Monday and Tuesday nights.

The 1921 season record was four wins and one loss to the YWCA. Teams played were within an hour and a half from Winona. The team traveled the greatest distance to Lake City about 45 miles north of Winona on the Mississippi River. They also played Kellogg and La Crosse, which is across the Mississippi River in Wisconsin.

The girls' and boy's teams played double header games.

The 1921 team photo lists- Coach MacCumber, Gertrude Schoniger, Marjorie Sawyer, Amelia Sievers, Lucille Seidlitz, Dorothy Engels, Elva Donehower, Louise Steiner, Edith Barton, captain.

Information on the 1927 team was limited to the names of the following players - Lila Schaub, guard; Jeanne Pehrson, jumping center; Edwina Schlueter, forward.

The 1928 *Radiograph*, shared that the team was coached by the physical director of the "Y," Miss Georgia Schori.

Winona 1928

308 Daughters of the Game

The team held tri-weekly practices. A squad of 13 girls composed the team. There were five returning players and many new recruits.

The team had different uniforms by 1928, wearing what appears from the photo to be shorts, with a white blouse and dark ribbon.

The 1928 photo lists - Front: Luella Biltgen, Bernice Haesley, Mildred Kalouner, Edith Wendt, Agnes Hangartner. Middle: Elsie Thurley, Harriet Meginnis, Ruth Bung, Margaret Nelson. Back: Dorothy Spanton, Margaret Kurth, Marguerite Venables. Back: Carlene Rose.

The high school switched completely to the Girls Athletic Association format in 1928-29.

Winthrop High School

South central Minnesota, 17 miles northeast of New Ulm on #19
Years Represented: 1918-1921

Mildred Lofthus Roepke played on the Winthrop girls basketball team from 1918-21. It was a three-court game.

Winthrop 1920

Team members listed on a photo of the 1920 Winthrop "Stars" were - Dora Webster, Mildred Lofthus Roepke, Viola Nylander, Gunhild Otterstrom and two unidentified players. A female teacher was the coach.

Games were played in city halls. Uniforms were full bloomers, with white middy blouses.

Teams played included: Gaylord, Arlington, Gibbon, Fairfax and Franklin.

The team traveled to away games on the Minneapolis & St. Louis Railroad.

The team always returned home after games. Mildred said, "They always had a midnight train."

The girls and boys' teams traveled to games together. The girls' game was played first, followed by the boys' game. The team always returned home after games. Mildred said, "They always had a midnight train."

Mildred reminisced that the boys' team and community were very supportive. She said, "They cheered for us. The *Winthrop News* always had coverage of the games."

Mildred's favorite memory was their undefeated season in 1921.

Zumbrota High School

Southeastern Minnesota, 25 miles north of Rochester on #52
Years Represented: 1904-1915

The 1904 Zumbrota girls basketball team photo lists the following members - Elsie Woodbury, Pearl Anderson, Grace Laughlin, Helen Biersdorf, Sadie Lothrop and Eva Maley.

Zumbrota 1904

The Centennial Booklet, *Zumbrota – The First One Hundred Years, 1856-1956*, referenced the girls basketball team. It identified the 1910 team members as - Front: Florence Anderson, Georgia Morgan, Stella Paulson. Back: Agnes Nerhaugen, Lena Svee, Ovida Berg, Constance Svee. The team uniform consisted of dark middy tops with ribbons and dark bloomers

In the same publication, it noted in a description of the boys' game that "today's sharpshooters do not have to worry about hitting low ceilings or dodging low-hanging light fixtures." The girls played in the same facilities.

In 1912, it was reported in the *Zumbrota News* that the team played against St. Charles, defeating the opponents 10-5 in the City Hall. There was a banquet before the game for both boys' and girls' teams.

Zumbrota 1910

The 1915 photo lists - Millie Fossum, Barbara O'Kane, Irene Biersdorf, Irene Nelson, Clara Miller, Cassie Stary, and Bernice Svee. Coach Mrs. Otto Steege

Zumbrota 1915

Fourth Quarter Free Throws

Here we are near the end of the game! So we have to get the ball and score!!

There is enough time to add points to your score and, if you are behind, to pull out a victory!! So, let's see how you play when the pressure is on!!

Thanks for playing with us!

Fourth Quarter Questions
1. What is the year of the earliest team photo? What is the name of the team?
2. What team traveled in the "Merry Widow?"
3. What team declared to be the state champion after defeating New Ulm in 1919?
4. What team played St. James in 1904 and again in 2005?
5. Which team was awarded a silver trophy when it won its 1925 invitational tournament?
6. What kind of award was presented to each player?
7. How did one player lose her award?
8. What team traveled to games in a street car?
9. Name one of the early teams to switch its uniforms from bloomers to shorts.
10. What was the name given to the high scoring player from Rapidan?
11. What was the name of the player's team who was featured in the St. Paul rotogravure?
12. "Myrt's parents feared basketball would ruin her health. What was her team's name?
13. When Willow River won its game, what kind of cake did they eat?
14. When the Willmar teams traveled by train, what was the name of the railroad?
15. Heidi Robbins modeled her great-grandmother's uniform that her family had preserved. What was the name of her great-grandmother's team?
16. What 1930 Montgomery team player was her town's second Kolacky Queen?
17. Thea Sletkolen Stay of Montevideo played during what hard economic times?
18. What was Ruth Olson Kleven's mother's reaction when she went to a game and saw her daughter playing wearing shorts instead of bloomers?
19. Name the school of Mabel Thompson Erickson who was good at winning at marbles.
20. What player from Hutchinson led the Gopher Women to national recognition?
21. Name the team that ended the Litchfield 72-game winning streak.
22. What is the name of the team in the first era to win 94 consecutive games?
23. Which team marched into Odd Fellows Hall to demand that their team not be dropped?
24. How did the Buffalo boys' team help the bus driver in one 1920s severe snowstorm?
25. Jeannette Page Wright of Crookston nearly died during what epidemic?

Score: Home_____ Visitor_____

Answers:

1. 1901; Crosby-Deerwood
2. Grand Rapids
3. Owatonna
4. Northfield
5. Sherburn
6. A silver ring with a basketball on the top
7. Swimming in a gravel pit
8. Excelsior
9. Milan, Browns Valley, Sherburn, Mabel, Jordan, or Underwood
10. "Point-a-Minute Just"
11. Ellendale
12. Windom
13. Angel food
14. Great Northern
15. Pelican Rapids
16. Irma Malone Foley
17. The Great Depression
18. She looked mostly at the floor.
19. Mabel
20. Lindsay Whalen
21. Buffalo
22. Grand Meadow
23. Cromwell
24. They wrapped the girls' wool scarves around their heads and walked in front of the bus
25. The influenza epidemic of 1918-1919

FINAL SCORE TALLY

Total the scores for each team from each quarter.

First Quarter	Home_____	Visitor_____
Second Quarter	Home_____	Visitor_____
Third Quarter	Home_____	Visitor_____
Fourth Quarter	Home_____	Visitor_____
Total Score	**Home**_____	**Visitor**_____

And the Winner is:_____

"We had fun!!"

Overtime

Some games do not end in regulation time and go into "overtime!" The history of the first era of girls high school basketball is a game that cannot end here. There is so much history left "out there" in the memories of women who played, in their family archives and in local historical societies.

So, the game must go on until each school's history has been uncovered and preserved. Each day, more history comes into the game.

Just as the final layouts were being edited, Eden Prairie and North St. Paul flew in the door! So they lead off our "overtime" period!!

Eden Prairie High School

Southwest metro area, west of #494 on Highway #5
Years Represented: 1926-1935

In the first issue of the school newspaper, *The Buzzer*, October, 1926, the Sports section included an article on "Gymnasium Work By Girls." It stated,

"Gang Way! Here comes the army of girls. If Eden Prairie school does not get a blue ribbon team out of that number of girls, there is something wrong. The girls are going to be held back somewhat because there are a great number who have not played basket ball before. They will need a great deal of practicing. They have practiced throwing the ball, catching it from each other, making baskets from different positions on the floor and dribbling. We have our star center with us this year which we thought was going to another school. Her name is Astrid Anderson. She was good in every game because of the way she played to get the ball to the right basket."

The Buzzer, March 1927, reported, "On Tuesday, February 15, the Eden Prairie boys were to play with the St. Louis Park boys' team. The St. Louis Park team did not come, so the girls agreed to play with the boys. In order to be fair we played boys' rules half of the game and girls' rules the other half. The score was 14-17 in favor of the boys." The girls later won a game against Deephaven 24-11 and against Bloomington 48-0.

During the 1927-28 season, the team played Carver and won 29-6. They received their middies and had a dress rehearsal wearing them in practice. The middies were paid for with the subscription money from the sale of Curtis magazines. Team captain was Abbie Tuckey.

Inter-school games were revived in 1929-30. The team played Carver, losing 18-15. Team members included Ruby Mlinar, Ethel Anderson, Lyda Anderson, Margaret Tuckey, Abbie Tuckey and Captain Jane Frissell.

The 1930-31 team included Boyd, Margaret Tuckey, Ruby Mlinar, Harriet Abel, Kortz, Beryle Pemberton. Substitutes were Vernice Neidenfuehr and Boyd. The team lost to Chaska, playing the three-court rules.

The 1931-32 team consisted of Vernice Neidenfeuhr, Anita Mlinar, Betty Hulbert, Jean Page, Marjorie Rosendahl, Harriet Abel, Beryle Pemberton and Captain Anita Mlinar. The team lost to Carver 12-11. A game against Victoria was cancelled.

During the 1933-34 season, the team won a game on January 19th against Carver, 15-7. The team members were Vernice Neidenfeuhr, Jean Page, Hulbert, Marjorie Rosendahl, Helen Kopesky, Emily Nechas, Shorba and Clark. The team won a game against Victoria, 14-10.

The Buzzer stated, "Victoria evidently does not have the same interpretation of the girls' rules of the game as Eden Prairie has. They played a very rough game. Their floor is quite small compared to our own. The ceiling is low."

The 1934-35 team photo caption listed: Ruby Nechas, Emily Nechas, Pauline Kakach, Marjorie Rosendahl, Letha Moats, and Helen Kopesky.

North St. Paul High School

Northeast of St. Paul on Highway #36
Years Represented: 1917-1918

Olga Hanson Bowman played on the first girls basketball team at North St. Paul High School in 1917-1918. She has lived in North St. Paul for all of her 103 years.

The first girls high school basketball team was formed when she was a senior. Olga has clear memories of playing the game. The team was composed of five players and they played full-court basketball. According to Olga, "we played like they do today."

Olga played center. She said, "I was tall at 5 feet 7½ inches so I took the jump balls and 'whacked' the ball hard to start the game and after baskets were scored."

Olga's teammates included Edna Schletk (whose father owned the hardware store), Edna Behrens, Ann Walser (whose father owned the saloon), Lucille Herrick (whose father owned the bank in North

St. Paul and Liz Krause, substitute.

The girls bought their uniforms that consisted of short-sleeved middy blouses and full bloomers worn below the knee. Black stockings and high-topoped canvas shoes completed their uniform. There was no other expense involved in playing on the team.

The girls did not travel with the boys' team nor did they play on the same nights. Travel was by train or horse and wagon. Both the girls' and boys' teams were popular and supported by the community. The teams cheered for one another and had parties and dances after the games.

Olga remembers traveling to play White Bear Lake and Mahtomedi. They practiced in the gymnasium at the new North St. Paul High School and their team photo was included in the school yearbook.

In 2005, at age 103, Olga feels there was no harm in playing girls basketball. She believed that she gained confidence playing front of spectators and "had a lot of fun."

Second Overtime

Then a call came from Jane Moening, Braham, who had just learned that her mother, Renee Otte, had played on the Melrose girls basketball team in the late 1920s. Her mother is now playing in our "overtime" period

Just as the buzzer was about to sound, a telephone call from Paula Gallagher, St. Paul, reported that her mother Marguerite O'Grady had played in the early 1920s on the St. Paul Cathedral girls basketball team. The history of the first era of girls basketball continues to be discovered.

You, like Jane and Paula, may find a family member of a school team to get into the game.

In the last section, "Family Memories," you can preserve information about your athletes and teams.

Now, as they say, "the ball is in your hands!"

Epilogue

The original goal of this book was to preserve the history of the first era of girls basketball in Minnesota. After listening, reading and talking with the women who played during that first era:

It has become so much more!

The research for this book exposed the essence of these wonderful women and the lessons they can teach us.

Basketball was the common denominator among the thousands of young women in Minnesota who played the game during those five decades of the twentieth century. As athletes, they learned about commitment and teamwork. They understood that they were role models representing their family, school and community.

The women took the lessons learned from their favorite sport and applied them throughout their adult lives. They challenged barriers that had limited women in their communities and careers and they made a difference in our state and well beyond.

After full lives, these marvelous women continue to be role models showing us how to face one's senior years with courage, dignity and grace.

There is a story to be told by each woman in this book as she represented the spirit of the remarkable women of Minnesota. They have set a high standard for today's athletes now enjoying the second era of girls' sports.

Our friend Marie Keeler would give us words of encouragement, "Hurry up with that book. I'm not going to live forever!" Now, with this book, we can say, "Yes, Marie, you will! You and all of the women of the first era of girls basketball in Minnesota will live on and your stories will be told from generation to generation."

You taught us the most important lesson of all: *how to live as women in the game of life.*

"The battle for the individual rights of women is one of long standing and none of us should countenance anything which undermines it." Eleanor Roosevelt[1]

The photo of a favorite coach preserved over a lifetime in a player's scrapbook - Belle Plaine 1925

Roster of Coaches

The following list of coaches includes those individuals named in the team profiles. Coaches were frequently referenced without a first name and were referred to as: Miss, Mrs., Mr., or by position, such as Coach, or Superintendent.

Sources of the names and years coached were taken from player interviews and questionnaires, newspapers, historical organizations, school publications and family archives. The individual may have coached prior to and/or following the years listed.

A

Aarder, Art, Hartland, 1910
Abbetmeyer, Miss, Stillwater, 1922
Albert, Paul, Northfield, 1904
Allen, Delores, Montevideo, 1933
Allen, Miss, Princeton, 1921
Alvin, Doris McCrady, elem. teacher, North Branch, 1931
Alway, Miss, Greenway, 1923-1925
Andrews, Miss, Starbuck, 1919
Armalore, Miss, Gaylord, 1920

B

Barrington, South St. Paul, 1922
Becker, Litchfield, 1932
Benson, Ann, Milaca, 1920
Bergesen, B.E., principal, Ellendale, 1925
Bergney, Miss, Rose Creek, 1919
Bjorklund, Miss, Windom, 1926
Blakeslee, Mrs., Mankato, 1929
Blanchard, Margaret, LeSueur, 1921
Bloom, Miss, Gaylord, 1924
Brack, Alice, Delavan, 1923
Brekke, Al, Riverton, 1927
Brennan, Irene Koll, Cass Lake, 1924-1926
Bryant, Miss, Windom 1920
Bunday, Grace, Arlington, 1929

C

Callaghan, Miss, Tracy, 1909
Carlstrom, Harold, Jeffers, 1928
Carss, Miss, Proctor, 1923
Cedarstrand, Miss, Brainerd, 1926
Christopherson, Julia Howe, Delavan, 1927
Clark, Alyda, Tracy, 1911
Cornish, Miss, Crookston, 1910

D

Dahl, Verna, Jordan, 1932
Dahlke, Ruth, East Chain, 1929-1931
Dales, Dr., Aitkin, 1910
Danielson, Vernon, Wheaton, 1936
Dasovic, Dan, principal, Toivola, 1933
Denmire, Miss, Byron, 1924
Diedrichs, Louis, Jeffers, 1930
Dittes, Miss, Grand Rapids, 1929
Dixon, Benny, Northome, 1936
Doremus, Fern, Willmar, 1914
Drew, Herbert, Cloquet, 1923-1925

E

Eckberg, Miss, Mountain Lake, 1923
Eggen, Bernice, Arlington, 1926
Ehnbom, Elvira, International Falls, 1925
Engbritsen, Earl, Rapidan, 1930
Erlandson, Mable, Franklin, 1929
Ernst, Mr., Windom, 1928

F

Foote, Raymond, St. Paul Central, 1915
Foss, Edith, Franklin, 1924
Foss, Thelma, Starbuck, 1930
Fraser, D.A., Frazee, 1939
Frasier, Miss, Bingham Lake, 1927
Fredrickson, Margaret, New Prague, 1930
Fuller, Mr., Windom, 1926-1928
Fuller, Norman, St. Mary's High School, Waverly, 1931-1933

G

Gaarder, Art, Hartland, 1910
Gerber, Northwest School of Agriculture, 1928
Gillesby, Miss, Proctor, 1922
Goldtharpe, Miss, International Falls, 1926
Graeff, Johnny, Montgomery, 1920s
Granger, June, Blooming Prairie, 1934
Gratzek, Miss, Proctor, 1923
Greckla, Miss, Cromwell, 1929
Greene, Miss, Proctor, 1922
Grow, Miss, Windom, 1921
Gugesberg, Miss, Bricelyn, 1928

H

Hallberg, Miss, Brownton, 1923
Handke, R.W. Supt., Brownton, 1924-1927
Hanley, Miss, Wheaton, 1937
Hanson, Miss, Albert Lea, 1914
Hartshorn, Herbert, Rapidan, 1928
Haubner, Miss, Warroad, 1925
Haugen, Cyrus, 1921
Haugland, Thor, Rose Creek, 1929
Hawker, Mr., Buffalo, 1924
Heberling, Mr., St. Paul Central, 1909
Hensler, Susanna, Arlington, 1926-1929
Hermanson, Ann, Buffalo, 1924
Hickisch, Miss, Cloquet, 1932
Higgins, Miss, Proctor, 1921
Hoffer, Bill, Buffalo, 1922-26
Holcombe, Inez, Cloquet, 1925

Herbert Hartshorn, Rapidan, 1928

Hollichek, Miss, Milan, 1935
Holton, Miss, Stillwater, 1926
Holzinger, Greenbush, 1924
Horman, Gertrude, Braham, 1929
Hughes, Lillian, Mankato, 1913
Hughes, Magdalene, Luverne, 1932
Hutton, Lee, Excelsior, 1917-1921

I

Iverson, Mrs., grade school teacher, Milan, 1927

J

Jacobson, Rachael, Franklin, 1928
James, Miss, Grand Rapids, 1911
Jansen, Victor, Mountain Lake, 1923
Jaynes, Mildred, Grand Rapids, 1925-1928
Jedlicka, Mr. and Mrs., Proctor, 1919
Jelstrup, Lillian, Roseau, 1925
Johnson, Carl A., Hendricks, 1928
Johnson, Ella, Windom, 1919
Johnson, Erling, Verdi, 1935
Johnson, Miss, Albert Lea, 1921
Johnson, Miss, mathematics teacher, Cloquet, 1921
Johnson, Miss, Greenway, 1929

Johnson, Sandall, South St. Paul, 1921

Jones, Miss, Austin, 1915

K

Kloster, Mr., Principal, Underwood, 1937

Knox, Dorothy, Westbrook, 1930

Kraft, Alvina, White Bear Lake, 1925-27

Krueger, Mrs. George, Westbrook, 1924

Kuehl, Miss, South St. Paul, 1925

Kuitu, Esther, Cromwell, 1931

L

Landus, Miss, Freeborn, 1927

Langlie, Thora, White Bear Lake, 1926

Lanning, Victor, Montevideo, 1929

Lansing, Miss, Blooming Prairie, teacher, 1905

Larson, Miss, Kasota, 1931

Lauman, Professor, Bingham Lake, 1927

Levine, Oscar, Warroad, 1923

Lofthouse, Miss, Crookston, 1910

M

Macomber, Miss, Winona, 1921

Madsen, Miss, Hutchinson, 1922

Makit, Miss, Cromwell, 1929

Malmen, Miss, Montevideo, 1918

Mann, Evelyn, math teacher, Owatonna, 1924

McIntyre, Marie, International Falls, 1926

McKenna, Miss, Greenway, 1926

McMullin, Miss, Aitkin, 1910

Menzel, Louise Fritsche, New Ulm, 1926

Mickelson, Edna, Deer Creek, 1924-1929

Miller, Daisy, Buffalo, 1926

Miller, Gladys, principal, Arlington, 1920

Mitchell, Mr., Cromwell, 1922-1928

Mohr, Gladys Wandersee, Rapidan, 1929

Montgomery, Miss, Excelsior, 1917-1921

Moonan, Grace, St. James, 1917

Mossberg, Miss, Braham, 1927

Muraski, John R., Montgomery, 1929-1932

N

Nelson, Miss, Jeffers, 1928

Nelson, Miss, Slayton, 1914

Nelson, Raymond, Ellendale, 1926

Nesbitt, Miss, White Bear Lake, 1928

Nestande, Marian, Grand Meadow, 1936-1938

Nibbe, Mr., Tracy, 1925

O

O'Connell, Miss, Montgomery, 1931

Oelke, Mildred, Montevideo, 1933-1935

Ogle, Ches, St. Mary's High School, Waverly, 1931-1933

Olson, Miss, Starbuck, 1918

Olson, Mrs. Swanville, 1922

Opp, Virginia, Wheaton, 1937

Ortman, Miss, Starbuck, 1920

P

Palmer, Miss, St. James, 1914

Parker, Miss, Grand Rapids, 1906

Peters, Miss, West Concord, 1925

Peterson, Mr., Austin, 1924

Peterson, Mr. H., Marshall, 1924

Pierce, Miss, Stillwater, 1928

Coach Pierce, Stillwater, 1929

Roster of Coaches

Pike, Miss, Olivia, 1937
Poppitz, Lillian, Hutchinson, 1922
Pothoff, Carl, principal, Rapidan, 1924
Potthoff, C.J., Slayton, 1928
Pritchard, Miss, Swanville, 1919-1922

Q

Quito, Miss, Cromwell, 1929-1931

R

Raberton, Lewis, school principal, Rapidan, 1926
Redding, Viola, science and math teacher, Willmar, 1917-1921
Reiersgard, Lila, Grand Meadow, 1929-1936
Rem, Carolyn, Grand Meadow, 1939
Robertson, Miss, Stillwater, 1924
Rosel, Mr. Brainerd, 1926

S

Sanford, Miss, Cloquet, 1926, 1930
Sassy, Miss, Olivia, 1924
Saul, Mr., Red Wing Seminary, 1926
Schmidt, Robert, Belle Plaine, 1926
Schori, Georgia, Winona, 1928
Schropp, Edna, Two Harbors, 1920
Selander, Mildred, Cambridge, 1925, 1928
Sheman, Margaret, Gaylord, 1924
Sherwood, Katherine, home economics teacher, LeSueur, 1925
Skogland, Miss, White Bear Lake, 1920
Smith, Marge, North Branch, 1932
Sommerville, Douglas, Glyndon, 1932-1934
Sorenson, Hannah, Freeborn, 1910
Sorlie, Miss, Ellendale, 1924
Speckel, Helen Allen, Lyle, 1929-1931
Sprague, Miss, Wheaton, 1935-1937
Squire, Helen, Cyrus, 1921
Steege, Mrs. Otto, Zumbrota, 1915
Stenson, Ruth, Starbuck, 1910
Stockton, Mr., Adams, 1927-1929
Strom, Vera, Franklin, 1930-1936

Studt, Ann, Buffalo, 1919-1921
Stutsman, Miss, Willmar, 1924
Sutton, Anna, Arlington, 1927
Swanson, Edwin, Red Wing Seminary, 1919-1921

T

Tallakson, Harold, Mountain Lake, 1923
Taylor, Irene, Faribault, 1923
Telander, Ruth, Preston, 1941
Thomas, Miss, Grand Rapids, 1911
Tobin, Miss, Greenway, 1923
Todnem, Mary Chadwick Dickmeyer, Cohasset, 1925-1927
Trydal, Lynda, Moose Lake, 1930-1933
Turbak, Miss, Buffalo, 1932

V

Van Cura, Lawrence, Hancock, 1923-1926

W

Waldo, Miss, Brownton, 1927
Waller, Miss, Brownton, 1927
Wandersee, Gladys, Rapidan, 1929
Ware, Pear, Rapidan, 1927
Weedel, Miss, Austin, 1913-1915
Wenstrom, Evelyn, Slayton, 1923-1925

Coach Williamson, Monticello 1928

Wiberg, C.C., Braham, 1927
Wiedenmann, Naomi, Gaylord, 1921-1923
Wilbrecht, Florence, Elkton, 1930
Williamson, Miss, Monticello, 1928
Wing, Auretta, Lake Crystal, 1932
Woods, Ruth, Blooming Prairie, 1925
Wyler, Marian, White Bear Lake, 1925
Wysochi, Mr., Milaca, 1920

Z

Ziebarth, Gertrude, Park Rapids, 1926-1928; White Bear Lake, 1928-1929
Zimmerman, Miss, Sherburn, 1925
Zollner, Miss, Windom, 1922-1925

"Much credit is due to their coach, Miss Hanson, for the amount of work she has done training the team." The 1914 Albert Lea yearbook

"Mrs. Blakeslee, the coach of the Basket-ball and Soccer Teams made the girls of the squads capable players. A great deal of the success in winning all the games is due to the coach. Night after night she practiced with the girls teaching each individual the way to play a good game of Basket-ball and Soccer. The coach taught the team tricks so as to outwit the other teams they played. The girls of the squads think themselves very fortunate in having for their coach such a splendid leader as Mrs. Blakeslee." Mankato 1921 High School yearbook

"Our coach didn't get after us for anything. We respected her so. No one would ever criticize her. She made you want to practice and nobody hardly ever missed practice. She expected us to do the right thing all the time. We kind of worshipped her, I think." Ruth Bratrud Jacobson, Grand Meadow, 1930.

"We had a real nice male coach. He was handsome and really tall. The rest of the female faculty used to fight over him. The thing I remember about him was during the half, we were given oranges and I thought that was so good. We didn't have oranges at home Eileen Grover and Blanche Kingsley Cromwell, 1930.

Are Modern Girl Athletes Risking Their Looks?

Judging by These Pictures, the Answer Is "No"

IS the modern girl in a sorry plight? Must she make a choice between beauty and brawn?

Can she spend hours on the tennis court, in the swimming pool, on the golf links or even on the basketball floor, and yet expect to be so attractive that she will be invited to senior proms and other nice parties?

Do the young men like the athletic type of girl or do they prefer the less energetic ones because they are prettier?

Apparently the answer is that a girl can be both athletic and pretty, that she can possess feminine fascination and charm, but at the same time have supple muscles and the vigor of an Amazon.

There was a time when it was considered unmaidenly for a girl to participate in any sort of sport. And she was barred from games and contests.

Of course, there were always a few who disregarded the dictates of convention, but they were called tomboys and pointed out as bad examples by careful mothers. But no one ever hears of a tomboy these days. Perhaps the new styles in clothes have liberated girls from the situation which denied them the opportunity of exercising; perhaps with the dismissal of the old ground trailing skirts went a host of other traditional inhibitions.

Dr. Anna Norris, director of athletics for women at the University of Minnesota, is an advocate of sports for girls attending the university.

"I am certainly of the opinion that a girl can take part in athletics and yet be very charming," she says. "In fact, I always believed that sports, by increasing grace of the body and flexibility of movement, add materially to the attractiveness of the girl. There surely can be no conflict between beauty and participation in athletics. The university recognizes this by requiring that all girls must engage in some sort of physical training during their first two years here. They all seem to enjoy it."

That athletics and personal charm go together is being proved by high school girls of the northwest whose pictures are shown on this page. They all are basketball players and have participated in many strenuous contests in recent seasons. Nor is basketball altogether a gentle game, as note the picture of Patricia Gritzner, who is a member of the New York University girls' basketball team. Miss Gritzner wears a regular football noseguard of rubber to protect her face from disfigurement during the rougher moments of the game.

— And Sports Are No Longer Considered Unmaidenly

Pictured in the row along the top of this page are girls who have played on basketball teams at Litchfield, Brainerd, Princeton, Buffalo and Montevideo. The full length figure in the middle top is of Marian McInerny of the First National Bank team of Minneapolis.

Below at the left is Dorothy Burshek of Buffalo, and over at the right, opposite her, is Winifred Roth of the same school.

Newspaper article, Circa 1930, see Credits

Roster of Players

The following list of approximately 2,000 players represents the names included in this publication. They were obtained from team photos, newspapers, school yearbooks, and other resources. Names are listed alphabetically. Each player's name is followed by her school team. When a last name is not followed by a first name, it means that a first name was not available.

The years listed reflect the information received in interviews, questionnaires, newspaper articles, yearbooks and from photos. It may not include a woman's entire playing career.

When years are combined, i.e., 1920-1925, it includes the years of 1919-1920 through 1924-1925. When a single year, i.e., 1931, is listed, it reflects one school year, 1930-1931.

A

Aaberg, Mabel, Starbuck, 1930
Aaker, Hilda Satren, Wanamingo, 1925
Aakre, Lillian Romo, Wanamingo, 1926
Aamodt, Mabel, Greenbush, 1924
Aanden, Annie, Underwood, 1937
Abel, Anna, Kasota, 1931
Aberle, "Babe," Alexandria, 1915
Abel, Harriet, Eden Prairie, 1930-1932
Abrahamson, Alma, Wadena, 1910-1912
Abrahamson, Myrtle Almlie, Milaca, 1920
Abrahamson, Ruth, Moose Lake, 1933
Abrehampson, Birdie, Bricelyn, 1928
Ackerman, L., Willmar, 1924
Adler, F., Marshall, 1922-1924
Adlesick, Vangeline, Greenway, 1929
Adlesick, Frances, Greenway, 1926
Ahlgren, Astrid, South St. Paul, 1925
Ahrens, Lois Eckhart, Morton, 1927-1930
Akre, Sylvia, Warroad, 1922-1925
Alberg, Eva, Aitkin, 1932-1936
Albrecht, Grace, Morgan, 1924
Alfe, Ethel, Glyndon, 1934
Allard, Tillie, Owatonna, 1924
Allen, Margaret, Willmar, 1914
Almquist, Thora, Moose Lake, 1929-1931
Altnow, Eileen, Arlington, 1920
Alton, Gladys, Alexandria, 1914
Alzant, Grace, Brainerd, 1926
Ambrose , New Prague, 1932
Amendson, Martha, Montevideo, 1918
Amundsen, Athelyn, Two Harbors, 1920
Amundson, Ethel, Moose Lake, 1933
Anderson, Alice Armstrong, Bricelyn, 1928
Anderson, Alvira, Adams, 1932
Anderson, Amy, Montevideo, 1933-1935
Anderson, "Babe," Buffalo, 1931
Anderson, Bea, Bricelyn, 1928
Anderson, Bernice, North Branch, 1931
Anderson, Bessie, Proctor, 1919-1921
Anderson, Edith, Litchfield, 1926-1928
Anderson, Eloise, Buffalo, 1929-1931
Anderson, Elsa, Cloquet, 1928
Anderson, Emma Lee, Lake Crystal, 1932
Anderson, Ethel Jaeger, Westbrook, 1924
Anderson, Ethel Lyden, Pelican Rapids, 1912-1914
Anderson, Florence, Zumbrota, 1910
Anderson, Helen E., St. Peter, 1924
Anderson, Hilda Zander, Brownton, 1926-1928
Anderson, Irma, Greenway, 1929
Anderson, Kathleen, North Branch, 1930-1932
Anderson, Lillian, Stillwater, 1923
Anderson, Lola, North Branch, 1932
Anderson, Lottie, St. James, 1916-1918
Anderson, Luella Bandelin, Arlington, 1924-1928

Anderson, Margaret, Litchfield, 1931
Anderson, Mildred, Jeffers, 1928
Anderson, Mildred, Litchfield, 1915
Anderson, Myrtle, Litchfield, 1927
Anderson, Nora, Starbuck, 1910
Anderson, Pearl, Litchfield, 1930
Anderson, Pearl, Zumbrota, 1904
Anderson, Rhoda, Litchfield, 1928
Anderson, Ruth, Alden, 1911
Anderson, Ruth, LeSueur, 1921
Andres, Alice, Montevideo, 1928-1931
Andrews, Rosemary, Glyndon, 1934
Anerson, Alta, North Branch, 1932
Aney, Delia, North Branch, 1908
Ankeny, Beulah Travis, Grand Meadow, 1936
Annand, Wilma, Duluth, 1924
Annexstad, Grace, St. Peter, 1924
Appell, Ella Beaver, Kasson, 1920's
Arf, Mildred, Cloquet, 1921
Armstrong, Alice, Bricelyn, 1928
Arneson, Dorethy, Clarkfield, 1924
Arnold, Helen, Brownton, 1927
Arntz, Violet Gregor, Hancock, 1924
Arpan, Velma, Greenway, 1929
Arscott, Grand Rapids, 1929
Arvig, H., Willmar, 1924
Augur, Dorothy, Albert Lea, 1917
Auger, LeNora, White Bear Lake, 1929
Auger, Rose, White Bear Lake, 1920
Augustine, Katie, Alexandria, 1915
Austed, Mildred, Two Harbors, 1920
Averill, L., Montevideo, 1935

B

Baird, Frances, Austin, 1914
Baker, Bernice, Aitkin, 1928
Bark, Sena, Northfield, 1904
Baker, Charmion, Litchfield, 1927
Baker, Marjorie, Slayton, 1923-1925
Baker, Virginia, Brownton, 1907
Bakken, Northwest School of Agriculture, 1928
Bakken, A., Willmar, 1924

Baldinger, Genevieve, St. Paul Central, 1909
Ballou, Helen, Northfield, 1904
Bangert, Pearl, Stillwater, 1926
Barger, Myrtle, Gaylord, 1907
Barncard, Ruth, Proctor, 1917
Barr, Dorothy, Austin, 1914
Barr, Mable, Austin, 1914
Barsness, Alice, Cyrus, 1921
Bartlett, Frances, Lake Crystal, 1932
Barton, Edith, Winona, 1921
Bassett, Nellie, Roseau, 1923
Bassett, Nina, Roseau, 1923
Bate, Margaret, Lake Crystal, 1932
Bates, New Prague, 1907
Bates, Mabel, Grand Meadow, 1933-1935
Batson, Cynthia, Wayzata, 1924
Batzer, Lydia, Royalton, 1904
Batzer, Susan, Royalton, 1904
Bauer, Willa, White Bear Lake, 1929
Baukol, Christie, Starbuck, 1930
Bauman, Grace Sunderman, LeSueur, 1925
Bauman, Hazel, LeSueur, 1925
Beasman, Mae, Cromwell, 1932
Beaulier, Brenda Stewart, Proctor, 1917
Beck, Ruth, Willmar, 1913-1916
Beckfelt, Carrie, Grand Rapids, 1905-1908
Beckfelt, Ruth, Grand Rapids, 1908-1911
Beckman, Lucille, Jordan, 1924-1928
Beckstrom, Ordella, Cambridge, 1928
Bedi, Mary, Greenway, 1929
Bedi, Rose, Greenway, 1929
Beebe, Irma Solvari, Toivola, 1933
Beggs, Helen, Brainerd, 1924-1926
Beise, Margaret, Windom, 1917
Bekkerus, Alvina, Glyndon, 1934
Bell, Iva, Greenway, 1922
Bemel, Evelyn, Proctor, 1923
Bendickson, Ferne, Litchfield, 1928-1931
Bendickson, Hazel, Litchfield, 1926-1928
Benson, Alexina Post, White Bear Lake, 1926
Benson, Alvida, St. James, 1916-1918
Benson, G., Willmar, 1924

Benson, Helen Smith, Byron, 1924

Benson, Lilia, St. James, 1914

Bentz, Irene, Grand Rapids, 1929

Berdan, Elsie T., Morgan, 1924-1928

Berens, Litchfield, 1932

Berens, Helen, Litchfield, 1928-1930

Berentzen, Ruth, Roseau, 1923

Berg, Cloquet, 1923-1925

Berg, Gladys, Wayzata, 1924

Berg, Marie Tommerson, Grand Meadow, 1929-1934

Berg, Marion, Luverne, 1933

Berg, Ovida, Zumbrota, 1910

Berg, Z., Montevideo, 1935

Bergan, Edith Anderson, Cloquet, 1920-1925

Bergwell, Effie, North Branch, 1908

Berger, Ellen, Rapidan, 1925-1928

Bergeson, Ethel, Willmar, 1916

Bergquist, Harriet Pederson, Westbrook, 1924

Bergquist, Marion, Moose Lake, 1929-1933

Bermel, Evelyn, St. James, 1915

Bernhart, Mabel Plumb, 1925-1928

Beseke, Norma, Arlington, 1926

Bhend, Esther, Le Roy, 1939

Bianchi, Laura Corbett, Elkton, 1927-1931

Bibus, Lola Belle, Blooming Prairie, 1934

Bieder, Margaret, Jordan, 1932

Biegert, Gladys, Montevideo, 1916

Biersdorf, Helen, Zumbrota, 1904

Biersdorf, Irene, Zumbrota, 1915

Bies, Marguerite Norstegard, Westbrook, 1924

Billet, Helen, Lake Crystal, 1932

Biltgen, Luella, Winona, 1928

Bjorkland, Windom, 1926

Bjorkland, Marie, Cloquet, 1926

Bjorklung, Nancy, North Branch, 1908

Bjornlie, Edith Dalen, Milan, 1924-1927

Black, Laura, Northfield, 1903-1905

Black, Velma, Northfield, 1904

Bladholm, E., Marshall, 1924

Blair, Northwest School of Agriculture, 1928

Blaisdell, Francis, Hayfield, 1925

Blake, Clara (Mary) Louise, White Bear Lake, 1926-1928

Blake, Ruth, Cloquet, 1930

Blanchard, Dorothy Allen, Grand Meadow, 1936-1939

Blanchard, Hazel, Greenway, 1925

Blanchard, Hazel Peterson, Grand Meadow, 1936

Blasyk, Wanda, Moose Lake, 1930

Blodgett, Margaret, Northfield, 1903-1905

Blom, Adelaide, Milan, 1935

Bloom, Aurora, White Bear Lake, 1929

Bloom, Harriet Rosamind, White Bear Lake, 1927

Bloom, Margaret, Northome, 1936

Blume, Florence, Belle Plaine, 1930

Bluntoch, Della, Greenway, 1923

Bogart, Minneapolis Central, 1901

Bohdanowicz, Aldona, White Bear Lake, 1929

Bonarher, Edna, Grand Rapids, 1906-1908

Booth, Edna, Litchfield, 1931

Booth, Eleanor, Brownton, 1926-1927

Bonin, Leona, Stillwater, 1924-1926

Borak, Pearl, Two Harbors, 1920

Borchert, Ruth, Gaylord, 1924

Bordewich, Janet, Olivia, 1937

Borsheim, Mildred, Cloquet, 1930

Botten, Myrtle, Montevideo, 1926

Bourquin, Ellen, White Bear Lake, 1919-1922

Bowman, Olga Hanson, North St. Paul, 1917-1918

Bowser, Violet Tolzman, Belle Plaine, 1923

Boyd, N/A, Eden Prairie, 1930-1931

Boyd, Emma, Willmar, 1916

Bradt, Dorothea, Sherburn, 1926-1927

Brabec, Katherine, Montevideo, 1925

Bracket, Alice, Minneapolis Central, 1901

Brayden, Eleanor, Proctor, 1918-1921

Bradash, Alma, Montgomery, 1932

Brandel, Ruth King, Belle Plaine, 1923

Brandjord, Evelyn, Franklin, 1928

Brandon, Mary, Grand Rapids, 1911

Brandon, Mildred, Wayzata, 1924

Brandt, Alice, West Central School of Agriculture, 1914
Brandt, Loretta, Glyndon, 1934
Brantsag, Emma, Starbuck, 1910
Brayden, Eleanor, Proctor, 1918-1921
Brazee, Minneapolis Central, 1901
Breffle, Helen, Franklin, 1931
Breiland, Northwest School of Agriculture, 1928
Breimhorst, Jane Varner, Jordan, 1928-1932
Brekke, Joy Moore, Milaca, 1931
Brenden, Jeanette, Starbuck, 1930
Brennan, Lucille, White Bear Lake, 1928
Brenneer, Viola, Stillwater, 1923
Brewster, Mildred, Slayton, 1927-1929
Briest, Gertrude, Gaylord, 1922
Brooks, Edna, Freeborn, 1910
Brooks, Ruth, Luverne, 1935
Brooks, Virginia, Frazee 1939
Brosch, Hiacynth, Morgan, 1924
Brown, Minneapolis Central, 1899-1901
Brown, Barbara, Litchfield, 1930-1932
Brown, Charmion, Litchfield, 1927
Brown, Elizabeth, International Falls, 1925
Brown, Lorraine, Cloquet, 1927-1930
Brown, Mabel, Brownton, 1907
Brown, Orpha Hendershott, Buffalo, 1926
Browne, Winnifred, Underwood, 1936-1938
Brundage, Marian, Sherburn, 1926-1927
Bryant, Helen, Monticello, 1924
Buck, C., Northwest School of Agriculture, 1928
Buckley, Eileen Bourquin, White Bear Lake, 1920-1923
Budde, Elnora Burke, Clarkfield, 1923-1925
Buehe, Ione, Paynesville, 1928
Buehe, June, Paynesville, 1928
Buesing, Charlotte, Cyrus, 1921
Bullert, Martha, Arlington, 1927
Bundy, Vearl Kennedy, Elkton, 1927-1931
Bung, Ruth, Winona, 1928
Burfening, Beryl, Litchfield, 1915
Buringsrud, Northwest School of Agriculture, 1928
Burke, Esther, Slayton, 1901
Burns, Loretta, Moose Lake, 1933
Burns, Nina McMonagle, Litchfield, 1902-1905
Burquin, Marva, White Bear Lake, 1920
Burshek, Dorothy, Buffalo, 1930
Butler, Mabel, Brownton, 1907
Butler, Marjorie, Brownton, 1907
Bye, Irene Mahoney, Grand Meadow, 1935-1939

C

Cain, Windom, 1925
Callahan, Gladys, Freeborn, 1910
Campbell, Blanche, Tracy, 1911
Campbell, Elna, West Concord, 1929
Campbell, Iris McGraw, Litchfield, 1932
Campbell, Zella, Tracy, 1911
Carlson, Claribelle Nebel, Braham, 1927-1929
Canfield, Hazel, Luverne, 1935
Canton, Lois, Montevideo, 1930
Canton, Thelma, South St. Paul, 1925
Card, Ruby Burrington, Grand Meadow, 1911
Carlquist, Florence, Warroad, 1922
Carlson, Sigrid, South St. Paul, 1925
Carrol, Edna, Hutchinson, 1921
Carrol, Ruth, Wadena, 1910-1912
Carter, Alice Dahlman, Cromwell, 1925-1928
Carter, Ruth, Windom, 1923-1925
Cartier, R., Marshall, 1924
Casey, Amy, Jordan, 1928-1932
Cassidy, Hazel, Litchfield, 1929-1932
Cassidy, Ina, Litchfield, 1924
Cassidy, Mildred, Litchfield, 1928-1930
Caswell, Helen, Cass Lake, 1924-1926
Catlin, Eileen, Buffalo, 1923-1926
Caylor, Vivian, Litchfield, 1931
Champlin, Mary, Lake Crystal, 1932
Chapman, Madge, Princeton, 1921
Chapman, Marjorie, Princeton, 1921
Chelberg, Ruby, Cambridge, 1928
Cherkezian, Rosalind Knutson, Clarkfield, 1929-1933
Cherrington, Ruth Miller, Freeborn, 1910
Chizum, Verna, Luverne, 1933-1938
Christenson, Hildegard Amann, New Ulm, 1926

Christiansen, Agnes, Luverne, 1935
Christianson, Norma, Adams, 1932
Christie, Orpha, Windom, 1922
Christofferson, Viola, White Bear Lake, 1927-1929
Clark, N/A, Eden Prairie, 1933-1934
Clark, Genevieve, St. Peter, 1924
Clark, Gladys Dahl, Cromwell, 1930-1933
Clark, Jessie Benn, Hancock, 1924
Clark, Thelma, Sherburn, 1926-1927
Claude, Rose, Delavan, 1927
Clement, Ruth, Proctor, 1921
Clewett, Myrtle, White Bear Lake, 1929
Cochran, G., Grand Rapids, 1929
Cochran, R., Grand Rapids, 1929
Coe, St. Paul Central, 1909
Cole, Anne, Kasota, 1931
Cole, Phyllis, Faribault, 1923
Coleman, Alice Kuhl, Grand Meadow, 1930-1935
Coleman, Frida Kottke, Owatonna, 1919
College, Iva, Bingham Lake, 1927
Collette, Catherine, White Bear Lake, 1929
Collins, Rebecca, Cloquet, 1924-1925
Collison, June, White Bear Lake, 1928
Comstock, Grace O'Donnell, Warroad, 1925
Conat, Elsie Parks, Grand Rapids, 1929
Cone, Avis, Windom, 1922
Cone, C., Windom, 1925
Cone, Jeanette, Windom, 1922-1925
Conway, Mary, Byron, 1924
Cook, Myrtle, Brownton, 1907
Cook, Pat, White Bear Lake, 1920
Cooke, Dot, Rochester, 1921
Coolen, Bigfork, 1933
Copeland, Grace, St. James, 1913-1915
Corbert, Marjorie Borland, Hancock, 1925
Corcoran, Helen, Gaylord, 1923
Cordes, Miriam, Grand Rapids, 1909-1911
Corkery, Margaret, Frazee, 1939
Cormier, Cathryn, Cloquet, 1929-1932
Costigan, Berniece, Owatonna, 1924
Cottrell, Alphreta, Alden, 1911

Couillard, Evelyn, Moose Lake, 1930-1933
Courrier, Joyce, Buffalo, 1929-1931
Cowen, Bessie, Windom, 1924-1926
Cox, Bessie, Minneapolis Central, 1901
Craig, Elsie, Minneapolis Central, 1901
Cramb, Lois, Milaca, 1920
Cramer, Armello, Delano, 1925
Crane, Lucille, Stanley Hall, 1909
Crane, Mildred, Windom, 1913
Crary, Lucile, Northfield, 1904
Crase, Marjorie, Rapidan, 1928
Crosby, Gertrude, Litchfield, 1929
Crowe, Mary, Le Roy, 1939
Cummings Ethel Anderson, Buffalo, 1924
Curran, Pearl, Willmar, 1913-1914
Curran, Thelma, Willmar, 1914
Curtis, Lucile, St. James, 1916
Cuta, Dorothy, Olivia, 1937

D

Dahl, Gladys, Cromwell, 1929-1933
Dahlke, Ruth McCarron, Sherburn, 1924-1927
Dahlman, Alice, Cromwell, 1927
Dahlquist, Anita, Roseau, 1917
Daigneau, Marcia, Austin, 1914
Dalen, Ione, Milan, 1935
Dalen, Junice, Milan, 1935
Danielson, Bernice, Cloquet, 1930-1932
Danielson, Della, Hendricks, 1928
Danielson, Iona, Hendricks, 1928
Danielson, Martha, Litchfield, 1922-1924
Dansmore, Bessie, Minneapolis Central, 1901
Darby, Ethel, Owatonna, 1924
Darrach, Bertha, Proctor, 1923
Daugherty, Pearl, Rapidan 1924
Davidson, Helen Johnson, Ellendale, 1923-1925
Davis, Doris, Proctor, 1923
Davis, Elizabeth, Deer Creek, 1925
Davis, Gladys Young, Milaca 1920
Davis, Sybil, Litchfield, 1915
Davis, Vivian, Proctor, 1918-1920
Davy, Irene, Grand Rapids, 1906-1908

Day, Elsie, Wayzata 1924
Day, Margaret, Wayzata, 1924
De La Hunt, Eleanor, Willmar, 1917-1921
DeLapp, Ruth Norelius, Luverne, 1936-1938
Delke, Litchfield, 1932
DeMotts, Elizabeth McLaughlin, Litchfield, 1902-1905
Dengler, Kathryn, Frazee, 1939
Dennis, Flora Peterson, Fairmont, 1926
DePoe, Martha, Cloquet, 1930
DePoe, Mildred, Cloquet, 1923
Derzai, Amelia, Greenway, 1921
Desparde, Aline, Le Roy, 1939
Determan, Anna Olson, Litchfield, 1902-1905
Deuhn, Mildred, Brownton, 1927
Devine, Sadie, Albert Lea, 1913
Dewey, Louise Just, Rapidan, 1923-1927
Dickerson, Geraldine, Windom, 1913
Dieter, Bessie, Brownton, 1907
Dietz, Rose, Montgomery, 1932
Dixon, M., Cloquet, 1921
Dobias, Northwest School of Agriculture, 1928
Dodds, Kate, Olivia, 1937
Doering, Thusnelda, Gaylord, 1924
Doherty, Mercedes, Grand Meadow, 1933-1935
Donaldson, Muriel, Tracy, 1925
Donavan, Molly, Grand Rapids, 1906-1908
Donehower, Elva, Winona, 1921
Donlin, Clara Mae, Excelsior, 1917-1921
Doran, Lucile, Stillwater, 1924-1926
Dorn, Mary, Jordan, 1932
Dougherty, Margaret, White Bear Lake, 1928
Doyle, Mary, Cambridge, 1928
Draheim, Dorothy, Northome, 1936
Drake, Doris Voorhees, Elkton, 1927-1931
Draxton, Annette, Litchfield, 1931
Drewry, Ruth, Windom, 1918
Drinkall, Verna Warner, Grand Meadow, 1911
Dryden, Ruth, Windom, 1915-1917
Duffy, Mary, Cass Lake, 1924-1926
Dumas, Laura, Cromwell, 1930
DuMoe, Pearl, Two Harbors, 1920
Dunkle, Elsa Jokinen, Toivola, 1933

E

Early, Katherine, Brainerd, 1926
Eastwold, Esther, Le Roy, 1939
Eckert, Belinda Corcoran, Gaylord, 1919-1922
Ecklund, Hazel, Greenway, 1929
Edmonds, Janice, Luverne, 1935
Effertz, Belle Plaine, 1932
Egerton, Lois, Slayton, 1927-1929
Eggena, Alice, Monticello, 1924
Eiden, Paulene Holmes, Sherburn, 1922-1925
Eilers, Lillian, Cloquet, 1921
Eilers, Martha, Cloquet, 1932
Einerson, Dorothy, Olivia, 1937
Ekanger, Viola, Glyndon, 1934
Elletson, Leona, Buffalo, 1931
Ellingson, Edith, Hayfield, 1925
Ellingson, Mildred, Ellendale, 1926
Elliott, Miriam, Grand Meadow, 1932
Ellwood, Stanley Hall, 1909
Elness, Esther Schwerin, Elkton, 1927-1931
Elness, Irene, Windom, 1915-1918
Elsenpeter, Marguerite, Buffalo, 1922-1926
Elsenpeter, Mildred, Buffalo, 1925-1927
Emberg, Ilda, Proctor, 1926
Emberg, Mabel, Proctor, 1919
Emlaw, Ellen, International Falls, 1925
Emmons, Myrtle, Albert Lea, 1910
Eng, Mable, Westbrook, 1930
Engel, Dorothy Lachmiller, Rapidan, 1930
Engels, Dorothy, Winona, 1921
Engfer, Dolores, Belle Plaine, 1930
Engfer, Mildred, Belle Plaine, 1925
Engle, Emily, Blooming Prairie, 1925
English, Jessie, Luverne, 1935
Englund, Evelyn, Starbuck, 1910
Englund, Marjorie, Jeffers, 1928
Engstrom, Marjorie, Le Roy, 1939
Enstrom, Margaret, Greenway, 1929
Eppley, Frances, Rose Creek, 1929
Erbstoesser, Margareta, Braham, 1929
Erickson, Litchfield, 1932
Erickson, Agnes Daberkow, Hancock, 1924

Erickson, Edna, Slayton, 1924
Erickson, Edna, Westbrook, 1930
Erickson, Eunice, Wheaton, 1936
Erickson, Mabel Thompson, Mabel, 1927-1931
Erickson, Oline Christianson, Greenbush, 1924
Erlandson, Mabel, Franklin, 1928
Esser, Katsy-Louise, New Ulm, 1926
Estenson, L., Windom, 1927
Estenson, Mildred, Windom, 1924-1926
Etter, Emily, Brownton, 1922-1925
Erickson, Eva, Duluth, 1924
Eugen, Josephine, Hayfield, 1925
Evenson, Bigfork, 1933
Evenson, Alvilda, Cloquet, 1930
Evenson, Cora, Litchfield, 1924
Evenson, Marguerite, Litchfield, 1931
Everson, Lillian, Cloquet, 1924-1926
Evling, Alice Jensen, Grand Meadow, 1939
Ewald, Leonora, Brownton, 1907

F

Fagerstrom, Dora, North Branch, 1908
Fairbank, Luella, West Concord, 1929
Fallon, Virginia Sandon, Rapidan, 1930
Farmer, Marjorie Crase, Rapidan, 1925-1928
Farrar, Miriam, White Bear Lake, 1921
Faust, Eileen Herron, Thief River Falls, 1920
Felt, O., Willmar, 1924
Fenske, Polly, New Ulm, 1926
Ferguson, Mildred, Proctor, 1923
Fernelius, Joyce Smokestad, Hancock, 1923-1925
Filk, Bertha, Hutchinson, 1920-1922
Findley, Lorraine, Braham, 1928
Finn, Julie, White Bear Lake, 1920
Fish, Florence, Monticello, 1924
Fiss, Mandy, Gaylord, 1907
Fitzgerald, Ethel Carlson, Monticello, 1924
Fitzgerald, Genevieve, Delavan, 1923
Flo, Anna, Rapidan, 1928
Flynn, Mary, Litchfield, 1902-1905
Flynn, Olive, Buffalo, 1931
Foedesi, Helen, Belle Plaine, 1930

Fogelstrom, Edna, Brainerd, 1924-1926
Foley, Irma Malone, Montgomery, 1929-1932
Forsberg, Nadine, Cambridge, 1928
Forsness, Ella, Greenbush, 1924
Fossum, Millie, Zumbrota, 1915
Foster, Harriet, Stillwater, 1924-1927
Foster, Wilner, Lake Crystal, 1932
Fournelle, Janet, White Bear Lake, 1928
Fournelle, Kathryn Schweizer, White Bear Lake, 1924-1927
Fox, Grand Rapids, 1929
France, Helen, White Bear Lake, 1920
Franklin, Iva, Roseau, 1917
Franson, Warroad, 1919
Franti, Vivian, Greenway, 1921
Frantz, Fern, LeSueur, 1921
Frantz, Helen, White Bear Lake, 1920
Fratzke, Helen, Hutchinson, 1922
Frederick, Emma, Grand Rapids, 1909
Freed, Florence Larson, Rose Creek, 1932-1936
Freeman, Gertrude, White Bear Lake, 1922
Fremont, Lillian, Greenway, 1924-1926
Friedrichs, Leila, Rapidan, 1930
Fritzner, Flora, Gaylord, 1907
Froiland, Audrey Moe, Dawson, 1930-1934
Fruth, Gladys Peterson, Grand Meadow, 1930
Fuchs, Ethel Whitcomb, Byron, 1924
Fuchs, Glenna, Montevideo, 1930
Fuller, Myrtle, Blooming Prairie, 1905
Fulton, Margaret, White Bear Lake, 1929
Furtney, Rochester, 1921

G

Gaard, Blanche, Grand Rapids, 1909-1911
Gaffney, Angeline, Greenway, 1924
Gale, Mary Alice, Duluth, 1924
Gale, Susan, Duluth, 1924
Gall, Freida, White Bear Lake, 1914
Gallagher, Luella, South St. Paul, 1925
Gamer, Blanche, Litchfield, 1924
Gandel, Ella Olson, Milan, 1923-1927
Garding, Pat, Paynesville, 1928
Garlie, Alvina, Hancock, 1926

Gay, Grace, Moose Lake, 1930-1933

Gearnes, Alice, Cromwell, 1930-1932

Gearnes, Mary, Cromwell, 1927

Gehrenbeck, Gladys, Monticello, 1924

Geib, Edna, Arlington, 1919-1922

Geib, Sylvia, Arlington, 1923-1925

Gerstenkorn, Clara, Franklin, 1924

Gertejejensen, Adeline, Arlington, 1927

Giantvalley, Eleanor, St. Paul Central 1909

Gibb, Melva, N/A, 1927

Giffney, Francis, Northfield, 1904

Gilmore, Anna, White Bear Lake, 1914

Gilbert, Katherine, Grand Rapids, 1906

Gilbert, Mildred Berg, Grand Meadow, 1930

Gillam, Edna, Windom, 1914-1916

Giroux, Alice, Tracy, 1925

Gjevre, Genevieve, Hancock, 1926

Gleason, Gertrude, Austin, 1914

Glewwe, Mabel, South St. Paul, 1925

Glynn, Alvena Travis, Grand Meadow, 1933-1935

Goar, Clara, Montevideo, late 1920s

Goar, Mary Lou, Montevideo, 1931-1933

Goar, Winifred, Montevideo, 1927-1930

Gochnauer, Hazel, West Concord, 1929

Goeman, Anna, Jeffers, 1928

Goette, Irene, St. Paul Central, 1909

Gole, Pearl, Grand Rapids, 1910

Goltz, Arlene, South St. Paul, 1925

Goodell, Pearl Sizer, Lake Crystal, 1932

Goodman, Edna, Paynesville, 1928

Goodman, Marjorie, Cambridge, 1928

Goodrich, Ruth Kuhn, Grand Meadow, 1930-1932

Gorden, Mildred Wick, Northome, 1934-1937

Goulel, Maria, Warroad, 1923

Grabert, Marcella, Jeffers, 1928

Graham, Janet, Duluth, 1924

Graham, Marjorie, Frazee, 1939

Graham, Min, Rochester, 1921

Grahn, Ruth, North Branch, 1908

Grass, Alice, Blooming Prairie, 1925

Graupman, Lillian, St. Paul Central, 1909

Gravlev, Mary, Bingham Lake, 1927

Gray, Leona Siewert, Byron, 1922-1924; and Dodge Center 1924-1926

Greaves, Gertrude, Northfield, 1904

Greene, Irma, Proctor, 1926

Greene, Leonore, Sherburn, 1926-1927

Greenwald, Norma, Jordan, 1932

Gregg, Florence, Albert Lea, 1917

Grenau, Mildred, South St. Paul, 1925

Grendahl, Agnes, Litchfield, 1927

Grendahl, Carrie, Litchfield, 1929-1931

Grendahl, Myrtle, Litchfield, 1926-1928

Griebler, Pearl, Granite Falls, 1910-1915

Griffin, Helen, Glyndon, 1934

Griffin, Lucille, Glyndon, 1934

Grimes, Clare, Franklin, 1936

Grimes, Lorraine, Franklin, 1927-1929

Grimstad, Tillie, Windom, 1913

Grogan, Cecilia, St. James, 1914

Gronner, Merelle, Underwood, 1937

Gross, Mae Harvey, Grand Meadow, 1938-1939

Groth, Hilda, Brownton, 1927

Groth, Marlys, Cromwell, 1935

Groupman, St. Paul Central, 1909

Grove, Lulu, Stillwater, 1928

Grover, Eileen Maxner, Cromwell, 1930-1933

Groves, Gladys, Aitkin, 1928

Groves, Margie, Stillwater, 1924

Gruetzmacher, Verna, Ellendale, 1924-1926

Gunderson, Helen, Grand Meadow 1930

Guttersen, Jean, White Bear Lake, 1929

H

Haar, Eulalia, Proctor, 1926

Haas, Marian, Frazee, 1939

Haesley, Bernice, Winona, 1928

Hagen, Gladys Dougal, Gaylord, 1920

Hagen, Jeanette, Starbuck, 1930

Hagen, Mary, Brownton, 1926

Hagstgrom, Grace, Stillwater, 1927-1929

Hahnke, Olive, Litchfield, 1927-1930

Haines, Jean, Paynesville, 1928

Hajicek, Mary, Hutchinson, 1920-1922

Hakes, Mantie, Windom, 1922-1926
Halbrook, Viola Funnesan, Rapidan, 1930
Hall, Audrey, Greenway, 1925
Hall, Leila, Northfield, 1904
Hall, Ada Mae, Rose Creek, 1919
Hall, Margaret, Stillwater, 1924-1926
Halley, Lilly, White Bear Lake, 1928
Halloran, Margaret, Belle Plaine, 1930
Halverson, Jeanette, Slayton, 1927-1929
Halverson, Leveta, Kasota, 1931
Halverson, Marion, Hancock, 1926
Halvorson, Laverne, Bingham Lake, 1927
Halvorson, Leone, Adams, 1932
Halvorson, Laverne, Bingham Lake, 1927
Halvorson, Mavis, Milan, 1927
Hamilton, Montevideo, 1927-1930
Hamlin, Lois, Warroad, 1925
Hammer, I., Marshall, 1923
Hamre, Northwest School of Agriculture, 1928
Hancock, Eileen, Greenway, 1929
Handke, Norraine Thorson, Grand Meadow, 1935-1939
Handsaker, Bertha Skartvedt, Lake Benton, 1910
Hanefeld, A., Windom, 1927-1929
Hanefeld, Merle, Windom, 1924-1927
Haney, Margaret, Morgan, 1924
Hangartner, Agnes, Winona, 1928
Hanlon, Kate, Blooming Prairie, 1905
Hanse, Ruth, Cyrus, 1921
Hanson, Adelia, Alexandria, 1915
Hanson, Clara Digre, Hendricks, 1928
Hanson, Eloise, Owatonna, 1919
Hanson, Eva, Rapidan, 1928
Hanson, Hazelle, St. James, 1913-1915
Hanson, Leona Briard, Gaylord, 1920-1924
Hanson, Maisie, LeSueur, 1921
Hanson, Roberta Fritz, International Falls, 1925
Hanson, Velma Hanlin, Roseau, 1917
Hanson, Verna Miller, Rapidan, 1925-1929
Hanson, Grace, Windom, 1917-1919
Hanson, Irene, Windom, 1913
Harding, Grace, Wadena, 1911
Harmann, Harriet, Litchfield, 1926-1928

Harper, Mildred, White Bear Lake, 1927
Harper, Shirley, Delavan, 1926-1927
Harpel, Vivian Randall, Ellendale, 1924-1926
Harrington, Jane, White Bear Lake, 1927-1929
Harris, Bergetta Sorenson, Roseau, 1925
Harrison, Hazel, Elkton, 1927-1931
Hartje, Ida, Austin, 1914
Hartje, Marie, Austin, 1914
Hartley, Mollie, Minneapolis Central, 1901
Hartung, Gertrude, LeSueur, 1921
Hastings, Mary Swanson, Buffalo, 1925-1927
Hatelid, Lillie, Cyrus, 1921
Hatelili, Gina, Grand Rapids, 1908
Haugan, Belle, Neilsville, 1928-1931
Haugen, Lorene, Tracy, 1925
Haugland, Charlotte, Montevideo, 1918
Havel, Rosalia, Montgomery, 1929-1932
Hawes, Cameon, Rapidan, 1924-1927
Hawkins, Erma Jacobson, Rose Creek, 1919
Hawklund, Willmar, 1913
Hayes, Elmyra, Buffalo, 1930
Headland, Maxine, Glyndon, 1934
Hebbel, Helen, Windom, 1914-1917
Hebert, Cloquet, 1925
Hedges, Stella, Milaca, 1920
Hedlund, Myrtle, Olivia, 1906
Heegard, Virginia, Starbuck, 1930
Hegland, Maxine, Roseau, 1925
Hegstad, Ione, Slayton, 1925
Heidman, Ruth, Arlington, 1919-1922
Heilig, Doris, Milaca, 1920
Heineman, Maud, St. Paul Central, 1909
Hellman, Geniveve, Delano, 1923-1925
Henderson, Ella, St. James, 1925
Hendricks, Thelma Stewart, Proctor, 1916-1919
Hendrickson, Florence, North Branch, 1908
Hendrickson, Helen, Cloquet, 1932
Hendrickson, Ida, Northfield, 1904
Hennen, New Prague, 1907
Hennissey, Eva Hanson, Rapidan, 1925-1930
Henry, Marguerite, West Concord, 1929
Hensler, Susanna, Arlington, 1919-1922
Hepfel, Mary, Grand Rapids, 1906-1908

Herbert, Grace, White Bear Lake, 1920
Hermes, Annabel, Grand Rapids, 1908-1910
Herron, Eileen, Thief River Falls, 1920
Hettly, Gunia, Grand Rapids, 1907
Hezs, Gertrude, Montgomery, 1930
Hezs, Mildred, Montgomery, 1930-1932
Hickman, Ethel, Slayton, 1901
Higgins, Gertrude, Arlington, 1929
Hildahl, Shallborg, Greenbush, 1924
Hill, Marie, Cromwell, 1935
Himley, Helen, Montevideo, 1929
Hintikka, Thelma Pellika, Toivola, 1933
Hintz, Helen, New Ulm, 1926
Hochsprung, Helen, Brownton, 1927
Hoershgan, Lucy, Gaylord, 1920
Hoff, Ellen, Dawson, 1931-1934
Hofstad, Jenny, Starbuck, 1930
Hogan, Margaret Zwiener, Blooming Prairie, 1934
Hohn, Mildred Carlquist, Warroad, 1925
Hoiuch, Jessie Line, Cromwell, 1932-1936
Hokeness, Bernice Swenson, Elkton, 1927-1931
Holdahl, Inga, Roseau, 1925
Holden, Helen, Aitkin, 1928
Hollingsworth, Ione, Brainerd, 1924-1926
Holmeid, Bonnie, Luverne, 1935
Holmen, Marion, White Bear Lake, 1929
Holmen, S., White Bear Lake, 1929
Holmes, Florence, Stillwater, 1924
Holmes, Helen, Sherburn, 1925-1927
Holmes, Jean, White Bear Lake, 1929
Holmes, Martha, White Bear Lake,
Holmes, Mary, White Bear Lake, 1924-1927
Holte, Dena, Moose Lake, 1933
Holz, Margaret, St. Peter, 1924
Holzheid, Florence, White Bear Lake, 1919
Homme, Charlotte, Franklin, 1931
Homme, Genevieve, Franklin, 1931
Hompe, Lola, Deer Creek, 1920's
Honi Delores, Franklin, 1936
Hook, Eunice, Slayton, 1924
Hopkins, Lucille, Westbrook, 1930
Hopper, Wilma, Hutchinson, 1922

Hoppke, Violet, Stillwater, 1926-1929
Hoppin, Helen, Northfield, 1903-1905
Hoppin, Myrtle Rabine, Elkton, 1927-1931
Horjem, Anna, Starbuck, 1910
Horman, Gertrude, Brownton, 1923
Horne, Phyllis, Luverne, 1935
Horst, Isabel, Delano, 1925
Horton, Grace, Litchfield, 1929-1931
Horwitz, Ruth, St. Paul Central, 1909
Hosmer, Minneapolis Central, 1899-1901
Howard, Mae, Princeton, 1921
Howe, Iris, Alden, 1911
Howland, Carol, Neilsville, 1928-1931
Huelscamp, Julia, Gaylord, 1922-1924
Huffman, Margaret, Gaylord, 1924
Hulbert, Betty, Eden Prairie, 1931-1934
Hull, Margaret, White Bear Lake, 1919
Houck, Darrel, Cromwell, 1935
Houck, Jessie Line, Cromwell, 1932-1935
Hougan, Luella, Alexandria, 1915
Houle, Mildred, White Bear Lake, 1920-1922
Huebsch, Evelyn Miescke, Rapidan, 1928-1930
Hull, Margaret, White Bear Lake, 1914
Hunter, D., Marshall, 1923
Hursh, Grand Rapids, 1929
Hyovalti, Elsye, Aitkin, 1928
Hyslop, Jeanette, Slayton, 1924
Hyzer, Bertha, Gaylord, 1922-1924

I

Illstrup, Signa, Cromwell, 1932
Ingvalson, Ardella, Blooming Prairie, 1925
Ische, Ella, Belle Plaine, 1930
Isermann, Lenore, Stillwater, 1920-1922
Iten, Betty, Frazee, 1939
Iverson, Kathryn, Grand Meadow, 1936
Iverson, Lillian, Cloquet, 1923-1926

J

Jacobson, Aina, Cambridge, 1928
Jacobson, Anna, Windom, 1918
Jacobson, Muriel, Wheaton, 1933-1937

Jacobson, Pearl Tommerson, Grand Meadow, 1929-1931

Jacobson, Rachel, Franklin, 1928-1931

Jacobson, Ruth Bratrud, Grand Meadow, 1930

Jacobson, Vera, Wheaton, 1933-1936

Jaeger, Edna, West Concord, 1929

Jahns, Theresa Nelson, Grand Meadow, 1931-1935

Jahreiss, Edna, Owatonna, 1919

Jahren, Corinne, Austin, 1914

Jalonen, Narma, Cromwell, 1930-1932

James, Mary, Lake Crystal, 1932

Janes, Lucille, Hayfield, 1925

Janilla, Gertrude, Stillwater, 1929

Janke, Corrine Zimmerman, Brownton, 1921-1926

Janssen, Marie, Sherburn, 1935

Jasken, Anna, Arlington, 1929

Jasperson, Florence, Tracy, 1925

Jeffers, Gladys, Windom, 1915-1917

Jelinek, New Prague, 1907

Jensen, Warroad, 1919

Jensen, Helen, Albert Lea, 1912-1914

Jensen, Irene Angier, Hancock, 1923-1926

Jensen, May, Albert Lea, 1917

Jensen, Orell May Judd, Morris, 1938

Jensen, Violet, Ellendale, 1924-1926

Jerokovsky, Helen, Cromwell, 1935

Jerokovsky, Mary, Cromwell, 1933

Jindra, Julia, Montgomery, 1930

Johnson, Windom, 1927-1929

Johnson, Abbie, Albert Lea, 1910

Johnson, Alice, Cloquet, 1928

Johnson, Arlene, Luverne, 1933

Johnson, Bertha Smith, Bingham Lake 1927

Johnson, Blanche, Stillwater, 1921

Johnson, Charlotte Johnson, Hutchinson, 1920-1922

Johnson, Clara Digre, Hendricks, 1928

Johnson, Doris, Cass Lake, 1926

Johnson, Dorothy, Cloquet, 1927

Johnson, Dorothy, Cromwell, 1935

Johnson, Eldora, Moose Lake, 1933

Johnson, Eleanor, Cromwell, 1935

Johnson, Estelle, Owatonna, 1924

Johnson, Ethel, Litchfield, 1929-1931

Johnson, Evelyn, Braham, 1926-1928

Johnson, Florence, Cloquet, 1930

Johnson, Frances, LeSueur, 1921

Johnson, G., Marshall, 1923

Johnson, Genevieve, Braham, 1926-1928

Johnson, Geraldine Othoudt, Lake Crystal, 1932

Johnson, Gladys, Hancock, 1924

Johnson, Goralene, Braham, 1927-1929

Johnson, Grace, Wheaton, 1936

Johnson, Helen, Rose Creek, 1919

Johnson, Helen, White Bear Lake, 1929

Johnson, Hilda, Greenbush, 1924

Johnson, Jeannette, South St. Paul, 1925

Johnson, Juliann, Blooming Prairie, 1934

Johnson, Leah, St. Peter, 1924

Johnson, Leona, Owatonna, 1924

Johnson, Luella, Stillwater, 1921-1923

Johnson, Mable, Rose Creek, 1929

Johnson, Marjorie Nelson, Preston, 1941

Johnson, Mildred, Buffalo, 1927

Johnson, Myrtle, Willmar, 1921

Johnson, Pearl, Willmar, 1921

Johnson, Ragnhild, Cloquet, 1928

Johnson, Ruth, Mountain Lake, 1923

Johnson, Signa, Slayton, 1928, 1929

Johnson, Signa Niemi, Eveleth, 1915

Johnson, Wilma, Litchfield, 1927-1930

Johnston, Maureen, Buffalo, 1931

Jollymore, Helen, Proctor, 1926

Jones, A., Windom, 1927

Jones, Elizabeth, Luverne, 1933

Jorvig, Edna Linee, Montevideo, 1913

Judd, Frances, Windom, 1922, 1924

Juni, Ann Sticha, New Prague, 1927-1931

K

Kakach, Pauline, Eden Prairie, 1935

Kaldahl, Hanna, Starbuck, 1910

Kalouner, Mildred, Winona, 1928

Kamish, New Prague, 1932
Kamleiter, Anna Milbert, Wayzata, 1922-1924
Kampen, Mary, LeSueur, 1925
Kamunen, Lydia, Cromwell, 1932-1935
Kanne, Windom, 1927-1929
Karon, Esther, Duluth, 1924
Kasel, Catherine, Adams, 1927-1929
Kazunas, Valeria, Cromwell, 1927
Keefe, Kate, Blooming Prairie, 1905
Keeler, Marie Weibeler, Belle Plaine, 1922-1926
Keenan, Nan, Blooming Prairie, 1905
Keesling, Rosella, Wayzata, 1924
Keinitz, Lorraine, Arlington, 1926-1929
Keller, Carrie, Wayzata, 1924
Keller, Louise, Buffalo, 1930
Kelly, Ellen, Franklin, 1924
Kenely, Olive Farwell Peterson, West Central School of Agriculture, 1914
Kent, Catherine, Stillwater, 1920-1923
Kerwin, Wynifred, Franklin, 1928
Kester, Mildred, Underwood, 1937
Kettlewell, Elsie, Windom, 1913
Kiel, G., Marshall, 1924
Kielb, Ruth Erickson, Hancock, 1923-1925
Kienitz, Lorraine, Arlington, 1927-1929
Kieren, Feim, Rochester, 1921
Kiley, Nellie, Ellendale, 1926
Killian, Evelyn, Jordan, 1928-1932
Kilmore, Virginia, Northfield, 1904
King, Marilyn, Frazee, 1939
Kinney, Ruth, Aitkin, 1928
Kinter, Vivian, Greenway, 1920-1924
Kintzi, Frances, Mountain Lake, 1923
Kintzi, Marie, Mountain Lake, 1923
Kirwin, Valeria, Franklin, 1924
Kirwin, Winfred, Franklin, 1929
Kjonaas, Clara, Starbuck, 1930
Klavu, Esther, Cromwell, 1927
Kleven, Ruth Olson, Milan, 1925-1929
Kibert, Edythe, Cromwell, 1930
Kielb, Ruth Erickson, Hancock, 1924
Kidd, Rose, Greenway, 1924, 1925
Kingsley, Blanche Line, Cromwell, 1926-1931

Kinter, Vivian, Greenway, 1920-1924
Kirkeby, Dolores, Clarkfield, 1929-1933
Klanke, Ruth, LeSueur, 1921
Klavu, Esther, Cromwell, 1927
Klemz, Ruth, Cambridge, 1928
Klers, Annabelle, Belle Plaine, 1930
Kleven, Bertha, West Central School of Agriculture, 1914
Kleven, Ruth Olson, Milan, 1925-1929
Klokow, Helen, St. Peter, 1924
Kloos, Belle Plaine, 1932
Knoerr, Anna, Brownton, 1907
Knowles, Norma, Stillwater, 1925-1927
Knowlton, Marguerite, Slayton, 1925
Knudson, Clarine, Westbrook, 1929
Knudson, Evelyn, Westbrook, 1930
Knutson, Dorothy, Slayton, 1928
Knutson, Irene, Herman, 1913
Knutson, Pauline, Rapidan, 1930
Kobe, Otella, Royalton, 1904
Kobe, Theresa, Royalton, 1905
Kodadek, New Prague, 1932
Kohls, Ethel, Brownton, 1926
Kohn, Anna Karppinen, Cromwell, 1926-1930
Kontola, Linda Turkula, Toivola, 1933
Konz, Helen Jolson, Blooming Prairie, 1934
Koops, Florence, Glyndon, 1934
Kopesky, Helen, Eden Prairie, 1933-1935
Kopplin, Ada, Litchfield, 1915
Kording, Alvina, Hayfield, 1925
Kortz, N/A, Eden Prairie, 1930-1931
Koski, Allie, Greenway, 1920-1922
Koski, Alma, Greenway, 1921-1925
Kotek, Marcella, Montgomery, 1931
Kottke, Frieda, Owatonna, 1918
Kraft, Alma, Windom, 1922
Kramer, June Wright, Grand Meadow, 1939
Krantz, Helen, Hutchinson, 1922
Krats, Norma Booth, Big Falls, 1939-1943
Kratz, Lucy, Gaylord, 1920-1925
Kratzke, Irene, Franklin, 1929
Kraus, Evelyn Vales, New Prague, 1927-1930
Krautkremer, Mary, Jordan, 1932

Kremer, Erma, Grand Rapids, 1906
Kremer, Henrietta, Grand Rapids, 1908-1911
Krmpotich, Anna, Greenway, 1924
Kroeger, Lois, Luverne, 1935
Krogh, Mable, Cromwell, 1927
Krueger, Viola, Rapidan, 1930
Krugar, Lydia, North Branch, 1930-1932
Krugar, Verna, North Branch, 1931
Kruger, Virginia Irwin, Belle Plaine, 1920-1924
Kubat, Florence, Montgomery, 1929-31
Kubat, Rosemary, Cromwell, 1932-1933
Kuekler, Frances, North Branch, 1931
Kuka, Mary, Delano, 1924
Kukkola, Evelyn Olson, Underwood, 1934-1937
Kulkey, Delores Bloom, White Bear Lake, 1929
Kurth, Margaret, Winona, 1928
Kussky, Dela, Gaylord, 1920
Kvale, Gen, Rochester, 1921

L

Laaksonen, Irene, Cloquet, 1929-1932
Laaksonen, Lempi, Cloquet, 1923
Lachmiller, Dorothy, Rapidan, 1930
Lachmiller, Elsa, Rapidan, 1928
Lahr, Litchfield, 1932
Lamb, Bernice, Glyndon, 1934
Lamb, Beth, Wayzata, 1924
Lamb, Hazel, Wayzata, 1924
Lamb, Mary, Slayton, 1924
Lambert, Vernette, Royalton, 1905
Lammers, Margaret Ann, Stillwater, 1927-1929
Lampi, Hulda, Moose Lake, 1930-1933
Landin, Margaret, Sherburn, 1926-1927
Lane, Nell, Onamia, 1929-1932
Langan, Anna, Blooming Prairie, 1905
Langeness, Mae, Red Wing Seminary, 1926
Lanpop, Lucille, Windom, 1918
Laphan, Ruth, White Bear Lake, 1914
Larson, Addie De La Hunt Osterberg, Willmar, 1927-1929
Larson, Agnes, Windom, 1917
Larson, Alvera, Franklin, 1936
Larson, Ann Truog, Swanville, 1919-1922
Larson, Ellen, Cromwell, 1927
Larson, Emilia, Cromwell, 1927
Larson, Harriet, Montevideo, 1931
Larson, Helen, Greenway, 1920-1922
Larson, Hulda, Cromwell, 1930-1933
Larson, Ina, Cromwell, 1927
Larson, Lillian, Ellendale, 1924
Larson, Lorayne, Alexandria, 1914
Larson, Lyla, Cromwell, 1933-1935
Larson, Maree, Slayton, 1925
Larson, Marie Hippert, Our Lady of Good Counsel Catholic School, Wilmont, 1920's
Larson, Martha, Cromwell, 1927
Larson, Myrtle, Westbrook, 1930
Larson, Verna, Milan, 1935
Lathrop, Clara, Northfield, 1903
Laughlin, Grace, Zumbrota, 1904
Lavalier, Bernice, Greenway, 1926
Lawrenz, Clara Corcoran, Gaylord, 1919-1922
Lawton, Alice, White Bear Lake, 1925
Leach, Marjorie, Owatonna, 1919
Leach, Muriel, Faribault, 1923
Leahy, Agnes, Blooming Prairie, 1905
Lee, Alice, Northfield, 1904, 1905
Lee, Katherine, Northfield, 1904, 1905
Lehnert, Leila Fredricks, Rapidan, 1930
Lehtinen, Thelma Laine, Toivola, 1933
Lenhardt, Hazel, Litchfield, 1931
LeRoy, Anna Mae, Montevideo, 1932-1935
Lervold, Alice Aanenson, Nielsville, 1928-1931
Lescarbeau, Harriet, Stillwater, 1925
Leusman, Laura, Albert Lea, 1910
Levander, Margaret Bieder, Jordan, 1929-1933
Leversee, Florence Holzheid, White Bear Lake, 1912-1915
Levoy, Ariel, Montevideo, 1918
Lewis, Clara Ferris, Grand Meadow 1911
Lewis, Dorothy, Warroad, 1930
Lewis, Evelyn, Cambridge, 1928
Lewis, Ida, West Central School of Agriculture, 1914
Lewison, Olive, Ellendale, 1925
Lichtenegger, Edna, Gaylord, 1922-1924

Lickteig, Orene Hanson, Blooming Prairie, 1934
Lien, Alvera Knudson, Westbrook, 1924
Lien, Juletta Kasel, Adams, 1927-1929
Lienau, Mabel Siewert, Byron, 1924
Lignell, Bina, Duluth, 1924
Lilja, Dorothy Bradford, Monticello, 1924
Liljeblad, Hjordis, International Falls, 1925
Lillemon, Ruth, Greenbush, 1924
Lindahl, Helen Ohsberg, Willmar, 1924-1928
Lindelien, Bernice Nolan, Grand Meadow, 1911
Linden, Evelyn, International Falls, 1925
Lindmeyer, Dora Krueger, Westbrook, 1924
Lindquist, Ruby, Wheaton, 1937
Lindstrom, Edna Leveau, Milaca, 1920
Line, Blanche, Cromwell, 1930
Linner, Linnea, Litchfield, 1915
Little, Myra Sturges, Buffalo, 1915
Littlefield, Louise Klaehn, Elkton, 1927-1931
Lockwood, Hazel, Alden, 1911
Loehr, Margaret, Stillwater, 1929
Loff, Evelyn, Cloquet, 1926
Lofthus, Mildred, Winthrop, 1920
Logan, Rosemary, Grand Rapids, 1909
Logdahl, Evelyn, Northome, 1936
Loman, Olga, Cambridge, 1928
Long, Edith, White Bear Lake, 1921
Long, Edna, Proctor, 1921
Long, Elsie, White Bear Lake, 1919-1921
Longsvo, Margaret, Cloquet, 1923-1925
Longworth, Litchfield, 1932
Longworth, Geraldine, Litchfield, 1927-1930
Lord, Frieda Zander, Brownton, 1922-1926
Losey, Kathryn Skaran, Grand Meadow, 1939
Lothrop, Sadie, Zumbrota, 1904
Lott, Fannie, Stillwater, 1923
Loveland, V., Windom, 1915
Lowe, Mary, Slayton, 1928
Lowrie, Annabelle, Windom, 1925-1929
Luakkala, Wilma, Cloquet, 1925
Luman, Frances, Hendricks, 1928
Luman, Gertrude, Hendricks, 1928
Lund, Agnes, Windom, 1915
Lund, Eleanor, Two Harbors, 1920
Lund, Hedwig, Stillwater, 1921
Lund, Nedra, Bricelyn, 1928
Lunde, Elvina, Windom, 1916
Lundgren, Fern, Stillwater, 1924
Lundman, Ethel Fenton, Hancock, 1924
Lundmark, Florence Urdahl, Litchfield, 1928-1931
Lundquist, Vella, Willmar, 1921
Lundstrom, Elva, Cromwell, 1927
Lundstrom, Esther, Albert Lea, 1914
Lundstrom, Esther, Alexandria, 1915
Luther, Aileen Just, Rapidan, 1924-1930
Luther, Gertrude, Grand Rapids, 1910
Lynch, Evelyn, Montevideo, 1924
Lynch, Fergus, Montevideo, 1927
Lynch, Katherine, South St. Paul, 1925
Lynn, Luverne, Greenway, 1923

M

Madden, B., Marshall, 1922-1924
Madden, Helen, Arlington, 1927
Maenke, Cordelia, Belle Plaine, 1930
Magnusson, Nanny, North Branch, 1908
Mahoney, Madeline, Proctor, 1921
Malchow, Elsie, White Bear Lake, 1922
Maley, Eva, Zumbrota, 1904
Malm, Ordella, Braham, 1926-1929
Mangseth, Charlotte, Greenway, 1925
Manual, Stachea Mathew, Byron, 1924
March, Ada, Slayton, 1901
March, Cora Mae, Slayton, 1928
March, Marian, Litchfield, 1924-1927
Marholz, Montevideo, 1928-1930
Markland, Bonnie, Starbuck, 1930
Markland, Ione, Starbuck, 1930
Marks, Alice Tiedeman, Elkton, 1927-1931
Marks, Bethel, Westbrook, 1930
Markus, Maris Janssen, Sherburne, 1925
Marquette, Benita, Kasota, 1931
Marquette, Laura, Kasota, 1931
Marschalk, Rosalie, Warroad, 1923
Marshall, Adline, Willmar, 1916
Marshall, H., Marshall, 1922, 1924

Marshall, Nellie, Cass Lake, 1924-1926
Marstad, Tilda, Litchfield, 1931
Martin, Marie, Roseau, 1923
Martin, Ruth Wilson, Montevideo, 1925
Martins, Alice, LeSueur, 1921
Mason, Julia, Montevideo, 1927-1931
Mason, Mildred Hahn, Belle Plaine, 1922-1926
Mathison, Ella, Hayfield, 1925
Mathison, Isabel, Alden, 1911
Mathwig, Adella, Sherburn, 1925
Matkala, Cloquet, 1923-1925
Matteson, Margaret, Cloquet, 1928
Mattfeld, Violet, Frazee, 1939
Mattison, Dorothy, Buffalo, 1926
Mattson, Eloise "Honey" Anderson, Buffalo, 1927-1932
Mattson, Gladys, Braham, 1927
Mattson, Merle, Braham, 1928
Mattson, Myrtle, Adams, 1932
Matyas, L., New Prague, 1932
Matyas, M., New Prague, 1932
Matz, Carolyn Bandelin, Arlington, 1925-1927
May, Bessie, Brownton, 1922-1926
May, Jennie Ellen Sturges, Buffalo, 1926
Mayer, Florence, Greenway, 1924, 1926
McAlpine, Margaret, Grand Rapids, 1906-1911
McArthur, Millicent, Hancock, 1926
McBeath, Helen, Stillwater, 1921
McCarron, Ruth, Sherburn, 1925
McCarthy, Eleanor, Cloquet, 1923-1926
McClellan, Katherine, Wheaton, 1935-1937
McCloud, Leota, Jeffers, 1928
McCormick, Lucy, Grand Rapids, 1909
McCullough, Alta Berg, Grand Meadow, 1933-1935
McCurdy, Catherine, Proctor, 1923
McDougall, Carrie, Royalton, 1904
McDowell, Bette, Olivia, 1937
McFarland, Alice Schroeder, Franklin, 1926-1929
McFarland, Helen, Franklin, 1924
McGarry, Katherine, Brainerd, 1924-1926
McGrath, Margaret, Greenway, 1921
McGraw, Jeannette, Litchfield, 1930-1932

McGraw, Phyllis, Litchfield, 1930-1932
McHugh, Dorothy, Montevideo, 1929
McIllveen, Mildred, North Branch, 1908
McIntyre, Agnes King, International Falls, 1924-1926
McKee, Grand Rapids, 1929
McKee, Ethel, Willmar, 1916
McKeeby, Neva, Greenway, 1922-1925
McKenny, New Prague, 1932
McKenzie, Warroad, 1919
McKenzie, Mildred, Warroad, 1921-1923
McLain, Betty, Cromwell, 1935
McLain, Mae, Cromwell, 1935
McLain, Linda, Stanley Hall, 1909
McNamara, Elenor, Slayton, 1924
McNamara, Rita, Slayton, 1924
McNulty, Irene, South St. Paul, 1925
Mead, M.C., Windom, 1927
Meade, Lucille, Windom, 1925
Medeen, Fern, Braham, 1929
Meehl, I., Marshall, 1923
Meffert, Sarah, Arlington, 1920
Meginnis, Harriet, Winona, 1928
Mehlhorn, Lucille, White Bear Lake, 1927-1929
Meier, Belle Plaine, 1932
Meierbachtol, Marian, Belle Plaine, 1930
Meilke, Eunice, Sherburn, 1925
Mellquist, Eunice, Litchfield, 1924
Mennaga, Hilda Schwanberger, Rapidan, 1925-1927
Merill, Garnet, Warroad, 1925
Mertens, Jordan, 1932
Messer, Ethel Stephenson, Bingham Lake, 1927
Mettel, Agnes, Cass Lake, 1926
Mettel, Lauretta, Cass Lake, 1924-1926
Mettel, Theresia, Wadena, 1910-1912
Meyer, Irene, Arlington, 1926
Meyers, Anna, Delano, 1924
Meyer, Eunice Meikle, Sherburn, 1925
Meyer, Ruth, Arlington, 1923-1925
Michael, Miriam, Brainerd, 1924-1926
Michaelson, Rachel, Montevideo, 1933-1935
Michel, Dorothy, St. James, 1915-1918

Mickelson, Olea, Starbuck, 1930
Mielke, L., Montevideo, 1935
Mielke, Mildred, Montevideo, 1931-1934
Mieschke, Evelyn, Rapidan, 1929-1930
Mikkelson, Evelyn, Milan, 1935
Mikkelson, Margaret, Milan, 1935
Miller, B., Wadena, 1911
Miller, Beryl Regal, Big Falls, 1936-1939
Miller, Clara, Zumbrota, 1915
Miller, Ella Hunte, Freeborn, 1910
Miller, Florence, Princeton, 1921
Miller, Louise, White Bear Lake, 1925-1927
Miller, Lydia, Mountain Lake, 1923
Miller, Verna, Rapidan, 1928
Millimaki, Helen, Moose Lake, 1933
Milton, Florence, St. Paul Central, 1909
Minder, Marjorie, Slayton, 1924-1929
Minion, Lily Redding, Bingham Lake, 1927
Minnick, Charlotte, Wayzata, 1924
Mitchell, Windom, 1925-1929
Mithun, Doris Berg, Buffalo, 1926
Mladek, Ione, Montgomery, 1932
Mlinar, Anita, Eden Prairie, 1931-1932
Mlinar, Ruby, Eden Prairie, 1930-1931
Moats, Letha, Eden Prairie, 1935
Moe, Marilyn, Le Roy, 1939
Moelcher, Belle Plaine, 1932
Moenke, Belle Plaine, 1932
Mohr, Margaret, Stillwater, 1927
Molde, Inez, Montevideo, 1932-1934
Mones, Windom, 1925, 1926
Monroe, Ruth, Montevideo, 1931-1935
Moon, Mary, Slayton, 1901
Mooney, Willmar, 1913
Moore, Jessie, White Bear Lake, 1928
Moorman, Bernice, Arlington, 1926
Moors, Bigfork, 1933
Morearty, Betty, Belle Plaine, 1930
Morgan, Anna, Olivia, 1906
Morgan, G., Windom, 1914-1916
Morgan, Lucille, Proctor, 1923
Morgan, Priscilla, Adams, 1932
Morley, Marion, Jordan, 1928-1932

Morrill, Margaret Hauck, Madison, 1916-1919
Morrison, Ida, Albert Lea, 1910
Mortenson, Lucille, Litchfield, 1929-1932
Mortenson, Ardis, Underwood, 1937
Mortenson, Emma, Blooming Prairie, 1925
Mortenson, Sarah, Litchfield, 1917
Moser, Mildred, Windom, 1921-1924
Mossberg, Dorene, Braham, 1929
Mueller, Arlington, 1926
Mueller, Clara, Arlington, 1926
Munson, Ethel, Willmar, 1921
Murphy, Catherine, Greenway, 1923
Murphy, Ethel, Blooming Prairie, 1905
Murphy, Phyllis, Litchfield, 1931
Musil, Adeline Kamish, New Prague, 1927-1930
Musil, Lorretta, New Prague, 1927-1931
Myers, R., Windom, 1915

N

Naegele, Florence, Stillwater, 1924
Nagel, Cora, Brownton, 1926
Namock, Marjorie Elliot, Grand Meadow, 1931
Nangle, Ethel "Sis" Kalb, Rochester, 1921
Naplin, Northwest School of Agriculture, 1928
Nassif, Mabel, Rapidan, 1930
Nauman, Thelma, Le Roy, 1939
Nebel, Claribelle, Braham, 1927-1929
Nechas, Emily, Eden Prairie, 1933-1935
Nechas, Ruby, Eden Prairie, 1935
Necsik, Rosella Jensen, Grand Meadow, 1933-1936
Negland, Helen, Roseau, 1925
Neidenfuehr, Vernice, Eden Prairie, 1930-1934
Neitzle, Ella, Brownton, 1907
Nelson, Hutchinson, 1922
Nelson, Alma, Deer Creek, 1920's
Nelson, B., Willmar, 1924
Nelson, Beatrice, Milaca, 1920
Nelson, Cora, Litchfield, 1928
Nelson, Dolly, Deer Creek, 1920's
Nelson, E., Marshall, 1922-1924
Nelson, Elizabeth, Litchfield, 1931
Nelson, Esther, Deer Creek, 1920's

Nelson, Esther, Red Wing Seminary, 1926
Nelson, Evangeline, Belle Plaine, 1930
Nelson, Helen, Windom, 1924-1926
Nelson, Hilma, St. James, 1914
Nelson, Irene, Two Harbors, 1920
Nelson, Irene, Zumbrota, 1915
Nelson, Irma, Deer Creek, 1920's
Nelson, Laverne, Litchfield, 1930-1932
Nelson, Lillian, Cyrus, 1921
Nelson, Loretta, International Falls, 1925
Nelson, Magdalene Wellner, Westbrook, 1924
Nelson, Margaret, Winona, 1928
Nelson, Marian, Litchfield, 1928
Nelson, Mary, Tracy, 1911
Nelson, Naomi, Albert Lea, 1917
Nelson, Palma, Proctor, 1921
Nelson, Patty, Luverne, 1935
Nelson, Rosena Kraft, Elkton, 1927-1931
Nelson, Ruth, Blooming Prairie, 1925
Nelson, Ruth Krenz, Hancock, 1924-1926
Nelson, Ruth, LeSueur, 1925
Nelson, Violet, Milan, 1935
Nemitz, DeEtta, Montevideo, 1932
Nemitz, Loretta, Montevideo, 1932-1935
Nemitz, Lorraine, Montevideo, 1933
Nesburg, Harriet, Franklin, 1931
Ness, Northwest School of Agriculture, 1928
Ness, Claryce, Hendricks, 1928
Nessett, Gladys, Delavan, 1923
Neuman, Anna Martinson, Grove City, 1924-1926
Neunsinger, Hazel, Franklin, 1936
Neunsinger, Lucille, Franklin, 1936
Newgard, Helen, Ellendale, 1924
Newhaugen, Agnes, Zumbrota, 1910
Newman, Grace, Stillwater, 1921-1923
Newman, Ruth, Stillwater, 1927-1929
Nichol, Helen, St. Paul Central, 1909
Nicholson, Grace, Montevideo, 1918
Nielsen, Amelia, Alden, 1911
Nilsen, Margaret, Cloquet, 1926
Njus, Esther, Red Wing Seminary, 1926

Njus, Linka, Red Wing Seminary, 1926
Noack, Ruth, Arlington, 1920
Noonan, Florence, Alexandria, 1914
Norbeck, Selma, Red Wing Seminary, 1926
Nordgren, Rhoda, Milan, 1927
Nordquist, Avis, Montevideo, 1934
Nordstrom, Norma, North Branch, 1932
Nordstrom, Olga, Starbuck, 1910
Nordvedt, Irene Slavic, New Prague, 1927-1930
Norlander, Hannah, Roseau, 1925
Norman, Ida, Warroad, 1925
Norman, Louise, Montevideo, 1926
Norstegard, Irene, Westbrook, 1930
Nylander, Viola, Winthrop, 1920
Nyre, Solda, Montevideo, 1929

O

Oakes, Blanche, Princeton, 1921
Ohlen, Shirley, Luverne, 1933
Ohnstad, Idella, Ellendale, 1926
Ohsberg, H., Willmar, 1924
Oie, Ethel, Roseau, 1917
Olander, Sarah Mortenson, Litchfield, 1917
Olesen, Mary, Cloquet, 1920-1923
Olsen, Ellen, Cromwell, 1927
Olson, Belle Plaine, 1932
Olson, Agnes Peterson, Grand Meadow, 1930-1932
Olson, Allie, North Branch, 1908
Olson, Amanda, Litchfield, 1931
Olson, Carol, Belle Plaine, 1930
Olson, Clara, Rapidan, 1923-1927
Olson, Dorothy Quickstad, Grand Meadow, 1935-1936
Olson, Elsa Lachmiller, Rapidan, 1927-1930
Olson, Emily Day, International Falls, 1925
Olson, Evelyn, Braham, 1926-1929
Olson, Evelyn, Montevideo, 1933
Olson, Evelyn, Underwood, 1937
Olson, Helen, Cloquet, 1928
Olson, Lyla, Starbuck, 1910
Olson, Luvane, Moose Lake, 1931

Olson, Margaret, Braham, 1929
Olson, Mildred Wakefield, Grand Meadow, 1930
Olson, Myrtle, Starbuck, 1910
Olson, Orda, Franklin, 1924
Olson, Olga, Windom, 1915-1917
Olson, Ruth, Willmar, 1916
Olson, Willis, Underwood, 1937
O'Connor, Irene, Montevideo, 1933
O'Fallon, Mayme, Hutchinson, 1920-1922
O'Grady, Marguerite, St. Paul Cathedral, 1920's
O'Kane, Barbara, Zumbrota, 1915
O'Leary, Margaret Conroy, Hancock, 1923-1926
O'Malley, Ione, Blooming Prairie, 1925
O'Marro, Lucille, Cloquet, 1923-1926
O'Neil, Mary, Cloquet, 1923
Opheim, Alice, Tracy, 1925
Opjorden, Ella Nelson, Milan, 1927
Opp, Virginia, Wheaton, 1937
Oren, Charlotte, Montgomery, 1931
Ostrom, Joyce, Braham, 1927
Otsea, Mabel, St. James, 1914-1918
Otterness, Pearl, Willmar, 1916
Otterness, Ruby, Willmar, 1921
Otterstrom, Gunhild, Winthrop, 1920
Otto, Josephine, North Branch, 1931
Overby, Harriet, Roseau, 1925
Overby, Signe, Delano, 1925
Overgaard, Anna, Willmar, 1921
Overgaard, O. Willmar, 1924
Oveson, Inez, Roseau, 1917
Owen, Annie, Alexandria, 1915
Owens, Minnie Plumb, Rapidan, 1926-1928
Oyen, Agnes, Hayfield, 1925

P

Packard, Esther, Sherburn, 1925
Packard, Illa, Sherburn, 1925
Packenham, Dorothy, Wheaton, 1937
Paganini, Julia, Stillwater, 1924
Page, Jean, Eden Prairie, 1931-1934
Page, Klenora Olson, Grand Meadow, 1932
Palm, Beatrice, Litchfield, 1927
Palm, Violet, Cromwell, 1930

Palon, Mable, Moose Lake, 1932
Panek, New Prague, 1932
Parr, Maurine, Roseau, 1925
Parrhysius, Adelaide, White Bear Lake, 1922
Parsons, Gladys, Litchfield, 1924
Patnaude, Genevieve, Greenway, 1926
Pattridge, Emma, Tracy, 1911
Paulson, Stella, Zumbrota, 1910
Peacock, Lucille, Windom, 1921-1923
Pearson, Vega, Warroad, 1921-1923
Pease, Ella Mae Bauer, Delano, 1921-1925
Peavey, Grand Rapids, 1929
Pederson, Ethel, Nielsville, 1928-1931
Pedlar, Mildred, Montevideo, 1926
Pehl, Hattie, Mazeppa, 1905
Pehrson, Jeanne, Winona, 1927
Pelinka, Signe Benson, Blooming Prairie, 1925
Pemberton, Beryle, Eden Prairie, 1931-1932
Perkins, Nina, Wadena, 1912
Perrizo, Marceline, Delavan, 1927
Perry, Madeline McDonough, Grand Meadow, 1930
Perry, Olive, Stillwater, 1928
Peters, Bernice, Arlington, 1927
Peters, Doris, Litchfield, 1929-1931
Peters, Dorothy, Sherburn, 1926-1927
Petersen, Georgia, Albert Lea, 1917
Petersen, Lillie, St. Peter, 1924
Petersen, Pearl, Albert Lea, 1917
Peterson, Windom, 1926
Peterson, Alma, Bricelyn, 1928
Peterson, Ardis, Grand Meadow, 1936
Peterson, Audrey, Dawson, 1931-1934
Peterson, Bernice, Buffalo, 1931
Peterson, Bessie, Litchfield, 1903
Peterson, Blanche Heiny, Litchfield, 1902-1905
Peterson, Daniella Thompson, Grand Meadow 1939
Peterson, Dorothy Washburn, Rapidan, 1930
Peterson, Edith, Proctor, 1923
Peterson, Elene, Blooming Prairie, 1934
Peterson, Elsie, Tracy, 1925
Peterson, Evelyn Fox, Warroad, 1925

Peterson, Frances, Litchfield, 1932
Peterson, Genevieve, Stillwater, 1921-1923
Peterson, Goralene Johnson, Braham, 1927-1929
Peterson, Gretchen Harvey, Grand Meadow, 1930-1932
Peterson, Harriet, Litchfield, 1928-1932
Peterson, Hattie, Cloquet, 1932
Peterson, Helen, North Branch, 1932
Peterson, Helvi, Cloquet, 1923
Peterson, Ila, Litchfield, 1927
Peterson, Irene Wellner, Westbrook, 1924
Peterson, Joan, Litchfield, 1928-1932
Peterson, Josephine, Rose Creek, 1929
Peterson, Laura, White Bear Lake, 1922
Peterson, Lois, Stillwater, 1921-1923
Peterson, Lola, Slayton, 1927-1929
Peterson, Lorraine, North Branch, 1932
Peterson, Mable, Willmar, 1921
Peterson, Magel, Wheaton, 1936
Peterson, Margaret Forbes, Grand Meadow, 1932
Peterson, Marion, Bricelyn, 1928
Peterson, Mattie, St. James, 1913-1916
Peterson, Selma, Roseau, 1923
Peterson, Vernette, Moose Lake, 1929-1932
Peterson, Viola, Starbuck, 1930
Peterson, Winifred Goodsell, Grand Meadow, 1939
Petran, Ruth, Albert Lea, 1917
Pexa, Bernice Malone, Montgomery, 1926-1930
Pfeiffer, Arliz, Freeborn, 1939
Phillips, Lorna Lochmiller, Rapidan, 1923-1927
Phillips, M., Bingham Lake, 1927
Pickruhn, Alma, Buffalo, 1924
Pierce, Vera, Tracy, 1911
Pierson, Freda, Northome, 1936
Piper, Avis, Jeffers, 1928
Ploof, Phyllis, Franklin, 1931
Plumb, Mabel, Rapidan, 1928
Plumb, Minnie, Rapidan, 1928
Pogue, Grand Rapids, 1929
Point, Gladys, Slayton, 1923-1925
Pollard, Kathryn, Cloquet, 1932

Porath, Cleota, Delavan, 1927
Porish, Esther, Mountain Lake, 1923
Post, Irma Nelson, Deer Creek, 1924-1929
Post, Mildred, White Bear Lake, 1922
Potter, Beulah, Cass Lake, 1925
Pouliat, Catherine, Buffalo, 1931
Powell, Georgia, Grand Rapids, 1906-1908
Preston, Sadie, Minneapolis Central, 1901
Price, Edith Peterson, Grand Meadow, 1935
Price, Kathryn, Tracy, 1911
Proeschel, DeVera Bratrud, Grand Meadow, 1935-1939
Purdie, Lorna, Freeborn, 1910
Purra, Hilda, Greenway, 1929
Purra, Saima, Greenway, 1924

Q

Quade, Arlene, Le Roy, 1939
Quade, Maxine, Le Roy, 1939
Quale, Myrtle, Adams, 1932
Quam, Ada, Windom, 1921-1923
Quammen, Margaret, Cyrus, 1921
Quast, Leona, Arlington, 1926
Quick, Doris, Proctor, 1919-1921
Quigley, Ruby Strand, Rapidan, 1924-1926

R

Rabine, Elna Rubin, Elkton, 1927-1931
Radosevich, Rose, Greenway, 1926
Radosevich, Viola, Greenway, 1925-1929
Rafinski, Mary, Greenway, 1929
Raisanen, Zenya, Greenway, 1920-1922
Ramsey, Mabel, White Bear Lake, 1919-1921
Ramsey, Ruth Kelley, Grand Meadow, 1931
Ranfranz, Grand Rapids, 1929
Rappold, Katie, Proctor, 1917
Rasmussen, Nora Johnson, 1925-1928
Rathjens, M., Marshall, 1924
Rathlisberger, Gladys, Slayton, 1928
Raub, Doris Councelman, Rapidan, 1929
Raul, Margaret, Delano, 1924
Rawlings, Florence, Tracy, 1925

Rawn, Ruth DeLaHunt, Willmar, 1912-1914
Ray, Erma, Hancock, 1923-1926
Reagan, Monica, Rose Creek, 1929
Reagan, Muriel, Rose Creek, 1929
Rector, Una, Deer Creek, 1920's
Reedstrom, Lydia Kriel, Rapidan, 1924
Reedstrom, Stella Johnson, Rapidan, 1924
Regan, Maxine, Le Roy, 1939
Rehder, Ruth, Red Wing, 1917
Reif, Florence, White Bear Lake, 1914
Reilly, Laura, Northfield, 1903
Reilly, May, Gaylord, 1923
Reinhold, Helen, Cromwell, 1935
Reisrud, Agnes, West Central School of Agriculture, 1914
Revier, Mary, Franklin, 1927-1931
Reuter, Gladys, Brainerd, 1924-1926
Reynolds, Grace, Cromwell, 1927
Rhoades, Evelyn, Montevideo, 1927-1930
Rice, Margaret, Roseau, 1925
Richards, Violet, Glyndon, 1934
Richman, Marg, Rochester, 1921
Riechenbach, Helen, Arlington, 1926
Rieckert, Agatha, Arlington, 1925-1927
Rieder, Esther, Delano, 1925
Rieke, Grace, Franklin, 1927-1929
Rielly, Mildred, Litchfield, 1929
Riep, Anna, Delano, 1924
Rine, Lola, Cloquet, 1923
Ripka, Emily, Owatonna, 1924
Risdon, Frances, Litchfield, 1927
Rise, Helen, Roseau, 1923
Robarge, "Babe" Vivian, Buffalo, 1925-1927
Robasse, Delores, Buffalo, 1929-1931
Roberts, Warroad, 1919
Roberts, Grace, Windom, 1913
Robertson, Faith, Stillwater, 1925-1928
Robertson, Grace, Alden, 1911
Robinson, Rose, West Concord, 1929
Rodekuhr, Clara, Deer Creek, 1920's
Rodekuhr, Violet, Deer Creek, 1920's
Rodosevich, Rose, Greenway, 1925
Roemer, Bernice, Crookston, 1910

Roepke, Mildred Lofthus, Winthrop, 1918-1921
Roetman, Agnes, Slayton, 1924
Rogers, Edith Gilman, Grand Meadow 1911
Rogers, Frances, Windom, 1922
Rogers, Grace, North Branch, 1908
Rohlfing, Evelyn, White Bear Lake, 1921
Rohlfing, Naomi, White Bear Lake, 1920-1922
Rolf, Nora, St. James, 1915-1918
Roll, Gerdy, Bingham Lake, 1927
Root, Inez, Morgan, 1924-1929
Rorman, Bernice, Delavan, 1923
Rose, Carlene, Winona, 1928
Rosendahl, Marjorie, Eden Prairie, 1931-1935
Rosenquist, Luverne, Litchfield, 1927-1930
Rossetter, Ada, Proctor, 1920
Rossing, Daphne, Westbrook, 1930
Roth, Cleone, Cass Lake, 1925
Roth, Winnifred, Buffalo, 1930
Rowo, Lillian, Red Wing Seminary, 1926
Ryan, Edith, Proctor, 1918-1920
Ryan, Eileen, Arlington, 1920
Ryan, Lucille, Windom, 1925
Ryan, Marie, Arlington, 1923-1925
Rydland, Leora, Franklin, 1936

S

Sachs, Anna, Windom, 1918
Salmoiraghi, Lucy, Stillwater, 1921
Salmore, Dorothy, Stillwater, 1927-1929
Sampson, Beulah, Franklin, 1936
Sampson, Quanita, Franklin, 1936
Sandberg, Florence Akre, Warroad, 1925
Sandborn, Eileen, Paynesville, 1928
Sander, Ruth, Arlington, 1929
Sandon, Virginia, Rapidan, 1930
Sandstrom, Carol, Cloquet, 1932
Sandstrom, Martha Sorvari, Toivola, 1933
Sansome, Lorraine Bourquin, White Bear Lake, 1924-1927
Sarasin, Clara, Northome, 1936
Sargent, Leona Just, Rapidan, 1930
Sather, Elaine, Litchfield, 1924
Sathers, Mildred, Proctor, 1919-1921

Sauer, Eleanor, Stanley Hall, 1909
Savela, Saima Saari, Toivola, 1936-1938
Sawdey, Gwen, Le Roy, 1939
Sawyer, Marjorie, Winona, 1921
Schaub, Lila, Winona, 1927
Schauer, Ruth, Arlington, 1929
Scheflo, Alpha, Starbuck, 1930
Scheibe, Elinore, Cloquet, 1923-1926
Scheibe, Gladys, Cloquet, 1921
Schell, Leone Revier, Morton, 1929-1932
Schellenberg, Lillian, Slayton, 1927-1929
Schimnoski, Verna, Jeffers, 1928
Schissel, Inez Uglum, Adams, 1927-1932
Schlaet, Elenora, Faribault, 1923
Schlueter, Edwina, Winona, 1927
Schmalz, Lucyle, Westbrook, 1930
Schmidt, Gretchen, St. Peter, 1924
Schmitz, M., Willmar, 1924
Schneider, Ceil Stier, Grand Meadow, 1934-1938
Schneider, Ethel, Wheaton, 1935-1937
Schneider, Louise, Adams, 1932
Schneider, Margaret, Adams, 1932
Schneider, Minnie, LeSueur, 1921
Schnobrich, Ella, Gaylord, 1907
Schochet, Sara, Faribault, 1923
Schomberg, Charlotte, Northome, 1936
Schoniger, Gertrude, Winona, 1921
Schoregge, Iva, Olivia, 1906
Schottenbauer, Emily, Tracy, 1925
Schrier, Margaret, Blooming Prairie, 1925
Schrier, Marie, Blooming Prairie, 1925
Schroeder, Alice, Franklin, 1926-1929
Schroeder, Bertha, Franklin, 1928
Schroeder, Clara, Olivia, 1906
Schroeder, Esther, Franklin, 1928-1931
Schroeder, Marie, Franklin, 1936
Schrom, Kathryn Aldrich, Frazee, 1939
Schueler, Elsie, Gaylord, 1923
Schultz, Alma, Stillwater, 1925
Schultz, E., White Bear Lake, 1929
Schultz, Esther, Faribault, 1923
Schultz, Harriet Hahn, Belle Plaine, 1923
Schultz, Josephine, Sherburn, 1925

Schultz, Minnie, Montevideo, 1918
Schuster, Dorothy Schultz, Freeborn, 1924-1927
Schwartz, Blossom Renneke, Le Sueur, 1921
Schwerin, Edna, Elkton, 1927-1931
Scribner, Marcia, Northome, 1936
Scott, Irene, Franklin, 1931
Seashore, Helen, Duluth, 1924
Secker, Violet, Greenway, 1929
Sederberg, Dorthey, North Branch, 1931
Sederstrom, Elva, Litchfield, 1926-1928
Sederstrom, Muriel, Litchfield, 1928-1932
Seely, June, Windom, 1913
Seidlitz, Lucille, Winona, 1921
Seim, Corinne, Cloquet, 1921
Seltun, Ennis, Northfield, 1904
Sery, New Prague, 1907
Severinson, Amy, Willmar, 1912-1914
Seward, F., Marshall, 1924
Sexton, Margaret, Buffalo, 1924
Sexton, Ruth, Litchfield, 1915
Shambour, Anna, New Prague, 1928-1930
Sharkey, Marietta Moore, Belle Plaine, 1923-1926
Shaughnessy, Rosemary, Belle Plaine, 1930
Sheean, Sylvia, Cloquet, 1923-1925
Sheerin, Olga, Slayton, 1924
Sheffeld, Doris, Marshall, 1919-1923
Sheldon, Katherine, Brownton, 1923
Sherman, Grand Rapids, 1929
Sherman, Florence, Franklin, 1924
Shields, Jean, White Bear Lake, 1929
Shinn, Kathryn Meade, Browns Valley, 1926-1930
Shirk, Helen, Faribault, 1923
Shisler, Susie, Aitkin, 1928
Shoultz, Pauline, Litchfield, 1931
Shorba, N/A, Eden Prairie, 1933-1934
Sickman, Grace Peterson, Westbrook, 1924
Siel, Cora Meidl, New Ulm, 1926
Sievers, Amelia, Winona, 1921
Silliman, Windom, 1929
Silliman, Evelyn, Windom, 1922
Siltanen, Cloquet, 1925

Simon, Monica Janda, New Prague, 1925-1930
Simon, Ruth, Jordan, 1932
Simpson, Hilma, Wheaton, 1935-1937
Sinclair, Doris, Stillwater, 1920-1922
Sizer, Pearl, Lake Crystal, 1932
Sjoberg, Julia, Royalton, 1905
Sjostrom, Margaret, Northome, 1936
Skallman, A, Bigfork, 1933
Skaran, Opal, Grand Meadow, 1931-1935
Skelton, Dorothy, Moose Lake, 1931-1933
Skewes, Mildred Pettis, Rapidan, 1923-1927
Skieriski, F., Marshall, 1924
Skjod, Alice, Braham, 1927-1929
Skjod, Clarice, Braham, 1927
Skjod, Lucille, Braham, 1929
Skurtvold, Stella, Red Wing Seminary, 1926
Skuse, Lucille, Tracy, 1925
Slaba, Dorothy Meinhard, Sherburne, 1925
Sletkolen, Thea Stay, Montevideo, 1933-1935
Slocum, Helen, Stillwater, 1923-1927
Slocum, Phyllis, Stillwater, 1928, 1929
Smeby, Theodora, Albert Lea, 1914
Smedstad, Ethel, Starbuck, 1930
Smith, Beatrice, Bingham Lake, 1927
Smith, Bertha, Cloquet, 1924-1926
Smith, Elmira, Aitkin, 1928
Smith, Gladys, Brainerd, 1924-1926
Smith, Luella, Litchfield, 1922-1924
Smith, Mabel, Minneapolis Central, 1901
Smith, Mabel Nassif, Rapidan, 1930
Smith, Margaret, Greenway, 1922
Smith, Marian, Stillwater, 1926
Smith, Mildred, Willmar, 1914
Smith, Myrtle, Windom, 1917
Smith, Rosalyn, Cass Lake, 1926
Smith, Ruth, Bingham Lake, 1927
Snook, Jeffers, 1928
Snyder, Grand Rapids, 1929
Snyder, Doris, Hancock, 1926
Snyder, Ethel, Wheaton, 1935-1937
Soggie, L., Windom, 1924-1927
Soggie, M.M., Windom, 1926-1929
Solberg, Ina, Blooming Prairie, 1905

Solem, Arlene, Windom, 1917-1922
Solheim, Leola Huseby, Milan, 1927
Solvie, Esther, Cyrus, 1921
Solvie, Marion Halvorson, Hancock, 1925-1928
Solvie, Vivian, Cyrus, 1921
Sommer, Erma, Hancock, 1925
Sorenson, Willmar, 1913
Sorvari, Lillian Lahti, Toivola, 1933-1937
Sotaaen, Annie, Windom, 1921-1925
Soukila, Sally, Cromwell, 1927
Spaetgnes, Zoe, LeCenter, 1926-1930
Spanton, Dorothy, Winona, 1928
Spaude, Marie, Gaylord, 1922-1924
Spearman, Laura, Proctor, 1918-1921
Spencer, Ruth, Stillwater, 1921-1923
Spencer, Harriet, Wayzata, 1924
Spenser, Ruth, Stillwater, 1921-1923
Sperl, Ann, New Ulm, 1926
Sperry, Grace, Willmar, 1914
Sperry, Maxine, Owatonna, 1924
Sperry, Windom, 1926-1928
Spreck, Dorothy Tardiff, White Bear Lake, 1926-1928
Spreiter, Carmen, West Concord, 1929
Stadhem, Agnes, Albert Lea, 1913
Stanley, Edna, Slayton, 1928
Stark, Mary Nagel, Buffalo, 1924
Stary, Cassie, Zumbrota, 1915
Stay, Thea Sletkolen, Montevideo, 1931-1935
Stebens, Erma Christ, Westbrook, 1924
Steer Evelyn, Belle Plaine, 1930
Steffer, Sophie, Arlington, 1927
Steiner, Louise, Winona, 1921
Stempf, Dorothy, Glyndon, 1934
Stenke, Alice, Mountain Lake, 1923
Stenson, Ruth, Starbuck, 1910
Stephens, Jeanette, North Branch, 1932
Stephens, Katherine, North Branch , 1932
Stephens, Marjorie, North Branch, 1930-1932
Stephenson, Constance Torgrimson, Grand Meadow, 1932
Stevens, Grand Rapids, 1929
Stevens, Orpha, Slayton, 1925

Stewart, Colleen, Proctor, 1926
Stewart, Flora, Proctor, 1926
Stewart, Marjorie, Proctor, 1923
Stewart, Ruth, Proctor, 1919-1921
Stewart, Thelma, Proctor, 1919
Stiles, Adelaide, Delavan, 1923
Stipka, Annie, Proctor, 1926
Stoefan, Martha, Arlington, 1919-1922
Stolberg, Mildred, Cloquet, 1923
Stoner, Litchfield, 1932
Stonelake, Alice, Franklin, 1924
Storm, Alta, Brainerd, 1924-1926
Stowell, Margaret, Gaylord, 1922
Strand, Edith, Two Harbors, 1920
Strand, Eleanor DeLaHunt, Willmar, 1917-1921
Strand, Margaret, Albert Lea, 1917
Street, Beth, Northfield, 1904
Street, Edith, Northfield, 1904
Streich, Ida, Brownton, 1907
Streich, Goldie, Brownton, 1923
Stroberg, Dorothy, Cambridge, 1928
Stroble, Beatrice, Delavan, 1927
Stroeh, Lorraine, Luverne, 1935
Strom, Ethel, Cloquet, 1929-1932
Stromberg, Winifred Swanson, Milaca, 1919-1921
Struxness, Verna Dalen, Milan, 1927
Stufferd, Bernice, Hendricks, 1928
Stuhre, Emma Flynn, Buffalo, 1927
Stussy, Lorraine, Mantorville, 1930's
Styles, Elsie, Willmar, 1916
Sullivan, Aurelia, Belle Plaine, 1930
Summers, Harriet, Rapidan, 1929
Sundberg, Helen, Braham, 1927
Sundem, Marvel, Montevideo, 1932-1935
Sunder, Evelyn, Two Harbors, 1920
Sunderman, Lucille, Windom, 1923-1925
Svee, Bernice, Zumbrota, 1915
Svee, Constance, Zumbrota, 1910
Svee, Lena, Zumbrota, 1910
Swanstrom, Ruth, Greenbush, 1924
Swartz, Carol, Jeffers, 1928

Swedelius, Letta Farnum, Paynesville, 1926-1929
Sweeney, Mabel, Arlington, 1923-1925
Sweeney, Ruth, Arlington, 1920
Sweno, Doris, Milan, 1935
Swensen, Stella, Red Wing Seminary, 1926
Swenson, Charlotte, Starbuck, 1909-1911
Swenson, Ella, Jeffers, 1928
Swenson, M., Windom, 1929
Swenson, Ruth, North Branch, 1930-1932

T

Tagtgren, H. Bigfork, 1933
Tagtgren, V. Bigfork, 1933
Takala, Madeline Niemela, Toivola, 1933
Takle, Clarine Knudson, Westbrook, 1929
Tallman, Esther, Willmar, 1912-1914
Tasler, Lillian, Jeffers, 1928
Taylor, Alice Pulver, Rose Creek, 1919
Taylor, Marjorie, Alexandria, 1915
Tedford, Estelle, Cass Lake, 1924-1926
Teich, Lizzie, Brownton, 1907
Templin, Minnie, Buffalo, 1924
Templin, Vera Ilstrup Learned, Buffalo, 1922-1926
Tenjum, E., Windom, 1915
Terlinden, Helen, Grand Meadow, 1933-1935
Terlinden, Lillian, Grand Meadow, 1935
Tessen, Cora, West Central School of Agriculture, 1914
Tetu, Bernadene, Cloquet, 1932
Thake, A., Windom, 1925-1929
Theis, Lillian, Arlington, 1923-1925
Therrien, Margarite, White Bear Lake, 1921
Thiessen, Ann, Mountain Lake, 1923
Thomas, LaVon, Montevideo, 1932
Thomas, Lucille, Greenbush, 1924
Thompson, Hutchinson, 1921
Thompson, Eleanor, Faribault, 1923
Thompson, Gladys, Slayton, 1925
Thompson, Lillie, Bricelyn, 1928
Thompson, Lucille, Windom, 1921-1924

Thompson, Margaret Huffman, Gaylord, 1919-1924
Thompson, Marjorie, Albert Lea, 1912-1914
Thompson, Myrtle, Ellendale, 1924
Thompson, Nannie, Slayton, 1901
Thompson, Ruth, Faribault, 1923
Thompson, Ruth Bales, Blooming Prairie, 1934
Thompson, Viola, Buffalo, 1930
Thompson, Violet, Bricelyn, 1928
Thomson, Hazel, Austin, 1914
Thomtom, Clara, Montevideo, 1927-1931
Thornblad, Evelyn, Cloquet, 1927-1930
Thoreson, Margarethe Romo, Red Wing Seminary High School, 1921
Thorpe, Dorothy, Cloquet, 1932
Thorson, Loraine, Grand Meadow, 1936
Thorson, Marian, Adams, 1932
Throndson, Adeline, Underwood, 1937
Throndson, Hazel, Underwood, 1937
Thune, Clara, Albert Lea, 1910
Thurley, Elsie, Winona, 1928
Tierney, Margaret, Arlington, 1923-1925
Tietema, Ethel, Slayton, 1924
Timm, Clara, Arlington, 1919-1925
Timm, Deloris, Arlington, 1926
Timm, Edna, Arlington, 1925-1927
Timm, Elinore, Arlington, 1922
Timm, Helen, Arlington, 1926
Timm, Laura, Gaylord, 1907
Tingley, Helen, Albert Lea, 1910
Tinquist, Lily Parks, Grand Rapids, 1927-1929
Titus, Alzada, Greenway, 1929
Tjentland, Ivah Pietz, Bingham Lake, 1927
Todnem, Mary Thomas Chadwick Dickmeyer, Mankato, 1920-1923
Tok, Anna, Greenway, 1921-1924
Tok, Rose, Greenway, 1922-1925
Tok, Yentka, Greenway, 1924-1926
Toland, Genevieve, Ellendale, 1924-1926
Toland, Mary, Cloquet, 1929-1932
Tollefson, Esther, Montevideo, 1918
Tollefson, Lillian, Starbuck, 1930
Tomsche, Marie, Owatonna, 1919

Tonkin, Mary Champlin, Lake Crystal, 1932
Tonning, Hildur Lundeen, Litchfield, 1902-1905
Torgrimson, Phyllis Rother, Grand Meadow, 1929-1931
Torp, Christine, Tracy, 1925
Tostenrud, Edna, Litchfield, 1924
Totman, N/A, Windom, 1926
Trask, Grand Rapids, 1929
Trask, Iva, Brainerd, 1924-1926
Travis, Gladys Nelson, Grand Meadow, 1929-1932
Trboyevich, Dorothy, Greenway, 1929
Treadwell, Beatrice, Crookston, 1910
Tregillis, Amy, Greenway, 1924-1926
Trembley, Esther, Delavan, 1923
Trimbo, Arlington, 1926
Trimbo, Mae, Arlington, 1929
Trobec, Luretta Parker, Morgan, 1924
Trooian, Alyce Ness, Hendricks, 1928
True, Pauline Knutsen, Rapidan, 1928-1930
Tuckey, Margaret, Eden Prairie, 1930-1931
Tufte, Pearl Hanson, Elkton, 1927-1931
Tupper, Mildred, St. Paul Central, 1909
Turner, Edna, Brainerd, 1924
Tyndall, Alice, Grand Rapids, 1905-1908
Tyndall, Hazel, Grand Rapids, 1905-1908

U

Uhlhorn, Hertha, St. James, 1916-1918
Ulrich, Louise, Stillwater, 1922-1924
Ulven, Florence, Adams, 1932
Undlin, Ella, Milan, 1935
Upgren, Gladys, Moose Lake, 1930
Upgren, Ruth, Moose Lake, 1931

V

Vanasek, New Prague, 1907
Van Buren, Hattie, Minneapolis Central, 1901
Van Camp, Margeurite, Moose Lake, 1932
Van Cura, Christine, Hancock, 1924
Van Fleet, Marcella, Montevideo, 1932
Vande Velde, Ruth, Luverne, 1935
Vandyke, Ouida, Wadena, 1910-1912

Van Voorhis, Marion, White Bear Lake, 1929
Venables, Marguerite, Winona, 1928
Venoss, Margaret, N/A, 1914
Vibert, Jean, Cloquet, 1928
Vibert, Margaret, Cloquet, 1930
Viker, Northwest School of Agriculture, 1928
Viker, Dorothy Iversen, Hayfield, 1925
Vikesland, Luello, Red Wing Seminary, 1926
Vitha, Evelyn, Montgomery, 1929-1932
Vitha, Helen, Montgomery, 1932
Vold, Neda, Jeffers, 1928
Volkart, Lorrie, Le Roy, 1939
Von Eschen, Violet, Arlington, 1929
Von Lehe, Frieda, LeSueur, 1921
Von Lehe, Helen, LeSueur, 1925
Voss, E., St. James, 1915

W

Wahlberg, Clara Warroad, 1922
Wahlberg, Esther, Warroad, 1923
Wakefield, Irene Zweiner, Blooming Prairie, 1934
Waldhoff, Adelaide, North Branch, 1908
Waldron, Phyllis, Montevideo, 1934
Wales, Minneapolis Central, 1901
Walker, Elinor, Stillwater, 1929
Wall, Alma, Albert Lea, 1914
Wall, Florence, Brownton, 1926
Wall, Hazel, Brownton, 1925-1927
Wallace, Vera, Windom, 1921-1924
Walle, Alice, Nielsville, 1928-1932
Walleen, Vonnie, Olivia, 1937
Walm, Ruth, Jordan, 1932
Ware, Mildred, 1924
Washa, Eunice Wolfe, Montgomery, 1926-1932
Washa, Harriet, Montgomery, 1931
Washburn, Dorothy, Rapidan, 1930
Wasson, Katherine, Duluth, 1924
Watts, Marian, Cass Lake, 1926
Wayne, Iris, Ellendale, 1923-1926
Webber, Martha, White Bear Lake, 1919-1922
Webster, Dora, Winthrop, 1920
Webster, Genevieve, St. Peter, 1924

Wedum, Helen, Alexandria, 1914
Wegener, Laila Turkola, Toivola, 1933
Weibeler, Agnes, Belle Plaine, 1930
Weimer, Ercel, Cromwell, 1932
Weinrebe, Elsie Schmalz, Westbrook, 1924
Weir, Dorothy, South St. Paul, 1925
Weisbrod, Cora Carlson, Dawson, 1926
Weischelbaum, Blanche, Olivia, 1906
Weiser, Helen, Windom, 1918
Welch, Ella, Arlington, 1923-1925
Wellman, Myrtie, Windom, 1925
Welshons, Dorothy, Stillwater, 1921
Weld, Constance, Slayton, 1927-1929
Welter, Ida Picha, New Prague, 1927-1931
Welkele, Armella, Buffalo, 1924
Wendt, Edith, Winona, 1928
Wendtland, Miranda, Paynesville, 1928
Werges, Myrtle, Gaylord, 1920
Wermerskirchen, Veronica, St. James, 1913-1915
Werner, Martha, Litchfield, 1915
West, Gertrude, Brownton, 1907
Westby, Marcella, Moose Lake, 1930
Westerman, Catherine, Montgomery, 1929-1932
Westhoff, Belle Plaine, 1932
Westholm, Emma Lu, Moose Lake, 1929-1932
Westholm, Marie, Moose Lake, 1930-1932
Weston, Cloquet, 1925
Westrum, Beaulah, Albert Lea, 1912-1914
Wetter, Kay Nolan, Brainerd, 1924-1928
Wheeler, Bernice Halverson, Delavan, 1926-1930
Wheeler, Grace, Delavan, 1923
Whitcomb, Lucile Parker, Byron, 1924
White, Mae Beseman, Cromwell, 1930-1932
White, Marguerite, Cloquet, 1923
Whiting, Vera, Kasota, 1931
Wicher, Rose Robinson, West Concord, 1925-1929
Wick, Beulah O., Bigelow, 1926-1929
Wick, Mildred, Northome, 1936
Wick, Myrl, Cloquet, 1930
Widmer, Louise, Belle Plaine, 1930
Wiedenmann, Naomi, Gaylord, 1923

Wiegle, Rose, Grand Rapids, 1906-1908
Wiiret, Helvi, Cloquet, 1923-1925
Wiita, Harriet, Aitkin, 1928
Wilkes, Emilene, North Branch, 1908
Wilkinson, Ruth, Owatonna, 1924
Williams, Cora, Grand Rapids, 1906-1908
Williams, Helen Fisher, White Bear Lake, 1926-1928
Wills, A., Windom, 1928
Wilson, Dorothy, Montevideo, 1927-1930
Wilson, Hazel, International Falls, 1925
Wilson, Lavina, Northfield, 1904
Wilson, Mildred, West Concord, 1929
Windhorst, Flora, Olivia, 1906
Wing, Alice, Stanley Hall, 1909
Winje, Norma, Milan, 1935
Winters, Cora, Arlington, 1923-1925
Wise, Clare, Slayton, 1925
Wisuri, Arbuta Hendricks, Grand Rapids, 1925-1928
Woldy, Betty, Underwood, 1937
Wolframstorf, Eunice, Montgomery, 1930-1932
Wombacher, Ruth Carlson, Proctor, 1917
Wood, Cathline, Stanley Hall, 1909
Woodbury, Elsie, Zumbrota, 1904
Worner, Mae, Wheaton, 1935-1937
Wornson, Lenore, Slayton, 1923-1925
Wright, Grand Rapids, 1929
Wright, Jeannette Page, Crookston, 1912
Wright, Mabel, Cass Lake, 1925
Wylie, Ida, Blooming Prairie, 1934
Wynn, Leona, South St. Paul, 1925

Y

Yelle, Evelyn, Cloquet, 1930
Young, Evelyn Sponberg, New Richland, 1925-1927
Young, June, Rose Creek, 1929
Yount, Laura, Proctor, 1921, 1926
Yount, Thelma, Proctor, 1926

Z

Zachor, Grace, LeSueur, 1925
Zachor, Luella, LeSueur, 1925
Zander, Emma, Brownton, 1927
Zander, Hilda, Brownton, 1927
Zasoski, Helen, Moose Lake, 1933
Zebott, Eva, Proctor, 1923
Zebott, Gladys, Proctor, 1926
Zeller, Lorene, West Concord, 1929
Zimmerman, Arline, Brownton, 1927
Zimmerman, Carolyn, Arlington, 1926
Zimmerman, Florence, 1923
Zimmerman, Ilo, Brownton, 1923
Zimmerman, Lucille, Brownton, 1923
Zimmerman, Ruth, Brownton, 1927
Zweiner, Lena, Blooming Prairie, 1905

Composite List of Teams

This list includes over 350 Minnesota girls' high school basketball teams that surfaced during the gathering of information for this book. Each school might have its own team profile or is listed on the playing schedule of another team(s).

Teams may have played prior to and/or after the years listed. Schools in this publication can be located on the pages listed by their name.

A

Academy of Holy Angels, Richfield, 1939, 153
Adams, 1927-1932, 103, 119, 156, 172, 256
Adrian, 1929-1939, 204
Agricultural School, University of Minnesota, 1900s, 104, 263
Aitkin, 1910-1936, 105, 178
Albert Lea, 1908-1921, 107, 114, 230, 238
Alberta, 1920s, 184
Alborn, 1933-1937, 281
Alden, 1911-1930, 110, 152, 159, 166
Alpha, 1925, 268
Alexandria, 1904-1935, 110
Annandale, 1921-1926, 129
Anoka, 1921, 134, 243
Appleton, 1910-1935, 149, 220, 299
Arlington, 1908-1928, 111, 167, 309
Atwater, 1919-1930, 183, 302
Audubon, 1939, 165
Austin, 1913-1915, 114, 238

B

Badger, 1920-1930, 180, 289
Balleton, 1933-1935, 286
Barnum, 1920-1935, 139, 142, 225
Battle Lake, 1914-1929, 111, 150
Baudette, 1920-1930, 192
Beardsley, 1926-1930, 126
Beaver Creek, 1935, 203
Belgrade, 1924-1929, 183, 240
Belle Plaine, 1920-1932, 113, 115, 195, 221, 229
Bellingham, 1925-1929, 212
Belview, 1920s, 254
Benson, 1925-1928, 184, 220, 276
Bertha, 1924-1929, 150
Big Falls, 1936-1942, 119
Big Lake, 1925, 265
Bigelow, 1920s, 119
Bigfork, 1925-1933, 120, 208
Bingham Lake, 1921-1929, 120, 270, 304
Bird Island, 1923-1924, 237
Blackduck, 1924-1939, 192, 208
Bloomington, 1935, 313
Blooming Prairie, 1905-1934, 121, 159, 186
Blue Earth, 1926-1939, 108, 152, 204
Boyd, 1925-1933, 137, 149
Braham, 1925-1929, 122, 134
Brainerd, 1902-1926, 106, 123
Breckenridge, 1925-1928, 184
Brewster, 1923-1926, 305
Bricelyn, 1928, 125
Brookston, 1933-1937, 281
Brooten, 1926-1929, 240
Browns Valley, 1916-1930, 125
Brownton, 1906-1928, 127
Buffalo, 1911-1932, 129, 202
Buffalo Lake, 1923-1924, 128
Burtrum, 1922, 279
Byron, 1922-1924, 132, 186

C

Caledonia, 1927-1931, 206
Cambridge, 1902-1929, 122, 134, 243
Canby, 1923-1924, 137, 209
Cannon Falls, 1924-1928, 288
Canton, 1927-1931, 206
Carlton, 1921-1925, 138, 142, 244
Carver, 1924-1932, 116, 195, 313
Cass Lake, 1906-1929, 135, 175
Ceylon, 1924-1931, 267
Chaska, 1930-1935, 313
Cherry, 1933-1937, 281
Chisago City, 1926-1927, 142, 278
Chisholm, 1910-1911, 178
Clara City, 1931-1935, 220
Claremont, 1925-1929, 209, 290

Clarkfield, 1910-1933, 135, 149, 212
Clements, 1930's, 254
Cleveland, 1915-1924, 116
Climax, 1928-1931, 232
Clinton, 1926-1930, 126
Cloquet, 1903-1932, 138, 176, 181, 245
Cohasset, 1925-1927, 208
Cokato, 1921-1922, 190
Cold Spring, 1926-1929, 240
Coleraine (*See* Greenway)
Comfrey, 1927-1930, 193, 307
Cook, 1933-1937, 281
Correll, 1925-1929, 212
Cotton, 1933-1937, 281
Cromwell, 1922-1936, 141, 155, 225
Crookston, 1910-1912, 146
Crosby and Deerwood, 1901, 147
Crosby-Ironton, 1932-1936, 106, 123, 161
Cyrus, 1921, 148, 276

D

Danube, 1923-1924, 237
Dassel, 1914-1921, 201, 300
Dawson, 1909-1935, 135, 148, 207, 220
Deephaven, 1927, 313
Deer Creek, 1924-1929, 150
Deerwood, 1921-1936, 106
Delano, 1921-1925, 151
Delavan, 1921-1930, 152
Derham Hall, St. Paul, 1926-1939, 153, 278
Dodge Center, 1921-1930's, 154, 186, 209, 290
Dover, 1929-1930, 172
Drummond Hall, Mpls. 1899-1921, 216
Duluth Cathedral, 1917, 244

Duluth Public Schools, 1917-1931, 155
   Duluth Central, 142
   Duluth Denfeld, 155, 243, 284
Dundee, 1915, 156
Dunnell, 1921-1925, 266

E

East Chain, 1924-1931, 269
Eden Prairie, 1935, 313
Eden Valley, 1924-1929, 183, 240
Edgerton, 1920-1935, 179, 203, 270
Elbow Lake, 1921, 276
Elgin, 1922-1924, 132
Elk River, 1920-1930's, 243
Elkton, 1927-1936, 103, 156, 172, 256
Ellendale, 1923-1926, 157, 187
Elmore, 1924-1927, 152, 267
Esko, 1918, 142
Excelsior, 1917-1921, 161, 167, 296
Eyota, 1920s, 132

F

Fairfax, 1918-1924, 112, 167, 190, 237, 254, 309
Faribault, 1910-1923, 162
Farmington, 1920-1921, 276, 296
Floodwood, 1909-1930, 142, 177
Forest Lake, 1925-1929, 178, 296
Franklin, 1907-1929, 162, 254, 309
Frazee, 1924-1940, 165, 285
Freeborn, 1910-1927, 158, 165
Fulda, 1904-1935, 203, 270, 304

G

Garden City, 1924-1929, 248
Gaylord, 1907-1928, 112, 167, 309
Gibbon, 1918-1928, 128, 167, 309
Glencoe, 1919-1928, 112, 190
Glenwood, 1913-1915, 110, 275
Glyndon, 1932-1937, 169, 286
Good Thunder, 1924-1929, 248
Goodhue, 1910, 170, 288
Graceville, 1926-1930, 126, 293
Granada, 1924-1931, 267
Grand Meadow, 1911-1939, 103, 156, 170, 198, 205, 256
Grand Rapids, 1906-1930, 175, 182, 189
Grand Rapids, School of Agriculture, 1928, 104
Granite Falls, 1910-1924, 136, 179, 209, 299
Green Isle, 1919-1924, 128, 167
Greenbush, 1920-1930, 179
Greenway of Coleraine, 1921-1929, 139, 178, 180, 244
Grey Eagle, 1919-1922, 279
Grove City, 1924-1928, 183, 301

H

Hancock, 1916-1928, 184, 301
Hanley Falls 1924, 135
Harmony, 1927-1941, 206, 242
Hartland, 1910, 185
Hayfield, 1921-1930's, 121, 132, 159, 186, 209, 290

Hector, 1923-1924, 128

Henderson, 1907-1931, 112, 116, 194, 221

Hendricks, 1928-1935, 187, 286

Herman, 1913, 188, 293

Heron Lake, 1910-1925, 189, 260, 270, 303

Hewitt, 1924-1929, 150

Hibbing, 1909-1911, 142, 176, 189

Hills, 1935, 203

Hinckley, 1920-1921, 211

Holdingford, 1927, 260

Holloway, 1925-1929, 212

Holt, 1920-1924, 180

Hopkins, 1917-1921, 161

Howard Lake, 1912-1929, 130, 200, 299

Hutchinson, 1919-1926, 112, 128, 167, 190

I

International Falls, 1924-1937, 192, 235

Iona, 1920's, 302

Isle, 1929-1932, 142, 327

Ivanhoe, 1923-1935, 187, 209, 286

J

Jackson, 1924-1939, 204, 267, 305

Jasper, 1935, 203

Jeffers, 1925-1930, 193, 306

Jordan, 1907-1932, 116, 194, 221, 228

K

Kasota, 1918-1931, 196

Kasson, 1908-1930's, 132, 172, 186, 209, 238, 242, 290

Kelliher, 1939-1942, 119

Kellogg, 1921-1928, 308

Kenyon, 1921-1929, 159, 186, 288, 290

Kerkoven, 1939-1940, 183, 301

Kiester, 1925-1930, 152

Kimball, 1920s, 130

L

Lake Benton, 1910-1935, 187, 282, 286

Lake City, 1921, 197, 308

Lake Crystal, 1914-1932, 248, 261

Lake Mills, 1914, 108

Lake Park, 1939, 165

Lakefield, 1915-1939, 204, 270, 306

Lamberton, 1910-1928, 193, 209, 226, 282, 306

Lanesboro, 1940-1941, 114, 242

Lastrup, 1929-1932, 237

Le Center, 1926-1930, 221

Le Roy, 1927-1939, 103, 156, 172, 198

Le Sueur, 1920-1925, 116, 199, 229

Lena, 1905, 241

Lincoln, 1920-1925, 139, 263

Lismore, 1920's, 302

Litchfield, 1903-1932, 131, 190, 200, 240, 299

Littlefork, 1924-1942, 119, 192

Luverne, 1924-1939, 203, 272

Lyle, 1919-1936, 103, 156, 172, 205, 256

Lynd, 1933-1935, 286

M

Mabel, 1927-1931, 206

Madelia, 1914-1915, 261

Madison, 1913-1935, 136, 149, 207, 217, 220, 299

Mahtomedi, 1929, 315

Mankato, 1913-1923, 208

Mankato Loyola, 1922-1930, 248

Mantorville, 1925-1930's, 132, 209, 290

Maple Lake, 1924-1933, 129, 263

Marietta, 1925-1929, 149, 213

Marshall, 1923-1939, 204, 209

Mazeppa, 1905, 210, 241, 288

McGregor, 1932-1933, 142

Meadowlands, 1933-1937, 142, 281

Medford, 1923-1926, 132

Melrose, 1927, 260, 315

Middle River, 1920-1924, 180

Milaca, 1915-1932, 122, 211, 237, 242

Milan, 1913-1935, 149, 212

Minneapolis Central, 1899-1921, 114, 215

Minneapolis East Side, 1899-1921, 215

Minneapolis North Side, 1899-1921, 215

Minneapolis South Side, 1899-1921, 215

Minneota, 1923-1924, 137, 209

Montevideo, 1913-1935, 136, 149, 296

Montgomery, 1926-1932, 116, 162, 194, 221, 229

Monticello, 1907-1924, 130, 224, 265

Moose Lake, 1929-1933, 140, 142, 224

Morgan, 1924-1928, 226, 254

Morris, 1925-1928, 126, 227, 276

Morton, 1921-1932, 164, 190, 227, 254

Motley, 1925-1926, 123

Mountain Lake, 1923-1939, 204, 228, 307

Murdock, 1920-1921, 184

N

Nashwauk, 1921, 180

New Prague, 1907-1931, 116, 162, 184, 221, 228

New Richland, 1924-1928, 159, 230

New Ulm, 1915-1925, 190, 208, 230, 238, 261, 306

New York Mills, 1924-1929, 150

Nicollet, 1924-1929, 248

Nielsville, 1928-1931, 231

North Branch, 1929, 122, 134, 232

North Saint Paul, 1912-1924, 161, 276, 195, 314

Northfield, 1904-1905, 234, 260

Northome, 1924-1942, 119, 192, 235

Northwest School of Agriculture, 1928, 104

Norwood-Young America, 1919-1926, 112, 190

O

Oak Hall, St. Paul, 1927-1928, 153, 296

Odessa, 1925-1929, 212

Ogilvie, 1929-1932, 122, 237

Olcott (Marble), 1921-1929, 180

Olivia, 1906-1937, 190, 236

Onamia, 1929-1932, 237

Ortonville, 1926-1935, 126, 149, 184, 220

Osakis, 1922, 111

Owatonna, 1919, 107, 114, 238, 261

P

Park Rapids, 1926-1929, 77

Parkers Prairie, 1924-1929, 150

Paynesville, 1926-1929, 183, 240, 301

Pelican Rapids, 1911-1937, 240, 286

Pemberton, 1924-1930, 159, 166, 197, 248

Peterson, 1929-1930, 172

Pierz, 1929-1932, 237

Pillsbury Academy, 1914, 108, 114

Pine City, 1926-1932, 122, 225, 278

Pine Island, 1904-1928, 132, 241, 288

Pipestone, 1912-1935, 203, 269

Pleasant Valley, 1905, 241

Preston, 1940-1941, 242

Princeton, 1920-1921, 134, 211, 243

Proctor, 1917-1929, 138, 142, 178, 180, 243, 284

R

Randolph, 1925-1929, 290

Rapidan, 1922-1930, 197, 246

Raymond, 1913-1914, 299,

Red Wing, 1916-26, 217, 252

Red Wing Lutheran Seminary, 1920-1926, 252

Redwood Falls, 1907-1930, 168, 226, 254

Riverton, 1927, 212

Rochester, 1908 - 1921, 114, 242, 255

Rockford, 1931-1933, 130, 263

Rose Creek, 1919-1936, 103, 156, 172, 198, 256

Roseau, 1919-1937, 180, 257, 288

Royalton, 1904-1905, 258

Rush City, 1914-1936, 259

Russell, 1933-1935, 286

S

St. Charles, 1912, 310

St. Clair, 1924-1927, 166, 197, 248

St. Cloud, 1922, 111, 263

St. Cloud Cathedral, 1927, 260

St. Francis, 1928, 134

St. James, 1904-1921, 234, 260, 303

St. John's, 1934-1937, 286

St. Joseph's Academy, 1939, 153

St. Louis Park, 1923-1924, 313

St. Mary's of Waverly, 1923-1933, 263

St. Paul Central, 1901-1914, 263

St. Paul Humboldt, 1901-1914, 263, 295

St. Paul Johnson, 1901-1914, 263

St. Paul Mechanic Arts, 1901-1914, 263, 295

St. Peter, 1924-1929, 116, 167, 229, 265

Sanborn, 1924-1928, 193, 226

Sauk Center, 1913-1922, 279

Sauk Rapids, 1908-1927, 240, 260, 265

Sebeka, 1924-1929, 150
Sherburn, 1921-1927, 266
Silver Lake, 1912-1924, 128
Slayton, 1900-1933, 269, 303
Sleepy Eye, 1923-1924, 237
South St. Paul, 1901-1925, 161, 263, 274, 277
Spring Grove, 1927-1931, 206
Spring Valley, 1939, 156, 198
Springfield, 1924-1929, 226, 307
Stanley Hall, 1899-1921, 215, 263
Staples, 1925-1926, 123
Starbuck, 1910-1930, 275
Stewart, 1923-1924, 128
Stewartville, 1908, 132, 241
Stillwater, 1920-1929, 161, 276, 296
Storden, 1927-1930, 193
Swanville, 1919-1922, 279

T

Thief River Falls, 1920, 280
Thompson, 1927, 140
Toivola, 1933-38, 281
Tracy, 1909-1937, 204, 209, 270, 282
Triumph-Monterey, (Trimont) 1924-1925, 267
Two Harbors, 1920, 155, 244, 284
Tyler, 1928, 187

U

Underwood, 1934-1939, 165, 285
University High School, 1939, 153

V

Verdi, 1933-1935, 286
Vernon Center, 1924-1930, 248
Vesta, 1920s, 254
Victoria, 1933-1934, 313
Villard, 1915, 111

W

Wabasso, 1920's, 254
Waconia, 1917-1927, 111
Wadena, 1910-1929, 150, 287
Wahkon, 1929-1932, 161, 237
Waldorf, 1924-1930, 159, 248
Walnut Grove, 1927-1930, 193
Wanamingo, 1924-1929, 253, 266, 288
Warroad, 1919-1930, 180, 192, 288
Waseca, School of Agriculture, 1914, 104
Watertown, 1921-1925, 151
Waterville, 1907-1913, 107
Watson, 1925-1929, 212
Wayzata, 1923-1926, 290
Welcome, 1924-1927, 267
Wells, 1905-1927, 107, 114, 260
West Central School of Agriculture, 1914, 104, 184

Morgan, 1925

West Concord, 1925-1929, 209, 288, 290
Westbrook, 1914-1934, 193, 269, 292, 307
Wheaton, 1926-1937, 126, 293
White Bear Lake, 1912-1933, 276, 294, 314
Wilder, 1925-1927, 306
Willmar, 1913-1929, 184, 298
Willow River, 1931-1933, 225, 302
Wilmont, Lady of Good Counsel, 1926-1929, 302
Windom, 1914-1939, 120, 193, 204, 261, 270, 303
Winnebago, 1924-1930, 152
Winona, 1921-1928, 308
Winsted, 1931-1933, 263
Winthrop, 1910-1928, 112, 167, 309
Wood Lake, 1924, 136
Worthington, 1910-1939, 203, 261, 270, 304
Wrenshall, 1925-1935. 142

Z

Zumbro Falls, 1924-1928, 288
Zumbrota, 1904-1915, 253, 310

Post-Secondary Schools

Bethany College, 208, 248
Carleton College, 114, 217, 234
College of St. Catherine, 296
Duluth Normal, 243, 284
Hamline University, 200, 295
Lutheran Normal School, Madison, 213
Madison Normal, 212
Mankato Normal, 200, 208, 260
Mankato Commercial College, 260
Montgomery Normal School, 221
St. Cloud Normal, 105, 258
St. Olaf College, 234
Twin Cities Business College, 278, 296
University of Minnesota, 105, 295
Windom College, 218

Iowa

Chester, 172, 198
Lime Springs, 172
Little Cedar, 256
McIntire, 198
Northwood, 109
Osage, 114, 238
North Dakota
Caledonia, 231
Reynolds, 231

South Dakota

Clear Lake, 187
Flandreau, 187, 203
Sissiton, 126
Wilmont, 126

Wisconsin

Ellsworth, 253, 276
Hudson, 277
LaCrosse, 308
Nelson Dewey at Superior, 243
New Richland, 217, 276
Superior, 139, 155, 244
West Superior Normal School, 217

Canada

Ft. Francis, 119, 235

Rapidan trophy 1929

A photograph can be located on the page number shown in parentheses ( ); the page number follows the last year for photos on the same page.

Photo Credits — Teams and Players

Adams:	1932 team (103) — Courtesy of Inez Uglum Schissel
Agricultural Schools:	1928 (105) team of Northwest School of Agriculture, Crookston – Courtesy of Darie A. LaVoi;
	1914 (105) team of West Central School of Agriculture, Morris – Courtesy of Mary Ness
Aitkin:	1910 (105), 1929 (106), 1930 (107) teams — Courtesy of the Aitkin Public Schools; 1928 team (106) – Courtesy of the *Aitkin Independent Age* Newspaper
Albert Lea:	1908 (107), 1909 (107), 1913 (108), 1914 (108), 1920 (109), 1921 (109) teams — Courtesy of Albert Lea High School; 1910 (107) team – Reproduced by permission from the Freeborn County Museum, Library & Historical Village
Alden:	1911 team (110) – Reproduced by permission from the Freeborn County Historical Museum, Library and Historical Village
Arlington:	1926 (112), 1927 (113), 1929 (113) teams; Luella tells stories of her playing days at Arlington (xii); and photos from the Reunion of First Era Players — Courtesy of Luella M. Anderson
Austin:	1914 (114), 1915 (89, 115), 1976 (89) teams — Courtesy of Austin High School; Liz Erickson and daughters (89) – Courtesy of Liz Erickson
Belle Plaine:	1923 (115), 1925 (115), 1926 (book jacket, 116), 1927 (116), 1930 (116) teams; Marie and Mildred Engfer in 1925 (49) — Courtesy of Marie W. Keeler; Marie with ball (book jacket, 94) – Courtesy of Dorothy E. McIntyre; 1923 team (115) and scrapbook pages of 1923 team with coach (49) – Courtesy of Virginia Irwin Kruger
Bigfork:	1933 (120) team — Courtesy of Grand Rapids High School
Bingham Lake:	1927 (120) team – From the Cottonwood County Historical Society collection
Blooming Prairie:	1905 (121) team – *Blooming Prairie Update*, by Harold Severson, Rochester 1925 (121) team – Courtesy of Blooming Prairie High School; 1934 (129) team – Courtesy of Margaret Zwiener Hogan
Braham:	1927, 1928, 1929 (122) teams — Courtesy of Braham High School
Brainerd:	1902 (book jacket, 20, 123) team — Courtesy of Crow Wing County Historical Society
Bricelyn:	1928 (125) team — Courtesy of Alice Armstrong Anderson

Credits 357

Browns Valley:	1928 (126), 1929 (26, 126), 1930 (126) teams — Courtesy of James Shinn
Brownton:	1907 (127), 1923 (127), 1924, 1925, 1926, 1927 (128) teams — Courtesy of Max and Wilma West
Buffalo:	1915 (129), 1931 (131) teams – Courtesy of *Wright County Journal—Press*; 1924 (129), 1926 (130), 1927 (book jacket, 53, 131), 1930 (131) teams – Courtesy of Buffalo High School; Vera Templin honored at Lynx game (49) – Courtesy of Vera Templin
Byron:	1924 (133) team, guarding drill (133), Leona Siewert Gray (68) — Courtesy of Gray/Campbell family
Cambridge:	1928 (134) team — Courtesy of Cambridge Public Schools
Cass Lake:	1925, 1926 (135) teams — Courtesy of James Michaud
Clarkfield:	One photo before 1920s (135), one photo during 1920s (135), 1925 (137) team — Courtesy of Yellow Medicine East (YME) Public Schools and the centennial publication, *Clarkfield, Minnesota, 1884—1984*; 1931 photo of Rosalind Knutson and Dolores Kirkeby (50, 137) — Courtesy of Rosalind Cherkezian.
Cloquet:	1903 (20, 138) team — Courtesy of the Carlton County Historical Society, Octavie Morneau, Duluth, photographer; 1921 (138), 1923 (139), 1924 (139), 1925 (23, 140), 1926 (140), 1927 (140), 1930 (141), 1932 (141) teams – Courtesy of Cloquet High School
Coleraine:	See also Greenway
Cromwell:	1926 (142), 1927 (24, 142), 1929, 1931, 1932, 1933, 1935 (143) teams, three generations of Cromwell basketball (89) — Courtesy of Blanche Line Kingsley family
Crookston:	1912 (146) team, Jeannette Page Wright (iii, 91, 146) — Courtesy of Dr. Robert Wright; Lori Wright on 1982 St. Charles team (91) – Courtesy of *St. Charles Press and Lewiston Journal*
Crosby and Deerwood:	1901 (19, 147) team — Courtesy of the Crow Wing County Historical Society
Cyrus:	1921 (148) team — Courtesy of Beverly Reque
Dawson:	1910 team(88, 148) — Courtesy of Mary Froiland; 1926 team (148)— Courtesy of Carol Weisbrod Johnson
Deer Creek:	1925 (150) team, Irma Nelson Post (151) — Courtesy of Judy Becker
Delano:	1924, 1925 (152) teams, Ella Mae Bauer Pease — Courtesy of Ella Mae Bauer Pease
Delavan:	1923 (152), 1927 (24, 153) teams— Courtesy of Bernice Halvorson Wheeler
Duluth:	1924 (155) team, Duluth Central GAA 1936 (81) — Courtesy of Duluth Central High School

Dundee:	1915 (156) team – Courtesy of the Murray County Historical Society, Slayton
Eden Prairie:	1935 (314) — Courtesy of the Eden Prairie Historical Society
Elkton:	1930 (157) team — Courtesy of Bernice Swenson Hokeness
Ellendale:	1925 (60, 158), 1926 (159) teams, Helen Johnson Davidson (59), trophy (53) – Reproduced by permission of the Ellendale Area Heritage Society; Tournament medal (53) — Courtesy of the Helen Johnson Davidson family; Newspaper article (60, 158) – Courtesy of the *Ellendale Eagle*
Faribault:	1923 (162) team – From the collection of Marian Bemis Johnson
Franklin:	1924 (163), 1929 (163), 1931 (164), 1936 (164) teams, Alice Schroeder McFarland — Courtesy of the Alice Schroeder McFarland family; Michelle McFarland Bursch (91) — Courtesy of Mary McFarland; Lynn Trochlil Crist (91) – Courtesy of Lynn Trochlil Crist; Stephanie Hall Moran (91) – Courtesy of Stephanie Hall Moran
Frazee:	1939 (165) team — Courtesy of Debra K. Hoyhtya
Freeborn:	Postcard of 1910 team (165) — Courtesy of Jane Christensen and reproduced by permission from the Freeborn County Museum, Library and Historical Village; 1927 (165) team — Courtesy of Dorothy Schultz Schuster
Gaylord:	1920 (167), 1922 (167), 1923 (168) teams — Courtesy of Leona Hanson family; 1924 (68) team – Courtesy of Margaret Huffman Thompson; *Gaylord Hub* reports on Recognition Ceremony (97) – Courtesy of *Gaylord Hub* newspaper
Glyndon:	1934 (27, 169, 170) teams — Courtesy of the Douglas M. Sommerville family
Goodhue:	1910 (21, 170) team – Courtesy of the Zumbrota Area Historical Society
Grand Meadow:	1911 (170) team – Reproduced by permission from the Mower County HistoricalSociety; 1930 (64, 172), 1931 (55), 1932 (173) teams; Marie Berg (175) — Courtesy of Jackie McDonough; 1935 (173), 1936 (173) teams – Courtesy of Beulah M. Ankeny; 1934 (173), 1939 (64, 174) teams — Courtesy of the DeVera Proeschel family; Photo of Ruth Bratrud Jacobson (46) — Courtesy of Jacobson family
Grand Rapids:	1906 (175), 1907 (8, 21, 176), 1908 (52, 176), 1909 (176), 1910 (177), 1911, 1928 (178), 1929 (179) teams — Courtesy of Grand Rapids High School
Greenbush:	1924 (179) team — Courtesy of Oline Christianson Erickson
Greenway:	1921 (180), 1922 (181), 1923 (53, 181), 1924 (182), 1925 (192), 1926 (182), 1929 (182) teams — Courtesy of Greenway High School, Coleraine
Hancock:	1924 (184), 1925 (185), 1926 (185) teams; 1999 photo of teammates Irene Angier Jensen and Marian Solvie Halvorson (51) — Courtesy of Beverly Solvie Reque

Hartland:	1910 (185) team – Reproduced by permission from the Freeborn County Historical Society
Hayfield:	1925 (25) team — Courtesy of Dorothy Iversen Viker
Hendricks:	1928 (188) team — Courtesy of the Hendricks Pioneer
Herman:	1913 (188) team — Courtesy of Mr. and Mrs. Myron William Tiedt
Heron Lake:	1910 (189) team – Courtesy of the Murray County Historical Society
Hutchinson:	1921 (book jacket, 93, 190) team — Courtesy of Mary Hajicek Berry family; 1921 (book jacket, 93, 190), 1922 (191), Charlotte Johnson with her team photo (191) – Courtesy of Candace Barrick; Lindsay Whalen (book jacket, 93) – Courtesy of the University of Minnesota Athletic Communications
International Falls:	1925 (192) team — Courtesy of Agnes King McIntyre
Jeffers:	1928 (193) team, Teri Takle (92) — Courtesy of Roberta Piper Takle
Jordan:	1911 (92, 193) team – Courtesy of Earl Dean; 1932 team (27, 57, 195), Reunion of First Era Players, photo of gold basketball charm award (56) – Courtesy of Jane Varner Breimhorst
Kasota:	1930 (196), 1931 (197) teams and 1930 (50, 69), 1931 (50, 69) team activities — Courtesy of Judy Miner Hanson
Lake Crystal:	1932 (197) team — Courtesy of Mary Champlin Tonkin
LeSueur:	1920, 1921 (199) teams — Courtesy of Lucy Schwartz Sontag
Litchfield:	1903 (200), 1927 (62, 201) teams – eight-page tabloid developed for LHS Alumni Association, printed by the Crow Wing Press, Inc., owned in part by the *Litchfield Independent Review*; 1917 (201) team – Courtesy of Carol Barrick; 1931 (202) team — Courtesy of the *Litchfield Independent Review*; 1932 (32, 63, 202) team — Courtesy of Marlis Urdahl
Luverne:	1935 (204), 1937 (57, 204) teams — Courtesy of Ruth and Rollie DeLapp
Mabel:	1929 team (206), 1931 team in pyramid (50, 207), Mabel with athletic letters (57, 206) — Courtesy of Mabel Thompson Erickson
Madison:	1919 (89, 207) team — Courtesy of Margaret Hauck Morrill; Margaret Chutich (90) – Courtesy of Margaret Chutich
Mankato:	1921 (208) team — Courtesy of the Mankato Public Schools
Marshall:	1923 (209), 1924 (210) teams — Courtesy of the Marshall Public Schools
Mazeppa:	1905 (210) team — Courtesy of Lorraine Huffmeier
Milaca:	1920 (211) - team - Courtesy of Jeanette Stromberg Helmen

Milan:	1927 (90, 212) team, Ruth wearing first shorts uniform (book jacket, 26, 90), Ruth and two great-granddaughters (book jacket, 215) — Courtesy of the Ruth Olson Kleven family; 1935 (214) team – Courtesy of the Arv Hus Museum, Milan
Montevideo:	1913 photo and postcard (14, 218) — Courtesy of the Edna Linnee Jorvig family; 1918, 1919, 1929; 1930, 1931, 1932, 1933, 1934, (219), 1935 (62, 220) teams — Courtesy of Chippewa County Historical Society; Player Thea Stay (62), Thea Sletkolen Stay 2003 (62) — Courtesy of Thea Sletkolen Stay
Montgomery:	1930 (book jacket, iii, 56, 222), 1931, 1932 (223) teams, photo of Irma Malone and Evelyn Vitha with 1930 district trophy (56) — Courtesy of Irma Malone Foley; 1930 (222), 1931 (223), 1932 (223) teams – Courtesy of Montgomery High School
Monticello:	1924 (224) team; Coach Williamson in 1928 (Roster of Coaches) – Courtesy of Mary Lilja Bollman
Moose Lake:	1930, 1931, 1932 (225), 1933 (226) teams — Courtesy of Moose Lake Public Schools
Morgan:	1925 (226, 355) team — Courtesy of Luretta Parker Trobec
Mountain Lake:	1923 (228) team — Courtesy of Cottonwood Historical Society
New Prague:	1918 (228) team — Courtesy of Barta's Studio, and reproduced by permission from the Minnesota Historical Society
New Richland:	Laura Sampsell Hoffman and Evelyn Sponberg Young (90), Sara Sampsell-Jones (90) — Courtesy of Evelyn Sponberg Young family
New Ulm:	1924, 1925, 1926 (231) teams — Courtesy of New Ulm High School, with assistance from Harley Schneider, New Ulm
Nielsville:	1928 (92, 232) team, Heather Goodrich Schrider, Alice Lervold, Kathy Lervold Goodrich photo (92) — Courtesy of Kathy Lervold Goodrich
North Branch:	1929, 1931, 1932 (233) teams — Courtesy of North Branch Schools
Northome:	1936 (235) team — Courtesy of Mildred Wick Gorden
Olivia:	1906 (236), 1920 (236), 1937 (237) teams — Courtesy of BOLD High School
Owatonna:	1919 (52, 238) team — Courtesy of Matt Kottke; 1924 (239) team – Courtesy of Owatonna Public Schools; Game advertisement (238) – Courtesy of the *Owatonna People's Press*
Paynesville:	1928 (240) team — Courtesy of Letta Farnum Swedelius
Pelican Rapids:	1912 (92, 240) team — Courtesy of Pat Robbins; Heidi Robbins wearing her great-grandmother's 1912 uniform (92) — Courtesy of Tom Robbins
Pine Island:	1908 (242) team — Courtesy of *News-Record*, Pine Island
Princeton:	1921 (243) team - Courtesy of Princeton High School

Proctor:	1917 (243), 1920, 1921, 1922 (244), 1923, 1926 (245), 1929 (246) teams – Reproduced by permission from the Proctor Area Historical Society and Proctor Schools; 1919 (244) team – Courtesy of Jake Benson, *Proctor Journal*; Proctor Rails from 1893 to 1933 (37) — Courtesy of Proctor Schools
Rapidan:	1924 (247), 1925, 1926, 1927 (248), 1928 (61, 249), 1929 (249), 1930 (250) teams, photo of 1928 Aileen Just (book jacket, 61), poster announcing game (61), ball graphic, (315), Coach Herbert Hartshorn (Roster of Coaches 320) — Courtesy of James M. Luther; Rapidan team information from the personal collection of Vi Holbrook; 1928 (55) and 1929 (56, 356) trophies – Courtesy of Barb Knutson; Rapidan School (34) — Courtesy of Dorothy E. McIntyre
Red Wing:	1917 (252) team – Courtesy of Loraine Rehder
Red Wing Seminary:	1921 (252), 1926 (253) teams — Courtesy of Margarethe Thoreson
Rochester:	1921 (23, 255) team — Courtesy of Bob Nangle
Rose Creek:	1929 (256) team; Rose Creek 1928 school athletic letter (57) — Courtesy of Betty Rasmussen Hassenstab
Roseau:	1917, 1919, 1923, 1925 (257) teams – Reproduced by permission from the Roseau Historical Society - Marilyn Hanson Sharp Collection
Royalton:	1905 (258) team — Courtesy of Royalton Museum and the Gladys J. Clark family
Rush City:	1914 (259) team postcard - Courtesy of Marian Larson
St. James:	1914 (260), 1915, 1916, 1917 (261), 1918 (262) teams — Courtesy of Bill Nordgren, St. James Historical Society
St. Paul:	1902 (ii, 20, 88, 263), 1915 (264), 1976 (88) teams – Courtesy of St. Paul Central High School; 1915 (88, 273) team – From the *St. Paul Daily*
St. Peter:	1924 (265) team — Courtesy of Judy Miner Hanson.
Sherburn:	Tournament programs (53, 54), 1925 team (267) — Courtesy of Marjorie Pauline Holmes McNeal Eiden; 1925 team (262), Ruth and ring (54, 269), 1927 team photo (263) — Courtesy of Ruth Dahlke; Photo of Ruth Dahlke (54, 263) – Courtesy of Silker Photo-Graphic; Sherburn players reunited with trophy (54, 268) — Courtesy of *Martin County Star*; 1925 tournament trophy (xvi) – Courtesy of Jane Christensen
Slayton:	1901 (270), 1928, 1931, 1932 (273) teams – Reproduced by permission from the Murray County Historical Society; 1915, 1923, 1924 (271), 1925, 1927 (272) teams, one photo of early 1900s (270) – Courtesy of Slayton Public Schools
South St. Paul:	1920, 1921, 1924 (274), 1925 (275) teams — Courtesy of South St. Paul Schools

Starbuck:	1910, 1930 (275) teams — Courtesy of Minnewaska Area Schools
Stillwater:	1920, 1922, (276) 1923, 1924, 1925, 1926 (277), 1927, 1928, 1929 (278) teams, Coach Pierce in 1929 (Roster of Coaches 321) — Courtesy of Stillwater Area Public Schools
Thief River Falls	1919 (279), 1920 (280) teams — Courtesy of the Eileen Faust Herron family
Toivola:	1933 (280) team; Sports: The Toivola Athletic Club from *Echoing Footsteps, a 1988 History of the Toivola Community* — Courtesy of Lillian Lahti Sorvari; Photo of trophy and school letters (281) – Courtesy of Alex Sorvari
Tracy:	1911, 1925 (282) teams — Courtesy of Tracy High School
Two Harbors:	1920 (283) team — Courtesy of Laurie Newtson and the Two Harbors Public Schools
Underwood:	1937 (27, 285) team — Courtesy of Evelyn Olson Kukkola
Wadena:	1911 (286), 1912, 1913 (287) teams — Courtesy of Marjorie Ireland and Bob Zosel
Warroad:	1922, 1923 (289) teams – Courtesy of the Warroad Heritage Center & Museum; 1925 (289) team – Courtesy of the Warroad Public Schools
Wayzata:	1924 (290) team - Courtesy of the Anna Milbert Kamleiter family; 1926 (290) team – Courtesy of the Wayzata Historical Society
West Concord:	West Concord Hotel (35, 291), West Concord City Hall (34, 291) – Courtesy of Rose Robinson Wichser
Westbrook:	1924 (292), 1930 (293) teams, the reunion booklet, *Westbrook Schools–1910 to 1990* – Courtesy of Pat Robbins and Westbrook–Walnut Grove High School
Wheaton:	1936 (293) — Courtesy of Muriel Jacobson; 1937 (294) team — Courtesy of Mae Johnson
White Bear Lake:	1919 (294), 1920, 1921, 1922, 1924 (295), 1925, 1926, 1927 (296), 1928 (297) teams — Courtesy of White Bear Lake Public Schools
Willmar:	1913 (298), 1914, 1915 (299), 1916 (300), 1921 (300), 1924, 1927, 1928 (301) teams – Courtesy of Willmar Public Schools; 1927 team, 1927 (50) Lorraine Ackerman and Addie DeLaHunt – Courtesy of Anne Ripperger; Ruth Rawn and daughter Florence (95) – Courtesy of Ruth DeLaHunt Rawn and Florence M. Rawn
Windom:	1914, 1915 (303), 1917 (68, 304), 1922, 1923 (305), 1924, 1926, 1927 (306), 1928, 1929 (307) teams — from the Windom yearbooks, 1914 to 1929 – Courtesy of the Cottonwood County Historical Society collection
Winona:	1921, 1928 (308) teams – Winona High School yearbooks
Winthrop:	1920 (309) team — Courtesy of the Mildred Lofthus Roepke family
Zumbrota:	1904 (21, 310), 1910, 1915 (310) teams – Courtesy of the Zumbrota Area Historical Society

All-American Red Heads
Dolores Petersen Clack (85), Gretchen Pinz Hyink (86, 87), Sherry Mattson (86, 87), Lynnette Sjoquist (86, 87), Lynnea Sjoquist (86), and Jackie Wrage Zitlau (85); 1976-77 team (87), Coach Orwell Moore, (85) — Courtesy of Orwell Moore, former coach and current owner of the All-American Red Heads

Booklet
NAAF-WD Platform booklet (74) – From the collection of Ola Bundy, Bloomington, Illinois

Colleges and Universities
Max J. Exner (1), 1890 Gridley Hall (2), 1903 Women's Basketball team (3) — Courtesy of Carleton College

James Naismith with peach baskets and ball (4) – Reproduced by permission from the University Archives, Spencer Research Library, University of Kansas Libraries

Lindsay Whalen, University of Minnesota (book jacket, 93) – Courtesy of University of Minnesota Athletic Communications

Graphics
Little Girl Bouncing Balls and graphics (x, 28, 58, 70-71, 100, 311-312) — Bev Byington, Fairbanks, Alaska

Railroad map 1920s (x, 38) – Courtesy of Douglas Kruse, Hugo

Proctor rails, 1893-1933 (37) – Courtesy of Proctor Schools

Sherburne Invitational Tournament Program (53,54) — Courtesy of Pauline Holmes Eiden

Individuals
Janet Karvonen Montgomery and daughter Sophia (ix) – Courtesy of Janet Karvonen Montgomery; Janet Karvonen at MSHSL State Girls Basketball Tournament in 1979 (ix)– photo by Pete Hohn, Mpls Star Tribune, Janet Karvonen Montgomery and Kim Salathe Aker celebrating section championship (viii) — From the collection of Janet Karvonen Montgomery

Marian Johnson and Janet Karvonen Montgomery talk at state tournament, (xii) — Courtesy of Dorothy E. McIntyre

Elvera "Peps" Neuman (87) – Courtesy of Elvera "Peps" Neuman

Letter
Harold Jack letter to school superintendents (76) – reproduced by permission of the Minnesota Historical Society

Reunion of First Era Players
Marie Keeler and ball (94), Welcome to Basketball Pioneers (93), Sharing Memories (94), Jane Varner Breimhorst and Irma Malone Foley enjoying basketball (94), Receiving plaques (94), Lifelong friends, Paula Bauck and Mary Todnem (98) - Photos courtesy of Luella Anderson and Dorothy E. McIntyre; *Gaylord Hub*, "Reports on Recognition Ceremony" (97) – Courtesy of the *Gaylord Hub*; Ruth Rawn, Willmar and daughter Florence (95) — Courtesy of Ruth DeLaHunt Rawn and Florence M. Rawn; Cromwell teammates and friends for life (96, 145) – Courtesy of the Blanche Line Kingsley family

Social Attitudes and Fashions
"Are Modern Girls Risking Their Looks?" Newspaper article circa 1930, Source Unknown (324); From the collection of Nancy Bergert, Buffalo, MN

Fashion ads: Dowager and the Princess (16); Taking a Walk in 1902 (17) — The *Designer Magazine*, 1902

Special Teams

Women's basketball team, ca. 1900 (13) – Reproduced by permission from the Minnesota Historical Society

Travel

Early cars (43, 45) — Courtesy of John and Elizabeth MacLeod, Bovey

Heading for town with horse and buggy (36) — Courtesy of the Grimes family, West Union, Iowa

Horse-drawn school bus; First motorized school bus (44) – Courtesy of Blanche Line Kingsley, Cromwell

Horse and buggy on Main Street in Grand Meadow (36), Grand Meadow train depot (40); early cars on Main Street in Grand Meadow (46) – Courtesy of Jackie Berg McDonough

Horse-drawn school bus (36) — Courtesy of Port Wing Area Historical Society

Cromwell Schools horse-drawn school bus (36) – Courtesy of Cromwell Area Historical Club

Rural school van of 1910 (39) – Reproduced by permission from Harry Darius Ayer, Minnesota Historical Museum

Twin City Rapid Transit Company streetcar of 1902, Motorman (left) and Conductor (right) standing near Car #921, Class B3, taken near Lake Phalen, St. Paul, Minnesota (39) – Courtesy of Pete Bonesteel Collection

Rapidan train depot in 2005 (41) – Courtesy of Dorothy E. McIntyre

Notes

Abbreviations

AAHPER	American Alliance for Health, Physical Education, Recreation and Dance
A Century	*A Century of Women's Basketball – From Frailty to Final Four*
Lerner	Lerner Publishing Group
McGraw	McGraw-Hill Book Company
MNHS	Minnesota Historical Society
MSHSL	Minnesota State High School League
NAAF (WD)	National Amateur Athletic Federation (Women's Division)
NAGWS	National Association for Girls and Women's Sports
The Americans	*The Americans – A Social History of the United States, 1587-1914*

Epigraph

1. Ann D. Braude, Ph.D., "Answering God's Call to Speak," *The Magazine for the Mary Baker Eddy Library for the Betterment of Humanity,* http://www.marybakereddylibrary.org/news/answering.jhtml (accessed June 20, 2005).

Introduction

1. George Santayana, *The Life of Reason* (Amherst, NY: Prometheus Books, 1998), 82.

Chronology

1. Norene Roberts, "A Woman's Place in Minnesota," *Roots* (Minnesota Historical Society magazine), vol. 9, bk2 (Winter 1981): 11-18
2. Joan S. Hult and Marianna Trekell, eds., *A Century of Women's Basketball – From Frailty to Final Four* (Reston, VA: NAGWS and AAHPERD, 1991). Appendix, 427-430
3. Helen B. Lawrence and Grace I. Fox, *Basketball for Girls and Women* (New York: McGraw, 1954), 191-228.

First Quarter

A New Game Comes to Minnesota

1. Eric Hillemann, archivist, Carleton College, Northfield, MN. On September 30, 2004 Eric provided research and photos which documented the introduction of basketball by Max J. Exner at Carleton College.
2. Carleton College 1892-93 yearbook, *ALGOL, Gymnasium Work, Spring Issue* (Northfield, MN).
3. Max V. Exner, son of Max J. Exner. Co-author McIntyre interview with Max V. Exner, September 2004.
4. Dr. Naismith later became director of physical education at the University of Kansas, 1898-1937. He was the school's first basketball coach. Dr. Naismith would attend the 1936 Olympics where men's basketball was first held and award the medals to the winning United States men's team.

A Game of Their Own
1. Joanne Lannin, *A History of Basketball for Girls and Women – From Bloomers to Big Leagues* (Minneapolis: Lerner, 2000), 9.
2. Lawrence and Fox, *Basketball for Girls and Women*, 177-178.
3. "The Shot Heard Round the World," *Discovery YMCA, Spring/Summer 2001, 150th Anniversary Edition*, nos. 77 and 78 (2001): 26-29.
4. Ibid.
5. Betty Spears, "Senda Berenson Abbott – New Woman: New Sport" in *A Century*, 20.
6. Ibid.
7. Ibid.
8. Joan Paul, "Clara Gregory Bauer – Catalyst for Women's Basketball" in *A Century*, 37-52.
9. Joan S. Hult, "The Governance of Athletics for Girls and Women – Leadership by Women Physical Educators, 1899-1949" in *A Century*, 53-82.
10. MSHSL, *Official Handbook of the MSHSL* (Alexandria, MN: MSHSL, 1925), 28.
11. Joanna Davenport, "The Tides of Change in Women's Basketball Rules" in *A Century*, 83-108.

From Costumes to Uniforms
1. Harvey Green, *The Light of the Home* (New York: Pantheon Books, 1983).
2. Gerda Buxbaum, ed., *Icons of Fashion—the 20th Century* (New York: Prestel Publishing, 1999), 14.
3. Ibid.
4. J. C. Furnas, *The Americans – A Social History of the United States*, 1587-1914 (New York: G.T.Putnam & Sons, 1969), 492-494; and Amelia Bloomer, The *Lily* newspaper, with permission from the National Women's Hall of Fame, Seneca Falls, NY, http://www.greatwomen.org/women.php?action=viewone&id=22 (accessed March 28, 2005).
5. David Mozer, "Chronology of the Growth of Bicycling," *Bicycle History &Human Powered Vehicle History*, International Bicycle Fund homepage, http://ibike.org/library/historytimeline.htm (accessed June 26, 2005).
6. Victorian Station, Leisure Activities, "Bicycling," http://www.victorianstation.com/leisurebicycle.htm (accessed June 26, 2005).
7. Mary Bellis, "The Rover Cycle - The Tricycle," *Inventors-Bicycle History*, http://inventors.about.com/gi/dynamic/offsite.htm?site=http://www.tripnet.se/rcos/bike.html (accessed June 25, 2005)
8. Green, *The Light of the Home*, 163; and "Fashion-Bicycling," http://www.victorianstation.com/fashionbicycle.htm (accessed June 26, 2005).
9. Furnas. *The Americans*, 809-812; and David Hendrick, "Women and Bicycles," *The Possibility of Mobility*, http://xroads.virginia.edu/~UG02/hendrick/women.html (accessed June 28, 2005).
10. Susan B. Anthony interviewed by Nellie Bly, *New York World*, February 2, 1896, http://www.pedalinghistory.com/PHfaq.html (accessed June 25, 2005).
11. Hult and Trekkell, *A Century*, 11.
12. For reference to a history of the times: http://kclibrary.nhmccd.edu/19thcentury1890.htm

Second Quarter

Getting to the Game was Half the Fun
1. Richard S. Prosser, *Rails to the North Star – One hundred years of railroad evolution in Minnesota* (Minneapolis: Dillon Press, 1966). 1-63
2. Minnesota Street Car Museum, "Excelsior Streetcar Line History," *About Excelsior History*, http://www.trolleyride.org/ESL_Main/history.html (accessed June 9, 2005).

3. Christopher Muller, owner of Railserve homepage, "James J. Hill," http://www.railserve.com/JJHill.html (accessed June 11, 2005).
4. Mary Bellis, site curator, "The History of the Automobile, The First Mass Producers of Cars – The Assembly Line," *Automobile History – The History of Cars and Engines,* http://www.inventors.about.com/library/weekly/aacarsassemblya.htm (accessed June 26, 2005).
5. David Hendrick, "The Automobile Takes Over," *The Possibility of Mobility,* http://xroads.virginia.edu/~UG02/ hendrick/auto.html (accessed May 15, 2005).
6. Casey Cooper, "From Dirt Paths to Superhighways," *History of the US Highway System,* http://www.gbcnet.com/ushighways/history.html (accessed June 27, 2005).

Minnesota Hospitality and the Game
1. Bill Beck, company historian, *The Energy to Make Things Better, An Illustrated History of Northern States Power Company* (Minneapolis: Banta Corporation, 1999), 10-11, 29-38. (Foreword by James J. Howard, Chairman, President and CEO, Northern States Power)

Third Quarter

Darwin, Women and the Game
1. Steveda Chepko, "The Domestication of Basketball," *A Century*, 110.
2. George J. Engelmann, "The American Girl of Today. Modern Education and Functional Health," *American Physical Education Review* 6 (March 1901): 29-30.
3. J. Anna Norris, "The Beneficial Results and Dangers of Basket Ball" in *Official Basket Ball Guide for Women, 1918-1919,* ed. Florence D. Alden, Elizabeth Richards and L. Raymond Burnett, 71 (New York: American Sports Publishing Company, 1918).

End of the First Era
1. Original story by Dorothy E. McIntyre, book co-author.
2. Hult and Trekkell, *A Century*, 57.
3. Lawrence and Fox, *Basketball for Girls and Women,* 187-188.
4. Readers are encouraged to read a biography of Lou Henry Hoover to learn more about an exceptional woman who was born in Waterloo, Iowa and would become First Lady of the United States. Lou Henry Hoover was an independent spirit with a love of the outdoors, graduating with a degree in geology. She traveled the world as First Lady, challenged stereotypes and developed programs during World War I to aid women and children. Lou Hoover gave to the United States an unselfish lifetime of public service. Her leadership in the NAAF – Women's Division reflected her interests in providing an inclusive education program for all young women. (The Herbert Hoover Presidential Library-Museum, administered by the National Archives and Records Administration.)
5. Mabel Lee, *Memories Beyond Bloomers — 1924-1954* (Washington, DC: AAHPER, 1978), 74-75.
6. Brochure, "Community Athletics for Girls and Women, A few questions posed from a Study made in 1930, Platform of Women's Division, NAAF." (New York: NAAF-WD, April 1, 1931).
7. Lawrence and Fox, *Basketball for Girls and Women,* 188.
8. "Purpose of an Athletic Program," *Athletics for Girls – A Digest of Principles and Policies for Administrators and Teachers in Junior and Senior High Schools* (Washington, D.C. The Department of School Health and Physical Education of the National Education Association, 1933), 5-6.
9. Ibid.
10. Ibid., 6.
11. D. Stanley Eitzen and George H. Sage, *Sociology of American Sport* (Dubuque, Iowa: Wm C. Brown Company Publishers, 1978), 272.

12. *Women's Division of the National Amateur Athletic Federation (NAAF), Minutes of the Meeting: Resolutions adopted regarding Olympics, January 3-5, 1929, New York City.* From the files of Ola Bundy, former Assistant Executive Director, Illinois High School Association, Bloomington, Illinois.
13. Eitzen and Sage, *Sociology of American Sport*, 272.
14. Minnesota Historical Society. Records and correspondence of Harold Jack, Supervisor of Health and Physical Education, Minnesota Department of Education, 1938, 1939. 51H14F-Dept. of Ed. P.E. Division of the Minnesota State Archives, located in the Archives/Manuscripts Division of the Minnesota Historical Society.
15. State Historical Society of Iowa, "Iowa Girls' High School Athletic Union- Girls Basketball in Iowa," *The Palimpsest* XLIX, No. 4 (April 1968): 125-125.
16. Letter from Gertrude Ziebarth Bloom to co-author Johnson, 1978.
17. MSHSL, *Official Handbooks of the Minnesota State High School League*, 1924-1942, state tournament summaries.

A Team for Every Girl and Every Girl on a Team
1. The other phrase associated with the GAA period is *"The One Purpose of Sports for Girls and Women is the Good of Those Who Play." Standards in Sports for Girls and Women - Guiding Principles in the Organization and Administration of Sports Program*. A Project of the National Section for Girls and Women's Sports of the American Association for Health Physical Education and Recreation. A Department of the National Education Association. First Edition 1937. Copyright 1953, 5.

Finding Opportunities Beyond School Teams
1. *Spirit of '75, All-American Red Heads' 40th Anniversary, 1936-1976.* (Reunion publication) Moore's All-American Red Heads, owned and operated by Moore's Sports Enterprises, Caraway Arkansas.
2. Link to All-American Red Heads by John Molina: http://www.allamericanredheads.com.

Epilogue

1. Eleanor Roosevelt Quotes, http://www.brainyquote.com (accessed June 27, 2005).

Index

A

Adams

    team profile of, 103-104

    player information provided by Juletta Kasel family, 103; Inez Uglum, 11, 31, 103-104

Agricultural Schools

    team profile of, 104-105

    player information provided by the Olive Peterson Kenely family, 105; by the Clara Ness LaVoi family, 105

Aitkin

    team profile of, 105-107

    player information provided by Eva Turnock Alberg, 106

Albert Lea

    team profile of, 107-109

    research by student Mary Thomes, University of St. Thomas, St. Paul, 109

Alden, team profile of, 110

Alexandria, team profile of, 110-111

    Souvenir Edition of 100 Years at Alexandria's high school

Alexandria Alexandrian, 30, 110-111

All-American Red Heads

    information about, 84-86

    first owner and coach, C. M. "Ole" Olson, 84

    current owner and coach, Orwell Moore, 85-86

    player information provided by Gretchen Pinz Hyink, 85-86, Sherry Mattson, 85-86, Dolores "Dody" Petersen family, 85; Lynnea Sjoquist, 85-86; Lynnette Sjoquist, 85-86; Jackie Wrage Zitlau, 85

American Physical Education Association (APEA), 72-73

    Wayman, Agnes, 75

American Association of Health, Physical Education and Recreation (AAHPER), 77

Anthony, Susan B., 19

Arlington

    team profile of, 111-114

    coach information provided by Susanna Hensler, 112-114

    interview with players by Jane Helmke, KARE 11 TV producer, 113-114

    player information provided by Luella Bandelin Anderson, xii, 96, 112-114; Carolyn Bandelin Matz, 96, 112-114; Sarah Meffert, 33, 111-112

Arlington Enterprise, 111, 114

Arv Hus Museum, Milan, 214

Amateur Athletic Union (AAU), 71, 73, 75

Austin

    team profile of, 114-115

    legacy information provided by Liz Erickson, daughters, Megan and Annie, 89, 115

Austin Daily Herald, 187

B

Bancroft, Ann, explorer, book jacket quote by

Basketball, *See also* Girls Basketball

    name changed from two words to one word for, xvii

    inventor of, James Naismith, xv, xvii, 3, 13, 234

    origin of, 3-5, 234

original 13 rules for, 3-4

peach baskets as first goals for, 4, 13

site of first game of , 4

Bauck, Paula

book jacket quote by,

See also, Roseau, 257-258

Baer, Clara Gregory, inventor of game of "basquette", 5

Bell, H.C., first president of the Minnesota State High School League, 205

Belle Plaine

team profile of, 115-119

player information provided by Marie Weibeler Keeler, xii, 10, 22, 23, 30-31, 33, 40-41, 67, 95, 96, 115-119 317; Virginia Irwin Kruger, 30, 115

Belle Plaine Herald, 117

Berenson, Senda

editor of the first rules for women's basketball, 6

inventor of the three-court game for women, 5, 67

Bicycle, history of, 18

Bigelow

team profile of, 119

player information provided by Beulah O. Wick family, 119

Big Falls

team profile of, 119-120

player information provided by Norma Booth Krats, 33, 119-120; Beryl Regal Miller, 119-120

Bigfork, team profile of, 120

Bingham Lake, team profile of, 120

Blaesing, Dr. Ted, Superintendent of White Bear Area Schools, quote by, 297

Bloomer, Amelia Jenks, editor of the *Lily*, 17

Blooming Prairie

team profile of, 121

player information provided by Margaret Zwiener Hogan, 121

Blooming Prairie Update, 121

Bly, Nellie, interview of Susan B. Anthony, *New York World*, February 2, 1896, 19

Borton, Pam, University of Minnesota Women's Basketball Head Coach, book jacket quote by

Braham

team profile of, 122

player information from Goraline Johnson Peterson, 122

Brainerd

team profile of, 123-125

Flying Queens team in, 84, 124

player information provided by Kay Nolan Wetter, 22, 84, 123-125; Alta Creger Heikkenen, 80, 84, 123-124

Brainerd Daily Dispatch, 22, 80, 123-124, 147, 286-287

Braude, Dr. Ann, Harvard School of Divinity, epilogue quote by, vi

Bricelyn

team profile of, 125

player information provided by Alice Armstrong Anderson, 125

Browns Valley

team profile of, 125-127

player information provided by Kathryn Meade Shinn, 12, 25, 45, 125-127

Brownton

team profile of, 129-132

player information provided by Hilda Zander Anderson, 46, 128; Corinne Zimmerman Janke,127-128; Frieda Zander Lord, 49, 127-129

Buffalo

    team profile of, 129-132

    player information provided by Eloise "Honey" Anderson Mattson,131-132; Vera Learned Illstrup-Templin, 21, 23, 31, 42, 49, 129-132

Bundy, OIa, NAAF-WD information from, 72-75

Byington, Bev, creator of the Little Girl Bouncing Balls, x, xiii

Byron

    team profile of, 132-133

    player information provided by Leona Siewert Gray, 8, 31, 40, 68, 132-133

C

Cambridge, team profile of, 134

Cagers

    definition of, 13

    St. Cloud Times, reference to, 13

Carleton College

    ALGOL publication at, 1-2

    basketball introduced at, 1

    Gridley Hall located at, 1-2

    Hansen, Ele; Professor Emeritus, Carleton College, quote about, 3

    interview with Max V. Exner about his father at, 2-3

    Lamb, Pat; Professor Emeritus, Carleton College, quote about, 3

    location of, 1

    reference to, xv; 234

    role of Max J. Exner at, xv, 1-3, 234

Carleton County Historical Society — Cloquet, 138

Cars, reference to

    Case, 41, 213

    Ford Model T's, 43, 45, 237

    Franklin, Hutmobile, 41, 130-131

Cass Lake

    team profile of, 43, 45, 135

    information from Jim Michaud about, 135

Clarkfield

    team profile of, 135-138

    player information provided by Elnora Burke Budde, 135, 137; Rosalind Knutson Cherkezian, 137; Elvera Burke Lindborg, 135, 137

Clarkfield Advocate, 137-138

Clarkfield, Minnesota 1884-1994 Centennial Publication, 135

Cloquet

    team profile of, 138-141

    Octavie Morneau, Duluth, team photographer for, 138

    player information provided by Edith Anderson Bergan, 23, 37, 57, 139-140

    reference to, 7, 19-20

Cloquet Pine-Journal, 140

Coleraine, *See also* Greenway

Committee on Women's Athletics (CWA), 72-73

Cottonwood County Historical Society collection - Bingham Lake,120; Mountain Lake, 228; Windom, 68, 303, 304, 305, 306, 307

Cromwell

    team profile of, 141-145

    legacy information about June Collman, Tammy Hill, April Collman and Julie Collman, 89, 145

    player information provided by Alice Dahlman Carter, 37, 141-143, 145; Gladys Dahl Clark, 79, 96, 144-145; Eileen Maxner Grover, 96, 143-145; Jessie Line Houck, 144; Blanche Line Kingsley, 24, 32, 44, 89, 94, 96, 141-145; Anna Karppinen Kohn, 142-143; May Beseman White, 144-145

Cromwell Area Historical Club, 36

Crookston

    team profile of, 146-147

    legacy information, Lori Ann Wright Severson, 90-91, 147

    player information from the Jeannette Page Wright family, iii, 90-91, 146-147;

    Wright, Dr. Robert C. quote by, 146-147

Crosby and Deerwood

    team profile of, 147

    reference to, 19

Crow Wing County Historical Society – Brainerd, 20, 123, Crosby and Deerwood, 19, 147

Cyrus

    team profile of, 148

    player information provided by the Vivian Solvie family, 148

    Reque, Beverly, statement by, 148

D

Darwin, Charles, division of roles by gender, 65

Dawson

    team profile of, 148-149

    player information provided by Audrey Moe Froiland, 32, 88, 148-149; the Anne Jerde family, 88, 148-149; Cora Carlson Weisbrod, 148

Deer Creek

    team profile of, 150-151

    player information from Irma Nelson Post, 32, 43, 48, 68, 84, 150-151

Delano

    team profile of, 151-152

    player information from Ella Mae Bauer Pease, 10, 46, 151-152

DeLapp, Roland R. administrator, Minneapolis Public Schools, quote by, 204

Delavan

    team profile of, 152-153

    player information from Bernice Halvorson Wheeler, 10, 24, 45, 96, 153

Derham Hall, team profile of, 153

Dodge Center

    team profile of, 154

    player information provided by Leona Siewert Gray, 8, 31, 40, 68, 154

Douglas County Historical Society - Alexandria, 110-111

Duluth High Schools

    team profile of, 155-156

    Duluth High School, 155-156

    Duluth Central, 7, 155

    Duluth Central GAA (1936), 81

    Duluth Denfeld, 155

    Duluth Morgan Park, 155

Dundee, team profile of, 156

E

Echoing Footsteps, a 1988 History of the Toivola Community – Sports, The Toivola Athletic Club, 280-281

Eden Prairie, team profile of, 313-314

Eden Prairie Historical Society – Eden Prairie, 313-314

Elkton

    team profile of, 156-157

    player information provided by Bernice Swenson Hokeness, 156-157

Ellendale

    team profile of, 157-160

    player information provided by the Helen Johnson Davidson family, 59-60, 158-160; by Vivian Randall Harpel, 159 story by Ralph Wayne, 160

reference to, 53, 59-60

Ellendale Eagle, 37, 59, 157-160

Ellendale Area Heritage Society — Ellendale, 53, 59, 60, 158, 159

Engelmann, George J., p. 66

Euerle, Sharon, Activities Director, Mankato West, quote by, 83

Excelsior

team profile of, 161

player information provided by Clara Mae Donlin, 9, 21, 30, 39, 161

Exner, Max J., *See Carleton College*

Exner, Max V., information about his father, Max J. Exner, 1-3

F

Facilities where games were played,

Grand Meadow Opera house, 32, 171

Rapidan, 34

West Concord City Hall, 34

Faribault

team profile of, 162

player information about Elenora Schlaet Bemis, 162

First National Bank team, Minneapolis, 84, 324

Franklin

team profile of, 162-164

banquet information by Mrs. Rudolph Diekmeier, 162-163

legacy information about Michelle McFarland Bursch, 91, 164; Lynn Trochlil Crist, 91, 164; Stephanie Hall Moran, 91, 164

player information provided by Alice Schroeder McFarland, 91, 163-164

Franklin Tribune, 162-164

Frazee

team profile of, 165

Frazee Cane Women's team, 84, 151

Hoyhtya, Deb, statement by, 165

player information provided by the Kathryn Aldrich Schrom family, 165

Freeborn

team profile of, 165-166

player information provided by Dorothy Schultz Schuster, 44, 166

Freeborn County Historical Museum, Library and Historical Village — Albert Lea, 107; Alden, 110, 185; Freeborn, 165; Hartland, 185

G

Gaylord

team profile of, 167-169

Hanson, Susan, 169

player information provided by Belinda Corcoran Eckert, 32, 167; Leona Briard Hanson, 30, 167-169; Clara Corcoran Lawrenz, 30, 167; Margaret Huffman Thompson, 30, 42, 96, 167-169

Gaylord Hub, 167-169

Gaylord – Hub of Sibley County, 111

Girls Athletic Association (GAA)

Duluth High School, 1896-1900, 1923-1936, 155-156

Duluth Central (1936) GAA, 81

history of, 74, 76, 80-83, 278

reference to, xv, 75-77, 138, 193, 210, 217, 255-256, 278, 309

Girls basketball, early rules of, 5-15

Glyndon

team profile of, 169-170

coach information provided by the Douglas Sommerville family, 169-170

Godey's Lady's Book, 18

Goodhue, team profile of, 170

Goodrich, Kathy Lervold, *See also* Nielsville

Govednik, Anne, 78

Grand Meadow

    team profile of, 170-175

    player information provided by Marie Tommerson Berg, 63, 171-173, 175; Dorothy Allen Blanchard, 63, 172-174; Mildred Berg Gilbert, 172; Alvena Travis Glynn, 172-173; Mae Harvey Gross, 63, 174-175; Ruth Bratrud Jacobson, 32, 46, 63, 97, 171-172; Kathryn Skaran Losey, 63, 174; Margaret Forbes Peterson, 174; DeVera Bratrud Proeschel, 63, 172-174; Ceil Stier Schneider, 172-173

    reference to, 64, 79

Grand Meadow Record and Meadow Area News, 79, 174-175

Grand Rapids

    team profile of, 175-179

    player information provided by Lily Parks Tinquist, 178-179

    reference to, 7, 30, 47

Granite Falls

    team profile of, 179

    player information provided by Carol Fuller about Pearl Fuller, 179

Greenbush

    team profile of, 179-180

    player information provided by Oline Christianson Erickson, 12, 36, 97, 179-180

Greenway

    team profile of, 180-182

    reference to, 48, 52

    team information provided by Bill Hare, 181

Grove City

    team profile of, 183

    Elvera "Peps" Neuman, statement about mother, 183

    player information provided by Anna Martinson Neuman, 31, 43, 183

Gulick, Luther, 3

Gustavus Adolphus College, 117, 230

H

Hancock

    team profile of, 184-185

    player information provided by Irene Angier Jensen, 184-185; Marion Halvorson Solvie, 57, 184-185

Hansen, Ele, Carleton College, quote by, 3

Hartland, team profile of, 185

Hayfield

    team profile of, 186-188

    player information provided by Dorothy Iversen Viker, 24, 39, 49, 186-187

Hendricks

    team profile of, 187-188

    player information provided by Clara Digre Johnson, 37, 187-188

Hendricks Pioneer, 187-188

Herman

    team profile of, 188

    player information provided by the Irene Knudson family, 188

Heron Lake, team profile of, 189

Hibbing, team profile of, 189-190

Hill, James J., *See also* Railroads

Hodgson, Thomas A., Ed.D, University of St. Thomas, 109, 210, 273, 308

Hoover, Lou Henry, first chair of NAAF-WD, 72

Hutchinson

    team profile of, 190-192

legacy of Lindsay Whalen, book jacket photo, 93, 192

player information provided by the Mary Hajicek Berry family, 190-191; the Charlotte Johnson Johnson family, 9, 39, 190-191

I

Independent/Professional women's teams

Arkansas Gems, 87

Fillies, Minnesota, 86

First National Bank of Minneapolis, 84

Flying Queens, Brainerd, 84, 124

Frazee Cane Women, 84, 151

Marble City team, Marble, 181

Shooting Stars-Arkansas Lassies, 87

Texas Cowgirls, 87

International Falls

team profile of, 192-193

player information provided by Agnes King McIntyre, 15, 68, 192-193

Iowa girls basketball

Iowa Girls High School Athletic Union (IGHSAU), organization for, 77

preservation of as stated by Superintendent John W. Agans of Mystic Iowa, 77

J

Jack, Harold, State Department of Education, 75-78

Jeffers

team profile of, 193

legacy information about Teri Takle, 92, 193

player information provided by the Avis Hofslund Piper family, 92, 193

statement by Roberta Takle, 193

Johnson, Erling, coach, school administrator, Commissioner of Education, 286

Jordan

team profile of, 194-196

player information provided by Lucille Beckman, 33, 49, 194-196; Jane Varner Breimhorst, 11, 26, 33, 41, 56, 69, 95, 98, 194-196; Margaret Bieder Levander, 194-195

Jordan Independent, 50, 118, 194-196, 223-224, 228-229

K

Kasota, team profile of, 196-197

Klaen, Bruce, Supt. of Schools, Grand Meadow, quote by, book jacket, 171

Kruse, Doug, railroad map, x, xiii, 38

L

Lake Crystal

team profile of, 197-198

player information provided by Mary Champlin Tonkin, 69, 80, 95, 98, 197-198

Lamb, Pat, Carleton College, quote by, 3

Le Roy, team profile of, 198-199

Le Roy Independent, 198

Lee, Dr. Mabel, University of Nebraska, 73

LeSueur

team profile of, 199-200

player information provided by the Blossom Renneke Schwartz family, 199-200

Sontag, Lucy Schwartz, quote by, 200

LeSueur News-Herald, 199-200

Life magazine, 1890 Gibson girl description by, 20

Lily, The, newspaper, 17

Lissimore, Lisa, Associate Director, Minnesota State High School League

book jacket quote by,

legacy information about, 87-88

Litchfield

team profile of, 200-203

player information provided by the Florence Urdahl Lundmark family, 202-203; Edna McGraw Burns, 201-202; Iris McGraw Campbell, 63, 203

reference to, 62-63

Litchfield Independent Review, 131-132, 200-203

Luverne

team profile of, 203-205

player information from Ruth Norelius DeLapp, 69, 70, 95, 98, 204-205

DeLapp, Roland R., Minneapolis school administrator, quote by, 204

Lyle

team profile of, 205

coach information provided by Helen Speckel Allen, 205

M

Mabel

team profile of, 206-207

player information provided by Mabel Thompson Erickson, xii, 26, 98, 206-207

MacLeod, John and Elizabeth, cars, xiii, 43, 45

Macy, Dr. Kathleen, Superintendent of Schools, Stillwater, book jacket quote by

Madison

team profile of, 207

legacy information about Margaret Chutich, 89

player information provided by the Margaret Hauck Morrill family, 48, 89, 207

Mankato

team profile of, 208-209

player information provided by Mary Thomas Dickmeyer Todnem, 98, 208-209

Mankato Teachers College, 56

Mantorville

team profile of, 209

player information provided by Lorraine Stussy, 98, 209

Marshall

team profile of, 209-210

research by student Matt Irvin, University of St. Thomas, 210

Martin County Star, Sherburne, 264

Mazeppa

team profile of, 210

player information provided by the Hattie Pehl family, 210

Milaca

team profile of, 211-212

player information from Winifred Swanson Stromberg, 42, 211-212; Joy Moore Brekke, 212

Holmen, Jeannette Stromberg, 212

Milan

team profile of, 212-215

player information provided by Edith Dalen Bjornlie, 34, 45, 212-215; Ella Olson Gandel, 212-214; Ruth Olson Kleven, 26, 34, 69, 90, 212-215; Ella Nelson Opjordan, 215

Mille Lacs County Times, Milaca, 211

Minneapolis-St. Paul Magazine, 119

Minneapolis Journal, 158

Minneapolis Schools

team profile of, 215-217

Frances Kidd, physical education supervisor and advocate for girls sports for, 217

Minneapolis Star Tribune, 172, 192, 215

Rippel, Joel, 215

Minneapolis Tribune, 109

Minnesota Historical Society

    Clarkfield school newspapers – 136-137

    Barta's Studio of the - New Prague, 228

    Harry Darius Ayer, 39

Minnesota State High School League

    H.C. Bell, Supt., Luverne, first president of, 205

    MSHSL State Girls Swimming and Diving Tournament, 78

    MSHSL *Official Handbooks*, 7, 78

    Reference to, xi, 258

    Women in Sports Leadership Conferences conducted by, xii, 78, 118-119, 206, 221

Montevideo

    team profile of, 218-221

    player information provided by Thea Sletkolen Stay, 24, 32, 55, 61, 62, 219-221; the Edna Linnee Jorvig family, 218

    reference to, 62

Montevideo American-News, 62, 218, 221

    Olson, Bruce, staff writer for, 218-219

Montgomery

    team profile of, 221-224

    player information provided by Irma Malone Foley, xii, 99, 221-224; Bernice Malone Pexa, 99, 221-222; Eunice Wolfe Washa, 99, 221-223

    Karen Norell, 223

Montgomery, Janet Karvonen

    Foreword by, ix

    interview at state tournament by, xii

    reference to, 125

    reunion of first era players attended by, 93

Montgomery Messenger, 222-224

Monticello

    team profile by, 224

    player information provided by families of Ethel Carlson Fitzgerald, 224; Dorothy Bradford Lilja, 224; Mary Bollman, 224

Moose Lake, team profile of, 224-226

Morgan

    team profile of, 226

    player information from Elsie Berdan, 226; Luretta Parker Trobec, 226

    reference to, 355

Morgan Messenger, 226

Morris

    team profile of, 227

    player information provided by Orell May Judd Jensen, 227

Morton

    team profile of, 227

    player information from Leone Revier Schell, 227

Mountain Lake

    team profile of, 288

    Centennial Booklet, 1886-1996, about, 228

Mower County Historical Society – Grand Meadow, 170

Murray County Historical Society - Dundee, 264; Heron Lake, 189; Slayton, 265, 267

Murray County Wheel-Herald, 268

N

Naismith, James

    inventor of the game of Basket Ball, xv, xvii, 3-4, 234

    reference to, 1, 4, 13

National Amateur Athletic Federation - Women's Division (NAAF-WD)

    formation of, 72

    platform of, 73

National Association of Secondary School Principals, (NASSP), 74

National Girls and Women in Sports Day, 124, 175, 187

Neuman, Elvera "Peps"

    quote by, 183

    association with the Texas Cowgirls, Shooting Stars-Arkansas Lassies, Arkansas Gems, 87

New Prague

    team profile of, 228-229

    player information provided by Ann Sticha Juni, 99; Evelyn Vales Kraus, 229; Adeline Kamish Musil, 99, 229; Monica Janda Simon, 99, 229; Ida Picha Welter, 99, 229

New Richland

    team profile of, 230

    legacy information about Laura Sampsell Hoffman, 90; 230; Sara Sampsell-Jones, 230

    player information provided by Evelyn Sponberg Young, 23, 45, 90, 230

New Ulm, team profile of, 230-231

Nielsville

    team profile of, 231-232

    legacy information about Heather Goodrich Schrider, 91-92, 99, 232; Kathy Lervold Goodrich, ix, 91-92, 232

    player information provided by Alice Aanenson Lervold, 33, 91-92, 99, 231-232

Nordgren, Bill, St. James, quote by, 272

Norris, Dr. J. Anna, 72, 324

North Branch

    team profile for, 232-233

    player information provided by Lorraine Peterson Olson, 233

North Branch Review, 232

North St. Paul, 314-315

Northern Lights, International Falls, 193

Northfield

    team profile of, 234-235

    NHS athletic history by C.E. Sanberg, 234

    Richardson, Scott, and the *Commemorative Program: Game of the Century*, 235

Northfield News, 234-235, 270, 272

Northome

    team profile of, 235-236

    player information provided by Mildred Wick Gorden, 51, 235-236

O

Olivia

    team profile of, 236-237

    research by student Shelly Moudry, University of St. Thomas, 236-237

Olympics

    women's participation protested by NAAF-WD, 75

Onamia

    team profile of, 237-238

    player information provided by Nell Lane, 237-238

Owatonna

    team profile of, 238-239

    Boss, Sandy, quote by, 239

    player information provided by the Frieda Kottke Coleman family, 238-239

    reference to, 52

Owatonna Journal-Chronicle, 230, 238-239

Owatonna People's Press, 230-231, 238-239

P

Park Rapids, coach information provided by Gertrude Ziebarth Bloom, 25, 77

Paynesville

    team profile of, 240

    player information provided by Letta Farnum Swedelius, 240

Pelican Rapids

    team profile of, 240-241

    player information provided by the Ethel Lyden Anderson family, 92, 240-241

    Robbins, Heidi modeling her great-grandmother's uniform, 92, 241

    Robbins, Pat quote by, 241

Pfeffer, Maud, Hampton, Iowa, quote by, 21

Pine Journal, 241

Pine Island, team profile of, 241-242

Pine Island News-Record, 241-242

Pine-Knot, Cromwell, 143

Port Wing. WI Area Historical Society — horse-drawn school bus, 36

Preston

    team profile of, 242

    player information provided by Marjorie Nelson Johnson, 242

Princeton, team profile of, 243

Proctor

    team profile of, 243

    quote by school board member R. A. Silverness, 246

Proctor Area Historical Society – Proctor, 243, 244-246

R

Railroads

    Duluth Missabe Northern, 246

    Great Northern Flyer, 38-39

    impact on Minnesota of, 37-38

    James J. Hill, 39

    Merriam Junction, 40,

    Minneapolis and St. Louis, 40, 117

    Northwestern line, 40, 117

    Proctor rails, graphic, 37

Rapidan

    team profile of, 246-251

    player information provided by Aileen Just Luther family, 25, 31, 33, 61, 68, 246-251

    quote by Richard Just about sister Aileen Just Luther, 251

    reference to, 61

Red Wing

    team profile of, 252

    player information provided by the Ruth Rehder family, 252

Red Wing Seminary

    team profile of, 252-253

    player information provided by Margarethe Romo Thoreson, 11, 252-253, 288

Redwood Falls

    team profile of, 254

    legacy information about Isabella Ceplecha, 1976 MSHSL Class A Champions, 254

    player information provided by Lois Eckhart Ahrens, 254; Rowena Ceplacha, 254

Redwood Gazette, 162-164, 254

Referees in girls basketball

    Belle Plaine, 1930 — Jack Grafs, 116

    Gaylord, 1920-24 — Bell, 169

    Grand Rapids, 1909 — Lester Lofberg, 177

    Morgan, 1924-28 — Sam McNall, 226

    Park Rapids, 1926-28 — Gertrude Zeibarth, 77

    Proctor, 1920 — Miss Smith from Normal, 244

Rochester

    team profile of, 255-256

    player information provided by the Ethel Kalb family, 255

Rock County Star-Herald, Luverne, 204-205

Roosevelt, Eleanor, quote by, epilogue

Rose Creek

    team profile of, 256

    player information provided by the Florence Larson Freed family, 256; Helen Johnson, 256; Nora Johnson Rasmussen, 256

Roseau

    team profile of, 257-258

    player information provided by Paula Bruss Bauck, 99, 257-258; Muriel Quanbeck Turritin, 99, 257

    reference to, 30

Roseau County Historical Society

    Marilyn Hanson Sharp Collection of the, 257

Royalton, team profile of, 258-259

Royalton Banner, 258

Royalton Museum and the Gladys Clark family – Royalton, 258

Rural Electric Association (REA), 46

Rush City

    team profile of, 259

    information provided by Marian Larson, 259

    player information provided by the Ann Studt family, 259

S

St. Cloud Cathedral, team profile of, 260

St. Cloud Times, 12, 13, 260

St. James

    team profile of, 260-262

    2004 Game of the Century played against Northfield by, 235

St. James Historical Society – St. James, 260-262

St. James Plaindealer, 250-251, 262, 272

St. Olaf College, 234

St. Paul Daily News, 272-264

St. Paul Schools

    team profile of, 263-264

    research students Ryan J. Kavanaugh and Matt Jeppson, University of St. Thomas, 263-264

    St. Paul Central, 19-20, 87, 88, 264

St. Paul Pioneer Press, 59, 158

St. Peter

    team profile of, 265

    player information provided by the Genevieve Webster family, 265

Sauk Rapids, team profile of, 265-266

Sauk Rapids Herald, 266

Schumacher Hotel, New Prague, 117

Sherburn,

    team profile of, 266-269

    player information provided by Ruth McCarron Dahlke, 31, 43, 54, 79, 266-269; Pauline Holmes Eiden, 266-269

    reference to, 26, 53

    trophy located by former athletic director Ray Herman, 268

Sherburn Advance Standard, 267

Slayton

    team profile of, 269-273

    coach information about Evelyn Wenstrom, 272

    research by student Carleen Andert, University of St. Thomas, 269-273

Slayton Gazette, 737

Slayton Wheel-Herald, 296

Smith College, women's basketball at, 5

South St. Paul

    team profile of, 274-275

    research by student Sara Steichen, University of St. Thomas, 274-275

Spalding Athletic Library, rules in, 6

Spring Valley Tribune, 171

Stanton, Elizabeth Cady, interview of, 17

Starbuck

    team profile of, 275

    information from Matthew Pederson for, 275

    Starbuck Basketball, about, 275

    Starbuck Centennial History Book about, 275

Stibbe, Peggy Zimmerman, ix

Stillwater

    team profile of, 276-278

    quote by Dr. Kathleen P. Macy, Superintendent of Schools, book flap

Streetcar, reference to, 39, 161

Suffrage, 17

Sundeen, Carl, ix

Swanville, team profile of, 279

    player information provided by Ann Truog Larson, 279

Swimming and Diving

    state tournament for girls, 78

T

Thief River Falls

    team profile of, 279-280

    player information provided by the Eileen Herron family, 279-280

Todd County Bulletin, Brownton, 128

Toivola

    team profile of, 280-282

    Sports: Toivola Athletic Club, 280-281

    player information provided by Lillian Lahti Sorvari, 95, 99, 280-281; Saima Saari Savela, 95, 99, 281-282

Trains, *See railroads*

Tracy

    team profile of, 282-283

    reference to, 79

Tracy Headlight-Herald

    Seth Schmidt, staff writer for, 282-283

Twin City Rapid Transit Company Streetcar, 1902, St. Paul, 39

Two Harbors

    team profile of, 283-284

    player information provided by the Athelyn Amundsen Truman family, 283; Laurie Newtson, 283

    reference to, 8, 23

U

Underwood

    team profile of, 285

    player information provided by Evelyn Olson Kukkola, 27, 35, 48, 51, 285

University Archives, Spencer Research Library, University of Kansas Libraries, 4

V

Verdi

    team profile of, 286

    State Commissioner of Education Erling Johnson, quote by, 286

W

Wadena, team profile of, 286-287

Wadena Historical Society — Wadena, 286-287

Wadena Pioneer Journal, 286-287

Walters, Jean Frarey, swimmer, xii, 78

Wanamingo

    team profile of, 287-288

    player information provided by Hilda Satren Aaker, 287; the Lillian Romo Aakre family, 253, 288; Celia Vangsness Hostager, 287-288

Warroad

    team profile of, 288-289

    reference to, 30

Warroad Heritage Center and Museum – Warroad, 289

Warroad Pioneer, 48, 288-289

Waverly, St. Mary's of

team profile of, 289-290

player information provided by Sister Ellen Joan Malone, 289-290

Wayzata

team profile of, 290

player information provided by Marian Wise about Anna Milbert Kamleiter, 290; by the Cynthia Batson family, 290

Wayzata Historical Society – Wayzata, 290

West Concord

team profile of, 290-292

player information provided by Rose Robinson Wichser, 26, 44, 290-292

Westbrook

team profile of, 292-293

legacy information, Teri Takle, 293

player information provided by Clarine Knudson Takle, 92, 293

Westbrook Schools, 1910-1990, for, 292-293

West Central Tribune, Willmar, 215

Whalen, Lindsay, book jacket photo of, 93

Wheaton

team profile of, 293-294

player information provided by Muriel Jacobson, 293-294

White Bear Lake

team profile of, 294-298

player information provided by Eileen Bourquin Buckley, 295-297; Kathy Swietzer Fournelle, 295-297; Dorothy Bloom Kulkey, 295-298; Florence Holzheid Leversee, 294; Evelyn Rohlfing, 295-297; Naomi Rohlfing, 295-298; Loraine Bourquin Sansome, 295-297

Gertrude Ziebarth Bloom, change to GAA at, 77

quote by Dr. Ted Blaesing, Superintendent of Schools, 297

White Bear Press, 295, 298

Willmar

team profile of, 298-302

player information from Helen Ohsberg Lindahl, 301; Ruth DeLaHunt Rawn, 9, 20, 49, 95, 198, 298-302; Eleanor DeLaHunt Strand, 11, 38, 298-301

reference to, 8

Willow River

team profile of, 302

information provided by Donald Swartz, 302

Wilmont, Our Lady of Good Counsel

team profile of, 302

player information provided by Marie Hippert Larson, 35, 302

Windom, team profile of, 303-307

Windom Reporter, 303, 307

Winona

team profile of, 308-309

research by student Stacy Cordes, University of St. Thomas, 308-309

Winthrop

team profile of, 309

player information provided by Mildred Lofthus Roepke, 309

Winthrop News, 309

Women's Basketball Committee (WBC) of the American Physical Education Association (APEA), 6, 12-15

Wright County Journal-Press, Buffalo, 129

Woodman's Hall

Grand Meadow, 32

Underwood, 285

Y

Young Men Christian's Organization (YMCA)

    role in spread of basketball of, 1, 5

    James Naismith in Massachusetts at, 3

Z

Zumbrota

    team profile of, 310

    Centennial booklet, *Zumbrota: The First Hundred Years, 1856-1956*, 310

Zumbrota Area Historical Society - Goodhue, 21, 170; Zumbrota, 21, 310

Zumbrota News, 47, 310

Family Memories from Our Daughters of the Game

These are your pages to preserve the sports history of the women in your family.

Interview your family members. Review your family archives, photo albums and school yearbooks. Record the information on these pages. Share this book with the next generations of your family.

Questions for the women in your family who played basketball during the First Era, 1891-1942.
- Where did she go to high school?
- What years did she play basketball?
- What kind of game did her team play -- three-court, two-court or full court?
- Who were the teams played by her team?
- How did her team travel to 'away' games? Did they stay overnight and return the next day?
- Did her team participate in tournaments? Did the winning team receive any awards?
- Where did her team play its games?
- What kind of uniforms did the team wear?
- Who was the coach?
- Was the community supportive of the girls' team?
- What were her favorite memories of her days playing basketball?
- Was her team discontinued during her playing years?

Questions for the women in your family who were in high school during the 1940's – 1960's when interscholastic teams may not have been available for her.
- What kind of sports opportunities did she have?
- Did it involve intramural or Girls Athletic Association (GAA) activities?
- Did it meet her interests?
- Did she play in any community leagues or on teams sponsored by local businesses or organizations, such as the AAU?
- Who were her sports heroes?
- Was she satisfied with the sports opportunities she had during her high school years?

Questions for the women in your family who were in high school after 1970.
- What kind of sports opportunities did she have?
- What was the highest level of competition available to her? Did it meet her interests?
- Did she play on school teams or for community or sports organizations, or both?
- Who were her sports heroes?
- What were her reflections on her sports opportunities during high school?

Family Memories

Family Memories

Family Memories

Family Memories

Family Memories

Family Memories

Family Memories

Family Memories

Family Memories

Family Memories

Johnson, Marian Bemis.
Daughters of the game :
the first era of Minnesota
girls high school
basketball, 1891-1942
33500008778615   LX